HOUSE MUSIC

HOUSE MUSIC

The Oona King Diaries

OONA KING

BLOOMSBURY

First published 2007
This paperback edition published 2008

Copyright © 2007 by Oona King

The moral right of the author has been asserted

Bloomsbury Publishing Plc, 36 Soho Square, London W1D 3QY

www.bloomsbury.com

Bloomsbury Publishing, London, New York and Berlin

A CIP catalogue record is available from the British Library

ISBN 978 0 7475 9309 6

10 9 8 7 6 5 4 3 2 1

Typeset by Hewer Text UK Ltd, Edinburgh
Printed in Great Britain by Clays Ltd, St Ives plc

All papers used by Bloomsbury Publishing are natural,
recyclable products made from wood grown in well-managed
forests. The manufacturing processes conform to the
environmental regulations of the country of origin.

for Tiberio *for* ever

Aujourd' hui je comprends que nous sommes
à la recherche du temps perdu . . .

sul
ciglio
del
burrone,
gioia!

A NOTE ON THE AUTHOR

Oona King was born in Sheffield and brought up in Camden. She was first elected as an MP for Bethnal Green & Bow in May 1997. She has campaigned on issues including antisocial behaviour, domestic violence, housing, inner-city regeneration, comprehensive education and community cohesion. She lives with her husband and small son in Mile End, London.

Contents

List of Picture Credits

'Blair's Babes': the iconic picture of Tony Blair and some of the 101 Labour women MPs elected on 1 May 1997. © PA Photos

In my wedding dress, July 1994. Photograph by Slater King

With Tony Blair, John Prescott and local resident Brenda Daley on the Ocean estate in Tower Hamlets. © Getty Images

Addressing a packed House of Commons to second the Queen's Speech. © UK Parliament, courtesy of Parliamentary Recording Unit

Jack Straw visits Bethnal Green and Bow the day after the Brick Lane bombing. © PA Photos

Sharing a joke with Barbara Follet and Harriet Harman, one of the Cabinet ministers who helped me most. © Reuters/Russell Boyce

Tony watching me with a pained expression that was to become familiar. © PA Photos

The Prime Minister with London MPs during the ill-fated Frank Dobson mayoral campaign, January 2000. © PA Photos

Painting my constituency office in Bethnal Green (I had to begin again because the green paint came out blue). Photograph by Steve Bishop

On the campaign trail in the East End, Columbia Road Flower Market. © Getty

Congratulating George Galloway on his victory, 5am, 6 May 2005. © PA Photos

Life after being an MP: in New Orleans, reporting on Hurricane Katrina for the *Guardian*, September 2005. Photograph by Ted Soqui

Hosting a Q&A session with Gordon Brown during his leadership campaign, May 2007. © PA Photos

Campaigning for more youth services with young people outside Parliament as Chair of the Make Space Youth Review. © Getty

All other images are from the author's private collection.

Abbreviations

APPG	All Party Parliamentary Group
BGB or BG & B	Bethnal Green & Bow
CLP	Constituency Labour Party
DfID	Department for International Development
DTI	Department for Trade and Industry
DTLR	Department for Transport, Local Government and the Regions
DRC	Democratic Republic of Congo
FCO	Foreign and Commonwealth Office
GG	George Galloway
GLA	Greater London Authority
GMB	Britain's General Union
HoC	House of Commons
ICC	International Criminal Court
LP	Labour Party
NEC	National Executive Committee
NGO	Non-Governmental Organisation
ODPM	Office of the Deputy Prime Minister
PH	Patricia Hewitt
PLP	Parliamentary Labour Party
PM	Prime Minister
PMB	Private Member's Bill
PPS	Parliamentary Private Secretary
PMQs	Prime Minister's Questions
PQ	Parliamentary Question
SoS	Secretary of State
SpAd	Special Adviser
TB	Tony Blair

Part 1

The Human Boxing Ring
and the Helpful Sea Monster

Introduction

I don't remember exactly when I first decided to be Prime Minister, but it was soon after I gave up wanting to be an air hostess. I was probably four or five. I became the MP for Bethnal Green and Bow at twenty-nine. People told me I was a young parliamentarian, but from my point of view it took twenty-five years to reach the green leather benches. It seemed an eternity. I'm often asked why I wanted to be an MP from such an early age. It's difficult to remember, because I stopped questioning my career choice before leaving primary school. I just knew I wanted to be an MP, the way others knew they wanted to be singers, nuns or astronauts.

If I had to name the biggest contributory factor that pushed me towards the House of Commons, it would be my mother Hazel's intense belief in social justice. As a child I only ever saw her enraged by one thing: unfairness. Tears rolled down her cheeks when she saw starving babies on TV. No one said the world was fair but my Mum, a secondary school teacher, constantly said it should be fair*er*. I once asked why she was so upset and she replied, 'Because the politicians aren't doing their jobs properly.' I wasn't sure what a politician was, but if I was a 'good' one, I thought she'd be happy.

My personality profile also fits a politician: risk-taker, optimist, loudmouth. Funnily, being a politician turned my personality on its head: I became more risk-averse, my horizon clogged with pessimism, and I got sick to death of my own voice and tried to avoid it. The pessimism I felt wasn't the usual cynicism about politics and politicians. I continue to believe that politics is our planet's only salvation – only negotiated agreements between politicians can *systemically* tackle climate change, poverty and conflict. Individual responsibility is critical, but only prevails in the right environment – an environment governed by politicians. It is because politicians' choices are so important that we hate politicians when they fail.

My Mum's despair of politicians was a regular feature in my childhood, exacerbated by her experience as a poorly paid teacher bringing up two kids alone. When I was five, she took me on a teachers' protest march to the House of Commons. It was 1973 and her teachers' union was demanding higher pay. I sat in a committee room, under a table at my Mum's feet, and drew pictures with coloured crayons while trade unionists and MPs slugged it out above me. When the meeting was over we walked along a committee corridor lined with thick green carpet and Hansard volumes. I stopped outside one of the doors.

'Is that the room?' I peered through the door.

'Which room?' asked my Mum.

'The room where they give us the money. I thought we came to get the money.'

My early view of Westminster as a palatial cashpoint has withstood years of more detailed analysis. After all, politics is essentially the heated process of divvying up the cash.

I studied politics at school and university, and everything I did was geared towards entering the House of Commons. My parents instilled in me their strong belief that everyone has a responsibility to their community. In different ways they taught me there is no higher aspiration than public service. They were guided by principle, not money. My mother gave me myriad daily examples of her principles, some of which rankled. 'If something is wrong, it's wrong,' she'd say, explaining why she wouldn't make an insurance claim for a burglary (she refused to lie and say the locked door was also bolted), or eat factory-farmed meat ('I don't want animals tortured on my account'), or absolve her daughter from wrongdoing ('You can't let others take the rap, so I'm asking your teacher to include you in the group suspension.') My mother's main principle was honesty. She is probably the only person I've ever met who never lies – to the point where it's a real drag. 'Mum, can you tell Gran I can't speak right now 'cos I'm in the bath?' 'No, Oona, because you're not in the bath.' 'Oh *Mum . . .*'

My father Preston was a university lecturer. He has written books about political ethics, pluralism and authority, as well as poems and adventure stories for his children. Although his political writing was beyond my grasp it wasn't difficult to understand the moral of his own life story: he spent forty years exiled from his home and country on a point of principle. As an African-American he argued with the authorities in the segregated South, insisting that he should be treated like his white peers. He demanded equality regardless of the consequences. He was convicted by a white judge on trumped-up racist charges, but refused to submit to the court's jurisdiction. He waited decades to be exonerated, and only received a presidential pardon from President Clinton when the white judge, then aged ninety-six, admitted the conviction was racially motivated.

Going into politics was for me almost a point of principle: if you feel you *can* effect change for the better, then you must. My desire for change was driven by anger. It was blatantly unfair that in 1980s Britain, child poverty trebled while the richest received tax cuts. No one ever said the world was fair, but surely it didn't have to be a stitch up? It enraged me. I wanted to argue about it all day long, and I decided the best place to do so was Parliament. I still believe Parliament is the best place to have those arguments. That's not to demean the countless other fora for debate, or the other valuable ways people effect change. It's also not to ignore claims that Parliament has been diminished by power flowing to the executive. It is simply to recognise that being a legislator can be an extraordinarily direct – if frustrating – route to effect change. That's why becoming an MP was such a huge privilege.

However I soon discovered that there is a great difference between having a privilege bestowed upon you, and learning how to exercise it. That's why within months of becoming an MP, I was underwhelmed by the privilege. How could it be so difficult to change the smallest things? Early on I remember a group of women MPs wanting to change advertisements for positions in health quangos. The Government was embarrassed that there were so few women in these positions. An obvious starting point was advertising for health authority 'Chairs' instead of 'Chair*men*'. The then Health Secretary, Frank Dobson, assured us he'd get it changed – after all, it was such a small thing. Three months and four meetings later, Frank was a bit po-faced.

'Er . . . it was a bit harder than I thought. In fact it's impossible. The civil servants say it means re-writing the rest of the legislation going on to the statute book, which means buggering the parliamentary time-table, which means losing this health legislation and other legislation like the minimum wage . . . er sorry girls, can't do it.'

I didn't arrive at Parliament expecting revolution, but neither did I expect inertia. Change. Such a small word, requiring such great effort. The landslide victory of the Labour Party in 1997 created an overwhelming expectation of change, in part generated by the arrival of 101 Labour women MPs. We were meant to shake the cobwebs off Big Ben, give women a voice, and drag Parliament kicking and screaming into the tail-end of the twentieth century. It was a tall order, not least because after the 'historic' election of so many women, 82 per cent of MPs were still men.

Women in Parliament: The New Suffragettes by Boni Sones (with Margaret Moran and Joni Dovenduski) demonstrates that, notwith-standing our small power base, the 101 Labour women elected in 1997 eventually succeeded in transforming the Commons beyond recognition and giving a new direction to policy-making. It didn't feel like that at the time. Westminster bumbled along. Parliament was suspicious of modernity, and excelled in archaic ritual. The House of Commons wasn't merely a Gentlemen's club, it was a secret society, built on conventions with meanings lost in the mists of time. One new MP was impressed to find that each MP's coathanger had a pink ribbon attached – presumably to highlight AIDS or breast cancer awareness – only to discover that these ribbons were for MPs to hang their *swords* on. The sword ribbons are still there today.

The shock of arriving at Westminster was compounded by leaving a work place with computers and email, and arriving somewhere that wasn't even wired up. Although this has improved dramatically, it was never possible in my eight years as an MP to have my constituency and Westminster offices networked. MPs voted against electronic voting, and I was surprised to find that I spent my nights, literally and metaphorically, walking around in circles (through the voting lobbies). Westminster's very architecture was mysterious, almost a metaphor for British democracy: impressive, beautiful, bewildering and befuddled.

To a newcomer Parliament seemed a cross between *Harry Potter* and *Porridge*, with rules to match: when to stand, when to sit, where to sit, when to walk, how *far* to walk (never beyond earshot of the Division Bell), when to talk, *how* to talk, when to pray, and when to clap (never), to name a few. The rules that irritated me most were the 'how to talk' rules. 'Those words would never come out of my mouth,' I'd complain to the Hansard copywriters who record parliamentary debate, as I picked over the rubble of my latest speech: 'Why does not one understand? Is not the Honourable Member aware that when one is a young person one needs good quality housing?' [*Translation*: 'Why don't you understand? Don't you know that when you're young you need good quality housing?']

On the advice of Tony Benn, a devout Hansard quibbler, I beseeched the Hansard people regularly. 'I can't send this nonsense out to my constituents – you've got to change it. I sound like a twat.' They would stare back implacably and mouth two words: 'House Rules.' Occasionally, when I got really irate, a senior Hansard person would emerge from behind wooden desks lined with years of Hansard speeches, and peruse my speech briefly before gravely pronouncing, 'I'm afraid, as you know, House Rules must apply.'

To be fair to Hansard they also make gibberish intelligible. But the quid pro quo is that parliamentary debate sounds ludicrous to normal people, so they don't listen. It's a shame because British Parliamentary debate can be both outstandingly good and bad. The former inspires pride in our democracy, while the latter widens our pool of political talent (A *monkey* could do better than that, g'is a job! I'll be an MP too!). Good or bad, it's worth listening to the House debate.

The best way to describe the inside of the debating Chamber, the postage stamp crucible of democracy, is a human boxing ring. It's cosy yet ominous, your opponent is in your face, and just one performance puts you on the ropes, or makes you a champ. You're only as good as your last fight. Like any sport it offers great euphoria and great despair. Anyone can do it, but it's best to remember that Westminster politics is essentially a blood sport – war by other means. You watch MPs pull lumps out of each other, and some acquire a taste for it. A packed House of Commons loves nothing more than the scent of a kill – like any public humiliation, the crowd finds it thrilling and repellent. Being in a crowd of MPs is no different.

OK, MPs are a tad different: they're the country's representatives and they decide what Britain does, or they think they do. The House of Commons offers the simultaneous attraction of high drama and human farce. The Members' tea room is a glorious, glorified staff-room where Britain's political class plot the country's future and eat fried egg and chips. Journalists lie in wait along committee corridors hoping to squeeze words from their quarry, TV crews beckon MPs out on to Parliament Green, where photographers flash bulbs seductively. But while there is always the risk of self-aggrandisement, most MPs are no different to the people they represent. Most respect the office they hold, but don't take themselves too seriously. That's how it was for me, and on those occasions when I had a seat at the ring, speaking rights, the chance to influence Government *and* see the human side of it all – well, it was literally a dream come true.

So it came as a great shock to me, a personal bombshell, that after being an MP for less than four years I decided to resign. Being in the House of Commons didn't suit me after all. The rules, the surveil-lance, the strictures, the silly side of politics, the endless bargaining, the time it took to effect change, the pressure of 300 letters a day, the pound of flesh sought by Government whips and constituents alike who felt they owned me, the 'what-u-gonna-do-4-me' brigade cam-ped outside my front door, the cases of genuine desperate need that kept me awake at night, fifteen-hour days, few free evenings or weekends, financial debt because I borrowed money to keep my constituency office afloat (an office reeling under one of the highest caseloads in Britain), an extremely unhappy husband who had lost his wife, friends I barely saw . . . And that was before the death threats from white extremists started rolling in. Scotland Yard told me the threats were credible, and gave me a pole with a mirror on the end, so I could check for bombs under my car each morning.

But while the people who hated me preyed on my mind, they didn't take up my time. That was left to the people who liked me, nice people who just wanted a chat with their MP. 'You're so approachable,' they would say, as I discussed their rubbish shoot at one a.m. in the all-night Tesco. I started looking at the floor to avoid eye contact, wearing a headscarf or dark glasses. I half-seriously thought of buying a burka so I could choose my cornflakes without collecting half a dozen new constituency cases. I was my own worst enemy – if someone wanted to talk I never said no; I was a *people* person. But it gradually dawned on me that I didn't enjoy being public property.

By 19 January 2001, I had put a specific date on my resignation, it was to be the following Monday morning. My best friend Quincy counselled against it: 'Take two weeks off work to think about it. Don't be rash.' So I took four days off work and lasted another four years in the job. I walked along the canal in Victoria Park, in Tower Hamlets, where I live, cleared my head, and decided I had to step back and find a way to do my job without self-destructing.

I became better at dealing with an MP's workload – that's to say, I stopped imagining I could ever finish it. I swallowed my pride and begged for money from sympathetic friends so that I could employ more caseworkers. I gave up all-nighters at my Westminster office. I achieved a smidgen of work–life balance. I changed British law in five areas and contributed to changing it in many others; I founded the All Party Parliamentary Group on the Great Lakes and Genocide Prevention which was commended by the UN Security Council's expert panel for its work on conflict resolution; I received thousands of cards from grateful constituents saying I'd changed their lives. I knew many MPs who had been at Westminster for decades, and never changed the law in a single area. I even knew some Government *Ministers* who had never changed the law, unless they were given something off the shelf by civil servants. I felt I was achieving something.

As I began to understand the House of Commons better, I realised that in fact we had not sunk beneath a fog of political inertia. Instead the 1997 Labour victory triggered vast change in all areas – but like most seismic events it took years to reach the surface. First we had to wait two years for Tony Blair and Gordon Brown to throw off the Tory spending limits. Second, the 101 Labour women MPs dismissed by the media as 'Blair's Babes' were slowly but surely changing the nature of Parliament, and Britain. Childcare policy and the provision of early years education championed by women MPs like Harriet Harman, Patricia Hewitt and Joan Ruddock, backed up by the new battalion of women MPs, were transformed from fringe issues into key Government initiatives. For the first time, billions of pounds poured into areas that directly affected the quality of women's lives. The media reported the clothes we wore, our make-up and shoes, but missed the shifting political landscape.

And yet, having decided to remain in Parliament, I was about to illustrate that most reliable and often-quoted rule of politics: I would prove, more quickly than most MPs blessed with safe seats, that all political careers end in failure. I went into Parliament a human rights activist and trade unionist, and came out labelled a 'warmonger' and murderer. Where did I go wrong? The deafening answer from most of you reading this will be one word, 'Iraq'. And of course you are right. Yet any psephologist will tell you that if you lose an election by 800 votes, as I did, then *any* issue that costs 800 votes, costs the election. So of course it was Iraq. But of course it was other issues too.

In the Muslim community, for example, I lost at least 2,000 votes on the back of a deliberate rumour claiming I wanted to ban halal meat, and therefore effectively ban Islam. My Muslim friends told me repeatedly that the reason it was so widely believed was that I was Jewish, and people were also angry to hear I paid my parliamentary salary (according to another rumour) to the Israeli army to bomb Palestinian civilians. 'Really?' I asked, 'but the Palestinian Authority commended my work on Palestinian human rights in the Gaza Strip. And anyway, if you wanted to ban halal, you'd ban kosher too – so Jewish people would never support a halal ban. There's no logic in it.'

Logic was scarce. I couldn't complain though, because I held contradictory views myself. On Iraq I had argued that no military action should be taken purely on humanitarian grounds. (Where was the logic – if we were bombing countries with poor human rights records, why didn't we start with China, Saudi Arabia or Iran?) On the other hand I had argued for years that individual human rights were sacrosanct, the international community had a duty to protect civilians being murdered by their Governments, and of course we should take military action against tyrannical mass murderers whenever possible. Just because George Bush got away with murder, why should Saddam Hussein get away with genocide? I supported the invasion.

It's hard to pinpoint the moment I became irrevocably 'pro-war' or, as I would argue, anti-genocide, anti-Saddam. Was it when I set up the All Party Parliamentary Group on Genocide Prevention? Or when I joined the International Development Select Committee and took part in the inquiry into the deaths of 500,000 Iraqi children who died because of Saddam's manipulation of UN sanctions? Or meeting constituents like Risgar whose parents were tortured and murdered by Saddam? Was it because I couldn't bear to tarnish my chance of promotion? Or because I thought it might bring about progress in the Palestine–Israeli conflict? Or simply because I would do anything Tony Blair asked, right or wrong? I hope you will draw your own conclusions after reading these diaries.

What was clear to anyone involved in the 2005 general election campaign in Bethnal Green and Bow was that Iraq was the starting point but not the endgame. The endgame was what negative politics is always about: manipulating disaffection. Disaffection within the Muslim community mostly stemmed from Iraq, while in the white community it stemmed from feeling ignored, and deep anxiety about being a community in flux. There was also the persistent problem of deep-rooted poverty, which affected both communities.

This disaffection was greatly exacerbated by the Government's – and my own – failure to link improvements in people's lives directly to changes wrought by a Labour Government. Increased benefits, higher public sector wages, lower interest rates, a higher standard of living for pensioners and families with children, new school buildings and hospitals – the people that benefited often failed to make a connection between their improved circumstances and voting Labour. The result of this widespread disaffection, in different communities for different reasons, was that I crashed out of Westminster in the most bitterly fought battle of the 2005 election. I had fought three election campaigns, served two parliamentary terms, worked at the House of Commons for a decade and been an MP for eight years.

What I learned during those eight years is that 'wanting the world to be a fairer place' is not idealistic daydreaming; it is deliverable policy-making. I am proud to have been part of a Labour Government that pulled a million children out of poverty and helped allocate resources to families and communities that were previously excluded. I'm glad I helped thousands of people on a one to one basis. The main sadness I have is that whether you sit inside or outside the House of Commons, the promise of a representative democracy in Britain today remains little more than a chimera. Women are still scarce on the ground, ethnic minorities are barely visible, and a Muslim woman is yet to be elected, though this will surely change at the next election.

I am increasingly convinced that the *way* we do politics – and whether it is inclusive – is as important as the politics itself. We will only allocate resources more fairly if we allocate *influence* more fairly. We must open up the decision-making process to all, from top to bottom. In doing so we will encourage truly representative politics, and widen our pool of political talent. Our democracy demands it and our people deserve it.

The beginning

My earliest memory is being on a carousel, I'm tucked on one side of my mother's lap with my younger brother Slater on the other. We're giggling as my mum hugs us against gravity. Her arm is half-paralysed from a car crash in Ghana a few years earlier. It was sewn back together with thick needles that left giant stitches. As a child I was always fascinated by the imprint of the outsized fishbone that ran up the blue-white flesh of her inner arm.

On this first day of my memory, as the carousel spins faster and faster, it is my mum's torn arm with the decorative fishbone that stops us clattering to earth. The burly men operating the carousel don't realise that the young mother's laughs are now cries. She is terrified her children will slip from her grasp. Eventually, long after leaving the fairground, we do.

Another early memory is looking out of the back window of a car that my dad is driving, and seeing snowflakes fall through a dark night sky. The snow is illuminated by a lava-flow of headlights on a motorway. It is the first time I register snowflakes. I am thrilled and excited by the way they fall towards me, both heavy and light, like a mysteriously recurring dream. The snowy motorway leads to an airport in Switzerland where, unbeknownst to my mum, my dad flies us to Kenya.

We didn't see Mum again until she tracked us down in Nairobi four months later. I was four and Slater was two and a half, both unaware of the vicious custody battle raging around us. All I understood was that both my parents wanted us desperately. It didn't seem such a bad thing, and it was only at secondary school that I began to feel the light trace of stigma attached to a 'broken home'.

Our home, which we returned to after our mother won custody of us both, didn't feel remotely broken. It was a nice house that my dad had bought for £9,000 in the 1960s, in between Belsize Park and Gospel Oak in North London. Our street felt impossibly long to a five-year-old. The beginning of Upper Park Road was majestic but around the bend, where we lived, it became more prosaic. Vaunting Victorian houses with Corinthian columns gave way to brooding council housing. The two ends of Upper Park Road sat in different worlds. Our house was physically next door to the council housing, but in reality we were somewhere in the middle.

To be precise (and to be British) we were lower-middle class. Given that both my parents were teachers, we were textbook middle class. Mum taught English at a local secondary school. Dad lectured in political philosophy at different universities. In 1967 he was teaching in Sheffield which is where I was born, the year he published his first book. His next job was in Kenya, at the University of East Africa, where Slater was born in 1969, and where we lived until I was three.

My memory from those early times is mainly smells and sensations – mellifluous smoke from roasting corn near our house, the sweet fibrous sensation of juicy sugar cane bought at street stalls, and the sound of chickens squawking in the yard. When my Kikuyu nanny, Wanjiku, wasn't carrying me on her hip, I trailed Wanjiru, the garden lady, as she tended jacaranda trees, oleanders, and bougainvillea.

Wanjiru's son, Jackaio, was about my age and he and I had a particular soft spot for the chickens. A few years later when the time came to leave, the staff wanted to give us kids a big party. They got our favourite chicken and, as a surprise treat, cut its head off. The idea was a big celebratory roast. I clearly remember watching the astonished chicken run around the dusty yard while its head looked on from a distance. The headless chicken continued to run for longer than seemed credible. This event was far, far more traumatising than my parents' later divorce. It also provided much evidence for my transitory belief in life after death.

After the divorce, I lived with Mum and my brother in Upper Park Road for the best part of the next twenty years. We spent two months of each year, our summer holidays, living with our father. He was back in Nairobi for a few years, until I was six, and then moved to Australia until I was fifteen. Slater and I travelled as unaccompanied minors on flights from Heathrow to Sydney that took thirty hours. These flights seemed to be both intergalactic and interminable, because there is only so much felt-tip colouring a child can do.

For a decade we spent our summer holidays in an autumnal Sydney. We went to school there, mastered our times tables, and learned how to dive under giant waves at Coogee Beach. My father remarried an intelligent Lebanese woman with rich flowing hair called Nahla, who we often quarrelled with. Our young stepmother would complain in French to our father, and then look to the sky and demand a response from Allah in Arabic. 'Ya'allah, ya'allah' was the entreaty that floated around our Australian household.

Our childhood zigzagged between different worlds defined by geography, class and ethnicity. Continents swung in and out of view. But most of the time we were in Upper Park Road, playing with our neighbours, jumping over garage roofs near a thicket of brambles and tired trees ambitiously called 'the woods', or running around the estate next door.

Woodfield and Barnfield were huge squat 1940s brick flats that sat opposite each other across a concrete scrubland. Their under-bellies housed ominously dark lock-up garages littered with chip paper, broken bottles and the occasional dead rat. These cement runways next to the basement garages, partially hidden yet open to the elements, had huge scope for children's gun battles, hide and seek, smoking and snogging (for older children). It wasn't that we liked it down there, it's just where we usually ended up.

A few floors above, most of my playmates had nice, bright flats, the exact opposite of that subterranean gloom. These council flats often offered a combination of excessive heating (in my view always preferable to too little), and the smell of tea and boiled veg. While my mum stocked our cupboard with garibaldi raisin biscuits and sent me to children's birthday parties clutching carrot sticks, teatime in Barnfield or Woodfield offered a cornucopia of custard cream biscuits, chocolate Bourbons, and Angel Delight.

The only other place I got this type of illicit pleasure was my gran's house. It was stuffed full of Cadbury chocolates, which for some reason I thought unusual in an Orthodox Jewish household. My mum

Hazel was born at the beginning of the Second World War in 1939. Hazel and her sister Miriam were brought up by my grandparents in a meticulously kosher home. Their kitchen had separate cupboards, utensils, washing-up bowls, pans, cutlery and baking dishes for meat and dairy dishes. Two more sets of everything were kept in the attic and brought down for Passover.

The Un-chosen

Like all Orthodox Jewish children in Newcastle, Hazel and Miriam went to Hebrew night-school (*cheder*) three nights a week after school, and again on Sunday mornings. They attended synagogue on Saturdays with my grandparents, Sidney and Jenny Stern, and the family only differed from most others in the Jewish community by being a tad more observant, and a lot less affluent. They lived in a council house, didn't have a TV or telephone, and all their clothes were made at home. My grandmother Jenny had converted to Judaism in order to marry my grandfather. They had waited ten years to be married, until Sidney's father was dead – he would never have sanctioned a *goy* (non-Jew) in the family.

Despite being extremely bright, Hazel and Miriam were given a wide berth by the Orthodox Jewish community, partly because they were poor, and partly because it was known that their mother had converted. Each year the top girl's grammar school awarded full scholarships to the three girls in the region who scored highest in the entrance exam. Mum was one of those three. Miri was also a scholarship student. Miri once overheard her Jewish boyfriend's mother lament that her son had fallen for 'one of the Stern girls' who came 'from the wrong side of town', which at that time was the west end of Newcastle. Miri not only got through medical school – highly unusual for a woman in the late 1950s – but also became the youngest doctor in Britain (male or female) to receive her postgraduate medical qualifications.* When news of her achievement spread, Granddad must have taken some pride in receiving phone

---

* Miriam went on to become one of Britain's best-known doctors and to sell over twenty million books worldwide on childcare, parenting and grandparenting.

calls from Orthodox Jewish families enquiring if they might introduce her to their sons.

My grandparents were bitterly disappointed when neither of their daughters married Jewish boys. In Miri's case, Granddad turned her pictures to the wall and wouldn't let her set foot in the house for two years. When it was Mum's turn, the shock might have been greater – not only was her husband a *goy*, he was black too! But in fact it was easier. Dad had already published his Ph.D. thesis. Sid and Jenny placed great stress on education, and couldn't help but admire that their son-in-law was 'a man of letters' – even if he was black. And then there were the grandchildren. People tend to soften racist views when mixed-race grandchildren arrive.

Mum remembers walking with her parents, and the two of us as young children. An old white man called out, '*Bloody coons!*', which enraged Granddad. He ran over, grabbed him by the collar, and shouted, 'If you weren't so old I'd knock your teeth out,!' Mum thought it was funny because they were about the same age. Theirs was the generation that didn't meet a black person until the 1960s or later. As for Gran, she slowly got used to having black grandchildren, although Mum remembers her showing me to a neighbour as a baby and saying in hushed tones, 'Don't worry, she won't get any darker.'

The Georgia connection

Born in 1936, my dad, Preston King, was the youngest of seven sons. He confounded every stereotype of six-foot-two-inch black man. He was an adolescent of surreal intelligence who climbed out of the cauldron of 1950s Bible Belt Georgia, and whose father paid for him to take up a scholarship at the London School of Economics where he met my mother. He became an academic, a professor fascinated by Hobbes and Italian opera.

The year before he arrived in London as a nineteen-year-old, he and a friend in New Orleans hid the sign on the bus which said 'white people only beyond this point'. The sign would move up and down the bus, depending on how busy it was. The busier it was, the more seats were reserved for whites, and more blacks like Rosa Parks had to stand. Removing the sign disrupted the neat laws of separation that kept the races apart. When Dad arrived in London in the late 1950s, he entered an environment where myriad ethnic groups were coming together for the first time.

My great-grandfather Allen was born exactly a century before me in 1867, just two years after the Thirteenth Amendment officially abolished slavery. My great-great-grandparents Horacce and Eliza were slaves until their forties, but the 1870 Federal Census listed the following information for Horacce. Occupation: *farm labourer*; colour: *black*. Eliza's occupation was listed as: *at home*; colour: *mulatto*. Another column entitled 'deaf and dumb, blind, insane or idiotic' is ambiguously marked with a diagonal stroke. What is clear is that they had a remarkable grandson. My grandfather, Clennon Washington King, was born in 1893 in Florida. Like most free blacks of that time, Clennon's life was on the farm, where he worked for his father. His father would not, or could not, help him get an education, so Clennon set out on foot aged fourteen and made his way to a college that taught former slaves. This was the Tuskegee Institute in Alabama, run by Booker T. Washington. At college my grandfather taught himself to read and write, and met my grandmother, Margaret Slater. Clennon eventually moved to Albany, Georgia, and got a job with the federal government as a postman. Within a few years, he had acquired property and a variety of businesses. He was deacon in the Mount Zion Baptist Church – now a civil rights museum – and a pillar of the black community.

Despite daily insults due to their race, my grandparents brought up their children to be respectful of others. Unlike the prevailing attitudes around them, they were relaxed about religion, and never insisted on conformity from their own children, but all of them attended church because church for them was nothing to do with theology and everything to do with social belonging and loyalty. The family were all committed to their community, and hoped in various ways to defend it against widespread injustice.

Of the seven sons, my uncle Slater built the first affordable housing for black people in the area, Uncle Paul became a professor of linguistics, Uncle Chevene was Martin Luther King's lawyer, and Uncle Clennon, the eldest, was reputedly the first black man to run for president. Uncle Clennon also tried to desegregate Mississippi University, and for his troubles was committed to a mental asylum.

My Dad, like the others, was trained by his parents to stand up for his own rights, courteously but firmly.

The fact that my father refused to be treated differently on account of his skin soon led to trouble. Dad had to apply to the draft board to defer his military service. It was the late 1950s, after Korea and before Vietnam. Deferral was standard, though the students applying were virtually all white. When the military draft board in Albany, Georgia, discovered my father was black, they dropped the courtesy title of *Mr* and addressed him by his first name only – 'Dear *Preston*'.

Dad wrote back saying that he would only comply with their requests if they addressed him as they did his white peers. They refused, and instead arrested him on four charges of violating the Selective Service Act. To cut a long story short (and it's such a long and remarkable story that NBC News ran an investigative series on it, Madonna's film company travelled to the UK to discuss the film rights, and the *New York Times* devoted a full page to Dad's eventual pardon), Dad stuck to his guns; rather than accept inferior treatment to his white peers, he endured forty years of exile from his home and family. He wandered all over the place. He once told me during a casual conversation, almost as an afterthought, that he had become an Australian citizen. I was confused – did this suddenly make me Australian too? – and then pleased; I liked the idea of trying on a nationality, like trying on a hat. I viewed my British and American passports as travel ledgers with pretty stamps. I could not conceive that these small quadratic books – mine through an accident of birth – were life-giving treasures.

My automatic right to citizenship in two of the richest countries on earth only truly struck me years later, at a Red Cross centre on the border between the Congo and Rwanda. I was speaking to a thirteen-year-old child soldier who had lost family members in the Rwandan genocide, fled to the Congo, been kidnapped by the militia twice, escaped twice, and then spent years trapped on the no man's land at the border. I asked this child, if he could have anything, what it would be. Without hesitation he replied, 'A country'. I have never felt so humbled. He didn't want a new pair of trainers, a stereo, a car, or even a house and family. He wanted a country. Was it so much to ask? Most of us never think twice about this privilege we are born with.

But my dad did, because he didn't have a country either. As a teenager I didn't appreciate his situation at all. I understood it was sad, but no more. And I understood that I would be sent in his place to attend funerals, and see my American family, which happened about once every three or four years.

Waiting for a nuclear holocaust

Back in Britain, my mum Hazel brought us up on her small teacher's salary. She was always running, from home, to school, to work, to after-school clubs, to teachers' meetings, to parents' meetings, and then back again. She would get up very early each morning, usually five or six a.m., and prepare our lunches or her classes, or the car . . . My dream as a child was that I would buy her a new car. Her cars were always broken-down bangers that had to be coaxed and cajoled, warmed and begged. Every morning I listened to the revving engine, desperately hoping it would turn over. If it didn't, Mum's day was ruined.

Everyone liked my mum, especially the kids she taught. She is only five foot two inches, but I've seen her hold seething testosterone-popping giant teenagers at bay. She does it using a mixture of wit and irony, but mainly – I know it sounds corny – by showing unconditional empathy and kindness. Once I was incensed when one of her students tried to pin her against a wall with a chair. By this time she was running a special unit for 'troublemakers' expelled from secondary school. 'I'll kill him!' I shouted. 'The thing is, Oona,' she explained, 'he doesn't know how to behave, because nobody taught him. He and his four siblings, all under five, were found abandoned in a locked flat running around injured and terrified, basically left to rot in their own urine and excrement. You never know what another person's been through.' It wasn't that my mum excused bad behaviour, it was that she found a way to encourage kids out of it. She believed they could behave better and often, simply to repay her faith in them, they did. On countless occasions we met the parents of children who came to thank our mum for what she'd done for them.

Even though we admired our mother enormously, Slater and I could still make her life hell. Mum couldn't leave us with a babysitter

– her pleasant, polite children were highly inflammable beneath the
surface. Slater and I had a love–hate relationship. Until our late
teenage years it was mainly hate. Perhaps hate is too strong a word,
but the fact is, we often tried to kill each other. Because Slater is so
precious to me today – and other than my husband, he is the first
person I turn to for help – I often forget just how much I wanted to
garrotte him. I don't even remember what we argued about. 'You
should behave better,' I'd say, while trying to torture him or frame
him. We both still carry childhood battle scars. Today Slate is a top
professional photographer, he's the one I'm smiling at on the front of
this book.

I was conscious that we weren't an affluent family. Mum never
said I couldn't have things, but I knew not to ask. One time, when I
was thirteen, I asked for a shocking pink T-shirt dress that was
pulled into a big knot at the side – one of those desperate fashion
crimes of the eighties. Mum bundled me into the car and drove me
straight to Brent Cross shopping centre as though it was an emergency. She says it was only the second time I asked for something. I
doubt that's true but it's difficult to judge, especially when you know
two important things about my mum.

The first, as I mentioned, is that she never lies. The second is that
whatever I did was always, in her eyes, the best thing ever. She told
me constantly how much '*nachus*' I brought her, the Yiddish word
for parental pride and joy. And her praise was never meaningless to
me. She made me genuinely believe I could do anything, she gave me
an invisible shield of self-belief that has protected me time and again
from trauma. I know without a shadow of a doubt that I became an
MP because of that confidence she instilled in me. That, and her
intense attachment to social justice.

So maybe I didn't ask for things, or maybe she was good at making
us feel we didn't need things. I can only remember her once looking
me in the eye and saying, 'You can't have that, we can't afford it.' It
was 1979, the year of the Iranian revolution and the winter of
discontent. I was eleven, and thrilled because my primary school
class was going on the school's first ever skiing trip. I came home
clutching the piece of paper with the tear-off slip attached, elated at
the prospect of travelling to Europe. 'Ninety pounds,' said my mum
in a pained voice. 'I can never get that sort of money.'

Of the thirty-five children in my class, only five couldn't go. The rest left at three o'clock on a Sunday afternoon and I cried myself silly during my first lesson in social exclusion. I had a fantastic childhood because that's the worst that happened. Well, apart from once seeing Mum knocked unconscious and thinking she was dead. And apart from being sent to a doctor twice a year from the age of seven to check if I had cervical cancer. Mum had been given a drug during her pregnancy to prevent miscarriage, a drug called DES, diethylstilboestrol, later known as the 'silent Thalidomide' because of the abnormalities it caused in girls.

Ninety per cent of girls born to women who took the drug were affected. Some didn't have wombs, others had no ovaries. Most were infertile. A surprising number died before they reached twenty. I got more and more upset at being carted off to doctors for examination, and was devastated when, at the age of twelve, Mum and Miri tried to soothe me by explaining, 'You have a high risk of cancer and doctors need to monitor you.' I instantly interpreted this as a death sentence.

I spent my early teenage years thinking, 'Why me? Even if I don't die, I can never have children. No one will ever marry me. I'll never be normal.' I consoled myself that it didn't matter because we were all going to die in a nuclear holocaust. Like many of my generation, I was waiting for it to happen. I had CND stickers plastered all over my bedroom, and Joan Ruddock was my heroine. I lay in bed at night staring up at a huge poster of David Bowie next to silhouettes of nuclear warheads, and a couple of postcards from Greenham Common and Robbin Island. The 1980s had a dark narcissistic air to them, as if wrapped in filthy cling film. I didn't want to escape my home, I just wanted to escape my decade.

And yet I knew how lucky I was to live in this age, and not an earlier one. I was particularly grateful to my grandparents' generation for fighting off Hitler – the idea of being born a black Jew in Nazi Britain didn't bear thinking about. But even without the Nazis, what opportunities would a black girl have had in the 1900s? Or any woman for that matter. I thought of my gran, Jenny, a highly intelligent woman, whose job in the cigarette factory included taking random cigarettes off the conveyor belt and puffing on them to test that smoke came through properly: the literal definition of a dead-end job. But Jenny was clever and hard-working. By eighteen she was supervising hundreds of older women on the factory floor. She got out of the fag factory and became a dinner lady, and then worked her way up to be supervisor. 'So you see, Oona,' she told me proudly, 'if you work hard, anything is possible.'

Goodbye to *The Black & White Minstrel Show*

On Christmas Day 1978 Mum gave me a green velvet diary. I've kept a diary of one sort or another ever since. The word 'diary' was embossed on the green velvet in gold letters. I explained my purpose on the inside jacket:

'I am writing this Diary in the hope that someone in a billion years' time will find it and know what it was like for an average eleven-year-old to live in the 20th century.'

My entries have the interminable dullness you would expect from the average eleven-year-old, intertwined with mundane revelation. Glimpses of the winter of discontent filter through. Although in the playground and the street my national identity is constantly questioned ('Where are you *really* from?'), I am clearly a British child – half my entries mention the weather.

My first strong political memory is of the 1979 general election, watching TV footage of James Callaghan walking down a staircase, about to concede defeat. From the way the adults around me are groaning and moaning, it seems something very bad has happened. The main thing I gather is that my team is losing. My team, the Labour Party, is fighting for fairness, equality and socialism, but there's been a problem with the rubbish collection and rotting corpses, and we're being kicked out of power. My first awareness of my team being *in* power, is the moment at which it is ejected. A woman has elbowed her way into No. 10. I assume that can't be such a bad thing, because at least she's a woman. I am catastrophically wrong.

Although Margaret Thatcher took away my free school milk, on a personal level life wasn't bad at all. The after-school timetable at the front of my diary tells me I went swimming on Mondays and Fridays, did gym club on Tuesdays, piano on Wednesday, and hockey on Thursday. Fleet Primary School whisked me off to concerts and museums at every available opportunity, and when the school wasn't dragging me around an educational establishment, my Mum was. So basically, there it is. I led an utterly privileged, if not poncey, middle class life. I clearly remember skipping around as a young child thinking, 'I'm so happy, I'm so happy.' The only minor cloud to darken my horizon was the growing realisation that I was 'different'.

My primary school class comprised one black African boy, Howie Gondwe, one Asian girl, Monica Patel, thirty-two white children, and me. I always knew I was different. It wasn't a huge thing at all, but it was quite an obvious thing. And it wasn't just about how people reacted to me, it was how they reacted to my parents. More than once when my dad was visiting, girls in my class started crying when they saw him at the school gate. They were literally terrified of him. They had absorbed the prevalent idea of the time, that nothing was more frightening than a black man. Had I been my father's colour, as opposed to the light coffee colour I am, my 'darkened' horizon would have been even more frightening, even more crippled by the inherent racism of Britain's 1970s world view which equated all things black and dark with all things frightening and inferior.

There was also the fact that no one thought I was my mother's daughter. I didn't know any other children who had this problem, who were separated by colour from their parents. Not even Howie Gondwe or Monica Patel had this problem. Mind you, I can only imagine (I could be wrong) that they had far worse problems. Anyone who wants to understand the trauma that black children from African or Asian backgrounds suffered in 1970s Britain (as opposed to mixed-race or Afro-Caribbean children) should read the beautiful and powerful memoir *Black Gold of the Sun: Searching for Home in England and Africa*.

Written by ICA Director Ekow Eshun, born a year after me in 1968, *Black Gold* reflects some of the negative feelings from my childhood more closely than anything else I've read. But whereas the racism I encountered was minor, with Ekow it was major. That's because racism is . . . (doh!) racist. The darker you are the more racism you encounter. While mixed-race people have a whole raft of other issues to deal with – often facing racism from both communities – there is no doubt that from playground to boardroom, shade-ism rules. The darkest are most often at the bottom of the heap, the lightest sit on top.

In the North London caste system of my childhood, the only exception to this rule was that light-skinned Asian children ranked below dark-skinned Afro-Caribbeans. In my secondary school class I was the only mixed-race child. There was one black Afro-Caribbean boy, a black African boy, an Asian girl and me.

Although I was often quite content to be different (mainly due to my mum's brilliant work to boost my self-image) I went through phases when I desperately wanted to be the same as other children. I wanted to be 'normal', and this meant sometimes wanting to be white. I inter-nalised my 'difference' in a variety of ways, mainly negatively until early adolescence, and then increasingly positively. Britain's mood music was changing. Black people were no longer confined to *The Black & White Minstrel Show*. The National Front was fighting a losing battle. For the first time people like me slipped into the national consciousness. Two mixed-race fairies in the shape of Neneh Cherry and Sade sprinkled magic self-esteem over my teenage years. For every taunt of mongrel, or 'yid-nigger', there was now a positive image of a self-assured, respected, beautiful mixed-race woman.

A 2003 survey asked British young people which group they thought faced most discrimination in Britain: was it blacks, Asians, Muslims, disabled people, gay people, the old, the young, or other minorities? Their overwhelming reply was *ugly* people. In our image-obsessed world it's easy to see why, especially in relation to women. There are few things worse for a teenage girl than being called ugly. The playground taunts of '*ugly mongrel*' made my eyes sting. I linked it to a vague feeling of being soiled, marked, maybe ruined. My nose was wider than most, my lips much fuller, my skin slightly darker, and my hair a frizzy tangle. Looking in the mirror before I left for school I would damp down my hair and say to myself, 'I am not ugly, I can even be beautiful. Today they'll see that.' And yet later that day in the school toilets, with my hair frizzed up again, I looked in the mirror and saw *ugly*. And when the boys called me that, I felt they were right. Why did I seem attractive to my own eyes in the morning, and ugly in the afternoon? Was it just a bad hair day? Every day? It took me years to understand that the prevailing attitudes of a place shape your view of yourself. And the prevailing attitude in the school playground was clear: black was ugly, ugly as sin. And of course it was a bad hair day every day – because black hair could never match the white aesthetic.

I hated my hair. As early as eight years old I took a pair of scissors and cut off my two plaits, creating a ludicrous zigzagged frizzy bob that made me cry even more. Like most black or mixed-race British girls I was searching for what Zadie Smith described perfectly in her novel *White Teeth* as '*flickability*'. Princess Diana had it. George Michael had it. Michelle and Sharon from *EastEnders* had it. At thirteen I straightened my hair so I too could have it, so I too could look like the white girls. But still I worried about being an adult because I couldn't envisage a solution to my uncontrollable hair. How could I be Prime Minister, I fretted, if I had to wear my hair in two plaits like a ten-year-old? I never imagined a day would come when my hair was my favourite feature. (Nor, for that matter, when white girls up and down the country would straighten their hair even more fastidiously than black girls.)

My two plaits provide me with many memories, not all linked to race. The most extreme occurred in the playground when I was in my first year at Haverstock, my secondary school. The bell had gone for the end of lessons and I was filing up the stairs to go to class. In the middle of the stairway, barring entry to the building, was a menacing third year girl called Nadine.

By common consensus Nadine was mean and big, and you didn't mess with her. She was also Afro-Caribbean which lent her an extra-hard air. Nadine put her leg in front of each child, and demanded, 'Say please.' One by one each child said 'please' and she let them pass. My turn arrived.

'Say please.'

'No thank you, I just wanna pass.'

'Fucking say please.'

'No, I just wanna pass.'

'Are you gonna fucking say please or am I gonna rearrange yer fucking face?'

'Just let me pass.'

At this point the crowd began to chant, 'Fight, fight, fight.'

'OK you bitch,' said Nadine, 'let's fight.'

Like an instant pop-up carnival, young ushers bundled me from the stairs into the middle of the playground and formed a circle in preparation for a proper fight.

'I don't wanna fight, I just don't wanna say *please* to walk past you.'

'You're gonna say *please*, just watch.' And with that, Nadine laid into me. It wasn't quite as bad as I expected, mainly consisting of pushes and shoves against the circle of kids that was now deep enough to bounce off, like a human boxing ring. I could feel the blows but they weren't really hurting.

Just as I was thinking, 'This isn't that bad,' Nadine grabbed both my plaits. She started to pull me round by my head, and as the chanting got louder and louder, she gathered speed like a pilot cranking up a propeller engine, until eventually she achieved lift-off. To the delight of the assembled crowd she managed to swing me in circles a full two feet off the ground, by my plaits. It probably would have been the second time my plaits were parted from my head, if a teacher hadn't made a late tackle and caught hold of my flying legs. Then I was on the floor, dirt in my face, and it was over. Spitting the gravel out of my mouth I turned to Nadine as we were led away to the head's office.

'I never said *please*.'

Expanding horizons

Within a few weeks of starting Haverstock School in 1979, my middle-class accent morphed into the new London 'mockney'. This new accent, as rampant as the grey squirrel, has shaped a generation of middle-class Londoners from Jamie Oliver to Guy Ritchie, and continues to overrun its prettier cousin with rounded vowels, spreading to leafier parts of the capital and taking no prisoners. I picked it up partly to avoid attack by people like Nadine, but mainly because it suited me better than the one I had. My Mum was dismayed to hear my new glottal stop – it developed over a weekend, and has proved unshakeable over a lifetime.

But worse was to come in my French classes. My French teacher Madame Borelle was one of those lovely young teachers who are sweet and helpful and get massacred by a classroom of cruel children who scent any sign of weakness. I found French frustrating and difficult. I can't remember exactly how I behaved, but I know I must have been a gobby upstart. So one day Madame Borelle chucked me out of the classroom, and I stood for half an hour kicking my heels behind the door. It then occurred to me to express my frustration, so I got my pen and started to scratch a sentence into the woodwork using a new-found swear word.

'My French teacher is a *cun*–'

As I was adding the stroke to the *t*, the door opened and out popped Madame Borelle. She looked at me, I looked at her, and then the power of guilt involuntarily turned my eleven-year-old head towards the words I'd scratched on the wall. My informant eyes led her gaze directly to the crime. Within minutes the head of department was summoned, and Mrs Baxter stood shaking me by the shoulders, appalled at my misdemeanour. It wasn't that I'd done something entirely uncommon; it was that the daughter of *Hazel King* had done such a thing. Mum taught at the school for years, was one of the most polite women you would ever meet, and Mrs Baxter found it inconceivable that her daughter could be guilty of such a heinous crime. As the end-of-day bell rang, and children and teachers spilled into the corridor, she held me in front of everyone saying, 'Can you *believe* what Hazel King's daughter has done? Just *look* at what Hazel King's daughter has done.'

Suffice to say Mum was devastated. She explained how demeaning the word is to women, how it typifies their subjugation, and how extraordinarily rude it is. I cried bitterly because I couldn't bear to see her so upset. I promised I would never use the word again. I failed by a wide margin. Worse, I was among a generation of uncouth urban feminists who reclaimed the word to hurl at misogynistic men. I'm not proud of it. Using female genitalia to describe the worst human behaviour just shows it's a man's world.

That man's world shifted slightly on its axis during a maths lesson when I was thirteen. We were set a question that asked: 'If a student is cycling from X to Y, and covers a distance of three miles, travelling at fourteen miles an hour, how long does it take her to arrive?' How long? That wasn't the point! I remember bursting with wonder and amazement. It was the first time in my life that an unidentified active person was a *girl*. It could have been a boy, but for no particular reason it was a girl. A girl who *did* something. Normally the default position in classroom exercises was that the *boy* did something – he cycled, flew the kite, threw the ball, or saved the day. Imagine, I thought, what it would be like to grow up a boy instead of a girl, a man instead of a woman. It would just be so . . . *empowering*. It wasn't a word I knew, but it was a feeling I glimpsed. And if boys or men think it isn't empowering to grow up like that, it's because they don't notice. They take it for granted that they're always in the default position. And until that maths class, so did I.

At about that time, my horizons really did expand beyond the classroom walls, because I started skipping a few lessons to break into the Swiss Cottage Odeon with a crew whose parents claimed gangster links to the Krays. Playing truant gave me some life lessons. The most vivid was my first interaction with a police officer. 'Oy you black bitch!' he shouted after I burst out of one of the cinema's fire exits and scaled a wall to get away from the cinema ushers in pursuit, 'Get down off that wall!'

I was surprised – not because he called me a black bitch, but because I managed to jump off the wall and lose him. He has often revisited me, this police officer, not his flesh but his face. The face of authority. It was clear the authorities weren't mad keen on black people. Years later, as Vice-Chair of the London Group of Labour MPs, I often met with the Metropolitan Police Commissioner, who wanted to improve race relations. I spoke to rank-and-file police officers, many of whom said they had to state the truth, which was that black people were obsessed with race.

When I hear this still prevalent complaint (that black people are obsessed with race), the policeman's face floats back to me, reminding me of the irritating thing about race. Black people have it shoved down our throats from the word go – and then white people turn round and tell us *we're* obsessed. And yes, sometimes we become obsessed and paranoid, because whenever a thing tracks you from birth, hunts and haunts you, or at the very least is used by others like the policeman to define you, you'd be stupid not to see its glaring face everywhere. Yet sometimes you look twice and there is nothing there at all, and the paranoia gets worse not better.

The other thing that's galling is to have something pointed out to you again and again and again. It's like hearing the same joke twenty times a day for twenty years, and then someone turns around and says, 'Haven't you got a sense of humour?' It's not only black people who have this experience. Recently I watched Jonathan Ross, the English TV presenter, interview Dylan Moran, the Irish comedian. Ross spent much of the interview making dismal jokes about Dylan being Irish, and then asked him earnestly, 'Do you find people constantly typecast you as an Irish person?'*

When I arrived at secondary school I wasn't so much paranoid as realistic; I expected to be lightly typecast. I knew which part of my identity most defined me to others. Apart from my brother, I was the only mixed-race person I knew. So for example, regarding that most important thing for a young teenage girl – her first kiss – there was only one choice in my class: the black boy. All the white boys were ruled out by the invisible yet immovable race matrix that placed me below them.† My first kiss was therefore with a boy I was drawn to, or paired with, for no other reason than skin colour.

As for my first boyfriend, that was different. I was with Tom, on and off, for five years, for no other reason than love – I loved him the way fourteen-year-olds do, consumed yet detached. It's only now that I realise it wasn't different at all. Apart from being a great person, Tom is also mixed race, born to an Asian father and white mother. How did I miss that? How did I think I was the only mixed-race person I knew when I went *out* with one for five years? Did I miss it, just because his mix was Asian and mine black? Or because he was called Tom instead of Krishnan? Or was it a coincidence that my boyfriend was the only mixed-race person (half-breed said the kids) in his class, and I was the only one in mine? I recently said to Tom, 'It's strange, I never thought of you like that.' He replied, 'Well you probably did, because you always said how much you liked it that our skin colour was the same.'

It's a ridiculous remark worthy of the far right – 'I'm so glad our skin colour is the same.' And yet I recognise it immediately, as I've said it to my olive-skinned Italian husband repeatedly. I thought I had escaped being shaped by colour, but it was my imagination. In my childhood, being the same colour as the rest meant a sense of belonging and

---

* *Friday Night with Jonathan Ross*, 1 December 2006.
† See 'An American Journey', my *Guardian* article of 18 October 2005 (www.oonaking.com).

entitlement that I envied. Whether subconscious or not, race shaped my thoughts, and I yearned for someone the same colour as me.

Nowadays mixed-race people are two a penny. I sometimes wonder where we all came from. I mean these mixed-race people I see everywhere, reading the news or presenting children's TV, they have British accents like me, they look like me, they act like me, but where were they when I was growing up? We haven't all just got off a boat, so presumably they were also in British classrooms surrounded by white kids, wondering why they were different.

My earliest political passions were Amnesty International, and the Anti-Vivisection campaign. In my early teens I channelled my energies into drama and politics, two skills that are often intertwined. I helped my friend Quincy set up a United Nations Association, though I'm not sure whether this was because I was impressed with her vision, or because my name is spelt Una on my passport and I wanted UNA stickers for my bedroom. At fourteen I joined the Labour Party. I went to my first Labour Party meeting soon after and was so traumatised by boredom that I didn't go back for eight years. I can't say when I became a Labour person, as I've never thought of myself as anything else. The Labour Party seemed an obvious choice for anyone concerned about social justice. But neither of my parents were members of the Labour Party, although Dad was later an active member of the Fabian Society.

As the 1980s gathered pace, everything seemed wrong. It seemed wrong that millions of people were on the dole, that Margaret Thatcher won elections, and that the British Prime Minister was a misanthrope, genuinely convinced that society did not exist. I wanted to prove her wrong. If anybody had asked my primary purpose in wanting to be an MP back then I would have answered, 'To fight poverty and get rid of the likes of Margaret Thatcher.'

When I was seventeen and studying politics A Level, I wanted to visit the House of Commons with my class.

'You could always contact my cousin Ted,' said Mum, 'I haven't seen him since childhood but apparently he became an MP, and then a Lord.'

I was gobsmacked to hear of a Labour MP in the family. Uncle Ted, as I came to call him, devoted his whole life to the Labour movement. He was leader of Enfield Borough Council for ten years, then MP for Edmonton between 1974 and 1983, after which he was given a life peerage as Lord Graham of Edmonton.

Ted is a big-hearted man with a fantastic number of dubious jokes that he shared with me throughout my time at Westminster. His favourite involved slapping me on the back at the House of Commons tea room and saying, 'It's all *relative*!' before explaining to bemused MPs that we were blood cousins. I'm proud to say that at eighty-six Ted is still in Parliament as Lord Graham of Edmonton, having outlasted me by several decades.

After finishing my A Levels Mum waved me goodbye as I left for my Oxford interviews. It's the only time I remember her realism getting the better of her idealism.

'Oona, darling, wouldn't it be a good idea if you took that huge silver CND pendant off, just for the interview?' It was on a large chain, obscured half my chest, and looked at least twice the size of a Mercedes sign.

'No Mum, the CND sign stays.' In the event, at least for one of the interviews, I don't recall the interviewer looking up from his newspaper long enough to notice the pendant. I wondered if I was supposed to follow the example of the apocryphal Oxford hopeful who set the paper on fire to win attention and a place, but in the end I bottled it. And I probably didn't have the skills required to get through an Oxford entrance exam. After receiving a rejection on Christmas Eve, I threw caution to the CND wind and wrote in my diary, '*When I'm Prime Minister I'm gonna nuke Oxford.*'

Like most eighteen-year-old left-wingers, I was desperately seeking revolution. With nothing doing in Britain, I looked up Nicaragua in the phone book. The Nicaragua Solidarity Campaign gave me a means to see revolution, or at least coffee beans, first hand. I travelled with about thirty other British members of the La Pasionara Brigade to a remote mountain village in northern Nicaragua. We lived in a wooden hut, slept on wooden bunks, and ate rice and beans every day except for Sunday, when we would walk two hours to a wooden shack to eat roast chicken. I was the youngest at nineteen, and the oldest was seventy-four.

I was profoundly affected by what I saw in Nicaragua, and returned soon after, drawn less by a desire for revolution and more by a little boy called Luis. I often think of Luis. He was my first flesh-and-blood introduction to murderous poverty. Luis sat with his stick-thin legs and distended stomach on the threshold of his family's mud hut on a coffee plantation in the mountains. He would stare at me in a vacant kind of way. I played games with him and went to great lengths to squeeze a flicker of a smile from his solemn face. He was no more than three years old, yet he had wrinkles on his forehead where his skin hung loosely. He looked like an ancient toddler, if such a thing were possible.

Often we would just sit at the end of the day, him in my lap, watching the village transact its business. I loved Luis. I had a black and white picture of him by my bed for a decade. I was really excited to return to the village to find him, and it took me years to get over the fact that he had died before reaching the age of five. Your first death can stay with you even more than your first love, and that's how it was for me with Luis.

Luis's death, and my visits to Nicaragua, shaped my choice of politics courses at university: American Imperialism and Latin American politics. I'd been at York University for less than twenty-four hours when I got involved with wannabe revolution-aries much closer to home – the Socialist Workers Party. I didn't really know who the SWP were, but I was looking for the socialists, and the SWP stall was nearest the entrance.

'So you're the socialists? Cool, I'm a socialist, sign me up.' I don't deserve to live that down. Ever. But there was a particularly nice guy, Andy, running the stall, and I wasn't yet properly initiated into the Judean People's Front of left-wing politics. I even imagined that being a member of the Labour Party *qualified* me for joining the SWP rather than disbarred me. I was soon a working socialist, standing outside meetings selling copies of '*Socialist* Worker! Buy your *Socialist* Worker!'

During my first year at York I was elected on to the Student Union executive without party affiliation. I loved the Labour Party, and had been a member since joining at fourteen. But I liked socialist *work-ers*, and Andy and his mates seemed to be out *working* more in York than the Labour lot. Or at least *shouting* more. It was the SWP who eventually made me determined to move from the group of howling people on the outside, to the group of negotiating people on the inside. So I was a member of the Labour Party, working with members of the SWP, elected as an independent. A decade elapsed between election on to the Student Union executive and election to Parliament, where I finally made it into the very inside.

Most people I know who went to York University loved it. It has world-renowned academics, some of whom I'm still in touch with, and boasts exceptional academic achievement and a beautiful rural setting. York gave me a fantastic degree, and offered me astonishing opportunities. But as for being a student there, for some reason I couldn't abide it. I felt completely out of place. It was a very white environment, even more so than school. Why that bugged me so much, I don't know, though many black and mixed-race people brought up in white environments have told me they sought to 'rebalance' themselves as young adults by seeking out a black environment. If I was looking for a black subculture, York was the wrong place to look.

The answer was a scholarship to the University of California, Berkeley, to study politics and philosophy. I was transplanted from York to San Francisco for my second year. The idea of swapping the Jorvik Viking Centre for the Golden Gate Bridge was too good to be true. Yet as escape became imminent, the good memories of York came to the fore. There was the fantastic time I had directing Alan Bennett's *Kafka's Dick*, with an outstanding cast. And of course there were some things I would miss, like my boyfriend at the time who, with impeccable musical taste, handed me a tape at the airport of George Clinton's album *Parliament* featuring the legendary Bootsy Collins. With Bootsy's funkadelic tunes ringing in my head, I set off for San Francisco via my cousin Peggy's flat in New York.

I walked through the arrivals lounge at JFK on a sunny afternoon wearing a grubby T-shirt, dodgy multicoloured trousers, and half-crippled by a student backpack that towered over my head. At the luggage carousel I chatted with the young New Yorker I'd sat next to on the plane. Rachel was an original JAP (Jewish American Princess), with brown corkscrew curls and a vivacious sixteen-year-old's laugh that bordered on a whine. When her parents didn't arrive she was crying within seconds. I offered to accompany her home, got a cab, paid the fare, and subsequently found myself in an unknown part of Brooklyn sitting in a Jewish household with a menorah on the mantlepiece, drinking tea from bone china teacups. When Rachel's parents arrived home in the early evening, they were disturbed to find me in their living room. Rachel's mother held her wallet close to her body as she reimbursed me for the cab. Rachel's father stood in the doorway, gestured down the hill, and hurriedly shut the door.

The sunny afternoon faded to dusk, and by the time I found a subway platform I felt as though my rucksack might pin me to the ground. I gave up trying to decipher the subway map, and gratefully slunk on to the first train, where I got out my Walkman and listened to Bootsy Collins. A few stops later a black guy with a wild Afro boarded the train and sat opposite me. He carefully placed a cake box on the seat next to him, and then looked around the carriage. By this time I'd pulled out the subway map again and was trying to work out how to get to Riverside Drive on the Upper West Side.

'Need some help?' asked the wild Afro.

'Yeah, I have no idea where I am. Where's this train going?'

His eyes bulged, and then he started laughing.

'Oh, man, a black girl with an English accent!' The wild Afro thought I was the funniest thing he'd heard in a long time, and even called out to another black guy a few seats away, 'Hey bro, you heard this English chick? Unreal! She talks like the Queen!'

After he'd shown me where I was going, and got over the initial shock of my accent, he wanted to know more about England. Had I ever met the Queen? Were there any other black people in the UK, was our weather as bad as everyone said, what sort of places did I hang out, what sort of music did I listen to?

'I like *Parliament*,' I said, 'and it's funny cos I'm gonna work in Parliament, so you should remember me cos I'm going to be Britain's first black . . .'

'*Parliament*? As in Funkadelic?'

'Yeah, and also as in the Houses of . . .'

'Unreal. You is one *unreal* li'l English chick!'

'Why's that?'

'Cos you just named the best goddamn group around. My name's Bootsy. Bootsy Collins. Pleased to meet you.'

The wild Afro was apparently the same musical legend I was listening to on my Walkman. I tried to work out how much of a joker he was, and then replied gently, 'Fuck off.'

'I am, I'm Bootsy Collins.'

'Fuck off.'

'Oh, lawd, she don't be-*lee* me. Anyway, this is the deal. It's my friend's birthday, thas why I'm carryin' this cake, she in a play on Broadway, I'm playin' a gig for her, and Peter Gabriel's playin' – y'all hearda Peter Gabriel? Anyway, thing is, you invited, cos like I say, you is one *unreal* li'l English chick. So you gonna get off the train with me at the next stop? You wanna come?'

I sized him up again. The odds were stacked against him being Bootsy Collins. He probably just wanted to chat me up, rape me, and chop me into pieces. Maybe he was a mental patient. Or maybe he was Bootsy and he was going to Broadway. I made him quote his lyrics, 'I want the bomb, I want the P. Funk, I wants to get funked up.' Problem was, I always found slightly crazy people preferable to boring people, and I was never overly persuaded by risk. My attitude was, 'It'll be all right.'

'OK, I'll come, but I gotta ring my cousin.'

Half an hour later we turned up a dark alleyway. This is it, I thought, what did I expect?

'It's just a shortcut,' explained the wild Afro, 'it's around the corner, listen you can hear the people.'

And sure enough, from around the corner came a hum. A queue of people, narrow at our end, grew thicker as it sloped towards a brightly lit entrance.

'Yo Bootsy!' came the first shout.

'Hey Bootsy, whatup?'

'Thas my man Bootzilla!'

The wild Afro was Bootsy Collins, a man widely considered to be the Jimi Hendrix of bass guitarists, the genius who rocked the groove with James Brown before moving on to George Clinton's Parliament. In fact by the time I met him, Bootsy's crew at Parliament-Funkadelic, otherwise known as P. Funk, had overtaken James Brown as the most sampled artist in the world. They were responsible for No. 1 dance classics like 'One Nation Under a Groove'. Those who thought they'd never heard of Bootsy Collins had actually heard him a hundred times. Bootsy led me to the front of the queue. Near the door, bodies packed closer together, almost heaving and sighing in unison, all yearning to get through the door. Then the photographers made an appearance. 'Bootsy, over here!'

Flashbulbs popped, and somewhere there must be a picture of Bootsy Collins, the legendary funkster, arriving at a Manhattan nightclub in September 1988, with a chubby teenager in a grubby T-shirt and a towering backpack, on her way to meet Peter Gabriel.

I've had so many Bootsy nights in my life, I can't even remember most of them. I don't mean with Bootsy himself – he gave me his number but I never rang or saw him again. That one night was enough, and will always bring a smile to my face. By a Bootsy night I mean either having a really funny time with a person I didn't know at the beginning of the evening; or relying on the kindness of strangers and finding that my faith in their good nature pays off. I realise that many young women with a similar attitude don't live to tell the tale. But I just can't shake this attitude, I can't help it, or rather I don't *want* to help it, I don't want to live a life where you can't just meet someone new and do something unanticipated. In my life I want to rely on the fact that most human beings will be kind. I don't just rely on that fact, I relish it. And obviously I always help a stranger too if I can. Otherwise what's the point in human existence?

The secret life of tables and chairs

When I finally made it from New York to California, I studied at Berkeley under philosophers like Bernard Williams and John Searle. It wasn't long before philosophy drove me mad. Either it was intractable tomes of Heidegger, or it was imbecilic questions about a table. That bloody table. When you walk out of the room, does the table still exist? This is a respected philosophical question. Sometimes it's a chair. The fact is, it's there when I come back, so I really don't need to worry about what it does when I'm away.

A lot of my life philosophy is linked to the 'life's too short' school of thought. Life is far too short to worry about the secret lives of tables and chairs. I know I'm being unfair to philosophers, not least my father, but I've always had other worries on my mind – like getting rid of Tory governments, feeding hungry children, ending factory farming, unfair trading, global warming, helping freezing pensioners . . . Philosophers would say you can't deal with any of those pressing problems unless you have a coherent life view based on philosophical tenets. I agree, but not to the point where I theorise about what the table does in its spare time.

In 1988, while at Berkeley, I dropped philosophy, freeing myself to concentrate on the two political questions that interested me most, and on which I wrote my two degree theses. The first was Islam, and the struggle of Islam to interact with democracy, and reform. The second was the warped psychology of American foreign policy, and the astonishing ability of Americans to shoot themselves in the foot – and everyone else in the head – when prosecuting their wars on behalf of 'liberty, freedom and democracy'. Those two areas seem more relevant today than they did even then.

I had a brilliant tutor at York, Haleh Afshar, who taught me about Islam. She inspired me more than any other teacher at university. I immersed myself briefly in the world of Sunnis and Shias, Mohammed and Fatima. I read the Koran, and wondered why I was studying an area that no one else seemed to bother with. I couldn't imagine that two decades later a copy of the Koran would be *de rigueur* in most political and intellectual circles – not to mention the living rooms of half my constituents.

When I found out I'd been awarded a first-class degree I was filled with delight. Now I could become an aerobics teacher without being labelled a bimbo. I wanted a self-sufficient skill or trade, something I could do if my plan to become Prime Minister didn't work out. Something that would help me earn a living during a recession when a degree might be worthless. And I wanted to exercise and stay fit. I avoided regular gym classes like the plague, and decided the only way to guarantee my attendance was to become the teacher. The plan worked, and although I was temping as a secretary at the same time, I often exercised up to five hours a day. There were times as an MP when I was so unfit I could hardly stagger up the stairs to the voting lobby. On these occasions an image of me as an aerobics teacher would haunt me, the way an image of youth might haunt a care-home patient.

The tea lady's news

Around the time the Berlin Wall fell, I landed my 'get-out-of-jail-free' card. A doctor gave it to me. I was in my early twenties, and he told me to count my lucky stars. I was among the 10 per cent of girls exposed to the drug DES who were unaffected. He assured me I was completely normal, and I would be able to have children like anyone else. 'Do you know how lucky you are?' asked the doctor. 'Yes, I know how lucky I am.'

Every day I think I'm lucky. Even when I found out that, actually, I was infertile, or that my 'job for life' at Westminster was an illusion, I always felt lucky. I still do. I am eternally grateful that my cup is half-full, because pessimism is so exhausting.

After I graduated from university my first job was as an office temp in Vauxhall. It was November 1990 and I sat on the sixth floor of a skyscraper, entering medical data into a computer, and dreaming of storming up the road to Westminster. One morning the tea lady arrived with her trolley, took our orders, then added, 'Have you heard? Margaret Thatcher's resigned.'

I jumped up from the computer. 'What? Maggie's resigned? . . . Then I gotta go!'

My supervisor looked at me nonplussed. 'Go where?'

'To Westminster of course!'

'Why?'

'Because I've dreamed about Thatcher resigning for as long as I can remember, and today's the day!'

'You can't,' said the supervisor, pointing at my pile of work. 'No one leaves this office until their lunch hour.' It was 9.30 a.m.

'OK, I'll take my lunch hour now.' I grabbed a thick ink marker, a piece of cardboard, and ran for the lift. In the foyer I drew up my impromptu placard: 'I'm 23 years old and I've waited *exactly* half my life for today: bye-bye Maggie.'

It's the only time I've run the two miles between Vauxhall and Westminster. When I arrived breathless at Parliament Square, I squeezed in among the large crowds around the gates of 10 Downing Street. I stayed for a couple of hours, extending my lunch hour, soaking up the atmosphere and doing an interview with a French TV crew who liked my banner. In fact Maggie didn't leave No. 10 for another six days. By midday the focus of events had moved a few hundred yards down the road to the Treasury, where John Major made a brief appearance after announcing his decision to run in the Conservative leadership race.

Journey to the inside – via Brussels

It was round about then that I wrote to Labour MPs asking if there were any jobs going. The vast majority didn't reply. Bernie Grant, the fiery black MP for Tottenham was the exception. My dad, who was a trustee of the International Slavery Museum in Liverpool, spoke to him and I'm sure that like most middle-class kids I got my break because of my parents. For whatever reason, in late 1990 I sat in a draughty Central Lobby, staring up at a brass chandelier the size of a small elephant, waiting for my first appointment with an MP. I was twenty-two and terrified.

Bernie chatted to me for a while, and told me he would be able to help me with a job. I was overjoyed. He told me to go along for a 'ratification' interview later that week at a Labour Party office at Queen Anne's Gate, near St James's Park. I was already dreaming about my first desk at Westminster. When I turned up for what I thought was a formality, there were twenty other hopefuls vying for three places.

'What are your two European languages?' asked a woman at reception.

'What?'

'Anyone applying to be a *stagiaire* for the Socialist Group at the European Parliament must speak two European languages other than their mother tongue. What are your two European languages?'

I didn't dare ask what a *stagiaire* was. 'French and . . . er . . . German,' I stuttered.

In the interview I trotted out my two German phrases that have stood me in good stead for decades: '*Hilfe, hilfe, mein bein ist gebrochen; und der himmel ist aber dunkel.*' Help, help, my leg is broken; and the sky is dark. It clinched it. I became a *stagiaire* (which fortunately turned out to be a researcher, not a cleaner) for the Socialist Group at the European Parliament, and arrived in Brussels in January 1991. I came to love the fact that Brussels had great food, wonderful architecture and accommodation, and it became my political university; that is to say that Brussels is the place where I grew up politically. But I hated how grey and dull it was, and the narrow-mindedness that seemed to overflow within the Belgian state.

One time I'd gone on the monthly Strasburg parliamentary trek, only to find that my car, left legally parked outside my front door in Brussels, had disappeared. When I went to the police they told me it had been moved for 'street maintenance work', and I would have to pay a £300 fine. Two weeks' wages. I was incensed.

'But that's crazy, I parked legally! Outside my front door! You can't fine me for that!'

'Oh yes we can,' replied the Belgian policeman, a faint smile playing on his lips. 'There is a law that you cannot leave your car parked anywhere in Brussels for longer than twenty-four hours. That is in case we put up a notice to say you must move it. So you were not parked legally.'

'Well that's the stupidest law I ever heard.'

'Oh no it's not,' said the policeman, and pulled a huge statute book out from under his desk. '*This*,' he said triumphantly 'is the most stupid law you ever heard.' He ran his finger down a well-worn page until he found the entry he was looking for. '*It is illegal for a person not to have net curtains in their window*.' He looked up, satisfied. 'You see?' I conceded his point and got out my cheque book.

I lived in Belgium for five years, but wondered constantly when I would get out. It wasn't just the number of net curtains; the racism was the worst I'd encountered on a daily level, far more in-your-face than in Britain. When I was looking for somewhere to live I was turned down on five consecutive occasions by landlords who said the flat was vacant over the phone, but when I arrived told me it was for '*uniquement les Belges*' – Belgians only, code for whites only.

Bernie Grant had put me in touch with a black Italian MEP Dacia Valent, who met me for lunch after the fifth rejection from a white landlord. 'I can't find anywhere to live,' I wailed. Dacia threw back her head and laughed raucously. 'You thought Belgians would give a black girl somewhere to live? Even one as light-skinned as you? That's *hilarious*.' We were sitting in the airy member's dining room of the Rue Belliard building, all pastels and Kir Royale sparkling aperitifs. As she fell about laughing I started to cry.

'Oh, don't worry *bella*,' she said, 'you'll just have to come and live with me.' Dacia was generous and mad, with a beautiful apartment round the corner from the Parliament. I lived with her for my first two months in Brussels, before finding permanent accommodation with some of the many non-racist Belgian landlords.

From a work point of view, my first months in Brussels were the most carefree I've ever had. I was paired with another British *stagiaire*, Susie Jolly, and we both had to report to a *functionaire* in the Socialist Group, who would be our manager. Our *functionaire* was a nice British guy who was too busy (so he said) to assign work to others. Each time we went to see him he'd say, 'Look, can't talk right now, gotta work crisis, can you just, er, go away, and come back, say, Wednesday next week?' 'No problem,' I'd reply, and sidle off to get the gym timetable.

Being at the European Parliament was a lesson in British ignorance. There were hundreds and thousands of bright young things from all over Europe, and they all knew more than me. They had languages for a start. I could barely say a word in French, and was stalked by the ghost of Madame Borelle. Yet all these young Europeans conversed effortlessly in different languages. We Brits didn't. A few years later I was Glenys Kinnock's assistant. Glenys was the darling of Europe. She is one of my political heroines. Yet on more than one occasion she hid under her desk (literally) when the French teacher came to give her a lesson. I aspired to be that rare thing – a normal British person who spoke French.

I got ahead of myself when Bernie Grant asked me to be his interpreter at a conference in Portugal. Bernie always looked out for me, and offered me and many other young black people opportunities we wouldn't otherwise have had – not least because we weren't qualified. The trip included a meeting with the President of Portugal, President Soares. We arrived at the presidential palace, and were taken through half a dozen majestic antechambers. The President emerged, handshakes were exchanged. And then the first flurry of French from the President. Bernie turned to me expectantly.

'What did he say?'

'Um . . . I know it's not a good time to tell you Bernie, but my French hasn't come on as well as I hoped.' *If only* I'd paid more attention to Madame Borelle.

Bernie looked from me, to the President and back. And then he burst out laughing. Really laughing. 'Tell the President it's the funniest thing: I brought an interpreter all the way from Brussels, and she doesn't speak a word of French!' There was no one to translate the joke for the President. But Bernie invited me to stay for the rest of our time in Portugal as his assistant rather than his interpreter.

A decade later, when I was thirty-three instead of twenty-three I was able to repay Bernie's kindness. We were both MPs on the International Development Select Committee, travelling around Africa. Bernie's health had deteriorated, and his wife Sharon asked me to look after him on the trip. One of his symptoms was painful swelling of his legs and ankles. Although I disagreed with some of Bernie's politics, I loved him dearly for the help he'd given so many young people like me. And that's why I'm not ashamed to say that for a two-week period I soaked, washed, and moisturised Bernie Grant's feet with painstaking devotion every night!

The wedding and the spare rib

There were only two things I knew more about than the other European *stagiaires*. The first was how to write a good speech. The second was dance music. House music. It was a shared love of house music that brought Tiberio and I together. We came from very different backgrounds, both culturally and politically. Although we were both on the left, he was more Trotskyite, I was more Fabian Society. The only thing we had in common was a grey office in the nether regions of the European Parliament. We were Socialist Group researchers; he worked for the Italian Socialists, and I worked for the European Parliamentary Labour Party. We both went on to work for MEPs.

I was initially suspicious of Tiberio. The fact that he was Italian and beautiful seemed a sure sign he couldn't be trusted. Worse still, he wore suits. Sharp-edged, expertly tailored Italian suits. On balance I hate suits. They have 'boring' tattooed all over them. Boring is my swear word. I dismissed Tiberio as a boring Italian playboy.

It turned out that Tiberio was a laid-back twenty-seven-year-old who was passionate about European politics, music, his grand-mother's pasta recipes, and reading French literature in the original (given my failure with Madame Borelle this impressed me no end: I thought it was on a par with being a concert pianist or brain surgeon). Tiberio was also a one-time Buddhist, often quiet and reflective, a welcome antidote to my loudmouth tendencies. He confounded my own prejudice; despite being a southern Italian man he didn't have a sexist or racist bone in his body. What he did have was an eclectic sense of humour, and a personality that successfully married two divergent sensibilities: cast-iron reliability and spontaneity. We lived across the road from each other, and Tiberio might lean out of the window on a Saturday afternoon and shout, 'D'you wanna drive to Holland?' 'Yeah,' I'd reply. We'd bundle into the car with my Parisian flatmate Carole and break for the border.

Tiberio's experiences almost seemed to contradict themselves. Although he appeared quintessentially Italian, he travelled to Tokyo at twenty because he wanted to immerse himself in a different culture. While there, he picked up Buddhism and trained to be a karate black belt. His five fluent languages include Japanese. He studied to be an Air Force pilot, but then decided to join the Foreign Office, and passed the entrance exams, before deciding to go to the European Parliament instead. He wasn't sure what he wanted, but he knew he wanted to explore other cultures.

We became good friends. Admittedly we had a small fling about six weeks after we met in 1991, but we decided to leave it at that. Or maybe I was *thinking* of leaving it at that when Tiberio decided to go out with a Spanish woman for a year, allowing me to make Casanova jokes for the next decade. These premarital facts remain disputed, but what we agree on is that by New Year's Eve 1992 we'd been platonic friends for almost two years. We often gave each other relationship advice. I was moping about after another romantic disaster when Tiberio invited me to Naples to cheer me up – and say goodbye. He had a new job in Milan, and although we'd enjoyed knowing each other, our friendship wouldn't stretch to becoming pen pals.

I got my first introduction to Tiberio's Italian background when I boarded the plane to Naples. I was taken aback by the general noise and hand-waving, not to mention the passengers trawling up and down the aisle hawking contraband fags. Two men were throwing a laughing baby back and forth over seated passengers. It seemed like a typically boisterous Neapolitan scene. But Tiberio's family was not typically Neapolitan. His parents were brought up in the north of Italy, and his family were the only people he knew without strong Neapolitan accents. He was the only child who didn't speak the local dialect, and was sometimes ostracised. The occasional street beatings he received encouraged him to take up karate.

A few days after I arrived in Caserta, near Naples, there was a

huge meal to celebrate New Year's Eve. I had no way of under-
standing how important food was for Italians in general, or Tiberio's
family in particular. Like too many British young people, I thought
that cooking involved adding water to things like Cup a Soup and
Pot Noodle. Yet here I was, surrounded by some of the best cooking
in the world. Although I can eat with the best of them, I gave up after
the sixth or seventh course. Every relative arrived with a different
dish, a speciality handed down over generations. It set the scene,
some years later, when Tiberio's parents arrived in London. They
opened their suitcase and pulled out more food than clothes: sun-
dried tomatoes, litres of olive oil, home-made sausages, wine,
artichokes, roast peppers, pumpkin ravioli, Bolognese sauce, vegetable pies, prosciutto, pecorino cheese, even a whole chicken and a
whole rabbit, not to mention cream tarts, cases of buffalo mozzar-
ella, and wild lettuce leaves rinsed and wrapped in cotton cloths to
keep them crisp during their journey. God knows what would have
happened if they'd been stopped at customs. It was their 'custom' to
take their own food everywhere. On another occasion they had two
suitcases, one with food and one with clothes. They were over the
weight allowance, and had to leave one behind. It was a terrible
choice for Italians, but better to be poorly dressed than poorly fed.
The clothes were discarded while the food boarded the plane.

As that first New Year's Eve meal drew to a close, I felt felled by
feasting. I could hardly move. A bit of *grappa* and *limoncello* helped,
and somehow Tiberio and I ended up in a club, dancing to deep house
music from Chicago. That's the main reason we're together today.
Within weeks we were sharing Tiberio's apartment in Brussels, though
we often travelled to London, the hub of underground house in the
early nineties, to buy records from Paul Farris at Uptown Records in
Soho. Our pet hate was the ubiquitous Euro-rock music or the cheesy
Euro-house that blared from every Belgian bar. We even organised a
couple of club nights in Brussels so that we could hear our music.

Like so many others we bought our own record decks and mixers,
recorded our own mix tapes, and imported the club experience into
the home. I'd never got over the joy of my first proper club nights at
the Hacienda, that legendary Manchester nightclub, where in the
late 1980s I stood on the balcony (a regular refugee from York) and
watched the birth of British house music. House music was overtly

participative and physical; that's to say, you only really 'got it' on a crowded dance floor with a serious sound system. It wasn't about money, clothes, or status, it was about a shared physical and emotional experience. It was known as 'the second summer of love', and it consumed a generation – my generation.

For many of those taking part it was a rejection of 1980s individualism. For some it was just about pill-popping. For most of us it felt like a triumph of collectivism, and it spawned the belief that we could take care of each other, although many commentators dismissed it as young people's hedonism. Needless to say when the age-old cycle of idealism-to-cynicism kicked in, house music became a global industry that was all about money and status, and nothing to do with the music and the shared experience. Still, millions of young British kids lived for the rave scene. The political establishment took fright, and even passed a law banning the vast outdoor house music parties, many of which had become synonymous with drugs and criminal activity.*

By the early 1990s house music was moving back indoors with the creation of 'super clubs' like Ministry of Sound, which is where Tiberio and I spent our wedding night in 1994. We had our party at The Crypt in Trafalgar Square, then went to a great club called Iceni near Piccadilly, and finally arrived at Ministry at about three a.m. The wedding dress worked wonders. It was a silver baby-doll dress with matching silver platform shoes and an eight foot veil. It's the only time club bouncers treated me like a VIP. 'She's a real bride, let her in.'

We pushed through crowds with locomotive hips and fizzing smiles, and into the main room where we danced under a silver glitter ball to a live PA from Jocelyn Brown's 'Somebody Else's Guy', agreeing that there was no better place to spend our wedding night than on the dance floor. We tumbled out of the club at daybreak and made it back to our wedding suite at eight a.m., accompanied by half a dozen soul survivors – friends who helped us open wedding presents on a hazy Sunday morning, even though our wedding list had been donations to Amnesty International.

---

* cf. 'Don't Take Away My Music', my Radio 4 documentary about the history of house music (www.oonaking.com).

That Sunday morning brought our wedding week to an end. The first wedding was in a beautiful eleventh-century church in Caserta Vecchia, followed by a reception overlooking the Bay of Naples, and the second wedding was a week later at Marylebone registry office in London. The Italian wedding had been eventful, as I recorded in my diary:

15 July 1994
. . . I could hear beautiful music coming from the stone church on the mountain side of the ancient village of Caserta Vecchia. I was ushered towards the entrance and everything seemed surreal. 'Atheist from Camden Town Overwhelmed by Catholic Wedding.' 'The bride's coming,' they cried. I saw Tiberio, stunningly beautiful as ever. And then, seated at the altar, all eyes upon us, we had a blinding argument. I was livid, shaking with rage. I wouldn't look at him, it was all I could do to remain seated like a good bride instead of walking the wrong way back up the aisle.

Tiberio had asked my mother to read a passage from the Bible – not a criminal act in itself – but as I sat surrounded by smiles and tears I realised I was listening to the Spare Rib extract, aka the 'Women Are a Mere Second Thought in the Grand Scheme of Creation So Stay at Home and be Grateful,' extract. The row only lasted two hours. By the time we arrived at the Bay of Naples to get the romantic small fishing boat to the reception, we were back on the 'This is our wedding, this is divine' trip.

The Spare Rib incident was the first of countless marital–cultural stumbling blocks. Outwardly I seemed like the Italian, all hand flinging and wringing. Tiberio's demeanour was more British – reserved and stoical. But under the surface, time and again, my Anglo-Saxon world view clashed with his Latin sensibilities. Tiberio never wanted a stay-at-home wife, but nor did he want a wife wedded to the ship of state. I told him I wanted to be an MP. Although he always encouraged me, he assumed I'd be in my forties or fifties if and when I managed it. In Italy the average age for an MP is sixty.

I started doing selection rounds to be an MEP when I was twenty-four. Various women MEPs gave me invaluable help and advice.*

---

* Mel Read in particular.

But it was one of the older male MEPs that gave me the spur I needed.

'Oona love,' he said picking up the telephone on his desk as I walked past his door, 'do me a favour and ring Britain for me.'

'Sure, just give me a sec—'

'I need to be put through now.'

'Can't you do it yourself?'

'I don't know how.' He'd been an MEP for a decade, but he didn't know how to ring Britain. It was one of those moments when the Emperor's clothes come off, and you can't help thinking, '*Why* is this man the Emperor? Why do I imagine he has special powers that make him more suitable to be an elected politician than me? He can't even use a telephone.' Later that week I submitted my first selection application form.

One of the questions I am often asked is, 'How did you become an MP? And what should I do if I want to be an MP?' The answer is both obvious and elusive. First and foremost, join a political party. Secondly, be in the right place at the right time. This often leads to the grave digger tendency; high-flying young things tramping around branch meetings of soon-to-die or -retire MPs. The selection process itself is fairly straightforward. Local party branches nominate candidates. The Constituency Executive draws up a shortlist, based on branch nominations. There is then a hustings meeting where aspiring MPs give speeches and take questions. Local party members vote for the person they want. The winner becomes the party's candidate. If the candidate wins the general election, they become the MP. So far so simple. But in reality it's not enough to be a good candidate and give a good speech. Political machinations beneath the surface can shred a visitor's chances in seconds, like a shoal of piranhas at tea-time. That's where luck comes in. A lot of candidates, like me, are not favourites but come through the middle of local warring factions. If your enemy's enemy wants you as a friend, you're in with a chance.

By 1995 I knew that to have a chance of being selected, I had to leave the European Parliament, and get back to the UK. Tiberio was working for an Italian media company in Brussels, and got a transfer to London. I got a job as a trade union organiser with the GMB, Britain's general union, representing low-paid workers in the NHS. By early 1997 I had taken part in a dozen selection rounds, and lost all of them. I invariably won the branch nomination where I spoke, but crashed and burned on the final shortlist. I was good at giving speeches, but bad at lobbying. I was hopeful about Bethnal Green and Bow because it was a woman-only shortlist, which meant it would be a more open selection (the local favoured activists were invariably men). But by February 1997, just months before the general election, the woman-only shortlist was ruled illegal. It seemed I had no chance of arriving at Westminster. What's more, I wasn't sure I wanted to. My job as a trade unionist was changing me. I wanted to stay closer to the coalface, as the following diary entry shows:

28 February 1997
I'm on the steepest learning curve ever. I got a massive and un-expected temporary promotion due to a colleague taking maternity leave. Suddenly I'm doing pay negotiations, representing members at tribunals, negotiating with management over specifications for tenders submitted under CCT [Compulsory Competitive Tendering], PFI [Private Finance Initiative], putting in ITs over TUPE [Transfer of Undertaking Regulations, designed to protect employ-ees when a business changes hands] regulations, and dealing with the problems of the 2,500 low-paid members I represent in the NHS who are getting screwed.

Got in from work early last night (eight p.m.) but still had five pages of messages to go through from members. There are bills on the table, there's the Guardian *I haven't read – I should check to see if the LP has decided what it's doing in the Bethnal Green and Bow selection and whether it's imposing a candidate – there's a twenty page fax from Chris Smith's office (MP, aka Paul Daniels) explain-ing how Labour can save the NHS without putting any more money into it than the Tories, and there's a similar fax from Gordon Brown's office explaining how Labour can save Britain while imposing the Tory spending targets.*

There's a message from the Camden Commission for Racial Equal-ity; I've been nominated as a 'black heroine' of Camden, only they want to know what I've 'achieved in my life' – which is a stumbling block. Only two achievements mean anything to me. One is finding the partner of my life, the other is risking torture in El Salvador.

I didn't recover from a night I had in San Salvador in 1989 for many years. El Salvador was under a military junta renowned for its torture of political opponents. I was travelling with my best friend Quincy and another British backpacker, Caroline. We went to an anti-Government demonstration at the cathedral where Oscar Romero had been gunned down. Members of the FMLN were holed up there, and told us that the Army was poised to kill them. But the presence of foreigners like us would give them more time. Would we come again the next day, even though the secret service would follow us when we left, and there was a good chance we would be arrested?

We were already breaking the law by attending the demonstration. An Australian had been there the week before, and was picked up and badly tortured by the secret service when she left. I was determined to return to the demonstration but Quincy was exasperated. We both wanted to change things in Britain and beyond, but in different ways. She wanted to be a human rights lawyer. She had a legal mind, brilliant and concise. She had easily passed her Oxford entrance exams. 'There's no point wanting to be an MP if you're going to get killed first. You can't change anything if you're dead.'

After a night spent wide-eyed with terror waiting for footsteps on the hotel landing, I decided to go to the demonstration. Quincy took my two passports, British and American, along with her own, and went to both embassies. She wanted to register us in case we disappeared. The US consul was incensed at our foolishness.

'What the hell are you doing, back-packing around a war zone? Don't you realise there's a war going on? You and your friends have contravened immigration law by engaging in political activity, and can be legally detained for six months. Quite frankly I wouldn't care, but because one of you has a US passport it'll cause me too many problems. So fetch your pair of stupid student revolutionaries and drive them straight to the airport within the next two hours, or they won't be getting out.'

Even if the American consul thought it was the height of stupidity, for me the decision to return to the demonstration was a defining moment.

28 February 1997 [continued]
I always wondered whether I'd be one of those people who would put their safety on the line for their beliefs. For all I knew, I'd run a

mile. But – just briefly – I didn't, and it means I can look in the mirror . . . Which brings me back to my skin and eczema (I'm being euphemistic for acne) and stress, and my message book.

Paul pops into my mind. Paul is my member who has been sacked from his job as a cleaner with Initial Health Care Services (private 'expletive' contractors) for stealing four bread rolls worth a total of 50p. Paul is forty-eight. He can't find another job. I submit an appeal. The manager tells me our Recognition Agreement doesn't cover employees transferred from Whitley NHS contracts, so I'm not allowed to represent Paul at the hearing. No one is allowed to represent Paul at the hearing. 'Could we be reasonable?' I ask the manager. 'It's 50p. Could you make an exception?'

'Absolutely not.'

I ring Paul. While I'm on the phone Quincy comes round. I ask for her legal opinion on Paul's case. He doesn't have one, she says, not in law anyway.

'Paul, you don't have one,' I say, 'a case that is, or a job.' We discuss it a bit longer.

'Thanks for ringing,' says Paul in Thornton Heath, 'it makes a difference.' He's probably wrong. I want to spit on Initial Health Care Services – part of the Rentokill Group. Contractors of private misery, all over 50p.

In the end I didn't spit on Initial Health Care Services, I changed the law. It was because of Paul, and countless others like him, that when I became an MP I introduced a Private Member's Bill to prevent some of the cowboy tendering and contracting (Thatcher's loathed Compulsory Competitive Tendering) that effectively stripped workers of their rights.

The day it was incorporated into Government legislation and became law, I wanted to find Paul from Thornton Heath. I wanted to say, 'Look Paul, I'm really sorry that when I was your trade union representative I couldn't stop you getting sacked over 50p. I know it ruined your life, and God knows I'm sorry I couldn't win the argument with your manager. But I wanted to let you know that eventually, after a year's negotiation with the Government, the CBI (Confederation of British Industry) and the TUC (Trades Union Congress), I finally won the argument. For you, for me, for all of us on the trade union side. We finally won the argument, Paul.' Winning arguments at Westminster was a long way from standing with SWP placards outside meetings at York.

When I got on to the final shortlist for the Bethnal Green and Bow selection, several people told me not to go along. 'Don't humiliate yourself,' they said. 'You'll need a miracle. You have to understand that 50 per cent of Labour Party membership is Bengali. The majority of votes are decided by elderly male patriarchs. They'll never vote for you. You have the bad luck to break their first rule – you're young. And their second rule – you're a woman. Thirdly you're the wrong sort of black – there's a lot of ill will between black and Asian communities. And even if you managed to get past all that, worst of all, you're Jewish. You haven't got a prayer.' I decided to give it a go anyway, because it's never over till it's over. As the first diary entry in this book reveals, it's wise not to pre-judge the prejudice of others. And in any case, bad luck can often come good.

Thank God it's not a shark

My favourite good luck/ bad luck experience happened on a deserted white sand beach in Costa Rica when I was twenty-one, shortly after leaving El Salvador. My nice boyfriend who got me the Bootsy Collins album had left me broken-hearted, and I decided I was better off dead.

My ambiguous suicide plan involved swimming out past the signs that said, 'Danger! Strong currents! Deaths reported!' I would swim away from shore for an hour. I put my fate in the lap of the Gods, or the lap of the tide. Each time I broke the ocean surface, the early light forged foamy fireworks. From within these gentle fireworks a solid shape emerged, perhaps fifty yards away. It was long, bony, like a giant sea creature's gnarled finger, and it was pointing at me. As my horizon see-sawed up and down on the waves, the one thing that remained steady was the gnarled finger, heading for me at some speed. It looked like the tentacle of a giant squid, or maybe a stick being dragged under water by what . . . a shark?

All I knew was that a creature was about to attack me. That's the funny thing about the human instinct for survival. You decide you want to kill yourself, but if something *else* wants to kill you, you'll break the sea-to-land world record to save your skin. Within a split second a gnarled leathery tentacle wrapped itself around my raised arm, from elbow to wrist, and pulled me underwater. I didn't even have time to think, 'Thank God it's not a shark,' because a sensational pain, almost like an electric shock, spread over my arm. As I thrashed about, my arm touched my eyes, and suddenly I couldn't see. I felt my arm come free, so I made a desperate attempt to turn and swim, but as I did so my leg got roped in and I felt this squid/octopus/ nightmare pull me backwards. It let go and I kicked wildly, my legs thrashing, trying to shake off the eight other legs slithering around me. By the time I scrambled on all fours out of the sea and collapsed on the beach, I still couldn't see out of my right eye. My arm and leg were pulsating with red welts. All I could think was, 'Attacked by a sea monster, just my luck to be attacked by a fucking sea monster . . .' I'd completely forgotten my suicide attempt.

The doctor who treated me said the red welts on my arms and face were a nasty type of jellyfish sting. I protested: a jellyfish doesn't look like a giant octopus. The doctor thought a while, and then offered another explanation. The octopus had been tangled with a jellyfish, and tried to clean itself on the nearest thing to hand. I had been used as a piece of oceanic toilet paper. What a stroke of luck. If the helpful sea monster hadn't chased me back to shore I might have killed myself. And that's sometimes the way with good luck and bad luck. Bad luck is often good, especially if you make it work for you.

I have George Galloway to thank for bringing me the best sort of bad luck; the energising sort. He made me fight for my job as though my life depended on it. It was the political equivalent of being in a shark tank. And it reminded me of my experience in Costa Rica. I had often thought of giving up my job – committing political suicide – but as soon as some *other* creature wanted me dead, I found reserves of strength I didn't know I had.

So fighting George Galloway wasn't all negative. And in any case, throughout my life the best things to happen have *always* been born of bad luck, or something bad happening. I had the best year of my life in San Francisco because I failed to get into Oxford. I met the man of my life at the European Parliament in Brussels because I failed to get a job at Westminster. I got a first-class degree in politics because I failed to make the grade in philosophy. I got a job as a full-time trade union organiser in 1995 because I failed to win a place on the GMB parliamentary panel. And I became the MP for Bethnal Green & Bow, despite the all-woman shortlist being scrapped (a disaster for me at the time). I lost my parliamentary seat in 2005, but as a result won my life.

Winning Bethnal Green & Bow and losing it are two of the three best things to happen to me in the last decade. Obviously it was politically devastating to lose to a man like George Galloway – I felt he behaved in what I might euphemistically call an 'unscrupulous' manner, and it's a shame when bullying tactics win. It's also not usually the way we conduct elections in Britain. But on a personal level I cannot regret it, because life outside Westminster is such a liberation. The point is that without the wisdom of hindsight, the twin fates of good and bad luck are often mistaken for one another. It is best to recognise them for what they are: just points of departure for what comes next. Happily, life is not generally governed by past disaster, but by future action.

Note about these diaries

Although these diaries span a decade, they were never kept as daily or even monthly diaries. Rather, like the diaries I have kept since I was a child, they are snapshots of a time and place. In the aftermath of becoming an MP (1998–2001), I almost stopped writing my diary completely, as nearly all my time and energy was focused on staying afloat in Parliament and the constituency. I couldn't understand how MPs had time to write diaries, or books of any description.

The entries that follow were mainly written in a journal at home in the small hours of the morning, but also include entries written on scraps of paper in the Commons, backs of envelopes on buses, tapped on to keyboards, or recorded on tape during parliamentary trips abroad. Apart from occasional grammatical corrections and tidying up, I have left my diary entries more or less as I wrote them at the time – any editing has been to condense entries and limit repetition. Therefore anything I have added is in italics, so the reader can be clear when I am indulging the luxury of hindsight.

For many years after becoming an MP, I usually only found time to write under three circumstances: when I was ill; on holiday or travelling abroad; or when I faced great stress. I used writing as a cheaper and more convenient alternative to counselling. The result sometimes makes for uncomfortable reading – when I first read these diaries in their entirety (in 2007), I was shocked by how unhappy I often seem; either unhappy, or ill, or both. The fact is, being an MP was the greatest privilege I ever had; but it was also an occupation that at times made me unhappier than anything else in my life. Therefore, both myself, and these diaries, are conflicted. Whereas in public I was cheerful, in private I was sometimes despairing.

Happily, this doesn't mean that what follows is cheerless, or that my public and private selves are incompatible. It simply means that like most people, I can be happy and sad. It seemed appropriate that the latter was saved for my private space, especially any sadness related to infertility, which had no place in politics. Given that the greatest stress I experienced was in the year before the 2005 general election, these diaries are disproportionately weighted around that period.

Now that I am no longer an elected politician, I feel freer to make the private public. But although both my private and public spheres were stressful, it is an acute embarrassment to me that in private, as reflected in the pages that follow, I sometimes ended up in tears – especially as women who cry are inevitably deemed unfit for public life. But I would rather these diaries reflected the truth of my experience than a stoical fiction. As I said during an office meeting, recorded in my diary entry of 26 November 2004: '*Ignore the tears, I can't do anything about them but they're not relevant to this conversation.*' I hope that some of the internal conversation I had with myself, expressed in these diaries, is relevant to the debate about how we conduct politics, run our democracy, and engage people who are currently excluded.

Although politics is my greatest passion, it is not my only passion. It probably takes up no more than half of this book. Those whose interest is purely political might be perturbed. Those who have no interest in politics might be deterred. But those who believe the personal is political should be fairly entertained.

Part 2

The Diary

1997

The Triple Sulco and the Road to Socialism

23 March 1997

The selection for Bethnal Green and Bow finally got underway. Because of 'irregularities' the NEC (Labour's ruling body, the National Executive Committee) decided to shortlist candidates. They received 100 c.v.s and whittled them down to eleven. I wasn't sure if I was supposed to lobby anyone, and if so, who and how. I wrote a letter to Robin Cook saying, 'If it is appropriate, and if you think I merit it, I would be grateful if you could mention my candidacy to colleagues on the NEC.' Yuck and triple yuck. I can't abide that side of politics. Networking and backscratching. The other aspiring hopefuls are networking away like the absolute political maniacs they are.

I spoke to Terry Ashton (the London Labour Party Officer), helpful as ever, who said it's best just to leave it all alone. I was delighted – I trust him not to jeopardise my chances, so if he says there's no point in lobbying, there's no point in lobbying. On the other hand, the first rule of politics (I now realise) is that there's *always* a point in lobbying.

I made it down to the 'first eleven'. This was the long-list of candidates from which the NEC would choose the shortlist. Claude Moraes was the favourite. Everyone I spoke to, everything I read, told me Claude would walk it in his sleep. Claude was the NEC 'preferred candidate'. We had to appear at John Smith House, Labour Party HQ. 'Stage one' of the interview would consist of a four minute speech entitled, 'Why I Would Make a Good General Election Candidate for Bethnal Green and Bow'. Chosen candidates would be selected, there and then, to move on to stage two, a mock press interview. It reminded me of *Come Dancing*. Sudden Death. If they tap you on the shoulder you have to leave.

I arrived on Tuesday morning at Labour Party HQ shaking uncontrollably. As usual it wasn't out of fear, it was because I had to look 'respectable' with a suit and blouse (precluding a polo neck), and the only overcoat I had was a Huggy Bear one I got in New York to go clubbing, which I couldn't wear and by the time I walked up the steps my fingers had turned blue. Six of the eleven candidates were there. I hugged one of the other candidates, Pola Uddin, enthusiastically – much to the surprise of the others.

Claude Moraes was sitting circumspectly in the corner. He turned out to be far nicer than I expected. The local front-runner, Nick Fox, arrived and stood on the other side of the small foyer. He seemed rather cold and aloof. There were three white candidates (two men, one woman, all doctors!), and eight ethnic-minority candidates. Everyone was petrified. It felt like waiting to go into the Star Chamber. We were ushered upstairs and informed that, due to further problems, a report into the membership of BG & B had been ordered, and the morning would only consist of stage one. From my point of view that was great – I hadn't had time to go over the policy questions. They announced which order we'd be speaking in. Pola was fifth, I was sixth. I went into the toilets with Pola and demanded she read out her speech. The whole procedure was weighted against her, because she wasn't trained in speech writing or the 'New Labour' presentational politics the NEC would be looking for.

Her speech was scribbled on different bits of paper, written out word for word. I implored her to use bullet points so she could talk more naturally and look at the panel. I started writing them out for her, outlining her background and her long and admirable involvement in Tower Hamlets. It was impressive. The problem was she couldn't present it impressively. We started to run through it but she kept stopping after the first few sentences. 'I can't do it, I can't do it,' she was almost wailing. 'They're just going to think I'm another crap Bengali who can't speak properly.'

I grabbed her by the shoulders and shouted in her face, shaking her hard. 'You can do it, and you WILL do it, or I'll KILL YOU! You've a responsibility to *all* black women to do this well. Now start from the top and DON'T FUCKING STOP!!' And miraculously, Pola pulled herself together. She did a good job. I understood her fear. I felt the sickness you feel at the top of a 500-foot rollercoaster ride. You've actually volunteered to do this, and at the last minute you realise you'd do anything to avoid going over the edge, but you're strapped in and there's no escape.

When it was finally my turn to go in, I was shaking like a leaf, and this time it wasn't to do with the temperature. Practising it a few minutes earlier I realised the verbal diarrhoea was worse than expected: 'I believe the Labour Party needs a criterion that fulfils four essential candidates. Oh no, I'm going to fuck it up, I'm losing it . . .' Out of control. So I started to shout at myself the way I shouted at Pola. 'You can do it, and you WILL do it, or I'll KILL YOU!' And then calm, and then walking into the room, smiling at the eight panel members, listening to their introductions, and then my speech.

Out of the corner of my eye I could see the Labour Party's Head of Communications ticking a grid with boxes as I was speaking. I assumed the little ticks were for presentation, content, style, etc. But knowing New Labour they probably also included marks for hairstyle, colour of suit (in a desperate bid for acceptance, I'd plumped for John Major grey), type of earrings (non-dangly essential), and shade of lipstick. There were five women, and I was the only one without lipstick. What was the spin on that? One of the panel members, Diana Jeuda, gave me great encouragement. I could see she was willing me on, wanting me to be good, and it made a big difference. All of the panel were friendly, but Diana was amazing.

And then it was over and I was over the moon. I knew I'd done well, I hadn't made a mistake. I'd made them laugh, but my message had been absolutely serious. I almost skipped out of the room. A month went by and I heard nothing from the NEC. I had a conversation with Claude, and he said he had it 'from the highest sources' (e.g. direct from Tom Sawyer, the General Secretary of the Labour Party) that three of the candidates performed particularly well. I wasn't one of them. Was he lying, or was I crap? Then Pola told me she'd been told the same thing – except the three candidates named didn't include her but *did* include me. Everyone was playing games. Finally a phone call. We were called back in for stage two.

Only two candidates had been knocked out. This time I wasn't so scared. I'd prepared for the questions. I knew they would be things like, 'How do you explain Gordon Brown's failure to match the Conservative spending pledges on the NHS?' (Correct answer: 'To get elected, Gordon Brown has deemed it necessary to move to the right of Genghis Khan.' NEC answer: 'The Labour Party has fully costed all its spending commitments. We will not make any promises we can't keep. The Tories have turned the NHS into a paperchase through the introduction of the internal market. Today there are 20,000 more managers and 50,000 fewer nurses. Labour will move money from bureaucracy into front-line patient services, cutting waiting lists by 100,000.')

The first question was, 'How do you account for the £30 billion hole in Labour's spending plans? Where will that money come from? Straightforward question, simple answer. But then to my horror I started to stumble over the words. Where was this sentence going? I didn't know. Instead of concentrating on what I was saying, a loud voice in my head was booming, 'You fucked it up! You fucked it up!' I couldn't believe it. I didn't mess up things like this. It wasn't me, it couldn't be happening, not at such an important interview. It was like an out-of-body experience. I heard myself constructing the most ungrammatical sentences imaginable. It sounded like German. It horrifying was. The daughter of an English teacher! Mum would be revolving in her bed.

When I came out of the interview, I knew that at best I'd been decidedly average. From my own point of view I'd been completely crap. Shell shock. The stage one interview I would score myself ten out of ten. This was five out of ten. That's it, I thought, selection process over. Back to Surbiton. I didn't mind going back to my job, I loved my job. What I hated was performing badly.

I wrote down on a piece of paper who I thought would be on the final shortlist. The only two I was certain about were Claude and Nick. Claude was their favourite, and it was inconceivable that Nick wouldn't be on it. Pola, because even if she performed as badly as me, or worse, they had to have a Bengali. And who would the fourth be? When David Gardner (a Labour Party Official) came in to read the results, he started by saying great weight had been given to the first presentation. Maybe I'll live to fight another day, I thought.

'The NEC has unanimously decided on the following shortlist of four: Sam Everington (who was he?), Oona King (my jaw, quite literally, dropped), Claude Moraes (everybody knew it) and Pola Uddin (people knew it but were still surprised). Once I put my jaw back into place, my next reaction was, 'What on earth happened to Nick Fox? Why wasn't he on the list?' I rang Tiberio, then my parents, then Quin (my best friend, Quincy). Her exact words were, 'Shit, looking bad. If you're not careful you're going to get selected.' She was right. It was a tightrope. I wanted to do well, but not too well. She agreed with me, it would be better to learn more in my job with 'real people' before being buried alive in the claustrophobic unreality of Westminster. But then, of course, there's the problem of momentum – when you're in a race you want to win.

I daydreamed briefly about the NEC imposing me, but I knew that was a delusion. Everyone was convinced they would impose Claude. The NEC said the shortlist would now go back to the constituency, and the constituency would decide. If that was the case, I didn't have a chance. Nobody knew me. The hustings would take place in nine days, the following Sunday.

Rumours were flying around about why the NEC had left certain local candidates off the shortlist. Nick's case, in particular, was a mystery. There were two theories: 1. The Labour Party would be embarrassed if a white man was selected. Everyone knew Nick was most likely to win in an open selection, he was by far the strongest candidate. So the NEC took him off and put the relatively unknown Sam Everington on. They were leaving it open for Claude. But they didn't understand the constituency, and they didn't understand the difference between a Bengali vote and an Indian vote. They thought they were the same because they were both Asian, but in fact the Bengalis wouldn't vote for Claude, and many others in the constituency disliked him because he was seen as the imposed candidate. 2. The Labour Party wants a white candidate, because otherwise the BNP will be the only party fielding a white candidate, and Labour will lose votes. That still doesn't explain Nick.

At this point (one week ago) because I'm supremely naïve, I think maybe I'll win because I'll give the best speech. I understand nothing about anything. On Sunday I'm told that Nick and his supporters would like a meeting with me. They're meeting all the candidates.

Nick wants to be constructive. Although he must be devastated, he appears genuinely warm, sincere and friendly when I meet him. I feel terrible for him. Everyone knows it's outrageously unfair that he's been denied the opportunity he deserves. He explains they want to back the best potential MP, but they also have to back the person they think will win. On paper, my chances look pretty slim. I'm the only outsider. I've never shown my face in the constituency before. People are asking who the hell I am. Nick's people are disaffected with the NEC. They believe, and I agree, that they have been treated in an unfair, undemocratic way. The veiled hostility towards me in the room is not personal, it's even unintentional. But it's still there. It recedes as the meeting progresses. I start to shake again. This shaking thing is really starting to irritate me.

When the meeting's over they say they'll contact me later in the week. They ask me what I've been doing to mobilise constituency support, they want to know who I've been lobbying. The truth is, I haven't been lobbying anyone, just submitted my c.v. They tell me I must be mad, I can't possibly expect to win, etc. I say I'll give a good speech, I'll swing it on the day. Someone explains, 'There's nothing to swing, the proportion of those undecided before the meeting will be, at most, 15 per cent – not enough to win.' So Plan A is out of the window and I don't have a Plan B. I feel incredibly stupid; after all, merit never has anything to do with it and yet I've been relying on it.

When I get home at eleven p.m. Tiberio has made grilled teriyaki chicken, Thai rice, and a vegetable salad. We discuss the impending doom of the hustings meeting. 'We both know you can't win this time, you don't *want* to win this time, you just want to do well, and you have to give a good performance.' He's right, and more importantly, we've booked a holiday for the following week – our first holiday alone for a year, but what feels like an aeon. We bought a cheap package to Kerala in southern India. The flight leaves next Sunday night, straight after the count. Sun, sea, sand, and spices, the other side of the planet. I need and want it so desperately, it's the perfect incentive to lose.

On Monday evening Nick rings me. He's decided to back me. We both know the risk he's taking. 'We've got six days,' he says, 'nobody knows you, your support in the constituency is zero, but I think you'll make the best candidate.' I'm honoured and amazed.

He takes the next day off work to help me plan a strategy. It's simple. I have to try and meet the 703 eligible Labour Party members in the next 144 hours. Because it is possible to meet with many among the Bengali community until two a.m., and because I must start most days at seven a.m., it's a round-the-clock job. I look terrible. My skin is flaking off, and everyone tells me, as if I didn't know, how terrible I look. But the selfless kindness of Nick and (his wife) Louise spurs me on. It is the first time in politics I've met people who are capable of looking so far beyond their own personal situation.

With Nick's backing, others in the constituency are now working incredibly hard for me, notably Dino, Elaine, David and Leanne. They have put such faith and effort into my campaign, I will be mortified if I let them down. It is the night before the hustings meeting. I'm so exhausted I can barely walk up the stairs to sit at the computer. Eight p.m. and I'm starting the speech for tomorrow. I can usually always work through the night. Tonight is different. It's not just one week of acute exhaustion, it's three months. I can't do it. I realise I'll have to engage in the high-risk, take-it-to-the-wire strategy I used for my finals. Go to sleep now, wake up at two a.m., and write it then.

I'm asleep in seconds, it feels as though I blink, and it's two a.m. I feel I've had, at best, a ten minute nap. I sit at the computer. Nick and Louise have reminded me I have to be 100 per cent serious. No jokes, no sarcasm; because I'm twenty-nine, anything jokey will make me less credible. I write something, I hate it. There's no humour, it's dry, flat, dull. I can't believe I'm about to give a dull, crap speech. Not *today*, please. The minutes turn into hours. I feel physically sick. What upsets me most is that I've been telling everyone I'll win it on the day. I'll give the best performance, 'Don't worry, you can rely on me to pull it out of the bag.' And yet now it's six a.m., and all I've produced is nausea. I hate myself. Worked like a dog all week, and was now about to humiliate myself, and, worse still, let everyone else down. Panic. Blind panic. Nine a.m., finish the speech. Tried to run through it, but I was like Pola in the toilets at the NEC interview. Flustered, unprepared, making mistakes. It was a decidedly poor show. Hadn't even begun preparing for the question and answer session. Got dressed, and into the car with Tiberio. I knew I needed to sit down on my own and go through the speech, and pull it together. My only hope was that I wouldn't be picked first to speak.

When we arrived, just before eleven a.m., I was shocked to see the number of people there. Queues outside, people selling papers. It had the air of a show, or maybe the Colosseum, with excitement, humiliation and even political death lurking in the wings. The candidates were agreed on one thing – everyone else was enjoying throwing us to the lions. Pola looked wonderful, Sam looked smaller and greyer than I remembered him, and Claude, like me, was murmuring incessantly, 'Why are we doing this, why are we *voluntarily* doing this?' 'Please God may the force be with me, please don't make me first!' I was desperate. An extra hour and a half would make the difference between the best or worst speech of my life.

Pola picked her piece of paper out of the hat first. Number two. Sam picked his next. My whole being was willing him to pick out number one. And he did. I was third. That was fine. I had exactly one hour and fifteen minutes, enough to swing it. I went over the speech again and again to get the nuances right – the things that make a difference in a speech – and to learn the links so I wouldn't have to look down so much. My only hope was to engage the audience, speak directly to them, *prove* I was the best candidate and the one who could articulate their beliefs.

In one hour, I more or less learned the speech by heart. I was shivering like my grandmother's pet chihuahua, but now I had a fighting chance. I went back downstairs. Claude was sitting in the candidates' room. We both agreed that Sam was going to walk it; there was a high Bengali turnout, and most would vote for Sam. So there was no need for us both to be semi-hysterical with fear. And then we both returned to our private, outwardly calm terror. The sound of rumbling thunder shocked me. It was Pola finishing her speech, and applause from the audience of 400 people.

It was my turn. I walked on to the stage. I could see Tiberio at the very back of the hall. Deep breathing, focus. There is absolute silence, and then I start to speak. After the first thirty seconds I know it'll be OK. If you fuck up in the first thirty seconds you're doomed. But even though I think it will be OK, I have an out-of-body sensation, like I'm watching an ice skater in the finals of an important championship. I could go down at any minute. To win, I must score maximum marks for content, presentation, style and technical ability, and the others must score low.

Despite a lack of preparation I have to go for the high risk triple sulco effect without landing on my face. I realise at one point that I'm literally holding my breath. I mention the word 'socialism' and I get a round of applause. I don't do it for effect, I do it because it's what I believe in. People can tell when you're bluffing. I talk about the MPs' 26 per cent pay rise. I'm a trade unionist. How can Labour MPs tell public sector workers they can only have 3 per cent, but then award themselves 26 per cent? I'd expect that from the Tories, but not from Labour. I won't be accepting that 26 per cent, not now, not ever. Instead it will go back into the constituency.

I talk about inequality, education, training, the wealth of the city, redistribution – I'm very amused to realise that in New Labour terms, I sound like a minor revolutionary. How did that happen? I've always worked for the Labour Party leadership, I've always been part of the Labour Party establishment, but now I feel myself drifting away. An electorally motivated march to the right is one thing; for Labour to become a Tory transvestite is another. I'm reserving my judgement for the moment, but I don't think many of the party members in the hall are. They are vehemently anti-New Labour.

I finish the speech. I'm so relieved not to have made any mistakes, but I'm also convinced I'm about to perish under the fire of questions. At this point my good fairy godmother alights in the auditorium. 'Should a Labour Government enter the first wave of a single currency?' I must be the only politician in Britain who's ecstatic to be questioned on Europe. Five years in Brussels, if nothing else, gives me an edge over the other candidates. Then a question on pensions. The more convincingly I answer the questions, the more convinced I am I'm riding for a fall. Then private schools, educational league tables in Tower Hamlets, the health service. Seven questions in all. And then the chair, Nick Fox, says, 'That's fifteen minutes up, that's all we have time for.'

The relief swirls in my lungs, and as I breathe out, the image of an ice skater landing a near-perfect triple sulco flashes across my mind. I know I've scored a perfect 10. I'm astounded. To leave so much to chance, and not pay a heavy price, seems truly miraculous. I hear loud applause as I walk off the stage, but I have no way of measuring the reception against that for the other candidates. More to the point, I *don't care*. I'm just so happy. Truly, madly, deeply happy. I haven't felt this happy and relieved since I got my finals result. *This* is the result – not the ballot that comes later this evening. The fact that I didn't let anyone down, didn't let myself down – especially given the hopeless state I was in at nine a.m. – was the only result I wanted.

I had categorically decided I didn't want to go to Westminster now, that I wanted some more of my life first. Only Tiberio and Quincy believed me. I knew, whether or not modesty permitted me to say it out loud, I had been the best candidate. Being the best candidate and being the winning candidate were unrelated. I had won, and the glorious prize was a holiday with my husband.

Tiberio arrived back in the candidates' room. We were all gibing Sam. 'So how does it feel to be on your way to Westminster? What's it like to be an MP?' Tiberio squeezed my hand. 'You were the best, by far the best, on another level completely.' I eyed him suspiciously. 'You're my husband, your opinion doesn't count.' He took me into the corridor outside. 'You're not going to win, we don't want you to win, but you were easily the best.' Apparently Pola's speech was much better than anyone expected, but she was massacred during the question and answer session. Sam's was low-key and dull.

Claude answered the questions superbly – better than me, technically – but his speech was flat (I crept up into the balcony to watch), and he looked scared. He had a right to be scared, he was the NEC candidate. I was told Bill Morris had leaned on NEC members to keep Nick Fox, who was seen as Claude's main rival, off the shortlist. The NEC put me in to make up the numbers, and only then because I passed all their tests. Being the NEC candidate had turned from a boon for Claude into a gilt-edged coffin. He was going under, and I felt really sorry for him. He didn't deserve any of the opprobrium Labour Party members had heaped on him.

Labour Party members were coming out of the auditorium foyer after voting. Claude and I went to stand by the door to do the final bit of political hacking as the curtain fell on this two year selection process. Shaking hands, smiling, thanking people. A surprising number of Bengalis came up to me to say they hadn't known who I was, they hadn't even considered voting for me before today, but after hearing my speech they'd given me their first preference. Were they genuine, or were they just hedging their bets? It flickered across my mind that I might win. 'Oh God no,' I thought, 'right now I need forty years at Westminster like a hole in the head.' It was too absurd to contemplate. After wanting it all my life, I now didn't want it. Call me short-termist, but I was wondering whether I could pick up a bikini at the airport at five a.m.

After the last voters left, we got in the car and drove home. It was four p.m., and we had to leave for the count at seven. The house was a disgrace, hundreds of bits of paper fluttered underfoot – research documents, newspaper cuttings, Labour Party policy papers. They could now be thrown together in a funeral pyre. There were also piles of washing, piles of dry cleaning (which for financial reasons I refused to hand in), piles of washing up, piles of bills, piles of piles.

I glanced over my filing system: Bethnal Green and Bow/ local business; BGB/ local authority; BGB/ environment; BGB/ transport; BGB/ health; BGB/ hospital closures; BGB/ poverty. It had been compiled over two years, heaving with facts, most of which I hadn't digested. Tiberio looked at me imploringly. 'Can you throw it all away now?' Tidy to the point of mania, he had been afflicted by these papers since 1995. It was an affront to him to live under the same roof. 'Yes, love – scorched earth policy. It's all going in the bin.' A broad grin appeared on his face. 'But first,' he said, 'pack for the holiday.'

Our package holiday to Kerala had to be cancelled, because we had to be at the count. We lost £500 each. Even though I had little chance of winning, not turning up wasn't an option. So after some agonising, we booked the only package left, to Eilat, leaving Monday morning from Manchester. That way, we could go to the count, hear the bad but predictable news that I'd lost, then get in the car, drive up to Manchester and fly off for a week of sun, sea and sand.

I was desperate for this holiday. I looked sick, yellow, red-eyed, with flaky skin. For the first time in my life lack of sleep had produced rings around my eyes. My shoulder blades had been hunched together constantly and I now had a continuous shooting pain in the back of my neck. I had been to the doctor the previous day to get painkillers for it, and she ordered me to bed for a week. As if.

Tiberio went upstairs to pack. He always packs before me and it always irritates me. This time though I had a feeling he might regret it. Not because I felt destined to win, more because of sod's law. I decided not to pack. My determination to clear up the house also dissolved, and I found myself dozing on the bed.

A few hours later we were outside the London Regional Labour Party offices in Charles Square, where the count was being held. It was 7.30 p.m. 'Shit, I've probably missed it all,' I thought, 'I'm probably out already.' It reminded me of a count a few years earlier when I was up for selection as MEP candidate for London South Inner. I arrived with my mum. They hadn't started counting yet, so we went to get a drink. We were only gone five minutes. When we returned one of the other five candidates was standing at the entrance. 'Ha, don't tell me,' I said as a joke, 'I've gone out in thirty seconds after the first ballot!' 'Yes, actually you have,' came his cheerful reply. It wiped the smile off my face. It was like being punched in the stomach. Losing, no matter what the circumstances, is never entirely palatable.

Earlier during this mind-numbing week, I had let myself picture what it would be like to win. Over the previous five years I had imagined the sheer joy that would overwhelm me at the precise moment of achieving my lifelong ambition to be come an MP. Well, again, not exactly joy, more relief. Relief that my life was going to go the way I always hoped it would – when I was younger, the way I always 'knew' it would. It was amusing watching that certainty fade. Maybe I'd been wrong all those years. Maybe I was never going to be an MP, a Minister, an anybody.

Would it crush me? Would I consider myself a failure? An aerobics teacher in Hackney? A regional trade union official in Surbiton? I decided I could hack it, but I'd still like to know that feeling of relief. I had seen the mysterious process of aggrandisement happen to others when they became MPs. Would it happen to me if I won? Would people interrupt me less, always offer me a lift home, look at me furtively when I walked into meetings, always ask my opinion and wait for my answer?

I walked up the steps, assembling my mental armour as I went, ready to hear, 'So sorry, you went out in the first ballot.' I'd heard it before, that I'd lost, and I'd hear it again. I clenched my abdominals as if preparing for a body blow. In fact, the counting hadn't yet started. The room was packed with about fifty people, maybe more.

There was an expectant hum, some forced laughter. I was relieved to see Pola with her lovely daughter. We encouraged each other with our women's knack for self-denigration.

'So what are we doing here?' I asked her.

'Wasting our time.' Her smile was gorgeous. Next to her was Claude, looking like a man about to hang himself. He was definitely the one with most to lose. I was surprised to be introduced to his girlfriend; ironically I'd earlier been told of a false rumour that he was gay. I had no idea who had started it. I ran through the various characters – Colonel Mustard in the kitchen? Presumably the whole story was invented to make him lose the Muslim vote.

How many votes did I expect to win? Throughout the selection contest I said I would either come first or last. My reasoning was that if I could stay in the first ballot, I'd pick up all the genuinely uncommitted second preferences by giving the best speech and would therefore win. If not, I'd be first to go out. A hush spread from the front of the room where A4 boxes with our surnames were in a row on the table. The first ballot was complete.

'Everington 138 votes,' I waited expectantly, defiantly, for my name to come next. When 'King' popped out of the air it sounded like a bell in my head: '105 votes, Moraes 85 votes, Uddin 55 votes.'

Wow, I hadn't even come third, I'd come second. There were some audible gasps in the room. People with pens and papers started scribbling wildly. Additions, subtractions, divisions. I felt sorry for Pola. No matter how much she might smile, I knew the feeling she had in her stomach. The same pain was also engraved on Claude's face. Certain victory a few weeks ago had turned into certain defeat. He was ashen.

In my head the most appalling string of obscenities jostled for space. 'Unbe-fucking-lievable. I just don't fucking believe it, for fuck's sake . . .' I was dumbstruck at having received that many first preferences. I was led to believe it was impossible. 'Ninety per cent of votes are sewn up. You're an outsider. Sam Everington's done a deal with Jalal, the previous front-runner. You can't win.' Would Jalal's vote pull Sam through? I didn't think so. It was like seeing the deck of cards coming down. You could see it on Sam's face. I didn't know what you could see on my face. Tiberio smiled from the other side of the room, widening his eyes in disbelief and suppressing a giggle. It was absurd and it couldn't possibly happen to us.

The second count began with Pola's votes redistributed among the three of us. 'Well that's just typical.' My silent diatribe continued. 'Absolutely fucking typical. I'm gonna win it, and that's just absurdly typical.' Someone slapped me on the back. 'You're doing really well.'

The room fell silent again. 'Everington, King, Moraes.'

Claude's defeat was now fact. An awareness of the immense, physical, crushing disappointment flooding his senses made me feel slightly sick. Politics really was a humiliating, ego-lashing, loathesome affair. Why did we do it? Were we power-crazed? Did we really want to change the world? Or were we just nasty people? I didn't think that. Pola, for example, was a mother, a Bengali woman who'd lived in the East End for twenty years. She'd overcome God knows how many obstacles, social, religious, cultural. She'd endured wagonloads of racism and sexism. She'd received scant help from her own community or the Labour Party. She had no contacts at all. She had many excellent qualities, although these did not include holding it together as a professional politician in this male-dominated arena which required barnstorming performances at a hustings meeting. But I hadn't found her nasty.

Claude was the professional politician, a lawyer from a tough, Scottish working-class estate, as he occasionally reminded us, but now decidedly middle-class New Labour. Sam I didn't know much about, but he seemed pleasant. He had some heavyweight shadow cabinet contacts up his sleeve – as a doctor, he advised Chris Smith and his team on health.

Nearly ten years later at ten a.m. on a Sunday morning I rang the emergency out-of-hours GP service in Tower Hamlets, desperate to speak to a doctor after a relative became ill. I left a message with an operator, giving the patient's name (not my own). I had no faith that a doctor would materialise before Monday morning. Less than thirty seconds later my phone rang.

'Doctor Everington here, how can I help?'

'Sam, is that really you?' I was stuttering with relief. Sam saw my family member within thirty minutes, and I will always be

grateful that he continues to help people in Tower Hamlets today, and spends his Sunday mornings working in an NHS hospital. Although I didn't know it then, now I know what a genuinely decent person he is.

Then again, most of the heavyweight contacts of political wannabes usually turned out to be thin on the ground. The sum total of my cabinet lobbying had been that pathetically self-conscious letter – a paragraph long – to Robin Cook. That was it. He probably never even saw it. Claude had disappeared into the ether and I didn't see him again for two weeks, until he arrived very magnanimously to help campaign with the candidate for Bethnal Green and Bow during the election.

The final count began. After all that, I wasn't going to win. I'd been rash. Sam was too far ahead to be caught. I started laughing at myself, there in that room. I thought it was the most hilarious thing. Imagine, I'd really thought I was going to be an MP. Talk about hubris. The count was finished. Interminable waiting, whispering, jostling. Then absolute silence. The piece of paper with the result was passed between various officials.

Dino, my agent, was standing at the front, pen and paper in hand, eyebrows knitted and a concentrated frown on his face. He made his final sum and then frowned. 'Have I won?' I half-mouthed the question. For some reason, the four-inch scar slashed from his cheek to his jaw, inflicted six years earlier by the BNP outside an anti-racist concert in Bethnal Green, made him look more dignified.

Dino looked at his sums, looked at me again, and then almost imperceptibly shook his head. I mimicked his movement. 'Is that a no?' Another imperceptible movement. I sat perfectly still, but in my mind I was beside myself.

'Dino, for God's sake, is it a yes or no, am I an MP or am I not?' My future see-sawed dangerously between those two words. Yes. No. Did I want to win? Yes. No. I felt seasick. It was like being in two places at the same time. 'Now I'm a trade unionist in Surbiton. Now I'm an MP in parliament.' The result was now known. The officials had double-checked it and nodded their confirmation. I think it was Terry Ashton who read it out.

'In the final ballot the result is Everington 160 votes, King 200 votes.' Shock. Surprise. Whooping and clapping filled the room.

Dino, like a football fan watching his team score the winning goal in a penalty shoot-out, threw his head up, clenched his fists and jerked his elbows back: 'Yeeeeess!' So un-Dino.

People started slapping me on the back. It was the sort of loud, raw, yet benevolent well-wishing you get when the underdog wins. People seemed genuinely pleased, if amazed. Here it was, after two years, the result they'd been waiting for.

'And wouldya believe it, a twenty-nine-year-old black Jewish girl from Camden Town, who most of us never even heard of until ten days ago, walked in and we gave it to her.'

Now the clapping turned to hugs. People hugging me, throwing their arms around me. One of the Labour Party members squeezed me, an enormous smile on her face. 'You were brilliant this morning, really sensational.' She kissed me on both cheeks.

'You'll never know how close it was,' I said.

And in my mind I thought, 'So close, you came so close to blowing it this morning. Maybe this never really happened. God, what a trauma. I need a hol–.' I bit my lip involuntarily. Oh, shit. The holiday. The second holiday to bite the dust in as many days. Tease (Tiberio) was going to go nuts. Throwing good money after bad. I could make money disappear with more panache than anyone I knew.

Significant life events are often too big to digest at the time, so your brain obsesses on a smaller detail. And that's how it was at the precise moment my life's dream came true: the feeling that washed over me wasn't the relief I anticipated – instead it was a sort of eye-rolling 'Oh, no, I've done it again, another £500 down the drain, my husband's gonna kill me . . .'

Selection to Election

The next thing I remembered, after that moment of winning the selection and being surrounded by back-slapping well-wishers, was the sensation of being whisked away. Two Labour Party officials whisked me out of the crowded room – which still reverberated surprise – and towards an adjacent room and a new life. They congratulated me, and moved straight to business. 'Have you thought about what you're going to say?'

'To who?' I asked, as one of them straightened my jacket.

'The press. There are television cameras on the front steps waiting to film you. We've had calls from a dozen journalists. You also need to think about your campaign. And your office. You're OK to start in the morning, right? We need leaflets printed. Pictures taken.' He was interrupted by a phone ringing.

'Yeah, I'm with her now,' he looked at me, one eyebrow raised. 'Very unexpected, yes. But she's fine, she's ready to go . . . Yes, I'll tell her.' He put the phone down and turned back to me.

'When you go out there, be relaxed, be confident. You've just won a helluva prize. Remember why you wanted to win it. You want to be part of a New Labour Government that builds a fairer Britain. You want to get rid of the Tories. Positive message first, negative message second. Are you ready to go?'

'Uh . . . sure.'

With those words of wisdom I was pushed through the front door of the London Regional Labour Party office, and out into public life. The TV footage from that evening shows a newborn professional politician, the umbilical cord barely cut. I look slightly shy, perhaps taken aback. My hair is unkempt, my face shiny and unpowdered, and on occasion I suppress a half-smile. It is a 'my friends will never believe this' smile.

The TV journalist asked me what my priority would be for the East End. This was my media baptism. It was the first of many occasions that I had to answer an important question on live TV with less than a second to think. Many priorities crowded my mind – poverty, the NHS, education, crime, fighting racism. I was conscious that four years earlier the BNP won their first council seat in Tower Hamlets on an openly racist platform. Black and Asian people had their homes firebombed. The local Labour Party mobilised a massive – successful – campaign to throw the BNP out of Tower Hamlets. So I told the journalist that my priority would be fighting racism and the BNP.

What I meant was that it would be one of my priorities. It was the wrong answer. Of course it's right to fight racism and the BNP. But first impressions are everything. I didn't realise that across Tower Hamlets the next day, the first impression many white residents had of me was that (in their words), 'You only care about ethnic minorities. They are your priority. We don't count.' From that point forward I found that although white people told me I only cared about Bengalis, Bengalis told me I only cared about white people. A more seasoned politician would have chosen a first priority that was perceived as ethnicity-neutral (fighting poverty), and followed it up with a second priority that was perceived as relevant to a particular community (fighting racism). I was less than ten minutes old as a national politician and this was an early political lesson: a moment on the lips can fuel a lifetime on the back foot. Misconceptions flourish in seconds but take years to undo.

That night, standing on the steps in front of a TV camera, my main worry was my husband. What had they done with him? What was he thinking? The impromptu press conference was over, and Tiberio finally emerged through the scrum, all smiles and hugs. He was ecstatically happy for me, and we both agreed it was a crazy, brilliant outcome. We drove to get something to eat, and in the car I rang my parents.

'Mum, I won . . . I know, I can't believe it.'

Mum was so delighted she started shrieking with joy and I could hardly make out what she said. I think she started crying.

Then I rang Dad. In his usual steady tone he said, 'Well done darling,' the way he might congratulate me on finishing an essay. I wanted to say, 'Yo Dad! I'm gonna be an MP! How 'bout some whooping?' But that's not his style. I knew he was thrilled.

Then I rang Slate (my brother): 'No way, way-da-go sis!', and after that the phone calls started pouring in. It was like telephonic monsoon. As we ate our meal it seemed everyone I ever knew was ringing me, as well as many I didn't know. When we got home at midnight Tiberio unpacked his holiday suitcase. The honeymoon, as far as our marriage went, was well and truly over. I looked at the piles of paper from my Bethnal Green and Bow filing system: BGB/health; BGB hospital closures; BGB/poverty. They wouldn't go on a funeral pyre after all.

The next day my general election campaign began. It was a whirlwind of door-knocking, visits to community groups, leafleting outside supermarkets, speeches at husting events with Tory and Lib Dem candidates, TV and radio interviews, standing outside school gates – run-of-the-mill electioneering that candidates do up and down the country. My first indication that Bethnal Green and Bow was not a run-of-the-mill constituency came in the form of John Major. He appeared on a Conservative campaign bus at the back entrance of the Muslim mosque on Whitechapel High Street.

The Prime Minister tried forlornly to get from the pavement to the mosque's door, through a whirlpool of demonstrators, supporters, and highly vocal onlookers, the majority of whom had just finished prayers. The Downing Street security men seemed taken aback by the noise and the 'boisterous' nature of the large crowd. It evidently wasn't what they encountered in Bournemouth or Bromsgrove. John Major was soon bundled back on to the campaign bus for his own safety, while I was bundled in another direction by Labour Party handlers.

Even though the Tories trailed the Lib Dems into third place here in 1992, they hoped to capitalise on Bengali dissatisfaction at my selection in Bethnal Green and Bow. I was the only candidate from a main party who was not Bengali. Despite my predecessor Peter Shore bequeathing Labour a majority of 12,000, the Tories decided that Bethnal Green and Bow was worthy of their Prime Minister's time. They knew there was understandable disappointment in the Bengali community that Labour had not chosen a Bengali candidate. The Bangladeshi community remained one of the most disadvantaged groups in the country – badly hit by eighteen years of Conservative government – and in great need of political representation at Westminster.

An article in the Independent on 2 April 1997 reported on speculation that bitterness at my selection could result in an upset. The headline read, 'Oona King may be black and Jewish but that cuts no ice.' The article went on: 'She can, and probably will, become Britain's second black woman MP. And in a very short time her face will, no doubt, be one of the better known in the new Parliament. But the selection of Oona King as the Labour candidate for a very safe seat does not escape controversy [. . .] With the polls as they are, she should in theory canter through. But there is a little local difficulty; among Labour members in the East End there is a sense of wonder over how, talented and personable though she is, twenty-nine-year-old Ms King got this prize.'

To describe a 'sense of wonder' in the local Labour Party was euphemistic. Many of the key activists were outraged. Virtually all prominent Labour members and councillors had thrown their hat into the ring, momentarily dreamed of being the MP, or backed another local front-runner instead. Those who had backed me, usually as a second preference, had done so to keep a rival out. Some of them didn't speak to me for months, even when I shared platforms with them. But they were matched by the number of party members, councillors and activists who swung behind me with great enthusiasm.

Still, the issue of my ethnicity came up repeatedly. Responding to the suggestion put to me by the Independent journalist that my ethnicity might be damaging I replied, 'I am proud of my heritage [. . .] The real issues are ones of poverty and deprivation, housing and education, as well as racism. These issues affect us all. The fact that my mother is Jewish could symbolically be an issue if there really is a Muslim fundamentalist presence here. But again, in the context of the real problems people face, this should not matter.' I was right in the short term, though if fundamentalism had anything to do with my eventual defeat it was less Muslim and more Christian, in the shape of the witless American Neocons who condemned post-Saddam Iraq to catastrophe.

My 1997 general election campaign was mercifully quick. Unlike many candidates selected years earlier in other constituencies, I didn't have to campaign endlessly before the starting gun was fired on 8 April 1997. I felt like one of those women who only find out they're pregnant when they go into labour. It was like being rushed into political A & E. But although the campaign was quick, it had a perpetual motion that seemed infinite. Estate visits and walkabouts went on and on. The green benches of the Commons seemed so far removed, I remember thinking I would never reach them. From where I was, in run-down parts of Stepney and Bethnal Green, they seemed as far away as Zanzibar or Tasmania.

Elsewhere in the country, Labour and the Lib Dems savaged the Tories on the issue of sleaze and the cash-for-questions scandal. The Tories accused Tony Blair of wanting to end 1,000 years of history through Labour's plans for devolution. Labour ridiculed Tory disunity, particularly over Europe. Gordon Brown took the sting *out of Tory 'tax and spend' gibes by pledging to stick to Tory spending limits for two years. And in the dying days of the campaign John Major likened his impending doom to the Battle of Britain.*

Meanwhile, in Bethnal Green and Bow, the BNP decided to draft in a new candidate to challenge me. His main attraction was that his name on the ballot paper could easily be mistaken for mine (D. King instead of O. King). It was a good old-fashioned electoral con trick. The BNP hoped to fool Labour supporters into voting for them by mistake. In the event they polled 3,350 votes – 7.5 per cent of the total cast. Their trick worked, because at the next election they got well under half that number of votes.

On a lighter note, I was plagued daily by a comical stalker, a nutter in a dark bobble hat called Joynal. The biggest thorn in my side was naturally a Labour Party member. Joynal diligently followed me wherever I went, and popped up from behind bushes, bus stops, Whitechapel Market vegetable stalls, parked cars – or roving TV cameras, and energetically assailed me.

'You! Yes you! Oona King! You are disgraceful *candidate! You must lose! You will lose! I make* sure *you lose!' At first I tried to reason with him.*

'Why am I disgraceful?'

'Because you disgrace us!'

'Why?'

'Because you have no shame!'

'About what?'

'About yourself!'

One afternoon I was on top of the open-air battle bus, rattling off the usual political rant.

'Hello, I'm your Labour Party candidate, Oona King. Please vote Labour on May 1st. Invest in public services, get rid of the Tories, vote for Labour, vote for Oona–'

Suddenly I saw a dark bobble hat crossing the road ahead. Strangely, Joynal hadn't noticed the Labour campaign bus bearing his favourite target only fifty feet away. I couldn't resist it. I turned up the volume on the megaphone and started shouting at the top of my voice.

'You! Yes you! In the bobble hat! Joynal! This is your favourite *Labour Party candidate Oona King here. Thank you for your*

*support! Take off your bobble hat! That bobble hat is a disgrace!
You have no shame! You! Yes you!' Joynal looked flabbergasted, as
did a couple of passers-by, and my Labour Party campaign team.
Despite being berated for an unprofessional lapse, it was my favourite moment of the campaign, and my last devil-may-care moment as a politician.*

*When election night eventually arrived I was overcome with
excitement. Here was the moment I'd waited for since I was eleven:
Labour was poised to sweep the Tories from office after eighteen
years. We were about to win a general election for the first time in my
memory. And my own dream of becoming an MP was about to come
true. Despite earlier speculation, the general feeling was that I would
win with a big majority. But I was chewing my nails about results in
the rest of the country.*

*The BG & B count took place in an ageing municipal sports hall
on Old Ford Road, usually used for boxing matches. I arrived at
about eleven p.m. and was shocked to discover there wasn't even a
TV screen to watch election results come in. The first predictions
were broadcast at about 11.30 p.m. By midnight, with election fever
soaring, more and more Labour Party officials slipped away to the
next-door venue which had a TV. Our result wasn't due for three
hours.*

'Can I go, just for five minutes?' I asked one of the officials.

*'No you're the candidate, you must stay here. It'll only be three
hours.'*

*They were a long, frustrating three hours, when I had only
negligible contact with the outside world. For some reason (unthinkable today) I didn't have a mobile phone with me, and I kept
desperately searching for the one or two people at the count with a
radio.*

*'It's not that I'm uninterested in my own result,' I explained to
another official, as I considered slipping out the back, 'it's just I've
waited my whole life to see the Tories trounced, and I can't bear to
miss it.' In the event I missed it all: Stephen Twigg's wide-eyed
ousting of Michael Portillo; a generation of Tory Government
Ministers turned to dust – Norman Lamont, Malcolm Rifkind,
William Waldegrave; the Tories wiped out in the whole of Scotland
and Wales. It was ironic that becoming a Labour MP meant missing*

the Labour landslide, but my deprivation was repaid with a see-
mingly impregnable majority of 11,285.

Part of me envied those MPs in marginal seats, all eyes upon them.
They were considered electoral barometers. Unlike my experience on 1
May 1997, their counts fizzed with drama and anticipation. Bethnal
Green and Bow would never stage an electoral drama, nor be a magnet
for news teams from around the world. Or so it seemed back then.

Tuesday 6 May 1997 – First Day at Westminster

First day of school. ITN arrived with me in the taxi. Filmed me
looking up at Big Ben. Then winding down the window and saying
to the security guard, 'Hello, I'm a new MP.' Followed Martin Bell
because I thought he'd be going in the right direction. Abandoned
him and followed signs to the new MPs' reception area. Twenty-
Twenty TV was there to film me.

'So, Oona, how do you feel on this momentous day?'

'Umm . . .' Couldn't think of anything to say. For some bizarre
reason it doesn't feel quite as incredible as it should. I think it's
because I haven't had a holiday for ages, and sleep deprivation saps
enthusiasm. This morning there were sixty messages (exactly) on my
two mobiles. It depresses me that sixty people are waiting for a
response from me, and it's not even lunchtime. 'Umm . . . it's
amazing to be here at last.'

Spend an hour finding out that we get the most sensational perks
(basically anything we want), but no office. So it's true. They won't
even give me my own desk. Instead I get a locker. Just as I'm
wondering where the prefects are, a gaggle of Labour Whips appear
in front of me, flush with the glow of government. They say it's not
true that we'll have to wait two weeks for an office – more like four.
Meet Stephen (Twigg) on the way over to the pass office. Hug each
other. Start to giggle because we know we shouldn't, and because
Radio Five Live are recording us. We agree it's a miracle we're both
here. Sit in the pass office for over an hour. Virginia Bottomley
comes in. She looks sick.

Chat with Angela Smith who won Basildon, and eventually go and
have lunch. First time in the Members' dining room. Now we have

passes which mean we're MPs (green and white stripes) doors open for us, literally and metaphorically. Staff bend over so far backwards to help us, it's almost indecent. After lunch, a woman says she'll take me for a little tour. She turns out to be an MP, Lyn Golding, and she shows me where the 'Lady Members' Room is, equipped with shower, hairdryer, iron etc.

At the post office they tell me I'm the only new MP to have been assigned my own grey hessian sack for all the letters. I've only been here five minutes and there are already 5,000 unanswered letters. I have no desk, no staff, no phone line, so I decide I should at least go and get some stationery. Carrying it back towards Central Lobby, I ask a guard if the quickest way out is through the Chamber. He nods. Hesitatingly I ask if I'm allowed to walk directly through the hallowed Chamber. 'Madam, you're a Member of the House,' he says, 'you're allowed to do anything you want.'

'Cool,' I reply under my breath, and walk into the Chamber. This is the intersection between TV politics and my own life. Suddenly, it *is* amazing that I'm here. I look around again at the benches, the hanging microphones, the Speaker's Chair, the Coat of Arms. I'm totally gobsmacked to be standing between the two rows of famous green benches. Yes, I'm finally impressed.

Three male Tories walk in, such a bizarre species with their relentlessly upper-class accents and public-school striped ties. They eye me suspiciously with my brown paper parcel. They're in two minds about calling security, and my presence clearly makes them indignant and worried in equal measure. And then they catch sight of my Member's pass. Their expressions of disdain and disbelief are priceless. They remind me why I worked so hard to get here in the first place. They look at me like I've gatecrashed their private members' club.

Later, I do another interview with TwentyTwenty TV. My interview style already irritates me. I sound either smug, trivial or both. Take another twenty messages off my mobile. Consider disconnecting it. Try and arrange a meeting with the fees office. Don't have any cash left at all. Reread letter from Abbey National explaining that despite my changed circumstances, they are unable to extend my overdraft.

Do an interview with Channel 4, then drive to the constituency office. It's deserted, still no staff. Pick up another twenty messages and two carrier bags full of mail. One of the Labour Party ward officers drives me home to my Dad's house, but then cements himself to the sofa for an hour. Slate has the pictures from the count, which are great, though he still hasn't developed our wedding photos from three years ago. Tiberio refuses to come downstairs, evidently he feels crowded out. He's not the only one.

Mum has made an omelette and salad, which I gratefully eat. She's started working through three bags of old mail I brought back from the constituency office, and begun writing letters for me to sign. They're great. Thank God, or I'd give up hope. The Labour Party person finally leaves at 9.45 p.m. Go over letters with Mum until midnight. It's now one a.m., still haven't spoken to Tiberio. He made me a hot miso soup which was delicious. Calculate that I have at least 160 phone messages to return. Even if I did ten an hour, it would take me sixteen hours. One of the messages is from a trade union colleague, 'You see, Oona, we told you you'd change . . . you don't answer our calls any more. You're just like all the rest of 'em!'

At 1.15 a.m., I switch off my mobile. Wonder if I can send the letter Mum wrote to Diane Abbott. Diane wrote, 'Dear Oona, congratulations on being selected. I look forward to working with you in Parliament. Please do not hesitate to contact me if I can be of any help with your campaign.' I'd been shocked rigid, because I know she hates me. (Mind you, she's allowed to, cos I once ran against her, and it's fair for MPs to hate people who run against them.) But then I noticed the date on the letter: 1 April. Respect. It was the best letter I'd received, and really made me laugh. Mum's reply was:

Dear Diane,
Thank you for your letter dated April 1st. It was so good of you to write to me on what must always be a busy day for you.
With best wishes,
Oona

Hilarious, my mum is too good to be true. But decided I couldn't send it if I wanted to get beyond point scoring. Politics is so boring, but I have decided to go for the boring option.

7 May 1997

Arrived at the Commons at 9.30 a.m. and met the two women who will help me for the next two months. Took them upstairs for a coffee. Yesterday I'd paid the canteen staff, but now they realised I was a Member, coffee was free. 'But you still have to pay for your biscuits,' said the attendant gravely.

'How much?' I asked.

'Three pence.'

Are they taking the piss or what? Why is it that the more you earn, the less you pay?

Went to a photocall for London Labour MPs. Seems like there are hundreds of us. Diane (Abbott), who was chatting to Bernie (Grant), threw her arms around me. I wasn't sure whether she was going to kiss me, or wrestle me to the ground. To my surprise, it was the former, after which we had a love-in and posed for the press together.

At eleven a.m., I went over to the special hall the LP had to hire in order to fit us in to the first meeting of the PLP. All very momentous and exciting, but I thought Tony (Blair's) speech was a bit low-key. After the press were booted out, complaints were made about Gordon (Brown) giving the Bank of England control over interest rates. Tony was asked why he had done it without consultation. 'Because it was the right thing to do,' he replied. I was vaguely surprised that a room full of professional politicians let him get away with an answer like that, but on the other hand, anybody who gets us a majority of 179 deserves a bit of leeway.

Trembling with trepidation at the prospect of making my first intervention in front of the entire PLP, I got up and asked the PM if he would incorporate the issues of overcrowding in council housing, and racist attacks – legislating for a specific criminal offence for the latter* – into the Queen's Speech? I hadn't worked out how the microphone worked, so don't know if anyone heard. But at least I raised two of the key issues facing Bethnal Green and Bow at the earliest opportunity with the PM, as I promised.

---

* Race attacks became a specific criminal offence in the Race Relations (Amendment) Act 2000. I campaigned for many years to change the Overcrowding and Space Standards under the Housing Act 1985 and, with three other MPs, succeeded in getting the law changed in 2004.

Went out for photocall with Tony and the 101 Labour women MPs.* Then lunch, then into the Chamber. Sat down at the end furthest from the Speaker. Glad to even find a space on the benches – looking up I saw some MPs forced on to the balcony. Tony came in and we all clapped. Apparently you're not supposed to clap, you're supposed to do this 'Hear! Hear!' in an absurdly posh accent.

Sat between Andy Love (Edmonton) and Yvette Cooper (Pontefract). Yvette is one of the 'under thirty' group. There are nine of us, all Labour. She was trying to work out what to tell the *Sun* her quirky ambition was – they were waiting to interview us on the way out. She settled on tap-dancing, and being Ginger Rogers. I said my quirky ambition would be to see my husband more than one night a week.

The history of the occasion finally hit me, though at one point I came perilously close to drifting off. It's so strange to see how shrivelled the Tories have become, just a rump of their former selves. Tony Benn entreated us to act independently, and made some funny jokes, none of which I remember. Went outside to do the *Sun* photocall with all the under-thirty MPs. Chris Leslie is the youngest, Lorna Fitzsimons the oldest. Go over the work with my two new assistants, then later get them into a reception at No. 11 for new Labour MPs. It's the first time I've ever walked up to No. 10. From No. 11's window, you can see they share a beautiful garden. Gordon Brown advises me to solve my constituency problems by doubling party membership. I thank him for his advice and beat a retreat back to the constituency.

24 May 1997

I now have my feet under the table, but no telephone on my desk. How is it possible that three weeks after I arrive, the mother of all parliaments can't even give me a phone line? Despite being hermetically sealed off from the outside world, I am receiving an avalanche of mail. If being a young, black, Jewish woman is a disadvantage in

---

* It never occurred to me at the time that this would be a seminal moment, a photograph that defined the media image of 'Blair's Babes' for years to come.

the outside world, here at Westminster it's hell on wheels. Each minority status generates its own mountain of correspondence. As far as the senior MPs go, they all know your name, and they prove they're good politicians by repeating it often. But you don't know any of them, and they all look the same.

And my constituency, being about the most deprived in the country, generates five times as much casework as many of the others. I am swamped. Every time I walk to the Chamber, attendants spring out from behind the message boards to hand me yet more messages. They say things like, 'Ring me urgently. I am your constituent. This is my third message.'

Even though I hand as many messages as possible to my assistants, it's utterly impossible for three of us, working flat out, to deal with them. Some of the new MPs don't even have staff working for them, and yet they're lounging around in the MPs' tea room all day.

Although I've worked at Westminster before,* half the time I don't have a clue what I'm supposed to be doing. Take the Oath for instance. I was standing behind Alan Clark in the queue, he of the infamous 'I'm gonna shag every woman in sight' diaries. It was a classic moment to hear him say, 'I, Alan Clark, swear by Almighty God to be *faithful* . . .' At this point he paused as if to let the irony fill the Chamber, before adding '. . . to the Queen'.

When it was my turn, the wig man (as my friend Ol calls him) said, 'Do you wish to affirm or take the Oath?'

'What's the difference?'

'One includes the Almighty.'

'Oh, OK, I'll have the other.'

'In that case Madam, you can return the Bible.'

I hadn't even realised I was clutching it. I handed it back and went up to shake Madam Speaker's hand.

And then there's all the palaver with voting. To a new person it seems inexplicable. You go round and round in circles in the middle of the night. Literally. Each vote takes about fifteen minutes, and you have to physically walk through the voting lobbies and then stand in

---

* I was seconded from my trade union job part-time to work for an MP for two years, from 1995–97.

a queue. Sometimes we do it for hours, but we never know how long it'll take before it starts. It takes Labour MPs longer than Tories or Lib Dems, because there are loads more of us waiting to get our names ticked off by the clerks with thick green felt-tipped pens. What a drag . . . that's what happens when you have a majority of 179 seats. It's not as much of a drag as Tory Britain was, but it's still a drag, especially at three a.m. And the thought that comes back to me, again and again, is: 'Surely this is no way to run a country?'

18 June 1997

Today was the first reading of my Private Member's Bill. The Private Member's Bill ballot is Parliament's equivalent of the national lottery. MPs choose a lucky number and have a flutter. Usually at least 500 MPs put their names down, but only twenty 'win' a Private Member's Bill (PMB) each year. If your number comes up you get the chance to change the law of the land. But a PMB virtually never becomes law unless it has Government backing. Another sort of PMB is a Ten Minute Rule Bill which gets half an hour of parliamentary time (ten minutes for the MP plus time for the Government to respond), and is even less likely to become law, but is a good way to publicise an issue.

I won the lottery when my name came up last month on the PMB ballot. Was flooded with ideas for legislation from virtually every lobby group in the country. But I knew that I wanted to change the law in the area of employment rights. My Bill helps people like my GMB members who lost their employment rights when their jobs were contracted out by local authorities. In essence, my Bill makes it illegal for employers to ignore equality issues, and other 'non-commercial' matters. So, for example, if a local authority contracted out its cleaning staff, it could no longer accept the lowest bid without considering the consequences. The consequences might be that all the cleaners (inevitably women) took big pay cuts, or lost their holiday pay, or lost their trade union representation. I saw it happen time and again. Another non-commercial issue (according to current law) is quality. So if a hospital contracts out its cleaning staff at bargain-basement rates, it only has to consider the money it saves. It doesn't have to consider the quality of the service, i.e. are the wards filthy or clean?

Of the MPs that win the PMB ballot only the first five get significant parliamentary time. I was quite far down the list, so I went to see Government Whips and asked them to support my Bill. They gave me a spiel about the Government rarely supporting PMBs, and then said they would support it if I could get the CBI and TUC and the Tory frontbench to support it too. Thanks a mil. Why not ask me to get the Israelis and Palestinians to issue a joint peace statement instead? It's like when the king says, 'Of course you can marry my daughter, just bring me the dragon's head on a sword.' Since when does the CBI back employment rights legislation? But I'm giving it a go . . . Today was the first reading. I thought that meant something quite grand, but in fact they just read out the name of a Bill. That's it. 'The Local Authority Tenders Bill.' The first step on the road to parliamentary socialism.

25th June 1997

I asked my first question during PMQs. The Chamber was packed. For a newcomer it can be dazzlingly frightening. I spoke about overcrowded housing, outlining how in the East End there are people living ten to a room. Afterwards, bizarrely, a lot of Tory MPs came up to me saying they were impressed. Low expectations of black people can sometimes be helpful.

1 July 1997

Today I made my maiden speech. There was a man and his dog in the Chamber. Well, maybe a dozen MPs, twenty at the outside. It was nice that Bernie Grant was there. Most of the time the Commons is empty. Unless it's for a big headline debate, MPs are in their constituencies, concentrating on their specialist subjects, in committee meetings, in their Westminster offices, or gossiping in the Members' tea room. Obviously I haven't yet given a speech when the House is packed, though I've spoken at PMQs. There's silence, until they start baying for blood, then it's electrifying and it's horrifying. People say I don't look as scared as many other MPs do. Don't know why not, because I think I'm gonna have a heart attack.

Because the chamber was mostly empty, giving my speech didn't feel too daunting. Obviously you don't want to bugger it up with the men looking on. In fact I don't mind being the only woman there; because they're so sexist, they expect women to be really bad. During my speech, you could see the few MPs still awake saying to themselves, 'Oh my goodness, it seems she can actually string a few words together, how amazing.' Anyway I'm glad I'm not another middle-aged, white man in a suit. I don't have anything against them, nothing at all, it's just the House of Commons is bursting with them.

18 July 1997

I've been told by the Whips office that I'm going to be appointed to the International Development Select Committee. I'm thrilled, and also over the moon that one of the other MPs on the committee is Tess Kingham. I met Tess the first time I walked through the voting lobby. I was surrounded by hundreds of middle-aged men, when I saw a young woman with short peroxided blonde hair wading through the grey suits. I did a double take. Then I followed her. What was someone like her doing in the voting lobby? I caught up with her, and tapped her on the shoulder.

'Excuse me, but you look nice and normal. I'd never have guessed you were an MP. How did you manage to get elected with a trendy haircut like that?' Tess explained that she had dressed old and boring to get selected by her constituency party. But once she'd been selected, she cut off her hair and dyed it blonde. I know she's going to be a good friend.

There are only two Select Committees in the House of Commons that have a travel remit – the Foreign Affairs Committee, and the newly created International Development Select Committee. It's a real stroke of luck that I gave my maiden speech during the debate on International Development – I was told there wasn't 'room' for me to speak on the education debate. I didn't realise it at the time, but under normal circumstances, a new MP is only put on to a select committee (a sought after position) if they speak in the relevant parliamentary debate at the beginning of the parliamentary term.

My appointment to the International Development Select Committee was the most significant and privileged experience of my parliamentary career. I decided to step down in 2001, so that I could concentrate on my first priority – improving housing in Tower Hamlets. I asked to join the Select Committee on Housing (then part of the Department for Transport, Local Government and the Regions), and later secured the first parliamentary inquiry into affordable housing, an issue that has finally climbed to the top of the political agenda.

20 July 1997

Spoke in the education debate today. My speech was pretty good, but I really tripped up over the rules on how you speak. You can't say 'you'. It's like a bad party game. The first time I said 'you' I apologised to the Deputy Speaker. I was talking about the impact of Thatcher's education policies – class sizes increased, and teacher numbers fell. It drives me crazy when Tories claim it didn't have a damaging impact. I experienced it for myself.

'My school saw class sizes increase and teacher numbers cut,' I was on my high horse, about to be thrown off. 'I could choose from a diminished number of subjects, so it's no good Conservative Members telling me it didn't affect my education – it did. I believe that you–'

Whoops.

'If I do that once more,' I looked towards the Deputy Speaker, 'I am sure I shall receive a severe reprimand.' The accepted practice is to grovel as much as possible. 'You are being exceptionally indulgent, Mr Deputy Speaker.' The only person you can say 'you' to is the Speaker. Why can't they just let you speak plain English? I suppose it would be radical, because then people might understand what goes on here.

22 October 1997

Politics ages you. I was thirty today, but listed in the *Guardian* as forty. My first appearance last month on *Question Time* probably aged me ten years. It was horrific. Terrorising. My heart was in my mouth for the full hour. At one point David Dimbleby kept coming back to me on a detail of student funding that I didn't know about. Just when I thought I'd got out of the woods, he came back *again* and I actually thought I might faint and slide off my chair. Can't remember if that was before or after we got on to cuts to the Lone Parent Benefit, but the whole thing was a bloody nightmare. Bizarrely received loads of messages and letters from people saying I came across well. Just goes to show that disaster isn't always perceived as such.

1998

The Garden of Eden and the Hired Guns

12 January 1998

Changing the law is a pain . . . Negotiations with the CBI and Tory frontbench about my Private Member's Bill go on and on. They won't quite kill it, but they won't give it full support either. And why should they, they're Tories. I want to ask my Government Whip, Jim Dowd, what's *his* excuse. The main advice he gives me is that it'll never become law, and I should forget it. But other Government Ministers tell me that even if it dies as a PMB, if I get an agreement signed with the CBI and TUC, and all the ducks lined up like they're asking me to, then it could still be incorporated into Government legislation. So I'll keep going with it.

The other problem is that Private Members' business is taken on a Friday, which sometimes means being at the Commons from nine a.m. until three p.m., and missing all the constituency visits I would usually do before my surgery begins. I must have about 2,000 outstanding constituency visits at present – requests from organisations and individuals in Bethnal Green and Bow who want to meet their new MP. It's a tough choice – prioritise changing the law, or prioritise meeting constituents. Obviously I try and do both, but sometimes it's one or the other.

16 January 1998

Today was a big day for me. It was the second reading of my Private Member's Bill. I've done everything in my power to get the CBI and Tories to back my Bill. I was way down the list of business on the

Order Paper, lodged between other MPs' attempts to change the law such as the 'Mental Health (Amendment) Bill', the 'War Widows and Pensioners (Equal Treatment) Bill', and the 'Widening of the M25 Motorway Bill.'

I'm working with great people on the TUC side, notably Jack Dromey (Deputy General Secretary of the Transport and General Workers Union), and he gave me hope. He said, 'Look Oona, there are some enlightened people in the private sector, we choose them carefully, we lobby them hard, and then we get them to persuade the CBI, and the CBI to persuade the Tory front bench. It's not impossible.'

Jack was momentarily forgetting the existence of Eric Forth MP.* Eric Forth was a Minister under Thatcher and Major, but now leads the awkward squad in Parliament. He thinks equalities issues are a waste of time, was a cheerleader for apartheid, says the Government shouldn't spend money on AIDS because it's self-inflicted, and openly claims to represent the 'white, Anglo-Saxon bigoted majority'. Even if I can get my Bill past the Tory front bench, I'll never get it past him. 'You've got to,' said Jack. 'Go and persuade him.'

Eric agreed to meet me last June, and we sat in the grand surroundings of the Pugin Room overlooking the Thames, surrounded by cream teas and lavish wallpaper prints. MPs come here to chat or bring guests or escape their offices. The room itself is physically in the House of Lords, hence the red carpet on the floor (like the NHS, Parliament has a colour-coding system so you can work out where you are; red for Lords, green for Commons). But the Lords foolishly swapped the Pugin Room for Committee Room 4 in 1906, and they've been trying to get it back ever since.

Eric, as usual, was wearing a screamingly loud tie. I gave him all the reasons to support my Bill.

'More red tape for business,' he replied.

'Talking of which, Eric, a delegation from the CBI would like to discuss the Bill with you later today.'

'It won't make any difference,' he said, smoothing his clashing silk handkerchief. 'You can't charm me, you know.'

It took eight months, but eventually he said I'd managed it.

---

* Eric Forth died in May 2006.

'Yours is the only Bill I'm going to let through,' said Eric, as we sat in our regular spot in the Pugin Room.

As Jack predicted, we had only got that far due to enlightened support from the private sector, in particular Norman Rose on behalf of the CBI.

'How can I trust you?'

'You can't. But as it happens I'm a man of my word. And anyway, if I was going to object I'd tell you now. That's what I've done with all the others.'

Eric's *raison d'être* is to shoot down Labour PMBs in flames. It's not difficult. When a PMB comes up on the floor of the House, any MP can destroy it by calling out one word: 'Object'. If a PMB is objected to, even if only by a single MP, it goes straight into the parliamentary bin. I sat in the Chamber listening in a distracted fashion to Teresa Gorman (MP for Billericay) arguing that English people were denied the rights of Welsh and Scottish people. Teresa wants a devolved English Parliament, and said that the English were 'A bit like the Tamworth pig that is running around: if we get caught, we shall be chopped up into pieces and fed to the European Union'. I've never felt particularly oppressed as an English person, and I was more concerned to find out if my Bill would be chopped into pieces. After five hours, Teresa's Bill was talked out. There was no time to debate any of the other PMBs, including mine, so each of them just had their title read out. If Eric, or any of the awkward squad, said 'object', it was curtains. Mine was first up.

'Local Authority Tenders Bill.' I looked at Eric, and then at the Tory frontbench. There was silence. And then survival was confirmed: '*Read a second time, and committed to a Standing Committee, pursuant to Standing Order No. 63.*'

It didn't sound like anything to write home about, but in fact it was a huge victory. The Chamber was soon littered with dead PMBs.

'Representation of the People Bill.'

'Object.'

'Chronically Sick and Disabled Persons Bill.'

'Object.'

'Representation of Gibraltar Bill.'

'Object.'

'Widening of the M25 Motorway Bill.'

'Object.'

Eric kept his word, he killed all the others, but now my Bill is on its way to the Standing Committee.

16 February 1998

Goddamn Whips are all over me like a rash. They want me to vote for military action against Iraq, and I don't want to. To be fair, the vote isn't strictly about bombing Iraq (though it could be), rather it's about forcing Saddam Hussein to comply with the UN resolutions that he keeps flouting. If he doesn't comply, then he'll be bombed. I know that Saddam has biological and chemical weapons, but air strikes should only be a last resort if all diplomatic routes fail.

My Whip got tired of cajoling me and sent me to see Tommy McAvoy in the Whips office. Tommy is a Scottish MP in his late fifties with greying sideburns and a plump smile which doesn't come too freely. He's number two or three in the Whips office, and is also the Comptroller of Her Majesty's Household, whatever that means. I don't know why I like him but I do. Actually he's been good to me, he's a nice man, but that doesn't mean I'm going along with a spot of bombing.

'So Oona, what's all this about you not wanting to vote with the Government?'

'I'm unhappy about it.'

Tommy raised his eyebrows in irritation. There were three other Whips in the office listening to our conversation.

'Why's that?'

'I can't vote for military action against Iraq if there hasn't first been negotiation through diplomatic channels.'

'Saddam Hussein's had seven years. How long d'you want to give him?'

'A bit longer.'

'Listen Oona, I think Robin Cook's considered all the options, don't you? He wouldn't consider military action unless it was necessary, would he?' Tommy wasn't about to get bogged down in the finer details of the UN resolutions being flouted by Saddam. 'You're a Labour MP and we need you to vote with the Government.'

'Oh, Tommy, you know that's going to be really difficult for me.'

'Well, think about it hard, and come back and let me know at the ten o'clock vote.' We were voting that night on the Second Reading of the Human Rights Bill. At the ten o'clock vote I told Tommy I had to think about it overnight.

17 February 1998

Tried to avoid the Whips all day today, but got two pager messages telling me to go to Tommy again. Told him I couldn't vote with the Government. For the third time he told me to come back after I'd thought about it some more. I was exasperated and willing to resort to stupid tactics to get him off my case. Went to the Members' library and got out a map to check how far Lebanon was from Iraq. Not far, only Syria in between. I went back to the Whips office.

'OK, I've thought some more, and I definitely can't vote with the Government. There's nothing you can say that will persuade me.'

Tommy was about to try to do just that, but I interrupted him. 'Look Tommy, my stepmother of ten years is from Lebanon, a near-neighbour of Iraq, and I definitely can't vote for military action in that region. You can't expect me to vote to bomb my family.'

One of the other MPs in the office with Tommy was from Newcastle.

'If the Government gave me the opportunity to bomb Newcastle,' he said in joking tones, 'I'd jump at the chance.' Other Whips chimed in with areas of the country they considered ripe for military action.

'Well see now, my Mum's from Newcastle,' I said, 'so I wouldn't be able to join you in that vote either. Look, I'm really sorry, but I just don't agree with this vote, and I can't do it.' Tommy was still suppressing a smile at the thought of bombing various parts of England, and somehow my stupid tactics managed to get me out of the Whips office having avoided a confrontation about a deadly serious matter.

I did not vote with the Government that evening to endorse military action against Iraq. It was five years later, in 2003, that I decided Saddam Hussein had been given enough time to comply with UN resolutions, and his failure to do so left no option but military action.

18 March 1998

Today I got my very own Standing Committee for my Bill. A Standing Committee gets its name because it 'stands' while a piece of legislation is considered in more detail off the floor of the House. By contrast, a Select Committee sits for the duration of a whole parliament. On the committee are fourteen MPs including me and the Chair. As usual, the legislative process got underway with a bit of begging.

'I beg to move amendment No. 1.' I said, glancing down a row of barely decipherable numbers, 'On page one, line five, leave out from beginning to end of line eight on page two and insert "(1) The Local Government Act 1988 is amended as follows" . . .'

I went on and on, throwing in a Statutory Instrument here, and a non-commercial consideration there. I explained how the Bill would permit the Secretary of State to let local authorities take proper account of quality, equality and employment issues during the tendering process.

'This Bill represents a new, sensible approach to public procurement, which is based on the politics of partnership.' Once I'd gone over the purpose of the Bill, it was time to get on to the thank yous. I've noticed that British MPs spend half the time trying to kill each other, and the rest of the time thanking each other. I was fairly restrained.

'I wish to thank my colleagues on both sides of the Committee for their huge support. I am particularly grateful to the Government for having accepted the thrust of the Bill and for suggesting such a sensible amendment, which will allow us to move forward to the next stage.'

Then the Minister for Local Government and Housing, Hilary Armstrong, got up and made the obligatory congratulations.

'I congratulate my Hon. Friend the Member for Bethnal Green and Bow on presenting the Bill. It is an issue about which people have been concerned and the Government have been happy to co-operate to ensure that the Bill is a measure that we can support and one that can enable the social partners to work together to form a consensus on how to proceed.'

Then the only opposition Member there, Margaret Ewing, added her congratulations. It was like a wedding. 'I congratulate the Hon.

Member for Bethnal Green and Bow on her Bill and for the very positive way in which it was moved. I feel sure that the whole Committee will accept it.' Then I did my obligatory bit of grovelling and thanking the Chair. Then the Chair did her obligatory bit of congratulating me, 'I add my congratulations to the Hon. Lady for bringing forward the Bill in such a cordial and pleasant manner. Question put and agreed to. Bill, as amended, to be reported.'

And then the Committee rose. I went into the corridor and thanked Stephen (Twigg), Jim (Fitzpatrick), and Phil (Woolas). Normally MPs get press-ganged on to committees by the Whips, but when it's Private Member's business, it's up to the MP to get the Members there. Stephen, Jim and Phil were among the eleven Labour MPs who turned up at the Committee to support my Bill. Spoke to Jim about lobbying for police funding in Tower Hamlets, and then got a Jaffa Cake from the Members' tea room to celebrate getting through Committee stage unscathed.

25 March 1998

People say politics is war by other means. I've only recently realised the extent to which parliamentary parties resemble miniature armies. As far as backbench MPs are concerned, it's important to distinguish between *fodder* – which implies an immobile food source like alfalfa beans – and *infantry* – which implies throwing oneself out of a trench, or, in our case, on to a bench, at all hours of the day and night.

The Tories have an army, and we have an army. Our army won the election, and therefore Labour generals enact Labour legislation by using their greater numbers of Labour infantry to push laws through Parliament. Although the Tories can't stop this happening through force of numbers, they are quite within their rights to pick off Labour infantry by wearing them out. The infirm and elderly, comprising a large number of MPs, are the first to go down. Usually down the pub in the basement. Strangers' Bar. But after many nights of many drinks and many votes, MPs sometimes go AWOL.

Luckily for the Tories, although a larger number of them are infirm or elderly, the opposition has the advantage of surprise. This means that every once in a while they surprise us by ambushing a vote (by turning up *en masse* at one a.m. when we thought they'd all gone home). Apart from these carefully executed ambushes, the infirm and elderly Tory infantry don't have to be there all the time. And sometimes, even when they are there, they still have us running round in circles while they've got their feet up on a leather footrest in the Members' library.

Last night, for example, we were voting to ban corporal punishment in schools. The Tories were outraged, maybe some of them were shaped by a good whipping, I don't know. For whatever reason they set their hearts on sabotaging our plan to stop kids getting flogged. We'd been expecting votes any time from 3.30 p.m., the first vote came some time after five p.m. At midnight I managed to grab a sofa (one of only three in the whole building) but despite marking my territory with everything I could find (clothes, bags, mail) another MP nicked it while I was voting.

MPs have to line up in different queues in the division lobbies to vote, according to their surname. I'm in the middle third of the alphabet which takes the longest. We queue up to have our surnames crossed off by a clerk. The Tories zoom through their queues because there are hardly any of them there. If you're a Labour MP in the middle queue, the other queues zip by, and inevitably you lose your place on one of the few sofas or computers.

So I was lying on the floor, under cushions to keep warm. The heating was off. By 3.30 a.m. I was totally knackered and freezing. My fault, should've packed a sleeping bag this morning, but didn't know we'd be here all night. They never tell you in advance. They can't tell you in advance, because the opposition likes to spring surprises. The Tories kept calling votes – at around 4.30 a.m., then five a.m., then six. Half the time when we staggered into the Chamber they cancelled it. The Tories weren't actually turning up. They were doing it to wear us out, to physically grind us down. It sounds stupid but it makes perfect sense. I left the House of Commons at about seven a.m., and when I got back there after grabbing a few hours sleep (Tiberio had already left for work when I got home) my Whip said I'd have to be in Parliament tonight until at least midnight. I told him to take a hike. OK, I will actually go, because the vote tonight is on Northern Ireland and power sharing and the end of war, but good God, what a stupid way to work.

27 March 1998

Today was another big day for me with my Private Member's Bill. I had to be in the Chamber at 9.30 a.m., but my Bill didn't come up until after one p.m. Another struggle with Eric Forth. It wasn't a good sign when he started messing about with amendments at the outset. I crossed the Chamber, and perched next to Eric on the Tory benches.

'Um, any chance you might withdraw your amendment?'

'Only if you get a signed letter from the Minister, giving me assurances on this point, in the next fifty minutes.' Eric was pretty pleased with himself, not least because he knew his request was virtually impossible. Under normal circumstances it takes weeks if not months to get a response from a Minister.

It turned out that the Minister I needed was in Manchester. I hurried from civil servant, to special adviser, to frontbench spokesperson, and then ran out into the corridor at the back of the Chamber next to the Table Office, and made frantic phone calls to the Department. I finally got through to someone who said they would contact the Duty Minister. I dictated the assurance I needed down the phone, and pleaded with them to OK it, get it signed by the Minister, and then deliver it to the Chamber, all within half an hour. The guillotine would fall on my Bill at 2.30 p.m. Miraculously at 2.22 p.m. the Duty Minister's driver arrived with a signed ministerial letter.

I rushed back into the Chamber and handed it to Eric. He looked momentarily taken aback. But his opening gambit was still to move the amendment, and then claim he wanted to 'deal with this matter very quickly'. He continued in a half-apologetic tone. 'The Hon. Member for Bethnal Green and Bow (Ms King), the Bill's promoter, has gone to extraordinary lengths to deal with the questions raised by my amendments.' With his brightly coloured ties and waistcoats Eric had the air of a circus master. Everyone had to jump through his hoops.

'I do not want to delay the House . . .' he said, and then went on to do exactly that. The clock ticked ominously behind him. It was 2.24 p.m.

'Because of the diligence of the promoter of the Bill (Ms King),' continued Eric, 'it just so happens that the Under-Secretary of State for the Environment, Transport and the Regions, the Hon. Member for Greenwich and Woolwich (Mr Raynsford), wrote to try to reassure me.'

Eric was using the existence of an arcane legislative procedure called 'hybridisation' as an excuse to wreck my Bill. Hybridisation gives the relevant Minister powers to split up the legislation – making it applicable to some local authorities and not others. It's just a fancy way of saying you can introduce pilot schemes. But Eric and his partner in crime, fellow Tory David Maclean, weren't having any of it. They jumped up and down, claiming that the hybrid elements in my Bill were unprecedented.

'I am not aware of any precedent,' intoned Eric in a doom-laden voice. I immediately got to my feet.

'The provisions that the Right Hon. Gentleman seeks to amend are fairly normal in such cases,' I reassured him, speaking at speed. 'Recent examples include section 79(4) of the Airports Act 1986, section 34(4) of the Police Act 1996 and section 87(9) of the Environment Act 1995. I shall not continue, but there are several other examples.'

Eric had a wry smile on his face and lavished me with compliments instead of what I wanted – his amendment withdrawn, and my Bill on to the next stage.

'I am grateful to the promoter of the Bill (Ms King),' said Eric, 'who obviously does her homework, too – extraordinarily thoroughly, as my Right Hon. Friend the Member for Penrith and The Border (Mr Maclean) can see.' I wanted to knock his block off. The Minister at the Despatch Box, Glenda Jackson, backed up my case, and finally Eric gave me what I was looking for.

'In view of the letter from the Under-Secretary and what the Minister has said, I beg to ask leave to withdraw the amendment.'

'Amendment, by leave, withdrawn,' said the Clerk.

Just in time. It was 2.29 p.m. And then up piped Eric, 'I beg to move amendment No. 2, on page two, line nineteen, leave out "two" and insert "six". I tabled the amendment because I was uneasy about the two-month implementation period in the Bill–'

The clock struck 2.30 p.m. Eric had done what he so often does, which is to destroy good sensible legislation that no one opposes. Instead of saying 'object', he talked it out, another of his favourite tactics. All my prejudices flooded out. Stupid bloody Tory, I should have known I couldn't trust him as far as I could throw him. My team tried to console me that my Bill could still become law. I would have to get it incorporated into Government legislation. After all, I had climbed through the most difficult hoop of all, the challenge set by the Government: getting the CBI and TUC to agree to it. In a way, Eric's machinations had helped me, because he had exasperated even the businessmen he sought to represent. They now gave my Bill unqualified support. I had, in effect, got the dragon's head on a sword.

15 April 1998

I'm still trying to digest what I saw during the International Development Select Committee visit to Rwanda last month. The first shock came as the plane landed in Kigali. I saw gentle countryside, rolling hills, peace and tranquility. I had associated Rwanda with scenes of terror, babies flayed alive, neighbour murdering neighbour, the end of civilisation. I didn't expect it to look like Devon. As it turned out, it was even more beautiful. Driving from the airport into lush countryside, we were lulled into a false sense of security, enchanted by the palm trees, hibiscus, papyrus, sunflowers and mangoes. It was the closest I'd come to the Garden of Eden. Maybe this is fitting, because what happened in Rwanda is of biblical proportions.

At a welcome dinner on the first night I was seated next to the Chair of the Rwandan Foreign Affairs Committee, Aaron. He was an intelligent man with a great sense of humour, a soft laugh, bright sparkling eyes. 'So I assume you must have a very low opinion of the international community?' I asked.

'I'm not the right person to ask,' he said. 'My wife was killed in front of me . . .' He trailed off, shaking his head. 'And they killed my three children; with UN soldiers right there, they killed my wife and three children. I'm not the right person to ask. I'm biased.'

'I'm so terribly sorry. And there were really UN soldiers nearby?'

'Yes' he replied. 'They were standing right there, my family was murdered under their noses.'

I stared in silence at my plate. After a while I felt compelled to ask another question. 'Do you have any children . . . now?' I hesitated halfway through, realising how terrible it would sound to ask 'Do you have any children *left?*' Why was I asking the question? Selfishly, I wanted hope.

'Yes,' he said, 'I have two.' Then he added, 'Of course, in reality I have a lot more – twenty-six, but only two are mine. The rest are orphans. I have to provide for them, they have no one else. Some are nephews and nieces, some are my neighbours' children, and some I'd never seen before, they were just wandering the streets after their families were murdered.'

Twenty-six children. The enormity engulfed me. The answer I thought would give me hope instead filled me with despair. Aaron could see I was shocked, and advised me to reconsider visiting the genocide site the next day. 'You can't imagine what you'll see,' he said. 'I think it will be too much.'

We were to visit a school where between 35 and 40,000 people were herded together, murdered and dumped in mass graves. The new Government wanted to preserve the act of genocide: they had exhumed the bodies, men, women and children, and returned their skeletons to the classrooms for the world to see and learn. If it wanted to.

When the Jews were herded into gas chambers, no international organisation existed to prevent genocide. When the Rwandans (Tutsis and moderate Hutus) were rounded up and hacked to death, the UN not only existed, but it was there in Rwanda when the killings began. Its response was to pack up and leave. 'Never again' was exposed as a slogan, not a policy.

The next day when we visited the school, the atmosphere was surreal. We drove again through that Garden of Eden, while our guides told us that virtually every Rwandan we saw had lost at least five members of their family. Can you imagine if every person in Britain had five family members murdered in one hundred days?

We walked into the first classroom. Up close, skeletal corpses have more expression than I imagined. Some of the faces were quite clearly contorted in a final scream. Many had their arms up in a desperate effort to ward off inevitable death. I couldn't understand why many of the children had no feet, until I was told it was to prevent them escaping while the adults were murdered. And only once the adults were dead (those most likely to get away) did the militia return to finish off the children.

Try and picture a classroom of children with amputated feet writhing in agony. The killing began at three p.m. and continued unabated until six p.m. the next evening. One woman told me how she hid under the bodies of four women killed in front of her. They were hacked to death with machetes. She lay under their flayed, dripping bodies for seventeen hours. She is the only surviving member of her family. She lost thirty-six members of her mother's family and forty-eight members of her father's.

Until my visit I had an average grasp of the situation: two tribes, Hutus and Tutsis, hacking each other to death. An international community spending US $1 million a day in refugee camps. Western governments doing what they could to sanitise hell, but atrocities continuing due to 'belligerent tribalism'. I was ignorant. The Hutus and Tutsis are not tribes. They share the same language, land and culture. They more closely reflect a class system, and it was a class system clearly and brazenly manipulated by the West. In the past Tutsis owned cattle (and therefore had assets, and were more wealthy), while the majority Hutu (85 per cent of the population) worked the land. When the Belgians arrived as the colonial power, they clambered on top of this loosely based class system and turned it into formalised apartheid. They ordered all Rwandans to class themselves as either Hutus or Tutsis, and issued ID cards to separate the two.

It was inspired divide and rule tactics, and it encouraged the wealthier Tutsis to help the Belgians hold the majority Hutus at bay, denying them jobs, education and political influence. Colonialism is never a pretty sight, but the Belgian colonial era was particularly brutal, dating back to King Leopold II's genocide of ten million Africans in neighbouring Congo a few decades earlier. When independence came to Rwanda, the Belgians fled and the Hutus sought revenge on Tutsis for co-operating with foreign occupiers. Pogroms and mass expulsions took place, leading to a generation of Tutsi Rwandans fleeing to surrounding countries – Uganda, Burundi, and Congo. It was from Uganda that these Rwandans eventually re-entered Rwanda to end the 1994 genocide under the leadership of Paul Kagame, now President. It's not possible just to dismiss the massacre as bloody Africans killing each other. Without European intervention in the preceding years (especially Belgian and French), the 1994 genocide could not have taken place.

At the time I remember thinking how terrible it was that Lake Victoria was full of bodies, but I inevitably turned the page. I was making arrangements for my wedding. I had to get the caterers sorted out, the invitations posted. I didn't see the point in writing to my MP. Ironically, I've had to become an MP to realise it can make a difference. It now occurs to me that if you don't fuss over genocide, why fuss over anything? For whatever reason, between April and July 1994, the most methodical slaughter of civilians since the Second World War took place, and our Government was not pressured by either MPs or voters to take a stand against genocide.

Worse, the international community was well aware that genocide was happening, but chose to ignore it. This was in direct contravention of international law – specifically the UN's Convention on Genocide. In fact the UN office which received some of the earliest and most graphic reports of systematic massacres was run by a young official named Kofi Annan (later the UN Secretary General). His hands were tied by the reluctance of member states – most importantly America in the wake of its bitter Somalian experience – to intervene. By the time outside troops went in, between 750,000 and one million Tutsis and moderate Hutus had been murdered. It is not too much of an exaggeration to say there were hardly any left to kill – those who survived had already fled. And our Government, and every other government, sat back and did nothing.

As I walked around this genocide site looking at the skulls, crushed bones, and silent screams, I couldn't help catching a cliché with every breath: 'Something must be done, something *must* be done.' I spent an hour staring at death, almost convulsed by it, and then climbed back into the air-conditioned Land Rover with a Union Jack flag on the front. I have decided what I'm going to do.

I am going to set up an All Party Parliamentary Group on Genocide Prevention. The aim of the group will be to raise awareness of genocide in general, and the problems facing Rwanda and the Great Lakes Region in particular. I need to raise money for it, and I'm going to ask the NGOs to help. We will try to ensure that next time around, British MPs can't say, 'Oh, sorry, no one told us it was genocide.' The group will aim to keep interested members of the British public informed, and then they can lobby their MPs to join, and to take an interest. Anyway, I think that many MPs do actually care – whether for moral, political, or purely electoral reasons. In 1994 the genocide was under way for six weeks before it was even raised in Parliament. And the British representative to the UN said we couldn't use the word 'genocide', because then we'd be obliged to act under international law.* It's an astonishingly shameful episode for which we cannot make amends. Having said that, under Labour we're trying hard. These days Rwanda receives substantial British aid, run by the Department for International Development (DfID), and our government has created one of the most successful aid agencies in the world.

12 June 1998

Watching a Prime Minister walk through a room of MPs is like watching a magnet trail through a dish of paper clips. MPs cluster close, drawn to the ultimate source of political power. That's what I saw last week as the Prime Minister walked into the Members' tea room. He went to the Labour end of the tea room (or I should say the Government end, which is currently Labour), nearest the refrigerators bearing drinks, chocolate biscuits and sandwiches. The tea room is long and narrow, with the Commons' signature green leather armchairs on one side grouped around low tables, and a single row of tables that each seat four MPs on the other.

I watched MPs pretending to act normally, and then did the same myself, flicking through a copy of the *Guardian*. The PM chatted jovially to colleagues while someone got him a cup of tea. Then something strange happened, a break in the electromagnetic force of politics. While the PM sat sipping his tea, the four MPs around him got up and left him alone at the table. Maybe they had a Select Committee meeting or a Standing Committee, or perhaps had to be in the Chamber. If your name is about to be read out by the Speaker in the Chamber, or you're a Minister on frontbench duty, you have to be

---

* See *Conspiracy to Murder* by Linda Melvin.

there. You can't be late, not even a minute late, not even if you're sipping tea with the PM. The PM sat there, and more strangely still, no other MPs filled the space. I couldn't see his PPS (Private Parliamentary Secretary) either. I sat for about a minute, turning the pages of the newspaper, looking at the strange spectacle of the PM alone.

A voice in my head was saying, 'Go and ask him for something. You're an MP, he's the PM. What d'you think you're here for? It's your job to go and ask him for something.' But another quieter voice was saying, 'Oh, give the man a break, let him have two minutes sipping his tea in peace.' In any case, I hate asking people for things, in fact I'm quite bad at it (it's only recently struck me that's all an MP does, so I'm in the wrong job). But I was already walking towards him when I thought, 'What? What do I ask him?' I only had a few seconds to decide because I knew there would soon be a stream of paper clips following my lead. I'd already raised the issue of housing not too long ago during PMQs, so I trundled over with another two items on my wish list, picked more or less at random.

'Hi Tony, d'you mind if I ask you something?'

'Not at all Oona. How are you? Come and sit down.' He smiled broadly and moved some cups that the other MPs had left so I could put my papers down.

'I'm well thanks. Listen, I know you don't have long but there are two things I'd really like you to do something about.'

'You credit me with influence.' He laughed in a relaxed way and stretched back in the chair. He always gives the impression to underlings of being laid-back and humorous. Not *too* humorous, as that would be inappropriate for a Prime Minister, but humorous enough for both parties to smile and relax before business.

'So what is it?'

'Landmines. The Ottawa Convention – Britain should sign the treaty banning anti-personnel landmines. They kill and maim thousands of innocent civilians every year. I'm on the International Development Select Committee, and it's shocking to see the damage they cause. There's no point DfID funding development programmes if people go on being killed by landmines after a conflict ends. There's also a political consideration.' He had leaned forward slightly, cup in both hands, giving the impression that he was interested in what I was saying.

'Following the death of Princess Diana, you're closely associated in the public eye with her memory and legacy. She campaigned on this issue. It's not going to look good if Britain hasn't signed the Ottawa Convention by the anniversary of her death in August this year. Civil servants are dragging their feet. Can you sort them out?'

'I'll have to see what I can do. It's a very serious issue.'

He didn't seem about to elaborate, so I went on.

'And secondly, I want to tell you about a constituent of mine who was assaulted and beaten. The attacker singled her out because she was wearing a headscarf. She is Muslim. Under new legislation her attacker would receive a higher penalty for a racially motivated attack, as she is Bengali. But if it's a case like this where he says he attacked her because of her *religion*, he will receive a lower penalty. It's a terrible loophole in the law. Can we close it?'

'So people are saying racially motivated attacks are religiously motivated?'

'Yes. Regardless of whether they are racially or religiously motivated they should attract the same penalty.'

Then the PM asked a series of quick-fire questions: Who was the Minister in charge? What were the civil servants saying? Were there ideas for tacking it on the end of legislation? What was the level of racially and religiously motivated violence in Tower Hamlets? I answered his questions as best I could. We'd probably been talking for five or six minutes.

'I'll definitely try to do something about these two issues.' He replaced his cup in its saucer, signalling that our discussion was drawing to an end. 'And thanks for letting me know about the loophole around religiously motivated violence, because I wasn't aware of it.'

With that last sentence, the electromagnetic force of politics snapped back into place. His PPS emerged at his side, trailing four paper clips and a Cabinet Minister. I slipped away while the PM turned his attention to threatened redundancies in Scotland. I'd internalised an important political rule: always be ready with questions, always be ready with demands. You never know what law change you might harvest from a five minute encounter.

Of course, you can't change the law in five minutes, which is what the negotiations around my Private Member's Bill taught me. But being ready to pepper Senior politicians with demands (at a moment's notice), is as important as engaging the people you represent. And quite often your five minute conversation, while not immediately resulting in change, has the effect of water on sand. Taken with many other similar whispers in a politician's ear, it erodes the status quo, *until eventually the landscape is irreversibly changed.*

There is a physicality to the House of Commons and its environs (like the Members' tea room) that gives MPs the chance to informally lobby Ministers, and in so doing to change the political landscape. Informal lobbying like this is possibly more successful than anything else. If a picture is worth a thousand words, then a face-to-face conversation is worth a thousand letters. That is why access is so important. It is harder to reject a colleague who fixes you with an imploring stare, or visible anger, than it is to throw a letter in the bin.

The next day I walked through the Members' lobby, on my way to the Members' Library. My name was lit up on the MPs' letter board, meaning there was mail waiting for me from within the House of Commons, or within Government. The MP's letter board is where MPs leave letters for each other, or Ministerial departments distribute press releases or briefings that they want MPs to receive immediately. In my box was a slim A5 cream envelope. I turned it over, and on the back it said, 'No. 10 Downing Street'. Inside was a handwritten letter in black ink from the Prime Minister. He thanked me for raising the two issues I'd put to him yesterday, and asked if I would send a briefing on each of them to his office, marked for the attention of Anji Hunter. He said that he would look into them.

I couldn't help thinking of all the people who had a quick word in my ear and asked me to do something. I knew that ideally I should respond to each of them in writing, even if only briefly to say I would look into it. But with the thousand and one things on my desk, I rarely found time. Here was the Prime Minister with a million and one things on his desk, yet he found time. Maybe that's why he is Prime Minister.

Britain ratified the Ottawa Convention on landmines on 31 July 1998.

From the BBC website: 'The British Government has announced a total ban on the use of landmines [. . .] The late Princess Diana championed the anti-landmine cause and the British Government's latest stand – a month before the first anniversary of her death – has been welcomed by the British Red Cross and Mines Advisory Group.'

26 September 1998

I spent a week in America filming a documentary for the BBC to mark the thirtieth anniversary of Martin Luther King's death. The programme looked at segregation between the white and black communities. In MLK's time segregation was legal. Now it's just *de facto*. After we filmed in Washington and Georgia, I asked the documentary director to look at the situation in Tower Hamlets. I remember being stunned during an early visit to two schools in the constituency. They shared a playground, divided by a wire fence. On one side of the fence were brown children, and on the other side were white children, joined by a smattering of Afro-Caribbeans. How could this be, I thought, how could schools in Britain segregate children by race in 1997?

The answer was easy to find: one of the schools was a faith school, a Catholic school, while the other was a state school. The Catholic school attracted most of the white parents in the local area, along with some Afro-Caribbeans. As the state school experienced 'white flight', it became a *de facto* Muslim school, where 98 per cent of its pupils were Muslim – the vast majority Bengali, and about 10 per cent Somali. The result was racially segregated education. I've been trying to publicise this issue since last year, and the documentary, called *The Trouble I've Seen*, was a good opportunity.

Given that we are where we are, and we can't wish faith schools out of existence, I think there are only three solutions. The first is to allow state schools in multicultural areas to remain just that – multicultural. Schools should reflect the population around them. So if they are slipping towards being mono-cultural, they should be able, if they wish, to select a balanced ethnic intake. The problem is, no politician wants to say this, because it means selecting children by race. Of course, we currently select children by intelligence, and no one bats an eyelid. But race is different. Race is incendiary. But our current approach is short-termist, because racial segregation in education will be far more explosive in the long run. Unfortunately no one's listening.

The second thing we can do is take the racially segregated schools, and physically bring the kids together for lessons. So, the Muslim school and the Catholic school might do joint citizenship courses. And the third thing we can do is increase the numbers from other faiths (or no faith) that attend religious schools. My preferred option is the first, which is what I say in the documentary.

When I was filming in Atlanta I also met up with my cousins Clennon, Chevene and Peggy, three of Uncle Chevene's five children. Clennon told me he'd arranged a press conference for me.

'What for?' I asked.

'So you can demand that your dad be allowed back into the USA. You're a British MP. They'll listen to you now.'

'Really?' I was embarrassed that it hadn't occurred to me. When I followed Clennon into the press conference, I'm not sure what I expected, but it certainly wasn't the bank of TV cameras that greeted me. I'd forgotten – Clennon used to be a sharp-suited assistant for the Mayor of Atlanta, Andy Young. He is practically a media mogul, infinitely more experienced than me at getting the press interested in a story. They were all there. NBC, ABC, CNN, the *Washington Post*, the *New York Times*, the *Atlanta Constitution*, PA, Reuters, a whole host of others, and even the BBC correspondent.

'So what is your campaign about Ms King?'

'My campaign . . .' I stuttered, 'my campaign is to ensure that the racist charges against my father Professor Preston King are finally revoked. I want my father to come home.'

After the press conference, Clennon, Peggy, and Chevene ran through a list of people I should write and speak to. One of them was Tony Blair.

'I can't write to Tony Blair,' I said 'it would be completely inappropriate.'

Clennon said something like '*Are you crazy?* We're talking about a gross miscarriage of justice. It would be *completely* appropriate for Tony Blair to ask Bill Clinton to reverse it.'

'I'm not arguing about the injustice bit. I'm just saying that if I raise something with the Prime Minister, it's got to be about my constituents, or about a policy issue. It can't be about me and my family.' In unison, all my cousins groaned and rolled their eyes. 'In any case,' I added, 'I'm sure Dad would agree with me.'

The conversation went around in circles for a while before we were interrupted by the film crew. The next day there was significant coverage of Dad's story in the press. The *Daily Telegraph* even rang from London saying they'd seen the press conference and they wanted to run a story about Dad, which they did.

Shortly after the Atlanta press conference, the NBC team produced an in-depth report that brought massive media coverage of Dad's case, and was instrumental in eventually securing Clinton's presidential pardon. I did not, in 1998, write to Tony Blair about my father's case. However, in 2000 when my father had decided to return to America for the funeral of his eldest brother Clennon and it seemed likely that he would be arrested and imprisoned, I wrote to Tony Blair asking him to write to President Clinton. In the event, President Clinton agreed to a presidential pardon before any intervention from Tony Blair was required.

I am often credited with initiating the campaign that secured my father's pardon. Although the campaign only took off because I was a Member of Parliament, as this diary makes clear, it is my cousins and family in America who deserve the credit.

11 November 1998

Got in from the Commons after midnight. Tiberio stayed up long enough to tell me I'd left the bedroom a complete mess, and that our marriage was pointless because we never see each other. Spent three hours tidying the house. It's true, all the mess is mine. Went to bed at four a.m., alarm went off at 6.30 a.m. Must improve ability to function on less than three hours sleep. Felt awful, looked worse, slapped on about two inches of make-up. Meetings all morning, then into Commons for International Development Questions followed by PMQs.

I got into the Chamber early, because the first question on the Order Paper was about the floods in Bangladesh, and I wanted to put a question to Clare Short (Secretary of State for International Development). It was two minutes before Prayers began, and Clare was sitting in her place in front of the Despatch Box.

'Hi Clare, I wanted to mention that I'm going to try and ask a question about debt relief to help the flood response in Bangladesh.'

'Yes, the floods have been awful,' said Clare in her low trademark tones. 'DfID's putting a lot of money in, £22 million so far.'

'Great. My constituents are contacting me about it, so they'll want to know what the Government's doing. I'm going to send them a copy of today's Hansard, so anything helpful . . . I'd appreciate it.'

My two inches of make-up felt conspicuously garish in contrast to her refreshingly bare skin, as though my lipstick was ideologically tinged: old feminist meets new feminist.

'That's fine,' she said.

Slipped into my usual place – second row, towards where the PPSs sit, i.e. more or less behind the ministers at the Despatch Box. If you're going to be in the Chamber, you might as well have a ringside seat. The downside is that when you ask a question, you're so close to the Ministers (sometimes less than a foot) that you can forget to project your voice, and your contribution gets lost.

Took the opportunity afforded by Prayers to close my eyes for five minutes. Given that I'm an atheist it's strange how much I like Prayers. I suppose they're a bit like meditation. Only MPs are allowed in the Chamber (apart from the Chaplain and a couple of hangers-on), and there's no one in the public gallery. It's the only time the Chamber seems calm, the calm before the storm. Just before Prayers begin, the Speaker, Betty Boothroyd, comes in after doing her procession with the Mace. She has people behind her holding her skirts, or at least they look as though they are. Betty nods regally at the frontbench as she walks past to take up her position on the Commons' throne, known as the Speaker's chair. She gives the nod to the Chaplain, and off he goes.

There's a great temptation to join the group poetry session, and begin chanting with the rest of them: '. . . Thy kingdom come,/ thy will be done, on earth as it is in heaven./ Give us this day our daily bread . . . as we forgive those who trespass against us . . .' It *is* a beautiful poem. Today, eyes closed, I sway while my afternoon headache taps gently at my temples. Give us this night our nightly sleep. As my prayer ends, so does the Lord's, and we're straight into debt relief for the poorest nations.

I bob up and down, hoping Betty will call me. I have the demeanour of most MPs trying to 'catch the Speaker's eye': half-demanding, half-begging. Jenny Tonge, the Lib Dem MP on the International Development Select Committee with me, is called first. She asks if debt-ridden poor countries who experience a natural disaster, such as Bangladesh, can receive debt relief more quickly. Clare thanks Jenny, in fact says she's grateful to her for raising the point, and goes on to say more flexibility is needed around debt relief. Then the Speaker calls my name, and I follow up the point by asking Clare if Bangladesh might become eligible under the Heavily Indebted Poor Countries Initiative, so that money is available to tackle the long-term effects of the floods. Clare's response is loud and clear:

'No.'

What did she mean, *no*? I'd already told her in advance it was important to me, that I needed something I could send out to my constituents. She could have warned me I was on the wrong track (it turned out that although Bangladesh is heavily indebted, it is domestic debt and not international debt, and therefore Bangladesh is not eligible for international debt relief). Or she could have given me some softer blather. She didn't have to make me look a complete idiot. We're on the same side, for God's sake. I have great respect for the way Clare has led DfID, but the fact remains, she wouldn't know the term 'team player' if it hit her over the head. It was the only time I'd ever been rebuffed on the floor of the Chamber. Never mind the embarrassment, her response also meant I had nothing to send constituents. As I sat behind Clare Short, fuming, a note was passed along the benches with my name on it. I opened it, and did a double take: *Oona King to go to the Prime Minister's office immediately*.

Fucking hell, I thought, what have I done now? A message like that could only be bad. If it was something good, you wouldn't be hauled off the benches *immediately*. I stood up and searched my mind for misdemeanours. Were they still angry because I was mouthing off about immigration policy? Because I had disobeyed the Whip on that Standing Committee? No, that was for the Whips office to deal with, not the Prime Minister's office. Was it because I'd refused to vote for bombing Iraq earlier in the year? No, that was months ago back in February, there was no immediacy to it. I walked out of the Chamber, through the door opposite the Table Office, across the staircase landing, and into the corridor on the right. It was marked by a hand with a pointing index finger, under the sign 'The Prime Minister, The Rt. Hon. Tony Blair'.

Two security men stood outside. I knocked on the open door and entered the first of two antechambers. Two people I didn't recognise were sitting at a desk, next to a whirring photocopier.

'They're waiting for you, please go in.'

I knocked peremptorily before pushing the door open, and closing it behind me. Inside were the three people who ran the court of Tony, if not the country. Alastair Campbell sat leaning against a desk to the left. Sally Morgan was sitting at a desk directly ahead. Anji Hunter leaned against a sideboard on the right. Next to Anji, the door to the main office was ajar, and Tony was sitting at his desk poring over papers in his red Prime Minister's folder, evidently preparing for PMQs which would start in twenty minutes. He looked up and nodded in my direction before returning to work.

'Ah, Oona, thanks for coming,' said Alastair jovially.

'No problem, what can I do?'

'We need your help with something,' continued Alastair.

'Always willing to help,' I said, with a bright smile and sinking heart.

'We need you to pen an article.' I breathed a sigh of relief. Maybe it wouldn't be so bad.

'About?'

'Ken Livingstone.'

'Ken?'

'Yeah, Ken.'

'Why?'

'Well, as you know, he's trying to undermine the Labour Party, and we have to ensure he doesn't succeed.'

It was worse than I thought.

'What sort of article?'

'An article saying he can't be trusted.'

I repeated the words to give myself a few seconds to think. 'An article saying he can't be trusted . . .'

I was entirely opposed to the way the Labour Party and specifically the Prime Minister had tried to prevent Ken becoming the
Labour candidate for Mayor of London. It wasn't that I was a
cheerleader for Ken. I simply believed he had the right, like any other
member of the Labour Party, to put himself forward. It was a
democratic process and we shouldn't undermine it. If he won the
vote and got selected – well, tough, that was democracy. Pathetically,
the first words to come out of my mouth were, 'Why me?'

'Well,' said Anji playing her good cop role without irony, 'You're
considered independent minded.'

'And you're an ethnic minority MP,' said Alastair, 'you're held in
high regard by the black community, and this election has a London
electorate that's 40 per cent ethnic minority. We need you to get the
message across.'

'Thing is,' I said, trying to force a smile, 'I don't go in for personal
attacks. It's not my style. And the other thing is, I don't agree with
the strategy. We're alienating everyone, and Ken's going to win.
Surely that's not what you want.'

This irritated all of them, and they each proceeded to tell me just how
much Ken couldn't be trusted, and what a danger he was to the party.

'Look,' said Sally finally in exasperated tones, 'he's out to *destroy*
the Labour Party, and we have to respond.'

'But you see, Sally, I don't agree that he's out to destroy the
Labour Party. He just has a different point of view.'

'*Bollocks*!' Sally slammed the desk with her fist, and I jumped
involuntarily. She had a knack for the bad cop role. I was leaning
against a radiator and I realised my legs were shaking slightly. How
embarrassing. A booming voice in my head was saying, '*Backbencher under attack. Mortal danger. Must retreat. Must exit Prime
Minister's office immediately. Repeat: must retreat.*'

'Listen, I'll have to think about it. When do you need to know by?'

'Now,' said Alastair.

I was silent for a moment, while three sets of eyes drilled into me.

'Hey . . .' I tried a half-hearted attempt at humour, 'so now I know
how Robin Cook felt in that airport lounge.' Alastair famously gave
the Foreign Secretary an ultimatum in an airport lounge: choose
your wife or your mistress, but decide now before you board the
plane. Poor Robin. But at least he was a Cabinet Minister.

Given that I was a backbencher in peril, I thought it was quite a funny line. Not necessarily the right line . . . but still, I'd met Alistair a few times socially, and I knew he had a dry, caustic sense of humour. In different circumstances he would have appreciated it. We had a smidgen of social history gleaned from his ties to Neil (Kinnock) while I was working with Glenys. But from the look in his eyes I could see all that was erased, our social interaction had never happened. Other than the predictably loud ticking clock there was silence. A television monitor in the corner said 'International Development Questions'. Prime Minister's Questions would start any minute. I knew they had to wrap this up.

'I tell you what I could do,' I said, hoping to come up with a compromise, 'I could write out for you in the next hour or so, what I'm prepared to say. But it won't include a personal attack.'

'Write it out and bring it back after PMQs,' said Sally, 'but I doubt it's going to help.'

'Look,' said Alastair, in a final, take-it-or-leave-it voice, 'this is a direct request from the Prime Minister. Is your answer yes or no?'

I instinctively looked towards Tony to see whether he was listening. Not that it mattered, he'd know everything. Alastair's question might as well have been phrased, 'Would you like a political career? Yes or no?' I was disconcerted that I had to answer immediately.

'If you need an answer right this second . . .'

'Yes we do.'

'Well then . . . I know it's the end of my political career, but the answer is no.'

Alastair fired back without a moment's hesitation. 'It's not the end of your political career, Oona. Just the next five years. You can go now.'

Just the next five years. It reminded me of the David Bowie song. And with those words I was ejected from the inner sanctum. Alastair was sort of joking, and sort of not. Their demeanour was deadly serious. That's why they're good at their jobs. They have to be nasty so Tony can be nice. I wasn't surprised – every Prime Minister needs hired guns, and as it happened, they were some of the nicest around. But still, I felt like I'd been kidnapped off the benches during a particularly bad day that had now got irretrievably worse.

A few minutes later I returned to the Chamber and sat behind the Prime Minister, writing out some bullet points to give his office after PMQs. I know they'll never be used, because I couldn't bring myself to write anything they'd want. Every now and then I looked up from my writing to boo the Tories and cheer Labour. Punch & Judy. Politics is mainly reductive and rarely redemptive. But in some respects I feel great relief. Since becoming an MP I'd known there would be a moment like this, a *'direct request from the Prime Minister'* moment. The time and place and subject were unexpected, but not the event itself. And although my career seems damaged, maybe for good, I'm relieved by the outcome.

28 November 1998

Finally, after a lot of hard work, got the SoS for International Development (Clare Short) and the President of Rwanda (Paul Kagame) to come to the Jubilee Room in the House of Commons for the launch of my All Party Group. The full title is 'The All Party Parliamentary Group on Rwanda, the Great Lakes Region, and the Prevention of Genocide'. Not exactly a snappy title, but I haven't yet thought of anything better. Thrilled that so many MPs and Lords have accepted my invitation to become members – over 100. It's our first day of existence, and we're already one of the bigger groups in Parliament. The NGOs have been fantastic – Oxfam, Christian Aid, WarChild, UNICEF, and ActionAid in particular. Now all we have to do is change the way the United Nations responds to cases of genocide.

11 December 1998

I'm Vice-Chair of the London Group of Labour MPs. You'd think our offices were based in Mogadishu or Islamabad, given the amount of time we spend on asylum and immigration policy. I try to escape it but my path is blocked at every turn. On the one hand I'm constantly berated by people who think immigrants get an easy ride and take all the housing; on the other, I deal with the immigrants who have survived war and are now destitute and live in the worst housing imaginable.

As an executive member of the London Group I meet with pan-London bodies, the Local Government Association and the Association of London Government. They tell us how everything's falling apart on the ground, and then it's our job to go and lobby the Government, from the Minister for Immigration up to the Prime Minister. For instance, despite a new dispersal policy (designed to move more refugees and asylum seekers away from the capital) London boroughs have more refugees presenting themselves as homeless. The Home Office is supposed to issue guidance to local authorities, but the only thing it's issued so far is deafening silence. It's hard to have much faith in the Home Office, because they simply don't have the staff to deal with the job at hand. And although the Tories talk tough on immigration, they left a backlog of 70,000 cases. So they can shut up.

I spoke to a civil servant who told me they were working flat out to clear the backlog. But with the best will in the world they haven't got a prayer. And quite often they haven't got the best will. This civil servant also told me that they write letters to people saying the Home Secretary has 'seen the correspondence'. Apparently, they wheel thousands of letters past his desk on a trolley. They trudge about with wheelbarrows full of letters, like bureaucratic gardeners. When the Home Secretary gives the wheelbarrow a once over, they can truthfully state that he has seen the correspondence. Or was that a joke? The apocryphal and the mundane blend together at the Home Office like absinthe. It blows your mind.

When I visited the headquarters of the Immigration and Nationality Directorate in Croydon, they took us into rooms the size of football pitches and showed us acres of correspondence. Somewhere among those dusty files lie old dreams of new lives. If we looked hard enough through the subterranean filing cabinets we'd probably find the bones of Franz Kafka. But in the meantime Karen Buck and I, as London Group executives (she's Chair, I'm Vice-Chair), arranged a meeting with the PM. Two days beforehand I got a message from Sally Morgan at No. 10 telling me not to come. I rang her to find out why the meeting had been cancelled.

'Oh, hi Oona. Thanks for calling. Listen, the meeting with Tony hasn't been cancelled. It's just that on reflection we decided it was better if you didn't come.'

'But Sally, I'm Vice-chair of the London Group. I asked for this meeting and you agreed to it.'

'Yes, and the meeting will go ahead with Tony and the others, but I'm afraid he can't meet with you. I'm sure you understand our position. Immigration is a highly sensitive issue. We can only have people we trust.'

Out there in media-land I'm described as a 'Blairista', but in the real world No. 10 don't trust me as far as they can throw me. There is no love lost.

1999

The Grim Reaper and the Gold Wand

8 January 1999

MPs return to the Commons on Monday, itching to get back to the hotbed of Westminster politics. Well, sort of, but don't believe the hype. The day before Christmas Eve I was working with my assistants in our Westminster office. The building was almost deserted. We turned on the TV and heard the breaking news of Peter Mandelson's resignation.

'Westminster is being rocked by shockwaves today,' said the reporter with an excited look on his face. We walked out into the corridor to see what was going on. No sign of shockwaves anywhere, just the hum of the vending machine. The building was almost deserted. Why is it so much more exciting to hear about a place on TV, than to be at the scene itself?

26 February 1999

Visit of the House of Commons International Development Select Committee to India and Bangladesh.

We're here to do a report on the situation for women, and to check whether British taxpayers get value for money from the British aid programme. We end up in a brothel in Calcutta. We're on business, but of a legitimate sort. We speak to the sex workers to hear about their lives. Most of them are born into it, they inherit prostitution from their mothers and grandmothers who did it before them. As for their fathers, they're just like anyone else's father who visited a brothel. The link between men's economic and social control of women and women's sexuality is made plain. Seeing it in such stark relief in the developing South of India helps us recognise the same themes more delicately woven in the fabric of the developed North.

Violence against women remains universal. In Britain, one in four of all murders are due to domestic violence – a woman murdered by her male partner or former partner. In India and Bangladesh an old saying goes, 'It is a lucky man whose wife dies; it is an unlucky man whose ox dies.' The ox has great value and means economic sustainability for the family. The wife – and the woman – has no value, no status and is easily replaced.

We met the Chief Minister of the eastern Indian state of Orissa, who mumbled under his breath and hardly looked up to acknowledge us. He was far worse than mediocre. In Bogra, Bangladesh, we met women who were astonishingly engaging and articulate, yet confined to serving men's sexual needs. It's funny how stupid it is and terrifying how savage it is.

Bangladesh seems more hopeful than India. The scale – 125 million people – is easier to comprehend than India's one billion. The thing I loved most about Bangladesh is its diversity. All the people, all the colours, all the heat, all the dust, all the art. Art is everywhere, particularly on the lorries. They are lovingly painted. The rickshaws and bicycle rickshaws criss-cross the streets of Dhaka in an anarchic whirl. They remind me of one of my favourite films, *The Wizard of Oz*. If the munchkins had transport, it'd be these motorised banana-yellow tricycles. Tens of thousands of them engage in fierce jousting battles, their brightly coloured plastic tassles flowing in the wind, a real-life bumper car bonanza with a dash of 'whacky races' and the Grand Prix thrown in. The bicycle rickshaw peddlers, with their carriages decked out in an improbably bright mosaic of art and Bollywood pin-ups, are the human equivalent of the peacock. The physical demands of their job, combined with Dhaka's lethal pollution levels, ensure life expectancy is minimal. Their art, perhaps in compensation, is maximal.

2 March 1999

Spoke in the debate on the Stephen Lawrence Inquiry last week. Doreen and Neville Lawrence were watching in the public gallery.

Waited three hours to be called, and just when I was, they popped out to get something to eat. The speech went quite well. The only aggravating thing, more aggravating than the Tories, was the bloody Deputy Speaker. OK, he was doing his job, but his job is stupid. His job is to stop me saying 'you' when I speak.

For example, I was talking about institutional racism, which the Lawrence Inquiry clearly illustrates exists. One of the Tories said my charge was outrageous, and that I shouldn't blame an institution as a whole. 'Well,' I said, 'let's see whether the point you make is correct or not –'

Obviously I didn't get any further because the Deputy Speaker popped up, like the Grim Reaper clad in black.

'Order. The Hon. Lady must use the correct parliamentary language.'

There are two rules relating to Speakers: they only get their name in Hansard when they interrupt you, so they do it all the time, and when they interrupt you the usual response is to grovel for Britain.

'You are absolutely right, Mr Deputy Speaker,' I grovelled. 'I suffer from an inability to get that into my mind – not to say *you* – even after two years in the House.' And then I tried to carry on with the speech. 'Let's take another example of institutional discrimination. Let's take a look at sexism and Parliament. When the Home Secretary rose to speak, there was one woman on the opposition benches – and twenty-six men. Surely that shows that Parliament is biased against women? Would the Hon. Gentleman deny that? I presume that he would not.'

'I *would*,' came the predictable reply from the Tory benches.

'Oh, you *would*' – would you, I was about to say. It was like setting off the buzzer in one of those game shows. *Drrrring*. Wrong answer. 'You would say – I am sorry,' let's try that again. 'The *Honourable Gentleman* would say–'

The Grim Speaker was already on his feet.

'Order. The Hon. Lady must think carefully before she chooses her words.'

No shit. I smiled bleakly.

'You are absolutely right, Mr Deputy Speaker.' I tried to make progress. 'The Hon. Gentlemen on the opposition benches deny that there is discrimination against women, yet there are now just two women Members sitting on those benches. I believe that there is institutional sexism. However, I also believe that Members on both sides of the House are not individually guilty of being sexist. I do not believe that Conservative Members, for example, get up each morning and say, "Today we are going to deny women the right to be represented in Parliament." Of course they do not. That would be an absurd proposition. What the Hon. Member is saying is that we cannot apportion the guilt where it lies – in the institution, rather than in the individual.'

I kept going, and went through all the things we're campaigning on: full implementation of the recommendations of the Lawrence Report, a new Race Relations Act, recognition of the fact that 50 per cent of those arrested for racist crime last year were under sixteen, and the need for more effective youth services to deal with them. Finally I highlighted the astonishing and dignified contribution made by Doreen and Neville Lawrence.

As I finished speaking and sat down, Doreen and Neville Lawrence walked back into the public gallery. Although I'd been interrupted by the Grim Speaker, it wasn't a bad speech. I thought, 'I've got the hang of this MP lark. I can do this. I can battle with the opposition, I can even take them apart.' And that's when it went pear-shaped. I was trying to intervene on a Tory MP who wasn't 'giving way'. In the end I thought, 'OK, move on to the next point, get him on something else.' But for the first time ever the Grim Speaker butted in on my behalf.

'Will the Honourable Member give way to the Member for Bethnal Green and Bow?'

The MP assented, and the Grim Speaker called out my name. I stood up, too surprised by the Grim Speaker's benevolent intervention to remember what I wanted to say. All I could think was that Doreen and Neville Lawrence would expect Britain's second black woman MP to say something relevant to this debate. Nothing came to mind. Not even a parliamentary parachute (any load of old cobblers) to avert abject humiliation. All I could think of was the truth.

'Um . . . I have entirely forgotten the point that I wished to make . . .'

Diane Abbott started laughing (I couldn't blame her). So did a couple of other MPs. It was purgatory. It taught me a great lesson though. Never think you've got it sussed in the Chamber – at least not when you've been an MP for less than two years. And never get up without a parachute – anything to say when your mind goes blank. Have something jotted down so you can find the pile of old cobblers deep within you, and keep the vultures off your back.

That night I woke up at two a.m. with a tingling sensation on my face. The embarrassment was still burning me up. The other thing I learned is that purgatory isn't necessarily reported as such. The next day the *Guardian* carried an article on my speech, with my photo next to it. They didn't mention the Grim Reaper. They didn't mention my lapse. They just said I gave a great speech. Result.*

8 March 1999

Last week met the Bangladeshi Prime Minister, Sheikh Hasina, of the ruling Awami League, and today met opposition leader Begum Khaleda Zia of the Bangladeshi National Party. The two women are locked in a bizarre Shakespearean tragedy that is being played out occasionally in their Parliament, more often in the streets, and sometimes back home in Brick Lane.

On my return home, had to deal with the first big protest against me. Over a hundred angry people marched on my office carrying a six-foot black coffin and said they were going to put me in it. Unfortunately for them, I was around the corner in Bethnal Green Road, so they couldn't nab me. My assistant Marc rang me to tell me not to come to the office. He made the mistake of trying to reason with them, and when he opened the door they pelted him with eggs. What that boy puts up with for me is unbelievable. Even more unbelievable is what they're demonstrating about: parking regulations. I know parking in London can drive you mental, and I know MPs are good to have a pop at; but for God's sake, I don't have any jurisdiction over parking. None at all. They might as well put me in a coffin because the sky is grey.

---

* Bizarrely this speech is still used today as part of the secondary school curriculum for students studying Parliament and politics.

MPs have recently voted me the new backbencher 'to make the biggest impact on Britain's public life' – though obviously not in relation to parking regulations in Tower Hamlets. This was the Channel 4 Political Awards. Gave a very short acceptance speech, saying I knew for a fact that in politics, the best candidate doesn't always win.

(Of the four nominees for this Channel 4 Political Award of 'Rising Star' – me, Stephen Twigg, Lembit Öpik, and Theresa May – I was predictably the only one never to make it to the frontbench.)

Thursday 18 March 1999

Appeared on *Question Time* tonight. Very relaxed this morning, rigid with fear by lunchtime. I remembered the first time I went on in September 1997, making this only the second most frightening hour of my life. Spent four hours today mugging up on the budget, petrol tax, rural poverty, joining the Euro, asylum and immigration, welfare reform, the Working Families Tax Credit, Overseas British Territories, the Lawrence Report, Northern Ireland, Child Poverty, Lone Parent Benefit, Kosovo, Housing Benefit, Manchester United, the United Nations, etc, etc. Party HQ gave me a briefing and then I went to see Ed Miliband in Gordon's office.

The point to remember,' he said, 'is that under Labour, Britain's poorest families will receive a 40 per cent income boost.'

'I don't believe that for a second,' I said. Part of me was doubtful that New Labour would significantly redistribute wealth. But it was true: an extra £6 billion to be spent on lifting children out of poverty, a clear plan for redistribution. No getting away from it. Wow. New Labour would anoint New Gordon. New redistributive Gordon. Old Labour might even concede that the New Labour Government had delivered more to the working classes than Tony Benn or Dennis Skinner could hope to. Tony and Dennis sounded better. They made you proud to be Labour. But they couldn't deliver Labour's most cherished prize: a real reduction in poverty.

24 March 1999

Ha! My revenge, finally, on Eric Forth and the other Tory reaction-
aries who tried to kill my Bill. Today it was incorporated into
Government legislation and became law. *My Bill became law*. I keep
repeating the words to myself like an incantation. I should be more
dignified in victory, but those Tories messed me about so much, it's a
tall order. I can't help thinking about my former trade union members
who got so unfairly hurt by Compulsory Competitive Tendering. It's
too late to help them, but at least others will be protected.

16 April 1999

My constituency surgery this afternoon started at 2.30 p.m. and
lasted six hours. As usual, I saw loads of desperate people suffering
the utmost misery. But, for the first time since I started doing these
surgeries filled with desperate miserable people two years ago, I felt I
couldn't face writing all those letters which might have no effect at
all. I looked at the woman across the desk, alone, petrified, disabled
with lupus, clutching her crutches, tears smeared across her cheeks.
Drowning but not crushed. No family, no friends, no money.
Anthea's only inheritance was a National Insurance number. Unlike
Anthea, the socially included will never know their National Insurance number by heart. She was only twenty-one. Where were her
parents? Who was looking after her? She'd been taken into care at
six, and then shuffled between local authority children's homes and
her dysfunctional family until she was fifteen. Abandoned by the
adult world, disabled shortly afterwards, every step a painful effort.
How did she get here?

'A friend put me in a taxi.'

'Oh, so you have a friend. Are they outside?'

'No, he left.'

'How will you get back?'

'He gave me five quid for a taxi.' She looked at me intently. 'Who
are you exactly?' Immediately her hand shot to her mouth. She
giggled.

'That's a very good question,' I replied. 'I often ask the same thing.'

Another giggle.

'I'm your MP. Do you know what an MP is?'

'Yes, a Member of Parliament.'

'That's right.'

'But what do you do?'

I searched for the answer. 'Well, my job is to help people in this area who have a problem, and try and think of a solution.'

My job was most often to sit and listen to problems that I didn't have the remotest chance of solving. 'Let's start with benefits. You get income support. What about Disability Living Allowance?'

'No. I don't get any of that, just £20 income support.'

'Do you know if you're entitled to DLA?'

'No. The forms are really complicated. I can't understand them.'

A blank social security form could be as daunting as a tax return in a language you didn't understand.

'I've rung them to get help,' she said, her voice cracking, 'but nothing ever happens. Now I've got bills coming in and I can't pay them. The telephone bill, for instance. Eighty pounds because I've been on the phone to the DSS over and over. I can't pay the bills so I just leave them. I have to use the telephone because I can't get on the bus.'

'Well, we're going to have to look at the telephone bills, because otherwise you'll get cut off.'

'And the flat's terrible,' she continues, tears welling up in her eyes. 'I've let it get terrible, it's disgusting.'

'Don't you have a home help?'

'They don't come. That's why I ring the DSS, to ask if they'll come. But nobody ever comes. Oh, I'm going to cry.' Again her hand went to her face.

'Don't cry. Hey! You know what?' She looked up at me with a tenuous composure and brushed the tears away. 'You did a very good thing today, because you came to see me. It makes me very happy to meet someone as courageous as you. Do you understand how brave you are?'

Anthea nodded her head slightly.

'Yes, you're very brave, darling.' Her luminescent brown complexion reminded me of baby's skin. She was so young to be sitting across the table from me, alone.

'So look, I'm going to write to the DSS and we're going to sort this out.' I wasn't sure how to phrase the next bit.

'Have you got any money apart from the £5?'

'No.'

'Can you get any more?'

'No.'

'Well that's not fair,' I said. 'So you won't mind if I give you £20, because I can go to the bank and get another £20, but you can't.'

'What do you mean?' she asked, perplexed. 'You don't mean you're going to give me £20?'

'Well, that makes sense, right?' In fact, I always felt uneasy when MPs gave people money, no matter what the circumstances. In these circumstances £20 was paltry. But a) I only had £25 in my wallet, b) £20 represented her total disposable weekly income, and c) I had never done this before and was hesitant at plunging beyond the edge of an MP's prescribed role. I couldn't give money to all the people who needed it, so what was the logic? The logic was the damaged child in front of me. Like a photographer in a war zone who puts down her camera to pick up an injured child, I ignored professionalism.

'Oh my God,' Anthea gasped, 'I can't believe you'd put your hand in your own pocket for me.' She burst into tears.

'Now listen darling,' I said, hugging her, 'you mustn't cry because then you'll make me cry and I can't see all those people out there if I'm crying.'

She fell silent, amazed at the sight of my tears. Her eyes fell on the £20 note. 'I can't take it though, because I can't spend it.'

'Yes you can,' I said, hoping I wasn't ignoring her disability. Watching how she had to drag her legs in painful jerking movements on two crutches, it wasn't clear whether she'd reach the door, let alone a shop. I gave her my private mobile number, squeezed her hand and kissed her goodbye.*

---

* During eight years as an MP I only gave one other constituent cash. He was an eighty-year-old war veteran whose daughter's car had been clamped when she ran upstairs to help him while he was having a heart attack. Despite a letter from the hospital backing up his story, he was forced to pay £125. I gave him £25 towards his ticket because it seemed so unfair (his weekly disposable income was £50), although it was mainly because he'd sat patiently waiting to see me for seven hours.

After another three hours packed with stories of human desperation, it was time for a drink. Neither Marc nor I had any money. I stopped at the bank to refill my wallet. 'Available balance £6.10. Choose amount in multiples of £10,' said the cash machine. Just £6.10, to last until pay day in two weeks' time. Almost 50p per day. This was exactly why I should never have cut up my credit cards.

27 April 1999

I was meant to be travelling with the International Development Select Committee to Kosovo on the weekend, but I got a phone call from Tiberio saying a bomb had gone off in the constituency. No one was dead, but six people were injured (and thirty-nine people had been injured in a similar racist attack in Brixton the week before). For some reason I actually considered continuing with the other MPs to Kosovo, which would have been political suicide. Thank God Tiberio soon dissuaded me.

MPs don't have a job description, but one of our really important functions is to be there when something bad happens. Part of our job is simply to be visible in times of crisis. This only dawned on me when I was heaped with plaudits just for standing at the site of the bomb blast for nearly seventy-two hours without moving. Loads of constituents seem to love me for it. Not because I'm clever, or inspiring or heroic, simply because I stand there and say what everyone else thinks: 'We cannot accept this.'

I spoke to Jack Straw (then Home Secretary) yesterday before his statement in Parliament, and got him to agree that he would come and visit my constituency within twenty-four hours. I must have had Kosovo on the brain, because there was no excuse for the tenuous link I made in the debate, between ethnic cleansing in the Balkans and in Brick Lane . . . the problem is that when extremists are on the rampage, you get sucked into responding with extreme propositions yourself. Must resist.

4 September 1999

Samos. Four hours left of a four week holiday. Twenty-eight days, a month of Sundays, a fear of Mondays. We wait the entire year for Greece, and the joy of being here is only equalled by the fear of leaving. When we left the island this time last year after a two-week break, I felt panicked, actually terrified, like a deep sea diver who's out of oxygen. The thought of going back to fifteen hour days, no evenings, running on empty, the constant clamour and sleeve tugging, the 'I only need five minutes of your time' sixty times a day, the end of any sort of peace . . . it was a dread and foreboding that swallowed me whole.

A small part of me even doubted my physical prospects of survival. How much stress does it take to kill you? Other people might be surprised when I died of a heart attack aged thirty, but to me it seemed quite possible. So stop fretting and resign, I told myself. No one made you do it. You asked for public life, in fact you beseeched people until they gave it to you. And now you say it's a curse, it makes you deeply unhappy, you don't want it. But the only thing that would traumatise you more than being an MP would be *not* being an MP. There's no getting away from it, you're trapped. And have the decency to admit that you built the trap yourself, with infinite care and attention, over a lifetime.

When I came up from the bottom of the sea last year, from Samos to Athens to Gatwick to Victoria to Mile End to Westminster, I decided to dive in again at the deep end on one condition. Next year we'd have a four-week holiday, not two weeks. That single thought kept me going the entire winter, and winter lasted almost the whole year.

There was crisis in May when Tiberio sort of asked for a divorce ('You're married to the constituency, not to me'); and the constituency got bombed; and I started getting death threats with the frequency that I usually receive thank you cards. I was terrorised, not so much by the fear of being killed, but the fear of being killed before my holiday.

Now I'm just about to leave Greek airspace. It's been a beautiful month, twenty-eight days of living and breathing and seeing and laughing and sleeping and swimming. My ambitions have changed so much. I used to want to be Prime Minister, and now I just want to live without an alarm clock or umbrella. Later.

Although twenty-eight days felt like a long weekend, it's definitely done the trick. I don't have the feeling of foreboding that hung over the last trip from Athens to Westminster. I can't wait to get back to the constituency and I'm not even that perturbed about Westminster and the old codgers. I'm looking forward to working twelve hours a day (perhaps that's a bit strong – I'm 'happy' to work twelve hours a day) and prepared to tell anyone who wants me to work more than that to sod off, including myself. I'm thinking of a Private Member's Bill banning breakfast meetings. I feel stronger than I have done since the general election, though unfortunately not fit, because I haven't lifted a finger for a month.

Tiberio on the other hand is a vision of taut rippling muscles under dusky brown satin skin. He's gorgeous. He does abdominals every morning, swims for at least forty minutes a day, never eats chips or sweets and is effortlessly divine. It's like being married to Kate Moss, except he is Italian (better accent) and looks like an Indian prince. Despite his loveliness, I haven't had much time to ravish him alone, because we're social animals, love our friends, and invited practically all of them out to visit. The dazzling colours, deep blue, bright white, are still in my head. Nothing could dislodge them – other than a month of Mondays.

27 October 1999

Got into the Chamber in time for Prayers at 9.25 a.m. Betty (Boothroyd), the Speaker of the House, arrived with the Mace. The House of Commons isn't allowed to meet without the Mace. It's basically a big, heavy, gold wand, and it represents the monarch. It represents sovereign power, which is why Oliver Cromwell called it a 'fool's bauble'. Maces are used the world over to signify authority. They're a slight improvement on the club, and humans parade them about – especially in the House of Commons – to prove we're no longer cavemen. Michael Heseltine dented this theory slightly after losing a vote in the 1970s when he pounced on the Mace, and swung it about like Tarzan, which is why he's had that nickname ever since.

So this morning I was contemplating sovereign power, and the need to override it when sovereign states murder their people. Crimes against humanity. That was the subject of my adjournment debate on the International Criminal Court (ICC). (An adjournment debate is a short, half-hour debate introduced by a backbencher at the end of each day's business in the House of Commons.) I began my speech by summarising the importance of the ICC as '. . . nothing less than humankind's efforts to outlaw gross atrocities: crimes against humanity. It represents 150 years of evolution in international humanitarian law. Above all, it represents the recognition that having laws alone is just not good enough: we must have the means to enforce those laws.'

That's the problem. We've got laws coming out of our ears, but we never enforce them. We started off with the Geneva Conventions in 1864, and we've been ignoring them ever since. Robin Cook summed it up when he said that a man who murders one person is likely to go to court, but a man who murders 10,000 people is likely to get away with murder. For instance, we've got the United Nations Convention on Genocide, signed in 1948. It recognised what Churchill described as a 'crime with no name'. More like a crime with no punishment. It took half a century to get the first prosecution.

So the ICC is another attempt to bring war criminals to justice. It took years to negotiate but finally in July last year the Rome Statute – creating the ICC – was agreed. One hundred and twenty countries voted in favour of it, and seven voted against. Who were the seven villains? The usual suspects: Iraq, the USA, Libya, China, Israel, Yemen, and Qatar. The next step is ratification – the ICC will come into being when sixty states have ratified the Rome Statute.

One of the problems is that we say 'crimes against humanity' without properly digesting what those three words mean. I gave an example of one of the crimes used by the junta in El Salvador. A rat was placed on a pregnant woman's stomach, and surrounded by a metal box, which was heated from above. When the heat became too intense, the rat burrowed out of the box by eating its way through the pregnant woman's stomach.

But the ICC still doesn't exist, because it is yet to be ratified by sixty states. Although Britain voted for it, we haven't ratified it. We keep saying we 'hope to be one of the first sixty countries'. I called this debate in Parliament today because Britain should be leading from the front, which is what we did during the negotiations. The British Government ensured that crimes against women and sexual violence were included in the Statute, which is extremely important. You can't have men using rape as a tool of war (as they did in Bosnia and Rwanda) without providing for it to be a war crime, so that there will be an international response to track down – hunt down – those who do it in future. Britain scores high for our involvement to date, and low for not having signed on the dotted line. Apparently this is for 'legal reasons' that are being ironed out. Let's hope we do it sooner rather than later.

The United Kingdom Government was one of the first sixty states to ratify the Rome Statute of the International Criminal Court, on 4 October 2001. The ICC came into being on 1 July 2002. The first war crimes to come before the court took place in the Great Lakes Region of Africa.

29 December 1999

I'm charmed by the millennium. Putting aside the fact that it's a random, meaningless date, I love it. Got a note from the White Wolves, an amateurish group of British white supremacists. They're a neo-Nazi organisation that nicked their name from a Serbian paramilitary death squad. They say that Jews and non-whites who haven't left the UK by midnight on 31 December 1999 will be exterminated. Two days left, and I'm worth double points. The letter they sent me said, 'When the clocks strike midnight on 31 December 1999 the White Wolves will begin to howl, and when the Wolves begin to howl the Wolves begin to hunt. You have been warned. Hail Britannia.' The silly sods were also linked to the nail bomb in my constituency, after which, because I appeared on TV to say unremarkable things like, 'We don't want nail bombs,' I received another thirty death threats. I only read a few of them, and handed the rest to a Scotland Yard forensic officer. He told me they can do amazing things with forensics these days, and I shouldn't worry. Two weeks later he came back, and said they'd identified one of the suspects.

'How did you do that?'

'Er – he wrote his name and address on the envelope.'

'Wow, good work. So have you arrested him?'

'Well we did, but there's a question as to the state of his mental health, so he's been released.'

'That means he's not a threat, right?'

The officer examined his fingernails. 'Put it this way, he's sixty years old, and he's spent forty of those years in jail for violent offences – rape, robbery, GBH. He says he's going to torture you and burn you alive, but on the whole, these sorts of threats don't get carried out.'

'Well thanks for putting my mind at rest officer.'

This year I stopped doing most of the TV I used to do. I've decided it's a complete waste of time, and just means more people come up to you in the supermarket, so it takes three hours to do the shopping. What else has happened? Tease (Tiberio) produced his first short film, *The Fiancée*, with original music composed by Nitin Sawhney, and it was chosen for ten film festivals; Dad's campaign for a presidential pardon got huge media coverage; I met Yasser Arafat in the Gaza Strip; had my office Christmas party in Paris (Eurostar clubber's ticket, £29 return!); was ninety minutes late for lunch with Prince Charles at Highgrove (*bad* – told him I'd like to *vote* for him – get it?), met the director of the WTO, Mike Moore, the day after the Battle for Seattle ('I haven't even had time to unpack the bags under my eyes'); funny and perceptive.

Millennium Eve – what a way to end 1,000 years

My whole life, I thought I'd be at a wild party at the end of the millennium. Instead, I was queueing outside Stratford tube station. It was the only way to get to the Dome. Our friends Keith Khan and Catherine Ugwu were staging the New Year's Eve show, and they'd worked on it for years. We queued for hours. The police and London

Underground apologised for any inconvenience caused by the un-expectedly large crowds. How could the crowds be unexpected? It was the millennium. Although the police knew 10,000 people would be travelling to the Dome via Stratford station, they only brought *one* X-ray machine. London Underground weren't blameless either. There was a forty minute wait for the first train – even though they'd had a thousand years to get it on the platform.

Saw a couple of other MPs waiting in the line. One of them was Chris Leslie. His claim to fame is that he was the youngest MP at the 1997 election. I think he pipped Claire Ward by three weeks. They were both twenty-four. I heard him make a fantastic intervention in one of the most eloquent speeches I've heard Tony Benn make against bombing Iraq. Tony Benn was saying, quite rightly, 'This is disgraceful. Thousands of people are going to die. It's a nightmare. We're colonialists, imperialists.' Chris got up and said something like, 'Well, the Honourable Gentleman has told us why the military strikes against Iraq are a very poor means of stopping Saddam Hussein. But what would he do to stop Saddam Hussein instead?'

I couldn't believe that Tony Benn was really thrown. He stuttered for a second, and hesitated. Hesitation is death, which accounts for the amount of rubbish politicians come out with, because we'll say anything rather than hesitate. Your enemies go for the kill if you hesitate. Tony Benn hesitated, and everyone started saying, 'Yeah, what would you do? What would you do? Give us your answer. Answer! Answer!' But he didn't have an answer. Nothing.

That's when I realised two things: I love Tony Benn, no matter what; but you've got to come up with an answer. You can't just drum your fingers on the table and say, 'Oh isn't it a shame he's gassing 14,000 Kurds. Those poor Marsh Arabs are for the chop.' So that was a notable intervention by Chris. I stood in that queue at Stratford for three hours. Had a chat with Trevor Phillips and Jon Snow. Played games with a five-year-old girl queueing next to me.

Finally, after what seemed like centuries, we arrived at the Dome. It looked spectacular. My heart leaped, and I thought, 'OK, let's just forget the wait. Celebrate. It's the new millennium. Have a drink.' There was nothing to drink. Tiberio and I were getting really irritated because New Year's Eve is also our anniversary. Not our wedding anniversary, but the anniversary of when we started going out together. We decided to be cheerful and go on one of the Dome's rides that we'd heard so much about. We walked up the gangway to the Body Zone.

'Sorry,' said the woman at the top, 'we've just closed it.'

'What do you mean you've just closed it?' I was indignant. 'You let someone in a minute ago. And anyway, have a heart, it's New Year's Eve. This is meant to be a party, not a funeral.'

'That was the Prime Minister,' said the woman with her nose in the air, 'no one else is coming in. It's closed.'

At this point I was thinking, 'Well *fuck* the Prime Minister.' We decided we really needed a drink. It's sad and bad to associate celebration with alcohol, but once every thousand years . . . Then we rejoiced because we saw a long bar with hundreds of glasses of champagne. It was eleven p.m., and we were about to get our first drop to drink. We went running up and tried to mask overt desperation as we stood behind a row four-deep of people trying to grab champagne. About half of them got a glass, and then suddenly the bartenders said 'Sorry, that's it.' There were hundreds of glasses full of bubbly behind them, and at least 200 bottles of champagne on display. People started to shout.

'Sorry,' said the bartenders, who were wearing headsets and earpieces, 'we've just received instructions. No more champagne is to be handed out.'

A woman about ten yards away started screaming. 'What do you mean? We've been waiting three fucking hours in a fucking train station for the fucking millennium and you're telling us you won't give us one of those fucking glasses of fucking champagne behind you? What do you fucking mean?!'

I couldn't have phrased a parliamentary question better myself. But they wouldn't give us any. Instead they gave us a little ticket, and told us to go into the main hall, where we could exchange it for a silver bag. In that silver bag, lo and behold, would be a glass of champagne. It turned out they were talking about those titchy champagne bottles you get on a plane, that are the size of a thimble.

We tried to stop obsessing about alcohol and went inside to our seats. Admittedly the Dome looked great. We sat down, cracked open the titchy thimble and had a mouthful each. We saved the other midget bottle for midnight. The show started. The first hour was a bit like a TV variety show. At least if I'd been watching TV I could've skipped channels. Pretty soon I was thinking, 'Give me some beats. Give me a dance floor. And get me away from people like the Prime Minister and the Queen on New Year's Eve.' You think if you're with the most important people in Britain, you'll have a cracking good time. Now there's a mistake. Big, huge, *galactic* mistake.

Finally it was midnight. We reached into our silver bag for the other titchy bottle of champagne. It had disappeared. There were thousands of suspects all around us, alcohol-deprived party goers as far as the eye could see. I wanted to throw each one against a wall and frisk them, but instead we did the traditional thing and all held hands. One hand crossed over the other, linked up in a big chain. The Queen had both her hands the wrong way round. Her advisers should look out for that sort of thing. But considering how old she is, she did pretty well. I keep forgetting how old the Queen is, because her photos are always thirty years out of date, a bit like politicians'.

The performance after midnight was spectacular. There were so many things going on, it was impossible to take it all in. I was mesmerised by an aerial ballet, one of the most beautiful things I've ever seen. Given I was stone cold sober it must have been good. But the problem was, I could hear the *real* London fireworks going off on the Embankment. I kept thinking, 'Why am I here with the great and the good, who are just so boring, when I could be having a laugh out on the street?' It's not a mistake I'll repeat, not least because I'll never live to see another Millennium Eve. Apparently the London fireworks were the best in the world. After the show I was really happy for Catherine and Keith. They had delivered an amazing event. They weren't responsible for the single X-ray machine at Stratford or the Saudi Arabian alcohol policy.

We got back on the tube, and then went to five parties in a row. They got progressively worse. Keith (Khan) and I decided it might be time to panic. There was no decent party. During this whole time we'd been in radio contact with Quin and Nora – my oldest friend – so we met up at Nora's. That was when the Keith Allen Show began. Keith had just been thrown off a TV show. I should begin by saying that Keith Allen is one of my favourite people. He's also a nutter. He's a comedian and an excellent actor, but his trademark is to take the piss. That's what he does. He can drive people insane.

So Keith A. starts telling Keith K. about his first show. His parents, aunt and uncle and other family members were there. For some reason Keith A took his clothes off. It was the first time his family had seen their son on stage. Big event, fantastic working-class family, appearances are important, none of this middle-class hippy shit. And without warning Keith's standing there, completely naked.

And then Keith picks up a bowl, pisses in it, and drinks it. There's hardcore and then there's *hardcore*. I don't know what you do with that. Where do you put it? Is he just a lunatic? It's not funny. That's the most irritating thing about Keith – he can be brilliantly funny, but also a nutter, often at the same time. But I love him dearly, and there you have the dichotomy of Keith A. Five hours later I wanted him dead.

So Keith's dad is sitting in the theatre with his head in his hands. His aunt is shaking her head. It almost looks as though she's crying and turning the other way. But his mum – well she's beaming, looking around the audience saying, *that's* my boy, *that's* my boy! That's probably Keith's take on it, not hers, but it's a good story.

By now it was midday on New Year's Day. The only people left were Keith A., his friend Steve, Keith K. and me. The four of us were desperate to find something to do. So Keith A. said, 'Why don't we go to Alex's?' Alex is the drummer in Blur, a bit of a celeb boy. He and Keith A. once recorded a single together. We arrived in Alex's kitchen, and one of his friends was laid out unconscious on the couch. It would have been better if we'd all been laid out unconscious, instead of beating New Year's Day to death.

I went upstairs to raid Alex's CD collection because by now I felt I would die without house music. But Alex's collection was a combination of loads of indie groups, and then people like Geri Halliwell, the Spice Girls, Barbra Streisand . . . Still, at least the boys played for us: Keith A. on the piano, Alex on double bass, and Steve on the bongos. These three mad boys made up in effort and energy what the Dome experience lacked. This is when Keith K. and I should have left, because everything then went *markedly* downhill. We ended up in a dodgy pub near Trafalgar Square. Keith A. carried on being mental.

I turned to Keith A. and said, 'Thank God you didn't marry us.'

Keith was meant to come to our London wedding reception to perform some sort of ceremony for us. Luckly he didn't, because he's too mad. So then Nira, my friend and his wife, rang him on the mobile while we were still in the pub. His kids Lily and Alfie were arriving at Nira's house, and she was saying, 'You've got to come home to see your children.'

'I'll be home in an hour,' said Keith, but while he was saying that to Nira, he was mouthing, *'No way'* to me and Keith K.

'How can you do that?' said Keith K. 'She's your wife, and those are your kids. You can't just not turn up.'

I explained that Nira doesn't believe what Keith says anyway. Finally at about three p.m. I said, 'Right, we're going.' Keith A. said he was coming. I said he wasn't.

When I tried to stop him ringing Quincy to get her address he held the phone out of my reach, so I grabbed his shirt around my fist, and I said, still laughing, 'I'll rip your shirt off your bloody back if I have to. Just get out of my life.' We carried on laughing, but then I'd had enough, so I ripped his shirt in two.

It was the dawn of a new millennium, and I had to switch off the Keith Allen Show. I wandered down to Trafalgar Square with Keith K. As you'd expect on New Year's Day we couldn't find a taxi. We got on the tube, but couldn't work out how to change trains. Eventually we got off at Liverpool Street and I could hardly walk because I was laughing so much. Can't think why. We walked along Bishopsgate and into Spitalfields market and I suddenly remembered. This was my constituency. I was the local MP. But I had silver platform shoes on, a mad outfit and silver ribbon in my hair. And I couldn't stop laughing. As you would expect, there were constituents everywhere. No lie, finding a taxi was the highlight of my Millennium Eve.

We arrived at Quin's and she was fantastic. She's *so* my best mate. Keith K. and I were grateful to arrive in a Keith Allen-free zone. Then the phone rang and it was Keith Allen. I begged him to go away. Always a mistake. If you start speaking to Keith he will reel you into a conversation. In the end I put the phone down. An hour later the phone rang again. He said he was coming round.

'You are *not* coming around *you stalker*.'

I slammed the phone down, and turned the TV on. Keith's face stared out from the screen. He was giving a masterful acting performance, and doing my head in completely. The phone rang again. It was ten p.m.

'Keith, I am begging you. I am on my knees. *Please* go away.'

'Oona,' he replied, 'you don't want it badly enough.'

'What do I not want badly enough?'

'To be Prime Minister. You don't want it badly enough.'

The thing about Keith is that he can be mad and spot on at the same time.

'I know,' I said, 'I told you that earlier, when everyone was saying "She's going to be the first black Prime Minister." I said "I'm *not* going to be the first bloody black Prime Minister, I would rather die."'

And now I know why. Because I would always be trapped in a place like the Dome on New Year's Eve. But it was good of Keith A. to remind me of my fatal political flaw on the dawn of a new millennium.

Finally got home in the small hours of 2 January. What a way to end a thousand years. Good news, though, no White Wolves. Not a paramilitary death squad in sight. Blacks and Jews of east London rejoice.

2000

The Dog's Breakfast and the Twelve Week Scan

27 January 2000

Spent an age in the International Development Select Committee on Tuesday amending and drafting our Sanctions Report on Iraq. My contribution was to get the Committee to express the sentiment that 'A sanctions regime which relies on the good faith of Saddam Hussein is fundamentally flawed.' Saddam manipulates the safeguards intended to protect the civilian population. The UN oil-for-food programme is a joke. People insist that sanctions work, but after spending almost a year preparing this report, it's quite clear they don't. Well, not unless you're willing to accept the deaths of *half a million Iraqi children*. That's how many children UNICEF say have died due to Saddam's insane mismanagement of his country's health service, coupled with Iraq's punishment for Saddam's invasion of Kuwait. Half a million dead children. In the short term we need 'smarter' sanctions, in the long term he should be indicted as a war criminal. That's never going to happen (although our Sanction Report calls for it). So depressing.

On a lighter note, in DTI (Department for Trade and Industry) questions the hot topic of the day is 'Ice cream (Impulse Buying)'. They are mad, but it does make me think I should go and buy some Häagen-Dazs Pralines & Cream right now.

20 February 2000

The selection process to choose Labour's mayoral candidate has ended in victory for Frank Dobson. But he hasn't got much to smile about. He polled 52 per cent compared to Ken Livingstone's 48 per cent. But he only won because the electoral college gives a few hundred Labour MPs more say than a few million Labour Party members and trade unionists. In the Party member's section of the electoral college, Ken got 60 per cent compared to Frank's 40 per cent. We can't even be sure Ken won't run as an independent. Or worse, Tory candidate Steve Norris might beat Frank and become London's first Mayor. What a dog's breakfast, all because the PM couldn't handle a bit of democracy.

4 May 2000

Inevitably, Ken has won the election to be London's Mayor. Hilarious. It's a great day for Ken, and a terrible day for Labour. We've only ourselves to blame. I'd almost go as far as to say I'm happy for Ken. I don't know who will be more pissed off – the current Labour Prime Minister, or the former Tory Prime Minister, who already abolished him once.

20 June 2000

Have been out campaigning with David Lammy a lot in the Tottenham by-election. David is replacing my beloved Bernie Grant, whose feet I washed with dedication. I've been designated David's political minder – that is, the MP who shows him the ropes and keeps him on the straight and narrow. David thinks it's hilarious that I'm an MP. 'You can't act like that,' he says, as I lean out of a speeding car window doing a victory salute in the June sunshine. Anyway, we get on really well, and I can't help feeling excited when a young person gets elected to Westminster. He'll be the first young black man ever elected. He's only twenty-seven and destined to be the baby of the House, and hopefully many other things besides.

29 July 2000 – Finally Pregnant

My new motto is, 'Don't count your babies before they're born.' I'm nine weeks pregnant, but I don't really believe it. I was convinced I'd never become pregnant. For three years I didn't. With work pressures piling up, I didn't get round to seeing a fertility specialist. That was bad, especially as I have medical complications which made me think it would be hard to get pregnant. I did five pregnancy tests before going to my GP, and even then I didn't actually believe him when he confirmed it. The consultant I saw said that these complications mean I have a high risk of miscarriage. So I have a rational reason to be paranoid. But the GP says the consultant was wrong, that I have no greater risk than anyone else.

Who to believe? The consultant, the GP, neither? In any case, one in three conceptions doesn't last beyond ten weeks. Miri, my real-life agony aunt (Miriam Stoppard) told me, 'If it's healthy, nothing will dislodge it. If it isn't, anything will dislodge it.' Personally, I think it's a goddamn miracle school playgrounds are full. How do all these women manage to carry healthy babies to term? If I could just be in this very un-select group, God I would be grateful. Just let me into the healthy baby club, and spare me the lifelong misery of the bereaved parent club. Those two things, those are the only two things I really want for my life.

10 August 2000

Tiberio and I celebrate reaching eleven weeks. We've started to feel 'established' in pregnancy. I'm even beginning to feel I can pack away my paranoia. Despite this I can't believe I could be just six months from having a real live baby of my own. You see them in the street, they're everywhere, so near yet so far. Tiberio's love for his embryo knows no bounds. He's stopped smoking (as he should), but he's also stopped drinking completely (is he mad?), and spent half his salary on organic *everything*. He cooks me a perfectly balanced, nutritious meal every evening, and after we've finished eating that meal he starts cooking my lunch for the next day. This weekend he's gone to Italy and left me six home-made ready meals.

Two of my best friends, Sasha and Sara, are also pregnant. Sara has the same due date as me, 28 February 2001. Sasha is due around that date too.

Sara is having her baby privately, but not at the Portland where the royals and the *Hello!* celebs have theirs. She had her last baby there, but they gave her the wrong baby. It's costing £7,000, but she gets weekly check-ups from week seven, and her own consultant. I ask my GP if he'll refer me to an obstetrician, given my fears about a miscarriage, but he says it's unnecessary. At week ten I write directly to my old consultant, and he agrees that I can see an obstetrician, but not until week sixteen.

A few days before reaching twelve weeks, we meet our midwife for our 'booking in' visit. It feels like we're now officially pregnant – after all, the State is taking an interest.

'Any bleeding?'

'No.'

'Any spotting?'

'No.'

'Any persistent pain?'

'No.'

'Wonderful,' says the midwife, 'everything looks as though it's going very smoothly.' As she's talking I feel slight cramping. Late that night I start crying uncontrollably. I'm not in agony. I'm just convinced I'm going to have a miscarriage. I've always been convinced I was going to have a miscarriage. I couldn't possibly be lucky enough to have a real, live baby. Despite what I've been saying since week six ('It's dead as a doorknob, I just know it'), I secretly love this embryo-child so much, I can't contemplate the thought of losing it.

Next morning, I cancel my first meetings, telling my assistant Marc, 'I'll be at the constituency surgery this afternoon, no matter what.' Soon decide this was hasty. The cramps are persistent. Ring my midwife after seeing the first trace of blood.

'It's very common, you probably have nothing to worry about,' she tells me. 'But if you're really worried go to the Accident and Emergency Department.'

It's nearly midday. If anything is guaranteed to trigger a miscarriage, it's four hours sitting on a plastic chair in A & E. On the other hand, my midwife tells me the hospital will do a scan to identify the source of the bleeding. I want a scan. I want to see the baby. I want to know there *is* a baby. Decide to go to sleep for an hour and see how I feel. Tiberio wakes me up at one p.m. He's come home from work and cooked me my favourite meal. Grilled chicken with caramelised soya sauce and sun-dried tomatoes. He leaves at two, and I try to make up my mind: should I stay or should I go?

Last night I asked Tiberio, 'What d'you do if you're miscarrying, I mean d'you just flush the baby down the toilet? Seems a bit of a harsh way to go.' Suddenly I've made up my mind. Whatever else happens, I don't want to flush my baby-embryo down the toilet. I walk, ever so slowly, the five minutes to the hospital A & E department.

It's sunny and warm, one of the few sunny afternoons this August. I ring Tiberio on the way, and then sit, waiting. A young, tall, slim woman sits down next to me with her partner, who's carrying a tiny but perfect one-week-old baby. Damn bloody mothers and their damn perfect babies. Makes me nauseous. The woman is very agitated and keeps walking up to the reception asking when she'll be seen. I'm very agitated, but I don't dare move.

The woman now starts grabbing anyone in a white coat. 'I really need to be seen *now*.' She looks perfectly fine, and so does the baby, but who knows? I look fine too, but part of me is dying. I need to be seen now, now, now, and then maybe things can be put right. Fifteen minutes later the triage nurse arrives. The slim woman gets up immediately and is nearly in the consultation room before I can stand up.

'Excuse me,' I ask in as level a voice as I can manage, 'are patients seen in the order they arrive?'

'Er . . . yes,' says the nurse.

'Well I got here first. I need to be seen. Please.'

'But–' the slim woman is ready to argue. I surprise myself and steam into her.

'No, I'm sorry. I've waited in line, I haven't tried to jump the queue, and now it's my turn to be seen. It's an emergency.' After all, if either of us were actually about to peg it, we'd be in the other A & E section, where you arrive in an ambulance.

'But–' says the woman.

'Look!' I explode in a whisper-shout between clenched teeth. 'Is your beautiful baby dying?' She shakes her head.

'Well mine is. So if you don't mind . . .' I push past her and sit down in the consultation room. My head is swimming. I'm shaking. The nurse asks what the problem is.

'I'm nearly twelve weeks pregnant and I think I'm having a miscarriage.'

The nurse assesses my situation as 'urgent' which means a one-hour wait. I walk as though on egg shells back towards the A & E entrance. I want to ring Tiberio. I need him. But I look up and he's already here, striding through the sliding doors, arms around me, soft kisses. He's always there, whenever, wherever I need him.

An hour later we go in to see the doctor. The contractions are getting stronger. The doctor is called Dominic. He's young, my age or less. He takes down the usual details – age, occupation, medical details.

'If I could just have a scan . . .'

I want the scan almost more than the baby, or rather I'm certain that one will lead to the other. And whatever happens, I just want to see my baby, just once at least on the screen.

'The thing is,' he says, 'I can't send you for a scan until I've examined you, but by the time I've examined you the ultrasound department will be shut. It closes at five p.m. on a Friday. After that, the first time they can see you is Monday morning.'

'But that might be too late.'

'I'll see what I can do.' He goes out into the scrum of the A & E department, and we stare at the door. Fifteen minutes later it flies open.

'*Now* . . . you've got to go to the ultrasound department now. If you get there in the next few minutes they'll see you. First floor. They're waiting.'

When we get to the ultrasound room I feel calm but excited. I've done my bit. I've got myself and my stomach to the ultrasound department. All will be revealed.

The technician rubs gel on to my stomach, and rolls the sensor – like a roll-on deodorant – from side to side. She and Tiberio are looking at the screen. I manage to stay silent for about a minute, and then I ask, 'Can you see a baby?'

The answer is quick and carefree.

'No. I can see a growth.'

'But can you see a baby?'

'No. I can't find a foetal heartbeat. How many weeks pregnant did you say you were?'

'Nearly twelve.'

She shakes her head. Motherhood is receding at breakneck speed. In a desperate attempt to stop its retreat, I turn my question on its head.

'But can you definitely say there isn't a baby?'

'I can definitely say this isn't a normal pregnancy.' Wham. And just like that we tumble from the happy expectant couple group into the devastated and bereaved group. It's so quick, I don't even have time to cry. Tiberio squeezes my hand. God knows how hard it is for him. His beloved embryo-baby, who he's been organically nurturing, is nothing more than a mutant clump of cells.

'It's possibly an ectopic pregnancy,' continues the technician, 'so you need to go back down to emergency immediately.'

First stage of grief: denial. 'But are you sure there isn't a baby, could you just check again? What if the scan's wrong? *Please* look again.'

Second stage of grief: anger. Why wouldn't my doctor let me see an obstetrician when I asked a month ago?

Third stage of grief: desolate sadness. Dead, dead, dead. No light, no life. Access to the healthy baby club is clearly prohibited. Do not pass go. Return to A & E. The doctor says it's a suspected ectopic which, so late on, means it's very serious. Whatever it is, it isn't going without a struggle.

Start to have spasms like a scene out of *The X Files*. Drips put into both arms. And then the grilled chicken and the sun-dried tomatoes make an appearance. Everywhere. I've never done projectile vomiting before. The sheer force flips you up from a horizontal position, like a corpse doing the Mexican wave. Just as things look as though they're getting really hairy – and statistics from my International Development Select Committee's latest report into maternal mortality float through my head (the equivalent of a jumbo jet full of women die every six hours from pregnancy-related causes) – Dominic slams me with some pethidine.

The physical pain drains away. My body comes back under control. The doctor delivers a 'pregnancy sac' and I'm told there's nothing in it. That's what upsets me the most: there was never anything there. Like an egg without a yolk. All that wishing and dreaming and hoping, it was just a con. It was a phantom pregnancy, the symptoms were there, but the pregnancy itself was just for show. Ultimately it was more in my mind than my womb. I did seven pregnancy tests in total, all of them positive, and in the end I believed them. Stupid girl. But in some way I am calmed by the saddest thing: there's no more hope. It's the hope that can kill you.

Slate arrives at the hospital and then I'm taken to one of the wards. They say I'll be here for a least four days. They'll monitor me and decide whether or not to operate. One of the nurses tells me the patient who just left my bed had her seventh miscarriage. I'm not there yet. I'm given a leaflet for women who've had a miscarriage, entitled 'So Soon to Part'. Feel like hanging myself. At least I can honestly say this is the first time in three years that I haven't worried about constituency casework.

At six a.m. I am miserable enough to make urgent enquiries about visiting hours. I have to see Tiberio. 'Visiting hours start at two p.m.,' says the nurse. 'If you ask the new staff nurse at ten a.m., maybe she'll let him come earlier.' Drift off to sleep. Woken up at nine a.m. by . . . Tiberio. He's always there, whenever, wherever, whatever.

Last night the doctor explained that very rarely, in about one in every 30,000 pregnancies, two eggs are released, and one gets embedded in the fallopian tube, and one develops in the womb. But things look different in the morning, and now the doctor thinks I might have had a normal, run-of-the-mill miscarriage. A 'normal' anything for me, in obstetric terms, is abnormal for me, and I'm quite grateful for it.

Begin concerted positive-thinking campaign. I didn't have an ectopic pregnancy. I didn't have a miscarriage at five months. I didn't give birth to a baby that died after five hours. All these things have happened to my friends. I didn't lack expert medical care in an emergency (unlike the women in the developing world who make up the jumbo jet statistics). The emergency's off, and I'm allowed home. We pull up in the car for a pregnant woman at a zebra crossing.

'Run her down, run her down! She's at least six months pregnant!'

I think of Sasha and Sara, still on course for their healthy babies in six months. And they've both already had healthy babies. I'm a statistic, and I just have to get used to it. No one ever said life was fair.

The TV phenomenon of the summer is *Big Brother*, and its theme tune is, 'It's only a game show, it's only a game-show.' I start singing to myself all the time,

'It's only a miscarriage, it's only a miscarriage.'

Three weeks later and I feel fine. The thing that upset me most at the time ('no baby') now makes me feel much better. I didn't lose anything. At any rate, that's the spin I'm putting on it. Otherwise I might mope around and become a baby snatcher. And hey, it's only a miscarriage.

8 November 2000

I am in shock. I went to bed last night after early exit polls predicted that Al Gore had won Florida – and therefore the presidency. I woke up this morning to the horrific news that Florida swung the other way, and George W. Bush is President. This news is so bad, so abominable, that nothing can make it better. I feel truly sickened. The leader of the free world is a moron, and the future of the world hangs in the balance.

20 November 2000

Voted against the Government today. You have to choose your battles carefully. You can't vote against the party line too often if you want to retain influence. (And if you don't want to have influence, why bother wasting your life at Westminster?) Anyway, I didn't want to do it, but didn't have a choice. The Government are completely wrong to put a price tag on justice. If this new law goes through, anyone who gets turned down for a visa to come to Britain can only put in an appeal if they can afford to. Naturally it will be Africans and Asians who get turned down most often, and who can afford it least. If they want their appeal to be heard they'll have to pay about £500 (or £125 for a written appeal). It runs contrary to natural justice.

On the other hand you could argue that people forego their right to appeal every day because they can't afford lawyers' fees. All I can say is that we shouldn't be making things worse. Only seventeen Labour MPs rebelled, so I was in the lobbies with the likes of Dennis Skinner, Bob Marshall-Andrews and Diane Abbott. Told Jack (Straw) I thought it was an outrage. He promised to have an internal review after three months, but that'll be after the horse has bolted.

Following the internal review, Jack Straw reduced the appeal fees to £125 for a hearing before a judge, and £50 for a written appeal. In May 2002 the fees were abolished, and the legislation relating to fees that we voted on that night was repealed.

13 December 2000

It's even worse than I first thought. George Bush didn't win the election (Al Gore polled more votes than him), but he is still President. George's brother Jeb, Governor of Florida, stitched it up for him. Bush won because he took Florida. Six million people in Florida voted, but Bush won by only 537 votes! That's the equivalent of a British MP losing a general election by less than one vote. The margin is so small, relative to the electorate, that it almost seems democratically untenable.

2001

The Petrol Attendant and
the Days of Milk

9 January 2001

It seems unbelievable that I just spent two weeks with Tiberio and Quincy in Tobago. Beautiful chilled-out Tobago. We had a fantastic stroke of luck: *en route* back to Heathrow our plane's windscreen shattered. They had to drop us in Barbados. It was such a low budget charter company that they only had one plane. They put us up in a luxury hotel in a *Fantasy Island*-style resort. It was a dream outcome – until I remembered that I'd promised 3,000 constituents I would speak in the House on the new Homes Bill. The Bill aims to tackle housing and homelessness, which is my top priority, bugger it, so it had to take priority over a freebie in Barbados. Had to get the British consul to help airlift me out in time. Tease had to come with me, and we were gutted to leave Quincy sunning herself on the beach, very happy indeed.

Arrived home in London at six a.m. on Monday morning, having broken my new rule of always getting home at least a day before work starts. You think you're clever getting an extra day's holiday, but in fact you're a mess – dazed and confused for a week. But my plan went astray in Barbados, so having landed at six a.m., was at Westminster by eight.

I went to the Members' Library, wrote my speech on the Homes Bill, and then sat in the Chamber from three p.m. for just under six hours, waiting to be called. Got called at 8.40 p.m. Sat in the Chamber for seven hours in total. I would have gone nuts if the Speaker hadn't called me – it's bad enough at the best of times sitting in the Chamber for eight hours without being called. But if you sit there having pulled strings *not* to be lying on a white sandy beach –

well it's a desperate thought. Anyway, I was jet-lagged up to my eyeballs. Sometimes I don't know how the words come out of my mouth. At least the Grim Speaker didn't mess with me, or it would have all unravelled.

I finished the speech, left Parliament at midnight, and decided to see if Quincy had arrived home by now, because she was about fourteen hours behind us, and was bringing our luggage, because it had stayed locked in the hold of the charter plane. We've got a new car – well, not new, but only six months old. After driving round the diabolical old rust bucket that we've had for the last eight years, this new car, a Renault Clio, is the best thing ever. The driver's door of our old one fell off when I was crossing Tower Bridge. It was so shameful that I naturally had a laughing fit because everyone was staring at me.

So, got into the new car at midnight, picked up our luggage from Quincy's, got back in the car, and crashed it on the way home. I can't explain how distressing it was crashing the new car the first time I drove it. I never crashed the old banger once in seven years. I finally arrived home at four a.m., and that was when I noticed my pager, which I'd left on the passenger seat. There was a message from T. (Tiberio), asking me to ring him at about 1.30 a.m. There's nothing that drives him more nuts than not being able to get in touch with me, because I don't answer my pager or because I've lost my phone . . . again. I hate my phone. Some people lose their marbles, I lose my mobiles. When Tiberio can't get in touch with me, he feels like I've cut him off.

Tiberio was standing with the light on in the bedroom looking out, and he'd been waiting for me for three hours. I had such a bad feeling. He calmly told me that he wanted to leave me, because he'd had enough of waiting for me all night, of me never being home because I was at the House of Commons, because I was married to the constituency and not to him. I said, 'What, you're going to leave me because I crashed the car? I'm really sorry I crashed the car but give me a break.'

'No,' he said, 'this is how I felt during the whole holiday, this is how I've felt for the past year.'

It boils down to this: he doesn't see me, he doesn't have a life with me, and he wants a partner who is a partner, not a ghost. He is going to find out if his office can move him to Italy, and if that happens we should separate.

I have this image of me clinging to the bottom of his trousers while he's trying to shake me off.

'I don't want to live without you,' I pleaded. 'You are the most important thing in my life.'

'Oona, you're bullshitting me, I'm not the most important thing in your life. If I was the most important thing in your life you would stop working the hours you do. You would stop having meetings on the weekend, you would stop doing a surgery on a Friday night, you would stop making phone calls day and night. And you would put me first, the same way I always put you first.'

I was left choking on that really bitter pill that so many women swallow, or so many *people* actually: the choice between your job or your life. Your job or your family. The myth of work–life balance. You have a partner who wants to share a life with you, but your job doesn't allow for that. Do you let your job become your life? I think I know the answer. Westminster isn't life. Some sad people make it their life entirely. But it's not. There's nothing there, beyond the chandeliers and the bars and the men in tights. It's not somewhere you want to live, and that's the worst thing about this job; you're forced to *live* there. It's a posh boarding school with crap food.

I admit that on Monday evening I was only forced to be there until midnight. But if you can't leave until midnight, there's no point in rushing home because Tease is asleep. The bottom line is, Westminster isn't the life I want. If you can only take it or leave it – that is, take a nine a.m.-to-midnight working day, or leave it, then I think I'll leave it.

So, twenty-four hours after arriving back from the Caribbean, I'm completely shattered. And so is the fantasy that I can have the man of my dreams, and the job of my dreams. Because there's one immutable rule: the rule which says women can't have it all. Not unless you marry a hack. You can only bend the rule if you marry someone who loves politics, someone who wants to live it, breathe it, with you. That's why MPs marry their researchers, or turn their partners into their researchers, because the only way you can have a partner and see a partner is if they do the job with you. If you have a husband like mine, who has a healthy disdain, in fact an utter contempt for many politicians, then there's no room for a relationship.

Another important lesson is that it takes one week to unwind from stress on holiday, but only ten minutes to get wound up again once you're home.

11 January 2001

The week has gone from bad to worse. Today my secretary Victoria resigned; she's been offered £10,000 more by the GLA. I am devastated. The problem with Victoria is that she's too wonderful, you couldn't ask for more. But I did. I said I could only give her the job if she could commit to a minimum of two years, at least until after the general election; it was a secretarial job, could she manage that? She didn't strike me as a secretary. She assured me she could, but she hated being a secretary. And it's really difficult working in my office. We all try so hard but because everyone puts their heart into it, it's easy to get too wrapped up, too emotional. I did once scrape together an extra £3,000 to increase her salary, and I was going to try and do it every year. The amount of time I waste as an MP trying to scrape together extra money so I can pay my staff without going bankrupt is crazy.

She'd be nuts not to take the GLA job, I would do the same in her position. But now I'm completely stuffed. It's the run-up to a general election, and I don't have a secretary. I don't even have the money to get a new one because the office cost allowance has run out and I won't get any money before 1 April. The fees office will take money directly out of my salary to pay for my staff, so I can't replace her. It makes me so unhappy. What will I do? I don't know. Actually I do know, I'll rely on Marc.

13 January 2001

Yesterday I had a casework surgery from nine a.m. to one p.m., which was enough to finish anyone off. After the surgery I did an estate visit with Marc. I usually do an estate visit on a Friday. I knock on doors and say, 'Hi, I'm your MP, do you have a problem I can help you with?' It's a bit of a stupid question in Tower Hamlets. Everybody's got a problem. I do it whether there's an election or not, week in, week out. I'll be doing it the week after the next general election, the same way I did it after the last general election. And yet people stand on their doorstep saying, 'You're only here because there's an election coming up.' After you hear that twenty times in a row it can drive you mad. I am *not* here because it's an election. For a start I have a totally safe seat and it doesn't matter a damn whether people vote for me or not. The only reason I'm there every week is because I genuinely want to hear what they've got to say. I take up cases most MPs wouldn't touch. Certainly no MP in a safe seat. I don't know many MPs in safe seats that deal with the rubbish collection, and the broken lifts and broken lights in stairwells. All the things that councillors should look after but so often don't.

Anyway, we're doing this estate visit when I get a phone call. It's Friday, about six p.m. It's Anji Hunter from the PM's office, and she's ringing because he's coming to the constituency on Monday. She wants to go over the details and make sure everything is just right. I'm on the phone to Anji for about five minutes and Marc starts to get really irate. He's been knocking on doors ahead of me, saying, 'I'm here with your local MP, would you like to meet her, do you have anything you want to raise with her?' So there are some people waiting for me, but it's the Prime Minister's office on the phone.

I'm speaking to Anji and Marc starts saying, really loudly, 'Oona, we don't have time for this right now.' I'm thinking, 'Give me a break, it's the Prime Minister's office, and I'm a backbench MP. I can't tell No. 10, "Look, I haven't got time for this, could you ring me back at a more convenient moment?" '

Anji asks, 'Is anything going on there?' I say, 'No, nothing, it's fine.' I finish talking to Anji, and Marc says, 'The problem with you is that you're just so arrogant. You think the Prime Minister's more important than your constituents. Well you make me sick.'

I tried not to lose it. I said, 'Look, you know how dear to my heart Tower Hamlets residents are, but how can you say I'm arrogant just because I'm talking to No. 10?' So I was trying to pacify Marc, knowing that no one works harder for me, or for people in Tower Hamlets than he does. And then I start thinking, 'Oh God, Tiberio, Tiberio, no matter what else happens I mustn't be late for Tiberio.' It's got to the point that if the Prime Minister's on the phone, and Tiberio's waiting for me, then I've got to go, because it doesn't really matter whether the Prime Minister leaves me, but it does matter if Tiberio leaves me.

We've arranged to go away for the weekend, to try and stitch our marriage back together. I've just got to get from Tower Hamlets to north London where he's waiting for me to drive up to this house in Suffolk. And this is another big problem, because I'd promised Marc that I'd be knocking on doors on Sunday. That was a bad idea. It just proves that Tiberio is right. And it also proves that Marc works far, far too hard – for his good or mine.

So I say to Marc, 'OK, I'm going now. If you think I'm arrogant because I speak to the Prime Minister's office, fine. I don't know any MP in the country who would agree with you, but whatever, I'm going.'

'So I'll see you at eleven on Sunday morning?' Marc says.

'No, sorry.' I tell Marc I can't go, and as I drive off, I get a pager message from him saying (and I like the tone of it considering that he works for me, not the other way round), 'If I don't see you at eleven a.m. on Sunday morning I will fax a copy of my resignation letter to the *East London Advertiser*.' At this point my jaw can't drop any lower. Ever since that plane's windscreen shattered and we were diverted to Barbados, it's been one ridiculous diversion after another.

I meet Tiberio. And I tell Anji in the PM's office that she can get in touch with me later. At that point I seem to have lost my mobile, so I'm ringing from a pager, but I promise that I'll have my pager on me at all times, no matter what. And Anji says that she needs to speak to me about a couple of other urgent things, so she'll ring me later. And so I say to Tiberio, look, I'm really sorry, although we're meant to be getting away from it all, I just have to make some phone calls to No. 10 later on.

We drive off to Suffolk and Tiberio has packed all this fantastic food to cook and a nice bottle of wine. We're going to have a civilised evening on our own together, for a change. But I keep worrying about Anji Hunter. I know I must ring her back the minute she pages me, because it'll look really bad if I can't even return a phone call. So we're about forty miles out of London, and I go to double-check my pager. Then I realise I've left it in the petrol station, forty miles back. And I know that the only thing worse than leaving my pager in a petrol station when the Prime Minister's office is trying to get hold of me, expressly on my pager, would be to tell my husband, who is at the end of his tether, that he's got to spend his whole evening doing a hundred mile round trip to find my pager. I think, 'I know what, I'll send a message saying I've left my pager with you, could you please ring me back on this number?' And sure enough, about three minutes later this nice dear old petrol station attendant rings me on Tiberio's mobile.

'Thank God you've got my pager,' I said. 'I'm really grateful because I was expecting an urgent call.'

'Oh, yes love,' said the attendant. 'Yes, you did get a call actually . . . it was about five minutes after you left, it was from an Anji Hunter, does that name ring a bell? The message said to ring her urgently.'

I tried to meditate.

'Oh, don't worry love,' said the man, 'I rang the number.'

'*You what*?!' I was almost screeching at him now. I couldn't believe the petrol attendant had rung No. 10 Downing Street.

He had got through to Anji on the Downing Street switchboard and said, 'Oh, hello, I'm ringing from a petrol station, yes, young lady's just left it here, so she won't be getting back to you.'

I rang Anji to apologise. Can you imagine? I mean, she's phoned my pager, is potentially sending me messages regarding the Prime Minister, and I leave it lying around a petrol station. Anyway, I explained that we were driving along, we'd be at the house soon, and I'd ring her from there. We finally arrived at the house and I thought, 'God, the only thing between me and a vaguely relaxing Friday evening (or what's left of it because by now it's ten p.m.), the *only* thing between me and that nice bottle of wine, and nice food with my long-suffering husband, the only thing is the call to No. 10.'

But there's been a power cut. There are no lights in the house, can't see a thing, can't find the phone. Can't even ring the owner to find out where the phone is, because there's no mobile signal either. Worse, there's no heating. It is actually below freezing, and Tiberio and I, we're not known for our resistance to the cold. I often go blue in a centrally heated house.

I said to Tiberio, 'Look, we'll knock on someone's door.' Turned out there weren't any neighbours, but I said, 'There'll be someone, some form of human life, up on the village road.'

In the end we drive back towards Sudbury and we see a pub with lights on and they kindly give us candles. Mission accomplished, we go back to the house. I cannot describe how cold it is. Well I guess people understand how cold zero degrees is. I'm biting my lip and trying not to be pathetic, but I can't work out why it's so hard to have a Friday night without frostbite, trauma, work pressure, emotional distress, or all of the above.

Tiberio, hero that he is, finally worked out which fuse had gone. We didn't have lights for the rest of the weekend, but we got the heating going, and that was all that mattered. And so we huddled in the dark in the kitchen and had a glass of wine and some Spanish cheese. I still hadn't rung Anji Hunter, and I'm thinking, 'What's worse? Not to ring her, or to ring her at midnight on a Friday night?' I'm stumped, I don't know what's worse, but I know that either is bad. I decide to ring her and she's good about it, very relaxed, and it's very obvious why she is the Prime Minister's assistant who keeps the country ticking over, because she's quite happy to deal with any old rubbish at midnight on a Friday night.

Anyway, considering what a truly diabolical time Tiberio and I have been having, we had a reasonably un-terrible time over the weekend. On Saturday night I rang Anji again, and I was reminded of the conversation I had with her in October 1997. It was my first Labour Party Conference as an MP.

'If you're going to be a successful MP,' said Anji, 'what you really need is a member of staff who will lay down their life for you. Have you got that Oona? Because that's what you need to survive in politics.'

At the time I remember thinking, 'Well, you know, my staff are great, Marc is great, Rushanara is great, but they're not going to lay down their lives for me. And I wouldn't want them to.'

Anyway, since then a lot has happened. As I said, Marc has worked harder for me than I think any assistant has done for any other MP in the history of Parliament – perhaps even more than Anji does for Tony: who knows, because Marc just works so much. So now I've got what Anji advised – a member of staff who would probably die for me. The only drawback is that on days like this we want to kill each other, so is it worth it? And that reminds me that now even Marc appears to be leaving me, Victoria has already resigned and my husband is leaving me. At this rate there'll be no one left.

15 January 2001

When I got home last night I decided that as I'm introducing the PM at this meeting in the morning, I should write a speech. (I never know what to call him, *Him* with a capital *H*? If you call him *Prime Minister* it sounds a bit pompous. If you call him *Tony Blair* it sounds like you don't know him from Adam. And if you call him *Tony* it sounds like you think he's your best mate and you're a ponce. So the PM is what I'll call him.)

Of course it's not good for me to be working on a Sunday evening, because it gives Tiberio the message yet again that my work is more important than him. So I get into bed at the same time as Tiberio, about ten p.m., and then I get up when he's asleep, at three o'clock in the morning, and work until five. Two hours is a long time to prepare a five minute speech, but I want it to be really good, not just because the PM will be standing there, but more importantly because some of my constituents are going to be standing there.

I can't work on the computer, because the computer's in our bedroom and that will wake Tiberio. We live in this one bedroom at my dad's, with everything in the same room, because we don't have a house. So once I've written the speech I decide to go to my Westminster office in Portcullis House, just across from No. 10. I've timed my speech, because I know there's nothing worse than MPs speaking for too long. It's the sin they commit twenty times a day. My speech is five minutes and twenty seconds. I think, 'Oh well, what's twenty seconds between friends?'

Before I go to Downing Street at ten a.m., to travel with the PM to Stepney, I also have to prepare a brief on the Right to Buy scheme for council housing tenants. I want to give the briefing to both the PM and John Prescott, because John's going to be in the car too. I want to lobby them on the problems over housing regeneration money. So I go to my office and of course I haven't done my hair or make-up or anything like that. And then, as you would expect, because my computing equipment is a crock of shit, the printer jams, the computer crashes, and I look at my watch and it's 9.45 a.m. and I'm meant to be there at 9.50 a.m.

Bugger the briefing, I think, it's all in my head anyway, just don't be late for the PM. So I grab all my things together and run across

Whitehall. When I arrive outside the Downing Street gates it's 9.51 a.m., so I race up Downing Street, pretending that I'm not running, half-running, half-walking, like John Cleese. The PM's car is outside No. 10. The policeman says, 'Ah, you're Oona King, they've been looking for you.'

OK, it's *nine* minutes to ten, but I'm only *one* minute late. I guess the No. 10 aides are fairly precise people. Anyway, I've got my Frizz-Ease, the stuff you put in your hair to make it look nice. It occurs to me that since all the national media will be there, maybe it would be a good idea if I put on some make-up and did my hair. And so I ask the policeman, 'Are we leaving right now, or have I got a few minutes?' And he said I had probably three minutes.

There are these little toilets hidden away on the left as you go in to No. 10, so I rush in and unscrew the top of the Frizz-Ease bottle. I'm desperate to get it on my hair so it looks as though I've washed it, or just so it looks neat and tidy, but then one of the No. 10 people starts shouting, 'Oona, Oona, come out now, he's leaving, he's leaving!' So I throw the Frizz-Ease back in my bag, I still haven't put any make-up on, and I go bombing back out the door, into the car, and he's not in the car. Another three minutes go by, and I think 'God I could have done all my make-up by now, and I could have done my hair.'

I decide to put a bit of Frizz-Ease on anyway. It's a bit of a problem because there's no sink to wash my hands in afterwards, but what the hell, I'll just put it on quickly. So I put it all over my hands and I'm just about to put it on my hair and the door opens, and out comes the PM. He says, 'Morning Oona,' and puts his hand out towards me. I say, 'Morning Tony,' and I've got Frizz-Ease all over my hands, and, you know, I just . . . I wonder why I do it really, *how* I do it, but it makes me smile.

So he gets in the car with a mug of coffee and John Prescott and Alastair Campbell get in too. It's a people carrier with two rows of seats in the back, so Alastair and I sit in the back seat and John and Tony (there, I've done it, I've just called him Tony) sit in the front row. There's the driver and a security person in the front. We tootle off. I keep my mouth shut because I think, 'Stray backbench MP with PM and Deputy Prime Minister in a car, not the best situation to be chatty in.'

John and Tony start talking about Railtrack. Alastair's on the phone and I'm studiously looking at my speech, and Tony's saying,

'So, John, what about the scandal about this train that took nine hours to get to Glasgow from Newcastle, I mean what was going on?' John says, 'Yes, it's bloody ridiculous, it was only seventeen minutes late when it got into Newcastle, but then it took another nine hours from there.' And Tony says, 'Yes, but how can it take so long? What's the solution?' And so John starts reeling off all these possible solutions, and I have to say he sounds really on top of the brief, he knows every single microscopic detail about that train journey.

And Tony says, just like anyone else in Britain reading the morning papers might, 'But it's just ridiculous, I mean, what's wrong with them? Why can't they get a fucking train from one part of Britain to the other?' That was fairly entertaining. Then I did my bit of lobbying, and I actually got some good news from John on that. Neither John nor Tony were aware of the problem we're having with regeneration money for housing. In Tower Hamlets we can't renovate run-down council estates, because the minute you announce plans for regeneration, everybody decides they want to buy their council flat. They didn't want to buy it when it was a hell-hole, but if you want to make it habitable, people are tempted to get in there and make a quick buck. Fair enough, it's what everyone else in Britain is doing. But you then spend all the money the Government earmarked for regeneration on buying people out. So you can't refurbish the estate. So everyone's left living in a slum.

I want the Government to change the law, so that people are allowed their Right to Buy, but not when an estate is about to be done up. Right to Buy should be suspended when a regeneration scheme is announced. It's public money, and it shouldn't become a mortgage repayment scheme for council tenants who can afford it. John said he would look into it, because our top priority had to be improving housing conditions, especially on pre-war estates. He also agreed to meet with Tower Hamlets council to look at our particular situation, which was a big result. So I thought, 'OK, that's good, you've done your job as an MP.' Even if I didn't have a pretty briefing covered in Frizz-Ease to hand them.

I went back to looking at my speech, and Alastair said it looked a bit long. I said I'd been asked to do five minutes, and that's what I'd done. 'You politicians,' he said, 'you never stick to your allotted time; you'll never do only five minutes.' I said, 'Alastair, I will do five minutes; it's a five minute speech.' We arrive, go in, and there are Cabinet Ministers coming out of our ears – Mo Mowlam, Alistair Darling and Stephen Byers are there, along with about fifty residents. And all of the media. We have a very good meeting. I give my speech much too fast because I don't want to go over five minutes. Then the PM speaks. Everyone's happy, and then we go on a walkabout around Stepney. We're there for over three hours, which is a huge amount of time in Prime Ministerial hours – Prime Ministers' hours are like dog years, you know, they're in a different time zone.

At the end of the visit I go back to the people carrier to get my bag. Anji appears. It's her job to make sure there's no one anywhere near the Prime Minister who shouldn't be. She asks me what I'm doing. Not horribly or anything, just, 'What are you doing?' I said I was getting my bag, and I climbed in the back seat. As I was about to get out, the PM appeared. Anji told him I was getting out. The PM asked where I was going, and I said, 'Oh, I'm not meant to be in this car, I think I'll go in another car.' Not that I had one. And he said, 'No, get in, get in.' I gave Anji a sideways glance, but when the Prime Minister says get in, get in, you get in. So I got in the front row seat, where he'd indicated, and he got in next to me, and Alastair got in the back. We drove off, and about five minutes later I said, 'What about John?' We'd forgotten the Deputy Prime Minister.

It took us about forty minutes to get back to Westminster, driving south of the river. Tony chatted to me about various things. Leo his baby is the love of his life. He said he's the best thing that has happened to him, and he kept asking why I hadn't had kids, what was I waiting for? If I wanted kids I should have them as soon as possible, I shouldn't hang around.

'I'd really like to have children,' I said, 'but I've heard this rumour that you have to be in the same room as your partner if you want them.' I didn't mention that I'd just had a miscarriage, or that I'd give anything to be pregnant. Anyway we spoke about Tower Hamlets, about my problem with the mosque. I can go into the mosque any time, but I don't have access to the young men who are there, who have become interested in Islamic fundamentalism. He was very interested in the residents he met that day.

Then Alastair pipes up. 'So, Oona, you broke your promise, you said you'd only speak for five minutes but you didn't.'

I was a bit taken aback because I was certain I'd spoken for less than five minutes. I asked how long it was.

'Seven and a half minutes,' said Alastair.

I don't think he was winding me up, although with him you never know. If he was right, then that was bad. You don't drone on when the PM's waiting to speak. Alastair even said he'd put his stopwatch on. That is exactly the sort of thing Alastair would do. And yet it couldn't have been that long, because I was speaking too quickly.

He kept coming back to it again and again, 'You see, I knew I couldn't trust you.' What is it with them, why do they always say they can't trust me? He was joking, but with Alastair it's always a joke, and then again it isn't. He came back for the fourth time and in the end I said, 'Alastair, give me a bloody break.' And Tony said 'Oh, don't worry about him, I was about to tell you I thought your speech was brilliant, absolutely superb.'

I was quite pleased with that, coming from the PM, and then Alastair replied, 'Well it doesn't matter what *he* thinks anyway.'

I like Alastair's sense of humour, when he has it.

Got back to Westminster after getting out of the car at No. 10, and went straight into a meeting on funding for my All Party Parliamentary Group on the Prevention of Genocide. We need to raise about £30,000 a year. Then went into the Chamber for Parliamentary Questions, and then had three other meetings. I think we finished just before midnight. Got home, and Tiberio was asleep. I had a car coming for me at seven a.m. the next morning, because I'm on a TV programme. In general I've stopped doing media. They turn you over every time, added to which you get a reputation for being a rent-a-mouth. You should be in the Chamber doing your job, not poncing about TV studios.

On the other hand, when you're completely bankrupt because your office cost allowance has run out, being an MP is ruining you financially, you can't pay your staff, and you can't pay the phone bill in your constituency office, and then you get the opportunity to earn £1,700 for three mornings' work – well you don't have a choice. I've been going around dodgy businessmen and trade unions begging for money, but if appearing on TV will pay the bills, then I gotta do it. I cannot believe that my constituency telephone was cut off. All those people in Tower Hamlets ringing me for help with their debt problems couldn't get through because I didn't have enough money to pay the phone bill. Tiberio paid it for the last three months.

At least I went on TV to talk about my two key issues: housing and genocide. Whenever journalists ring up I say on the whole, unless there is an emergency, I'm only willing to talk about two issues. Housing and genocide. It's amazing how the interview requests melt away.

18 January 2001

I haven't slept properly since the last night of the recess (ten days ago) and now I'm feeling ill. I've been at Parliament each night till midnight, home at one a.m., then up at six a.m. for this TV thing. I can feel my glands swelling. I've also got an abscess in my tooth, but I can't go back to my dentist because she's ripped me off so badly, it's outrageous. Last time I went she told me it would cost £350, and then sent me a bill for £1,800, and then told me that was just for the temporary filling, and if I wanted it all finished I'd have to pay £2,600.

If I wasn't an MP I wouldn't have paid it. That's what I hate about being an MP, you can't get into these arguments, because the result will always be an article in a newspaper saying, 'MP refuses to pay her bill because she thinks she has the right to everything free in life.' So I refuse to go back to my dentist, my tooth is killing me, it's infected and I've got swollen glands. In the end I go to Miri, because she is both a doctor and an agony aunt. So she gives me some stuff for it, and I try not to speak, which is obviously a tough ask in my job. I go home and sleep.

21 January 2001

Tiberio is really pissed off, and says he's leaving me again, because the one night I get home early to see him, I go to sleep. It's because I'm tired and ill. And he says, 'Why are you tired and ill? Because you work sixteen hours a day.'

He doesn't want to live like this any more. It makes me so desperate, and I can't bear the thought of losing him. I decide I'll do anything to try and keep him; whatever it takes. But the pressure is enormous because what it requires is for me to face down my Whips and say, 'I'm not doing these nights any more.' That's pretty difficult, and it rules out a promotion, but fair enough. And it also requires me to be home on time. But MPs can never be on time, I am constantly waylaid one hundred times a day by people who say 'I only want twenty seconds of your time.' Time just disintegrates; it unravels. So I feel like I'm unravelling. And by the time I drive to my surgery at eight a.m. on Friday morning at the end of a week like this . . . I feel desperate.

When I was in the car with the PM, we discussed that Scandinavian Prime Minister who resigned recently because of stress. And Tony said it was a bit much, you couldn't expect to be Prime Minister and then go off work with stress. He's right. And I also don't think you can be an MP and then go off work with stress. I know some people have to go off work with stress, but it's like abandoning ship, like leaving everyone else to clear up the mess. You don't do it. So either I have to change the way I'm working as an MP, or I will have to go off sick with stress, because I cannot deal with this any longer. Driving back with the PM from Tower Hamlets, I thought it was hilarious, the idea of a politician being off with stress. Alastair, Tony and I were laughing at the idea. I don't know why on Monday it seemed so funny that a politician would go off sick with stress, and then by Friday it seems my *only* way out right now. I do not think I can physically survive another week at Westminster.

On Friday morning it hadn't occurred to me that I could take time off, I was just desperate. That idea occurred to me over the weekend, in fact it was Quincy's idea. On Friday morning, I was just wondering how to deal with it all: approximately 600 organisations, 20,000 constituents' cases, forty MPs and three or four Cabinet Ministers at any one time wanting an answer or action on something. And my Select Committee, and my position as Vice-Chair of the British Council and the twenty organisations I'm patron for. I just don't want to do it any more.

A very nice woman stopped me in the street recently, a black woman. She made her daughter, aged eight, hold out her hand, and said, 'This is Oona King, and I want you to be like Oona King.' Then she turned to me, such a lovely smile on her face, and she said, 'I just want you to know we're *so* proud of you. We're pinning *all* our hopes on you.' And I wanted to hug her, but then I wanted to shake her by the shoulders and shout, *don't* pin all your hopes on me! I'll probably disappoint you.

Either get in or get out, but don't fuck about like this halfway between life and death; it's pathetic.

So I'm sobbing as I drive along to the surgery, and I'm wondering what's happening to me, how can this be *me*, I don't do this sort of thing. This could be breaking point, and the reason I've reached it, the reason it has been brought to a head is because my husband has quite rightly said he's reached *his* breaking point. And when he breaks I break. I say to Tiberio, I'll follow you, I'll come to Italy, let's just leave. The most important thing is not my job, it's us. Let's just go. But he says, *no*, I don't like you any more Oona, you're not the person I want to be with. I don't want you to come with me.

It's a terrible thing when the person you love says they don't *like* you any more; not even they don't love you, but they don't like you. So that's why I think I'm close to a mental breakdown. He says to me what they all say, 'You're a politician, I don't believe a word that comes out of your mouth. You'll never change.' I feel that I try really hard to be a better partner. I feel I try as hard as it's possible to try, but either I'm not trying hard enough, or what I'm trying to do is impossible.

I arrive at the surgery, and I'm thinking, 'Don't cry, don't cry, you cannot walk into the surgery where all these people come to see you, and start crying.' So I sit down and my constituents come in, one after the other. This is what I have every week. The Tower Hamlets refugee camp, the poorest place in Britain. The human misery that trails in and out of my office is un-fucking-believable. It's a miracle I haven't topped myself already, just out of sympathy with them all.

For instance, Sara comes in, who escaped the war in Somalia with her five children. Her husband sponsored her, or so the Home Office say, but her husband's disappeared. Maybe he hasn't disappeared, I don't know, how can I tell? What I *do* know is that she's got five kids she can't feed because she's living on £40 a week. So she comes and cries in front of me for a while, because her children aren't getting the food or shelter they need, here in Britain. They're malnourished. And then another man comes in, he's homeless and he has three children under four. His wife has vertigo, which is unfortunate because they've been offered a flat on the eighteenth floor of a miserable tower block that's sandwiched between railway tracks, and he's scared his kids will either fall out of a window, or be run over by a train.

I've heard this man's story too many times before, or stories like it. The fact is, he's been offered a flat. I have to deal with all the people who don't even get a flat. So I tell him to move onto the eighteenth floor and be grateful he's got a roof over his head. It's filthy and damp, the paper's peeling off the walls, it's probably infested with mice, but it is a flat. Believe me, I tell him, I'm doing all I can to get more investment into housing in East London, I raise it with the Prime Minister and the Deputy Prime Minister and everyone I can, but I can't build you a house with my own hands, and I can't put you to the top of the council's housing list. So the man with his three kids starts crying.

Then Rashid comes in. Rashid is one of my regulars; he comes at least three times a year. Rashid is in his thirties and has five children. His wife died in childbirth with the fifth one. Rashid is failing to give his kids the care they need, and the only way he can do this is to get a new wife. He wants to bring over a new wife from Bangladesh. And actually, you have to think about the children. They're either going to be put into care, which will cost a lot of money and won't do them any good, or he's going to remarry and have extra support so he can bring them up. But the Home Office won't let his wife in. Rashid doesn't cry, he just looks at me with accusing eyes, and says his life is a misery and his children don't deserve to live the hell they do.

And then Risgar comes in. Risgar has come to see me twice before. Risgar is from Iraq, and he is coming to see me this time because I actually succeeded – no, let me be truthful here – Marc succeeded in getting Risgar's application for asylum approved. The thing about being an MP in Tower Hamlets is that if you are successful in a case, it only leads to more cases, because people who are very, very poor are only ever out of the shit for a certain amount of time. There are two groups of people that come to see me: those that know their National Insurance numbers off by heart, and those that don't. I mean . . . do you know your National Insurance number off by heart? Do I know

mine off by heart? Of course not, because we don't have to. Our lives
don't depend on it, but these people's lives depend on it. They've got
numbers, they're branded, they've got poverty stamped all over them.

So I think, 'At least here I've got a result for Risgar.' But Risgar is
sobbing uncontrollably, because he found out last week that his wife
has been killed in Iraq, and he says one of the reasons it's so terrible
for him is because it brings back memories of his father being killed
by Saddam Hussein's regime. When they killed his father they hung
his body up in the square, and cut out his organs and left them
dangling out of his body. What do you say to that? I explain that I'm
going to help him as much as I can. I try and give him what he wants,
which is basically somebody in authority giving him the attention he
deserves; some care and attention. There isn't much else I can give
him. And eventually Risgar leaves.

By the end of the surgery I, as well as my staff, have post-traumatic
stress syndrome. You finish the surgery on a Friday night and you
want to hang yourself. Not only because you have to deal with more
human misery than it's reasonable to expect anyone to deal with, but
also because we don't have a break from beginning to end; which is
usually four or five hours, sometimes seven.

Anyway I get home late for Tiberio. What am I supposed to do?
Look, Risgar, I'm sorry you've been tortured and your family have
been killed by Saddam Hussein, but my husband's got dinner ready,
so check you later. Maybe I have to start doing that, because maybe
there is no end to the misery. I know there is no end to it. Virtually all
the people I see in my surgery are tortured – either literally or
metaphorically. In some ways I'm inured to their suffering because I
deal with it every week, and yet in others I'm angrier today than
when I was a teenager. It's just so unfair.

I have a miserable weekend. I worry about all the constituents I
haven't been able to help and I worry about my marriage. It's
intolerable, to the point that I decide to resign. Yes, that's it, on
Monday morning I will resign. At this moment I cannot imagine
anything better than walking away from it all, than saying, 'Look,
I'm not your MP any more. Sorry, it's not me.'

In the past I thought I would resign because I couldn't bear the
alternative, which seemed to be losing Tiberio. But I couldn't
actually *visualise* resigning. I've wanted to be an MP since I was

five years old. How can you give that up? How can you give up your
dream when you come that close to actually having some influence,
or even being promoted and becoming a minister? So few people
have that opportunity, so few young people, and so few young black
women. Only one other black woman has ever even made it into the
Chamber. For me to get that close and go, 'Er, no, actually it's not for
me, no thanks,' it makes me want to cry.

I realise I've reached the point in my life where I'm fucked
whatever I do. Either I stay in my job and I will be a deeply unhappy
person because I will lose my husband, and I'll lose my life, or I'll
save my marriage, keep my husband, and lose my job. So it finally
dawns on me that whatever I do I'm going to be a deeply unhappy
person. And that knocks me for six, because I'm inherently happy.
I'm not prone to depression. Something really bad has to happen to
make me miserable. And this is something really bad. Losing the
person you love is devastating; it's a bereavement. And losing your
dream is devastating; it's a bereavement. So which will it be? It will
have to be my dream. It will have to be my job, because at the end of
the day, Tiberio is more important than my job.

I speak to Quincy, who says I shouldn't make a decision when I'm
under so much pressure. She says I should take two weeks off work.
Suddenly I think that's a really good idea, even if it's only a week. I
decide that's what I'll do.

22 January 2001

I look through my diary for this week, and decide to cancel whatever
meetings I can, so that I don't resign. The first meeting I've got on
Monday morning is about raising £10 million to redevelop Mile End
Park, and I think, 'Oh God, I must go to that one.' After that there's a
housing meeting, which is really important because I've asked for
further homes to be built, so I feel I must be at that. And then after
that there's lunch with businesses at the House of Commons. I've
written to all these businesses, asking them to come to lunch, so I
decide I must do that. Before I know it I'm in the office the whole
day. So then . . . I'm *really* at the edge. I realise the only thing to do is
to go home and say to Victoria I'm not going to look at my diary for

Tuesday, Wednesday, Thursday or Friday, because if I look at it – actually not Friday, I always do surgery, I wouldn't ever cancel surgery – but if I look at my diary, I am not capable of cancelling meetings because I feel so guilt-tripped. I keep forgetting that if I went under a bus tomorrow, it wouldn't make any difference.

23 January 2001

Today I seek asylum in another life. It's a life where you go for a walk in the morning before you do some work. It's a life where women push children around the park, and where stress isn't the foremost sensation during every waking moment of the day. I want that life so much. I go for a walk for an hour, and it feels so nice. I have my pager on me of course, and then I start taking phone calls, and I end up working, but even just being out of Westminster is so good. You can't imagine how much I hate being locked up in Westminster.

In the afternoon I visit Miri, and within about four minutes I'm crying again. And she says, 'You're really in a bad way.' The upshot of the conversation is that she thinks maybe I should go on anti-depressants. Miri says at least they will stop me crying, and that's a bit of a major selling point. I mean, I'm sorry, but you can't be an MP and wander round the House of Commons bawling in the corridors.

In any case, maybe this isn't a good line of work to be in. You get crucified left, right and centre. When I spoke to Miri last week she was talking about setting up a childcare company, and I'm desperate for there to be a crèche at the House of Commons. We've got a shooting gallery, why can't we have a crèche? And Miri is fantastic in terms of childcare; she's one of the most respected names in Britain. So I say I'll speak to Margaret Hodge, the relevant Minister, and I'll ask her to have a meeting with Miri to see if we can sort something out, to see if we can get a crèche in the House of Commons.

But if I became a Minister there would probably be an 'Oona King getting special favours for her aunt' scandal. Labour sleaze. The point is, things that normal people do twenty times a week (i.e. ask a friend or an acquaintance or family member to help with something), in my profession amounts to criminal activity.

26 January 2001

Mum arrives from France, and it's fantastic to see her. But I don't really want to let her know exactly how unhappy I am. On Wednesday I stay home and do bills that I haven't done for months. I owe far more money than I thought, and everything is a financial disaster from every possible angle. It's just catastrophic. I don't know how I'm going to repay all the money I owe. But on Thursday I spend the day with my Mum. I haven't spent the day with her in London for years.

We went to the British Museum, which was really lovely. But then I made the mistake of thinking I'd better check what was in my diary, and I remembered that I'd begged one of the Whips to put me on the Standing Committee of the Homes Bill. Better go.

28 January 2001

I've run about all week, I sat for hours in the Standing Committee on the Homes Bill among other things. My cousin Ed got married at the weekend. His bride Amie looked a bit uncomfortable when someone gave a reading saying marriage should be this; marriage should be that . . . Tiberio and I were sitting next to each other going yeah, *right*.

Ed and Amie had the infinite good taste to have the reception in the East End, in my constituency, at Wiltons Music Hall. It's fantastic – an old East End music hall with the paper peeling off the walls, but it's a stunning building. Miri's gift was the flowers inside the hall. You've never seen anything like the flowers at this wedding. They could have decorated the Olympic opening ceremony. Anyway, Amy looked really gorgeous. Saw lots of people I hadn't seen for a long time.

And then, before the speeches, I had to do a typical Oona thing. I had to make my excuses, give Ed a kiss goodbye, and say, I'm really sorry, I must dash to Vietnam. And that's where I am now, I'm in Hanoi with the International Development Select Committee. Spent today visiting a crater where ten young Vietnamese women were blown up by the Americans during the war. It's put my life in perspective.

22 February 2001

I am so sad that my best friend in Parliament, Tess Kingham, is leaving. She says she can't stand being an MP any longer. She has three young children, including baby twins, and she can only be an MP if she misses the first ten years of their life. She won't do it. I wish people understood why Parliament desperately needs modernising. It's not just because it excludes people with families, and women; it's because the country is then run by an isolated group of people out of touch with everyday life. Tess is desperate to get out. So am I. But I won't, I've decided to stay. I've weighed everything up, and on balance I've decided I can do this. I've got things under control again. I can do this MP thing, it's just I don't want to do it without Tess.

6 March 2001

Nelson Mandela has joined the Labour Party. It's great to have God on our side. He says it's because Labour has consistently focused on international development and tackling world poverty. Spoke in the debate on the International Development Bill today. It is truly fantastic that this Bill puts into law our policy to spend all our international aid on poverty reduction. Under the Tories, British international aid could be tied to arms deals, or kickbacks for British companies. But with this Bill, it will be illegal if British aid isn't aimed solely at tackling poverty. Bad for arms dealers, good for starving children.

19 March 2001

Apparently this general election is going to be the most boring ever, in the whole history of democracy. We're gonna walk it. That's assuming that Britain doesn't turn into one giant abattoir. The outbreak of foot-and-mouth disease has given the country a medieval air. Images of upside-down cows in flames. It's like the plague, only it doesn't affect vegetarians. I didn't know we had so many cows and sheep to burn. Anyway, it's unsettling, not the backdrop you want for an election.

2 April 2001

What a nightmare. The general election has been postponed so we can burn yet more cattle. The Tories are relieved, in fact they want it postponed for as long as possible. It's their only hope of avoiding a thrashing at the ballot box. But in general, MPs are desperate to get the election out of the way. Otherwise you're trapped indefinitely in a phoney war that saps all time and energy.

Bright note, Sarah Brown (wife of Gordon) rang. She offered to come with her mum and campaign in Bethnal Green and Bow. Her parents lived in Bangladesh for some years, and her Mum still speaks Bangla. That'll go down well with the Bengali community, especially as Gordon Brown is a near-deity around here.

3 April 2001

Spoke on the International Criminal Court (ICC) today. I love the House of Commons research department. They come up with juicy little nuggets for speeches, such as the first instance of a war crimes tribunal: 405 BC in Greece. And more recently, in 1474, a panel of judges from the Holy Roman Empire ordered a military commander to be executed after his soldiers committed crimes against humanity. The military commander's defence was that he was only following orders. They hung him by the neck. Over 500 years later, we're still at a fairly rudimentary stage of institution-building. A lot of military commanders in the world today don't even get a rap over the knuckles when their soldiers commit crimes against humanity.

The Tories don't support the ICC. Or at least they take the American position – they are happy for it to deal with the soldiers of other nations, but they don't want British soldiers to come under its jurisdiction. As it happens, even if British soldiers committed crimes against humanity, they would only be brought before the court if the British Government refused to carry out an investigation itself.

Halfway through my speech the Tories start gunning for me. It's always quite scary when your opponents say things like, 'The Honourable Lady should consult Article 20, Paragraph 3(b) which refers to trials in the United Kingdom . . .' Pleased to get through it OK.

14 May 2001

My election campaign literature has been printed off and put through people's letterboxes. It says 'Our Oona' in big letters. Who comes up with this stuff? I think it was in case the BNP tried to do their silly name stealing trick again, by putting up another candidate called King. So we're running with 'Oona' instead of 'King'. Knowing the BNP they'll find some Irish immigrant called Oona who lives in Bethnal Green and wants to run against me. Still, it's nice to see fluorescent yellow 'Vote for Our Oona' stickers appearing in living-room windows. People don't know what a boost it gives a candidate when they bother to put those posters up. On a less positive note, I'm truly sick of my own voice. Also sick of everyone else's. Don't want to talk any more. And if I get one more frigging question about burning cows . . .

10 June 2001

Got re-elected just in time for Tiberio's birthday. It's the worst present I could give him. He hasn't seen me for months because of the general election campaign. At three a.m. on his birthday he was standing at the count in York Hall in Bethnal Green, playing the dutiful political spouse. Purgatory. Still, I was pretty pleased. My share of the vote went up from 46 per cent in 1997 to 50.4 per cent. MPs get excited about that sort of thing. And Labour MPs were also pretty excited about our 'historic second term'. Even though everyone knew we were going to win, there was still a lurking doubt, a Labour ghost that had to be laid to rest. At the back of my mind I couldn't help thinking, 'We've never won two elections in a row before. For the whole of the last century the Tories got things their way, electorally speaking, virtually every time. Maybe it's true, they're destined to be the party of government, just because . . . well they're bloody Tories.'

Nah. They got whipped. Anyway, the Tory party is *so* last century.

3 July 2001

My first speech in the Chamber since being re-elected three weeks ago. I was talking about housing. During the campaign I was accosted daily by people who wanted me to come inside their homes and see their appalling living conditions. I repeated in the Chamber what I say to them: 'No, I'm sorry, I can't come to see the twelve members of your family living in two bedrooms. I know there are six of you in each room, that the baby has to sleep in the bath, and that some of you are sleeping on the floor. I know that your children are sick, that they have asthma, that their education is suffering and that your life is being ruined by the lack of proper housing. But I must spend my time lobbying the people who can change this, and raising your problems at Westminster.' So that's what I did today in the Chamber, although I will understand if some of these people don't vote for me next time around. Politicians' words mean nothing if you have to watch your children's development stunted every day.

10 July 2001

Watched another reshuffle go by. Although I'm deeply loyal to the Labour Party, it's been a terrible career choice. I can't imagine joining any other organisation and not getting a promotion. Actually that's not fair on the Labour Party, because it's not the party's decision. It's the PM and his advisers. And it's to do with me. I've made choices, and choices have consequences. Still, I'm dammed if I'm going to be a PPS.

Although I didn't become a PPS at that time, I still had to come off the International Development Select Committee. Tackling global poverty will always be my passion. But I knew I had to come closer to home. Moving on to the Select Committee on Housing (then part of the DTLR) meant I got to work on issues around domestic poverty. But it meant I gave up world trips, meetings with Kofi Annan at the UN, work on the global stage, for visits to sink estates in Loughborough.

26 September 2001

When I got home, Tiberio was watching the news about the impact in America of September 11th. The world is still living through the initial aftershock. It's fifteen days now since the event. The shock of seeing the physical destruction was immense. It was like watching a sci-fi film, or perhaps one of those action thrillers like *The Towering Inferno*. Seeing those airliners crash into the World Trade Centre, and then demolish them, and hearing the last conversations of the people inside, and seeing people jumping out of the buildings, was like watching something at the cinema. It's difficult to distinguish fiction from reality. Horror creeps in when reality proves more terrifying than fiction.

You kept thinking it could never happen, it's out of this world. Seeing those certainties crumble with the towers, the certainties about what constituted real life, was deeply, deeply shocking. Its impact was partly due to the modern media. You saw people dying up close. People die all the time, but not usually on live television.

All the people who die in the Congo – their deaths don't register with us because they don't die live on CNN or BBC World. We don't hear what those Congolese women said before they were hacked to death by a group of militiamen. We don't hear, we don't see, we're not close to it, it doesn't traumatise us. We ignore it. Now, the initial shock of September 11th has faded, but the aftershocks are even more powerful.

All the papers have headlines and leaders saying that the world has changed for ever. There's always an inclination to exaggerate the scale of disasters when they happen. Calamitous events seen with the perspective of time don't seem quite so apocalyptic. Indeed they never *were* the end of the world.

If one positive thing can come from this, it must surely be that America has learnt a tragic lesson. The American people have finally felt the appalling effects of indiscriminate murder on a large number of innocent people. I think logic will make them understand that when you see indiscriminate murder happening elsewhere – for example in Rwanda during the genocide – you have to do something, you have to act. You can't just walk away, just because they're not your countrymen or your relatives, or they don't have American flags in their back yards.

So life as we knew it has ended. Actually I think not. People are saying the whole world will come to a standstill; the airline industry will shut down, the tourist industry will collapse, any industry relying on travel – a key component of globalisation – will fall apart. September 11th will trigger a depression like that of the 1930s. The days of milk and honey are over. I don't think they were ever here. But September 11th marks a change: because of this new terrorism, there is now the prospect of arbitrary death for a miniscule number of rich people in the West. Before, arbitrary death was mainly inflicted upon vast numbers of poor people in developing countries.

27 September 2001

I went to bed, and my eyes did the opposite of slam shut. I tried one of those self-relaxation techniques, where you imagine yourself in a soothing beach scene, gentle waves lapping at your feet. Almost immediately grenades started exploding on the beach. A serious military battle took place, shrapnel everywhere, people running for cover, widespread terror. It wasn't a relaxing day. Or maybe it hasn't been a relaxing year.

Vital statistics, what were they? Got up at seven a.m., went straight to the office, to prepare for interviews for new caseworkers. I've introduced a one hour test for the candidates, to see if they can write press releases, and if they can deal with casework. Actually, first and foremost to see if they can write decent English. It's always tricky to get them over that hurdle.

Marc and Janata are getting really badly strung out. They're less strung out than me, but last Friday after surgery a woman rang up Janata and said she was going to kill herself right then and there. And Marc had to deal with an instant eviction: a family who were being evicted at 9.30 a.m. on Monday morning. For the first time I caught both of them with a look of terror in their eyes. They are so stressed by the weight of human misery that heaps itself on this office. It's astonishing that there can be so many miserable, poor people. Poor, as in not having any resources at all, and no means to generate resources.

Although we're known as an office that goes wildly out of our way to help people, we can't always help. A couple of desperate people were caught recently giving the address of friends who live in the constituency, so that they could come and see us instead of one of the other local MP's offices. They say the other MPs' offices just give out standard answers, but they need more than 'standard' help. The terrible thing is, I'm starting to realise the other MPs have got it right. We should stop going out of our way so much, and instead just make sure everyone gets an answer, even if it's a crap standard answer. But we're not good at it. I can't put those standard letters out, I find myself choking on them.

So I decide I must rewrite the standard letter, I must do my own letter. That's all right for maybe five issues, ten issues, fifteen issues, but when people are writing in on everything under the sun, everything from stem cell research, to parking restrictions, to the Human Rights Act, to the mating habits of the beluga whale – well you either have to accept the standard letter, or you have to accept that people won't get a reply. Belatedly – more than four years after I got elected – we are coming to recognise that we have to accept the standard letter. Because in this age of client-focused, customer-driven service, it is not acceptable to write to your local democratic representative and not get a reply. That, unfortunately, is even more unacceptable than getting a crap answer. So we need a good caseworker. Actually, we need a miracle-worker.

Marc has worked for me since I was first elected. He's got a new job as a Parliamentary Officer for Shelter, which is fantastic. But he is my corporate memory. We'll be walking down the street and he'll say, 'Coming up on your left, Mrs Clarke, 75 Jackman House, her husband died two years ago, but you got his pension sorted out, she loves you.' Or, 'Crossing the road now with a walking stick, Mr Suliman, arrived from Somalia, lost his eye in the civil war, we couldn't sort out Indefinite Leave to Remain for his three children, he's desperate.' Or, 'Ignore Angela O'Sullivan, coming up on the right, she's an SWP loon and wants to kill you.' Can't imagine what I'll do without him. Am destined to get the Mrs Clarkes who love me, and the Angela O'Sullivan's who hate me, all mixed up.

Neither Janata nor I can envisage what we'll do without Marc, but we're going to try and put new systems in place: do less but do better.

That's pretty difficult, though, because no one could do better than Marc, both in terms of the outcomes he gets for the cases he deals with, and his level of involvement and care. It is quite extraordinary how much he puts into this job. His work means that 60 per cent of my constituents are thrilled with me, and think I'm the best thing since sliced bread. And the other 40 per cent think I am a complete wanker who never answers their letters.

We finish the interviews at 5.30 p.m., and I haven't written the keynote speech I'm giving to the Tower Hamlets Mediation Service, and the event starts at six. I'm supposed to speak for fifteen to twenty minutes (which is far too long considering it's not written), on conflict resolution in Tower Hamlets. So I knock something out in thirty minutes on the computer, just bullet points, but then pulling speeches out of the bag is what I'm very good at. After all, that's how I got this job. So I know I can do it, which is why I spent more time on the interviews rather than preparing the speech.

Anyway, so we interviewed for a caseworker and I found the most miraculously perfect person, whose mother is Welsh, and whose father is Bangladeshi, and who speaks Sylheti, and who worked for Harriet Harman and so understands an MP's office, knows what would be required of her, and who can be a PA, but who can also do casework. I was nearly falling over myself with excitement. Oh, and who also, by virtue of being mixed race, can do all that bloody mixed-race stuff I get day and night. All the boxes I'm put into, it starts to get on my fucking nerves. Anyway, must stop swearing. Neil Kinnock always told me that to become an MP I had to stop swearing. It's work in progress.

At the moment I still don't have a PA. Back in August, I found the perfect person. I offered her the job, she accepted it, she was starting in September. And then she rings me the week before to say that she's been diagnosed with cancer, and she understands if I can't hold the job open for her, but she would be immensely grateful if I could. My first reaction is, well, you can't tell someone who's just found out they've got cancer that they've lost their job as well, so I said, of course I'll hold the job open for you.*

---

* In the event, holding the job open for Rohema was one of the best decisions I ever made: she made a full recovery, and became not only one of my best assets, but also one of my best friends.

So, because I have no PA, I ask a lovely new volunteer called Tim to ring the Tower Hamlets Mediation Service and check they're expecting me at 6.15. They tell Tim it's in Hanbury Street, Spitalfields. So I drive down to Hanbury Street, and I look at my watch and it's only 6.06 p.m., and I think, 'Thank God for that, I'm going to be on time.' And when I'm there I check my diary to see what number it is in Hanbury Street, and the diary entry says it's actually another street, so I ring them again and they say it's at this other address off Cephas Avenue, near my office in Bethnal Green, where I just came from. And I still have to finish the speech, and I really need a taxi so I can write it on the way, but I can't waste any more money on taxis. So drive off, trying to avoid speeding. I look at my watch, and it's 6.18 p.m., which is OK.

So I regroup again, but realise as I'm getting out of the car that I've left the speech in the office; I curse myself, and then decide I'll just begin by saying that this is going to be an unscripted speech. But I can't get in, I'm pressing all the door buttons and a notice on the door says, 'Keynote Speaker, Oona King', and I'm thinking, 'Yeah, if you'd let me in.' I ring and leave a message saying I'm outside. In the meantime two Bengali kids, probably twelve or thirteen, say to me, 'You're the local MP, aren't you? What are you doing here?'

I tell them I'm meant to be giving a speech. They want to know what it's about, so I explain that it's about conflict resolution. And I ask them what's the biggest cause of conflict where you live? They both immediately say drugs. And we know that, but you can never hear it enough. Then one of them says, 'Yeah, drugs and housing.' And we know that too, so I'm not really learning anything, but it's nice to speak to them. And then this boy says, 'The family upstairs, they've got twenty kids.'

'What do you mean, they've got twenty kids?'

'Yeah,' he said, 'they've got twenty kids.'

'In how many bedrooms?'

'Three bedrooms.'

I told him I didn't believe him. I've had bad housing cases, but the most I've experienced is twelve people in two bedrooms*. But twenty kids in three bedrooms is off the Richter scale.

---

* On one other occasion, I encountered an extended family where there were sixteen children under one roof.

'If you don't believe me, I'll take you there right now,' he said. 'I'll show you, because they live right above me, and they're driving me mad. It's a husband, he's got two wives, and they've got twenty kids.'

He's a kid. Maybe he knows what he's talking about or maybe he doesn't. The phone rings and I think, 'Why am I speaking to these two kids about conflict in Tower Hamlets, when I should be speaking to a meeting of sixty people?'

The guy on the phone says, 'We're waiting for you, where are you?' I say I'm standing outside. 'No you're not,' he says, 'and there are people waiting to see you, but you're not here, and they think you're really rude for not turning up, and on the programme you're down to speak at six p.m., so they've been waiting for you for half an hour. Are you sure you're in Hanbury Street?'

It's like a bad comedy. Ministers just glide about, they don't have to worry about anything but making the speech, which is written for them by a civil servant anyway. But I have to worry about everything *and* the speech. I race back over to Hanbury Street, and speak on conflict. I say that a lot of conflict in Tower Hamlets stems from housing, and that we need a twin-track approach to solve it. The Council and the Government must each play their part by providing a greater level of investment in social housing. And the community must play its part by developing sustainable communities, i.e. by having fewer kids. So we don't end up with ten kids in a house.

I gave my own family as an example, my gran was one of thirteen, my granddad one of seventeen. Then a woman got really upset, and said, 'Why are you saying big families are negative?' I was trying to make the point that you can't expect the council to solve your problem if you have eight children, say, in a two-bedroomed flat. The council can't solve that problem, and nor can the British taxpayer. No one's going to vote for a 10 per cent tax hike to sustain the cost. So therefore those kids will live in misery, their development and educational prospects will be affected, and they won't have the same life chances as other kids. Parents and communities have to take some responsibility for the children they bring into the world.

Anyway, I finally got out much later than I was supposed to, I was late for Tiberio. He'd made a lovely curry. I spoke to Mum on the way home, she's just started going to the gym again. Where has my commitment to exercise gone? I was so good just three weeks ago, and now it's disappeared entirely.

19 November 2001

Spoke in the debate on detention without trial. Against the Government. Another black mark next to my name. But honestly, you can't go ripping up habeas corpus just because of Osama Bin Laden. *Especially* not because of Osama Bin Laden. You can't lock people up without a trial. We're talking about introducing a dangerous precedent to deal with an estimated fifty people (who are fanatical enough to blow up their fellow citizens) out of our population of sixty million. Yes, of course we have to deal firmly with suspected terrorists. But not by trampling on our human rights. The Government wants to derogate from Article 5 of the Human Rights Act (1998). Sat in the Chamber for nine hours just to get my five minutes' worth of outrage on the record. Left Parliament some time after midnight.

2002

The General Anaesthetic
and the Queen's Speech

16 May 2002

Former bigwig MPs get called to speak before the likes of me during debates. By the time it's my turn, we're nearly out of time, so I'm always cutting my speeches to smithereens. Today I lost half of a very good speech on the problems of housing in the north of England. I told the Speaker that I was looking forward to the next life, cos in the next life, I really hope I can give speeches in Parliament that I don't have to shred beforehand.

21 May 2002

My obsession with housing and affordable homes (lack thereof) continues. The average income in Tower Hamlets today is £12,000, while the average home in Tower Hamlets costs £180,000. What that means, as I ranted in the Chamber to Stephen Byers as the Minister responsible, is that no ordinary person can buy a house in my constituency. The way house prices are going in London, soon it will only be the very poor or the very rich who live here, i.e. those who qualify for social housing, or those who earn ten times the average income. We need housing schemes that allow people in the middle to get their foot on the housing ladder.

'Blair's Babes': the iconic picture of Tony Blair and some of the
101 Labour women MPs elected on 1 May 1997

Me at fourteen
months

With my father
Preston

With my mother
Hazel and brother
Slater, Kenya 1969

Me standing in front of my mother with my aunt Miri, my uncle Tom, Slater and cousins Oliver, Will, Barney and Ed

On Slater's 30th birthday in Greece, August 1999

With Tiberio in Greece

In my wedding dress, July 1994

Glenys Kinnock borrows some red hair from my best friend, Quincy, to lend to Neil.

My wedding, July 1994

With Tiberio, members of
his family and my mum

On our honeymoon, August 1994

My father receiving a presidential pardon from Bill Clinton
following a racially-motivated conviction in the civil rights era

My uncle, CB
King, an inspiring
civil rights activist
and lawyer

Visiting El Salvador when I was 22, in 1989: on an anti-government demonstration at the entrance to the cathedral where Oscar Romeo was shot. A political demonstrator tells me how his eyes were removed with forks by the Junta, and his left hand – and a finger from his right – had been amputated during torture sessions

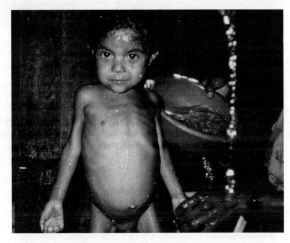

Baby Luis, who I spent time with in Nicaragua. Luis died before his fifth birthday, one of the twelve million poor children who die each year before the age of five

My first time on *Question Time*, with David Dimbleby, Lembit Öpik, Julie Morgan and Richard Littlejohn. September 1997

With Tony Blair, John Prescott and local resident Brenda Daley on the Ocean estate in Tower Hamlets

Addressing a packed House of Commons to second the Queen's Speech

Jack Straw visits Bethnal Green and Bow the day after the Brick Lane bombing

Sharing a joke with Barbara Follet and Harriet Harman, one of the Cabinet ministers who helped me most

Tony watching me with a pained expression that was to become familiar

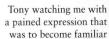

The Prime Minister with London MPs during the ill-fated Frank Dobson mayoral campaign, January 2000

Painting my constituency office in Bethnal Green (I had to begin again because the green paint came out blue)

With survivors at the genocide site in Rwanda that I visited in March 1998

With President Paul Kagame of Rwanda and members of his Cabinet and entourage

Sharing a moment with schoolchildren during a visit to Cambodia with the Select Committee on International Development, January 2001

With children in Burundi, the Great Lakes region, July 1999

Preparing to set off down the Congo river with the Rainforest Foundation and colleague Bob Blizzard MP in a trip organised by the All-Party Parliamentary Group on the Great Lakes Region and Genocide Prevention

Visiting a micro-credit financing scheme in Uganda, 1998

On the campaign
trail in the East End,
Columbia Road
Flower Market

Placades for the 2005
election, with supporters
including my assistant
Mohammed and
two campaign team
members, Anna and Joe

Congratulating George Galloway on his victory, 5am, 6 May 2005

Life after being an MP: in New Orleans, reporting on Hurricane Katrina for the *Guardian*, September 2005

Hosting a Q&A session with
Gordon Brown during his
leadership campaign, May 2007

Campaigning
for more
youth services
with young
people outside
Parliament as
Chair of the
Make Space
Youth Review

Elia diving into Tiberio's arms on his second birthday

5 June 2002

Another reshuffle last week.

A constituent came to see me, and said he needed my help to get promoted at work. He wanted to know who he could appeal to when his employer refused to give him the opportunity he felt he deserved. I gave him the info about industrial tribunals, but told him to disregard it. His case wasn't open and shut. It was one of those grey areas, where his manager didn't particularly like him, and wasn't going to give him a break. Most of the time in these cases (not all) there's very little point spending your life and your money trying to prove your treatment has been unfair. I told him that not getting promoted wasn't the worst thing in the world. Deeply unfair, yes, but quite run-of-the-mill. Better to leave your current job and find another where your talents are more appreciated.

So why do I stay at Westminster? Part of me wants to write to my MP and complain that I'm being unfairly passed over at work. I want the opportunity, given to others, to prove what I can do. And the other part of me says shut up. Work harder. Do better. Or go elsewhere. Last week during the reshuffle I made quite a good attempt to think about other things. I rang David (Lammy) about something entirely unrelated to the Government or the reshuffle.

'Oh my God,' he exclaimed, 'I just got promoted!'

'That's amazing . . .'

'Yes, I can't believe it, it's turning into quite a big day!'

And with that he was gone, another of my friends sucked into Government while I sit on the pavement outside.

Today I bumped into David behind the Chamber.

'You do know why you didn't get promoted, don't you?' He put his arm around me. 'Because you're a woman. Don't forget what you're up against. It's not fair, and that's all there is to it.'

It was a nice thing to say. Not necessarily true, but thoughtful.

I was in the Lady Members' room when I got the usual phone call from Downing Street following a reshuffle. I used to get it from Anji Hunter. The first time Anji gave me one of those calls she said, 'You were in, you were out, you were in, but then we had to make way for someone, and you were out. You know how it is. That's politics. But it's only a matter of time. Next time.'

Anji has since left the PM's office. Sally Morgan was exiled to the House of Lords, apparently following a long-running power struggle between her and Anji. But now Sally is back in charge. It was the Prime Minister's political secretary, Robert Hill, who rang.

'Tony asked me to ring you, because he wants you to know that he regards you highly.'

'You must have to make quite a few of these phone calls, Robert.'

'Seriously, we know it must be hard for you.'

'Really?' I was tight-lipped and non-committal.

'Seeing people who were elected after you, promoted ahead of you.'

'Oh, I'm sure I'll get used to it. In any case I'm delighted David has been promoted.'

I won't write to my MP just yet. I hear she has a backlog of constituency mail.

17 June 2002

Meet with TB today. He's irritated that on the day Kashmir and Pakistan looked like going to war, the media spent fifteen minutes at the No. 10 press briefing obsessing over whether his new glasses are the same as Sven-Göran Eriksson's. The press aren't interested in information any more, he says, instead it's all just a game of gotcha. He mentions the Tories' identity crisis – they're Thatcherite, and they know they need to move away from that, but they just can't bear to. They're taking refuge in all the furore around spin that we're dealing with, and they're not seriously looking at policy in the detailed way Labour did during the eighties. We spent ten years, from 1987 to 1997, engaging in genuine policy reflection. Perhaps it shouldn't have taken us ten years, says Tony, but at least we did it. The Tories are making a huge mistake in not doing it.

1 July 2002

Got called in to see the Chief Whip last week. After last summer's reshuffle, Hilary (Armstrong) said she'd had a request for me to become PPS for the Leader of the House of Lords, Lord Williams of Mostyn. It was nice of him to think of me, but I didn't want to be a PPS. I said no, and went on the Select Committee on Housing (part of the then DTLR) instead. That's how I instigated the first parliamentary inquiry into affordable housing: by *not* being a PPS. This time Hilary asked if I'd reconsider.

'No.'

'You've got to change your mind on this,' she says. 'You're not doing yourself any favours. Come and see me next week.'

So I went back yesterday, and she was really exasperated. She actually used that line out of the Tom Cruise film *Jerry Maguire*, though she probably didn't know she was quoting it.

'*Help* me to *help* you.' My resistance is starting to crack.

My resistance cracked. I was appointed PPS to Stephen Timms, then the Minister for E-Commerce, and subsequently Chief Secretary to the Treasury. Stephen is not a regular politician. He is enormously generous and by common consent one of the nicest men at Westminster. I enjoyed being his PPS because he gave me the chance to do more than railroad MPs. The job of a PPS is essentially to herd cats (sometimes sheep), so that MPs support ministerial initiatives. One of their most important functions is as a conduit between the frontbench and backbench. They are their Minister's eyes and ears. That sometimes means sitting in the Members' tea room for hours at a time, listening to gossip. Their most important role is to negotiate problems raised by MPs and be a go-between, smoothing over backbench concerns.

I liked working for Stephen because he didn't just make me sit in the tea room dishing out Parliamentary Questions to MPs. At its most boring this is the role of a PPS: to get MPs to physically turn up to your Minister's Parliamentary Questions, and raise 'friendly' issues, i.e. areas the Minister would like aired in the House. Stephen freed me from the tea room, and regularly let me fill in for him in his ministerial duties, giving speeches.

It was the closest I ever came to being Minister; picked up outside Members' Entrance in the Minister's car, the speech written by civil servants and laid out on the back seat, no need to find a parking space or work out where the venue was. I'd just sit back and enjoy

*the ride. It only got hairy once. I had to give a speech to 500
businessmen setting out Britain's energy policy, followed by a Q &
A session, and didn't have time to read the civil servant's 200-page
briefing document beforehand.*

*In order to become Stephen's PPS I reluctantly resigned from the
Select Committee on Housing.*

24 July 2002

Yesterday was our eighth wedding anniversary. I had a general
anaesthetic at the Homerton Hospital in Hackney. The anaesthetist
said, 'You're my MP,' before injecting me with drugs. I like feeling
consciousness recede in a calm yet breakneck fashion.

The doctors inserted a camera below my belly button and dug
around for a couple of fibroids. Good news: a week off work. Bad
news: a more serious operation required.

It's five a.m. and I can't sleep, which is strange, because I can still
feel the general anaesthetic making me drowsy. At least with a week
off work, I finally summons the effort to write something in this
diary. 'So, what up Oona?' as my twenty-year-old homeboy cousin
Chevene from Atlanta would ask. Good news: he's got me out
clubbing again. Bad news: I'm forgetting how to dance. It seems like
another life when I was twenty-four and used to be one of the
dancers on a stage looking out over 3,000 people. It's ten years ago
so I suppose it *was* another life.

So, anything new? Yes, an earthquake, a metaphorical car crash,
my life has been derailed. I was having the operation to find out
why I hadn't got pregnant two years after having the miscarriage.
At the consultation before the surgery, the doctor said he would
recommend me and Tiberio for IVF. I was at Westminster when
Tiberio gave me the news, on 17 July, the week before the
operation.

I was writing up a note for John Prescott on housing, in time for
his statement on Thursday. As I went into the Members' Library to
sit down and write it, the deadline on top of me, I was hit by how
much I missed Tiberio. So much. I was magnetically drawn back out
of the library, into the corridor to the phone near the Members' tea

room. I called him from there, hemmed in by glass cases holding ancient volumes of Hansard.

'I just want you to know, I know we're going through a bad patch, but I miss you so much.'

I can't remember his precise words, but he said, 'I'm sorry to say this over the phone,' (always a bad start) 'but I'm not happy in this relationship and I think I have to leave.' I looked at the green carpet, nodded and smiled at passing MPs, and then closed my eyes and tried to absorb this new information.

'Any reason?'

'The doctor said he was recommending us for IVF.'

'Yes?' I was incredulous, how could IVF be bad news – we wanted children so much.

'Well, it made me realise that if we do IVF you could easily be pregnant by October.'

'Yes, but that's what we've wanted for six years. When I was pregnant you were the happiest man on earth.'

'That was then. Now the prospect of a baby makes me understand that I don't want you to be the mother of my children.'

I looked down at the green carpet again. I didn't exactly feel dizzy, I felt ended. Bizarrely enough, John Prescott must have walked past at that point, because I kept thinking, 'My life is fucked. Fuck, there's John Prescott.'

When we spoke later that night, Tiberio expanded: 'I've given up everything for you – my family, friends, country, culture, language. And what do I get in return? Nothing. You're never here for me. I always have to wait for you. You never give our relationship priority. You never change.'

We'd been here three years earlier. My job was hell. When I was at home I was asleep, and when I was awake I was too tired to talk. I told Tiberio I was willing to resign. And I resigned myself to being unhappy whatever happened. Unhappy if I kept my job and lost my husband, unhappy if I kept my husband and lost my job. But most unhappy if I lost my husband. Tiberio wouldn't hear of me leaving my job. 'I won't have that on my shoulders, ruining your life's dream.'

'So what can I do?' I asked.

'Change.'

I thought I had. I made a huge effort at work to stop doing non-essential things. As an MP you risk drowning under an ocean of froth camouflaged as 'absolutely essential meeting/ engagements'. Some of it is critical. But much could be dealt with by a phone call or letter. And much is absolute nonsense. I even stopped working most weekends, which is unheard of for an MP, and especially for me. I did post and admin at home, but I wouldn't get suited and booted to do a local MP gig unless I knew it would really make a difference. I went to my Whips and said, 'My husband is leaving me unless you let me see him at least one evening a week. Just one night let me get home at eight p.m. instead of midnight.'

So Wednesday evenings were for me and Tiberio, and I was officially let off the Whip on those evenings. It's true that sometimes (I'd say one week in three, Tiberio would say one in two) Wednesday evenings got sabotaged by meetings I just couldn't cancel, or votes I couldn't avoid. Still, sharing one evening a week and weekends together was a world away from the ninety-hour-working-week hell of the previous three years. I also introduced a rule that my diary couldn't have more than twelve hours of scheduled meetings per day (of course it often did, but much less than before). If I had to be at Westminster at eleven p.m. then I wasn't willing to schedule eight a.m. meetings. I got loads of grief for it: 'Oona's not prepared to do morning meetings.' I argued with the Council Leader, Chief Executive, Deputy Leader, and the other local MP in Tower Hamlets, Jim (Fitzpatrick), asking them to start our leadership meetings at nine a.m. instead of eight. They said, 'Look Oona, we all work really late. There's no other time.'

I wanted to shake the whole lot of them. 'No, *you* look. Look at us. We're socially maladjusted sad bastards. Get a life. Or at least let me save mine while I still can.'

I got the hang of saying no. I perfected it when I was invited to meet President Clinton at the White House when my dad was granted the presidential pardon that ended his forty year exile. I got the invitation when I happened to be in a car with Paul Boateng, and discussed it with him. 'That's a tough one,' he said. Most politicians would do anything to have a picture of themselves and a US President on the wall. It's true, the US President is a very important man. But Tiberio was the most important man in my life, so I had to blow out the President. The 'old' Oona would never have done so. The new 'I gotta get a life for me and my husband even if it kills me' Oona didn't take long to make the decision. I'd changed.

Tiberio didn't see it that way. He felt that I now slept eight hours a night more often than four, so I wasn't as physically exhausted and drained, but we still didn't have quality time. 'The only time we live, really live, is when we go on holiday each year to Greece. I can't wait the whole year, just to live for three weeks. That's not life.' My problem is that I always think of genocide victims or slaves or people working down coal mines, or even just families in Tower Hamlets who live twelve people in two bedrooms. I know how lucky we are. I don't think it's such a bad life. Any middle-class person in the West leads an extraordinarily privileged life. And on top of all that I was now working 'only' a fifty-five hour week. I know lots of people with regular jobs who do that: lots of couples with at least one partner working those hours. But that wasn't what Tiberio wanted for his life. And I was starting to realise that neither did I. More and more I imagined the relief I would feel when I did my last MP's surgery and walked out the door. Over the last five years things had become clearer: politics could not be a substitute for life.

I was adamant that Tiberio wouldn't leave me. If he thinks he's getting away, I thought, he's so wrong. I'll follow him to Europe or America or wherever and I will never let him go. Of course, it wasn't that simple. Tiberio looked at me with sad eyes and said, 'It's too late. Even if you change your job, your house, your country, you'll still be *you*, and *you* don't make me happy.' One of the problems with Tiberio is that in so many ways he's perfect. It's difficult to keep up. He organises everything perfectly. He is amazingly generous. He helps everyone. He is the perfect host. He is the best friend. He will be the perfect father. He is so loving. He always goes the extra mile.

His main fault is that he often has unrealistic expectations, and too often the cup is half-full. One of my worst faults is that I'm overly optimistic. 'It'll be fine,' can be interpreted as taking things for granted. Tiberio said I had taken him for granted, and now it was over. I lost my temper.

'How can you do this to me? I'm thirty-five in October – every

year it's harder for me to get pregnant, but you've waited ten years to
tell me you're not happy, and you don't want to have children with
me. Well, you know what? I will forgive you for breaking my heart,
but if I never have children I will *never* forgive you for that. That's
my life ruined.'

'That's not fair,' he said, 'you can't blame me for that.'

'Yes I can.'

'The problem is that you want the child more than you want
me.'

'Don't be ridiculous! And anyway, how can I separate the two?
You're my husband and I'm supposed to have children with you. If I
hadn't had a miscarriage you wouldn't be leaving me.'

I was suddenly flooded with grief, real tearing heart-ripping grief. I
was losing my family, the children I'd dreamed of, the children that
already existed inside my head. This was a bereavement. I see-sawed
between wanting to throw myself at Tiberio's feet on the one hand,
and slap him senseless on the other. 'You've just murdered our
children! I'll kill you!' Maybe he was right. Maybe I wanted the
children more than him. Maybe my biological clock was going nuts.
Tiberio said it wasn't right to have children in a relationship where
he wasn't happy. Why was it so hard for him to be happy? For me it
was easy. I was very happy with him, very grateful to have him. We'd
had so many fantastic times together. Even just recently we had a
great holiday together. I was taking a fertility drug, Clomid, and we
were so excited about getting pregnant. It didn't work. Desolation.
But still, I was optimistic. Even Tiberio seemed optimistic. 'Don't
worry,' he told me, 'I know we'll have our children, don't get
panicked.'

Imagine, I'd been panicked when the only problem was getting the
egg and sperm together. Now I had to go back to the drawing board
and get a new life. Find a new life partner. How long would that
take? A year? Three years? Five years? The rest of my life? Alone for
ever? Tiberio said that fear of being alone wasn't the right reason to
stay together. I said that our marriage was for ever and if he left me
he would just end up going from one five or ten year relationship to
the next.

26 August 2002

At the beginning of the summer recess, I spent a week crying. So boring. But I couldn't come to terms with the end of my life as I knew it. Couples that were *half* as happy as us stayed together for ever, so how could we split up? The answer, obviously, which he kept repeating, was that only one of us was happy. He had to leave, and I had to let him go. It's times like this that you need a survival mechanism. The most reliable survival mechanisms involve clouds and silver linings. An ability to generate positivity from catastrophe. And slowly, sometimes over many years, the positive part becomes larger than the catastrophe.

So I started to concentrate on the positive. Maybe I could find a partner who loved me and could handle my job and my country. Maybe I could still have children. Maybe I could write my novel (my personal pipe dream), maybe I could spend more time doing what I wanted to do. Maybe if we split up and sold the house, we could pay off all our debts, and money would stop being such a problem. Maybe I had the mental and physical strength to 'move life' the way you moved house. We'd spent eighteen months building the most beautiful house in the world (OK, in Mile End – we live in a converted pub), and the only thing that kept me going through the worst of it was thinking, 'I'll never move again.' Now, less than a year after we finished, we were thinking about moving. On the positive side, moving is good, because it forces you to spring-clean your life. I decided it was a good thing to do. On our eighth wedding anniversary we went our separate ways – to Greece as always, but to different islands.

Everything has changed. I've decided I can't spend my life being a disappointment to my husband, so therefore we will have to separate. I crossed the Rubicon. 'It's over,' I thought. 'It's really over. This is the end of my marriage.'

Then the fear gripped me. What if I never met anyone else? What if I never had children? What if I wasn't strong enough to cope? I started to rehearse all the arguments Tiberio had made. He was right. The relationship must be right, babies can't be bandages. I knew he would never leave a marriage once he had children. It was the Italian Catholic in him. But the miscarriage meant I'd missed my chance. He didn't want to be trapped and I didn't want to trap him.

So I've let him go, and I'm on my way to Amórgos to say goodbye to him.

Meanwhile, Tiberio had spent another week thinking about our relationship, and decided that in fact he loved me. That's what he was waiting to tell me when I stepped off the ferry in Amorgos. Now it was my turn to say it was too late, and see the desolation in his eyes. I reluctantly agreed to six months' relationship counselling back in London. Roles reversed. He wanted to save the marriage, I no longer did. My determination to generate positivity from catastrophe had worked too well. I was actually looking forward to my new-found freedom. I kissed Tiberio at twenty-three, and got engaged at twenty-five. I had persuaded my thirty-five-year-old self that if I climbed outside the protective walls of our marriage I would find streets, if not paved with gold, at least lined with silver.

The counselling was helpful – not because it provided answers, but because it allowed us to ask the questions in a calm and rational way, without slipping into the dysfunctional patterns that govern many long-term relationships. I've learned that often with dreams (the love of your dreams, the job of your dreams) you have to be able to let the dream go before it can materialise. That doesn't mean it will materialise, simply that the possibility survives.

30 September 2002 – Labour Party Conference

Arrive on Sunday to speak at the Shelter fringe meeting, on 'Race and Community'. Even though Marc is no longer my assistant, he has written me an amazing speech. The reason he's such a good speech-writer is because he weaves together all the things I've ever said (in this case, in relation to race politics and communities) and somehow turns it into a tightly argued and compelling case. And if there's a gap, either in the argument or evidence, he fills it in better than I could myself. He mentions campaigns I forgot I'd done, campaigns I didn't know I'd won. At the end of one of his speeches I invariably think *damn* I'm good . . . but it's actually just that he packages me better than Saatchi & Saatchi could. Harriet Harman is also speaking.

29 October 2002

At the DTI departmental meeting this morning, Patricia (Hewitt) starts telling us about her trip to China. 'I was in Shanghai last week for forty-eight hours and I was amazed to see how the Chinese can build a new town from start to finish in eighteen months. It makes you weep. I thought to myself, 'Why can't we do it here to solve the housing crisis?' But then I reminded myself they've got no greenfield sites, no planning law and no democracy.'

A Minister at the other end of the table says, 'I feel draft legislation coming on . . .'

I wish they'd just sort the bloody housing.

9 November 2002

The drumbeat for war in Iraq is getting louder. Yesterday the UN Security Council unanimously passed Resolution 1441 giving Saddam one last chance. If he actually complies, which he won't, the Resolution also holds out the prospect of lifting sanctions. On Thursday I said in Parliament that Saddam Hussein was rightly being given one last chance to disarm. But I wanted to know under what circumstances sanctions might be lifted? Jack (Straw) gave me the only answer he could – they will be lifted whenever Saddam Hussein chooses to comply with the UN resolutions. Which means never, without military action. It's so enraging that everything depends on the whims of madmen – Saddam Hussein on one side, and George Bush on the other.

13 November 2002

Big day in Parliament for me today. I asked Hilary (Armstrong, Chief Whip) to let me 'second' the Queen's Speech. It's considered a great parliamentary honour, decided by the Chief Whip, and given to an MP that's going places. Tradition has it that one MP proposes the Queen's Speech (which outlines the Government's business for the forthcoming parliamentary term) and another seconds it. The first is an MP whose career is on the way down (the elder statesman MP), and the other is an MP whose career is on the way up (the whippersnapper MP).

So today I'm seconding the Queen's speech. Others get a tap on the shoulder and are asked if they would like the honour, but I went in and asked for it. I'm finally getting it into my dim head that if I don't ask round here, I won't get. Hilary had given me one of the 'sorry you haven't been promoted speeches' in her Chief Whip's office. A few months later I said to her something along the lines of, 'Well, if you won't let me be in Government, at least let me give a speech to a packed House of Commons. Just once. I'm good at it.' About a fortnight ago Hilary agreed, so I've just finished ironing my red silk suit.

The Times this morning says, 'Oona King, the "right-on" MP for Bethnal Green and Bow, has secured the highly prized speaking slot in today's Queen's Speech debate, traditionally awarded to a rising star. The honour suggests that Ms King may at last be on the path to high office. Ms King, one of only two black women MPs, has surprised colleagues with her slow progress into Government. Her decision to speak out against the Government over the bombing of Afghanistan and on asylum issues has held her back.'

Hmm. And the rest. Anyway, I've written a speech that covers my well-worn areas of obsession: housing, genocide, racism, sexism, enforcing UN resolutions, and representational democracy. Should have them rolling in the aisles. Oh, and I've also slipped in a bit about gorillas in the mist. Tiberio is coming in with Quin, and so are Mum and Miri. Scared to death. Hope I don't cock it up.

28 November 2002

I've decided it's a bit problematic that I only seem to write more than a few paragraphs in my diary when I'm on holiday or in hospital. This time I'm in hospital at the Homerton in Hackney. I'm worried they're giving me special treatment, because I've got my own room. Mind you, it hasn't got a window and I haven't seen daylight for forty-eight hours. Quin came to visit me today – she made me feel better by saying she also got her own room on the NHS at St

Thomas's. Maybe I should believe my own propaganda: the NHS is getting better. Certainly the treatment I've had here is first class.

Tiberio and I went to see our marriage counsellor last week. She said, 'This operation must be very frightening for you Oona.'

'Not really,' I replied. 'I haven't had much time to think about it, other than to be immensely grateful that I get a month off work. Rest, sleep. I can read novels. I can do things that under normal circumstances are entirely foreign to me.'

She persisted. 'But this operation must worry you, after all, it's about your *fertility*.' She let the word hang in the air.

'Yes and no,' I replied. 'Of course I'm desperate, if possible, at some stage to have my own children. But actually I spent this summer staring childlessness in the face. I looked it in the eye. I know I can survive it – not willingly, because I love children so much – but I can survive it. So I'm not terrified of this operation.'

Hopefully the operation will remove fibroids (the 'something unrelated to the pregnancy that looked like an ectopic' during the miscarriage). This will do two things: possibly reduce dysmenorrhoea (agonising periods) and possibly make it easier to get pregnant. And also, foremost in my mind at this moment, escape Westminster. A month off work. A month out of politics. Priceless. A month off skull-cracking fifteen hour days. For some reason they've reared their ugly head again. And the anaesthetic is a way out. I was *so* looking forward to oblivion. I wanted to throw my arms around it. 'So actually,' I concluded, 'I'm really looking forward to the operation.'

'I see,' said the counsellor. 'And what does this say about your life, the fact that you're so looking forward to oblivion?'

Ah. Good question. She got me there. Turning to Tiberio she said, 'What do *you* think this says about Oona's life?'

I took the cue to sit back and listen to how terrible my life was. I nodded humbly every now and then, but eventually just thought, 'Fuck it, give me the anaesthetic.' I was being childish. Tiberio was being constructive. That distressed me even more, as I normally pride myself on being constructive. But I really couldn't wait for them to strap me on a trolley and wheel me into theatre.

Tiberio came with me to the hospital. The consultant arrived, and was perplexed to find me in great spirits with a broad grin on my face. 'What's going on?' he asked. 'She's a changed woman, she was scared in July,' – the same consultant had seen me for the exploratory operation – 'but now she's jubilant.'

'She's in denial,' explained Tiberio, 'but it's true. She's looking forward to it.'

And I was. It's like going on a trip. I love going on trips. I love travelling. Anywhere. I recently got back from Rwanda, where I came face to face with genocide and gorillas. I'd regaled the Commons with the story while seconding the Queen's Speech, and was now equally wide-eyed at the prospect of being knocked unconscious and taken away somewhere different.

14 December 2002

The Queen's Speech! I forgot about it, mainly because it went well. Mostly, I take time to record catastrophe. However I'm reminded of the Queen's Speech because I just came across some letters about it, attached to the original Hansard report. I got loads of letters from MPs saying they liked it, including from about a quarter of the Cabinet. Unfortunately MPs are like GPs – you can't read their writing. It's taken me weeks to decipher half the letters I received. One was from – of all people – Quentin Davies MP, a devout Thatcherite.* The letter is dated 13 November, the day I gave the speech.

Quentin Davies wrote, 'Your speech today was superb – eloquent, *feminine*, with the exact balance of humour and seriousness . . . one of the most memorable speeches I have heard.' *Feminine*? I was just thinking how inappropriate even well-meaning Tories are, when I realised that instead of *feminine*, he'd written *genuine*.

Gordon (Brown) wrote, 'Congratulations on your great speech on the *Mormons*. It was magnificent.' From Jack (Straw's) letter I can make out, 'You managed the difficult task of combining great humus with some onions. So my sinuses lung rabulation – you were brilliant.' (Translation: You managed the difficult task of combining great humour with serious points. So my sincere congratulations – etc.)

---

* In June 2007, Quentin Davies defected from the Conservatives to Labour.

The letter from the PM read, 'Brilliant zit.' In fact he'd written, 'Brilliant. *It* is a difficult speech but you did it superbly.' When he got up to the Despatch Box on the day, he said well done, or words to that effect, and then added, 'The Member for Bethnal Green and Bow came into the House as one of the youngest Members of Parliament, and it is clear that she has a long and successful career ahead of her.' A volley of MPs immediately chimed in with, 'Ah-*ha*', as in, 'Does that mean you'll promote her?' Tony's measured reply, kicking my career into the long grass, was: 'How and when she will be successful I cannot say.' He's good.

The Leader of the Opposition, Iain Duncan Smith, was really funny, and his speech-writers had come up with better titbits than the lot at No. 10. He said, 'I gather that when the Hon. Lady was a teenager she said she wanted to be both Prime Minister and an air hostess. There is consistency in her ambition: air hostesses and the Prime Minister spend their days repeating the same pre-prepared and utterly predictable announcements before jetting off around the world.' And then, bizarrely, I listened to the Leader of the Opposition stand at the Despatch Box and quote *me* talking about Tiberio: 'He is Andy Garcia-gorgeous, speaks five languages including Japanese, has a black belt in karate, does all the shopping, and cooks the most fantastic Italian food.'

'Now we know,' continued IDS, 'why she has campaigned for so long and so hard to change the hours in this place: she wants to get home a bit earlier.'

And he is right. He is so right.

18 December 2002 – Re-selection 2003

Apparently I've got a problem with my re-selection by the local Party. Iraq means everything's up for grabs. The people who were outraged at my original selection now have grounds to attack again. It's not a full-frontal assault, more a limited insurgency in localised areas like Spitalfields and St Dunstans. They won't win. But I couldn't hold it against them if they did. It's my fault entirely. I didn't even make a single phone call to ask people to support me. Why not? Half of it is to do with integrity, and half of it is to do with stupidity. I've always thought it a bit distasteful to try to pre-empt the outcome of a meeting by ringing people up beforehand and asking them to vote for me. Let them go to the meeting, have their discussion, make their decision. Unfortunately, that's the most stupid approach a politician could ever take. It's not how it works. And I was lulled into a false sense of security by my easy re-selection in the last Parliament. I did no canvassing at all. But now Marc tells me that he made some phone calls on my behalf. And anyway, because of Iraq everything is different. In political terms, nothing will ever be easy again.

2003

The Worst-Case Scenario
and the Palestinian Ghetto

January–April 2003

I wrote virtually no diary entries during this time, and was constantly bombarded, day and night, about one issue only: Iraq. The feeling in the constituency, the country, and around the world, was reaching boiling point. Over a million people marched through London in protest. I spent weeks and months agonising over the vote for war in Iraq. I didn't want to vote either way. Both choices, of action or inaction, meant certain death for thousands of Iraqis.

I was plagued by two strongly held and incompatible beliefs, both of which I put on record many times:

- *First, we had to take action against sovereign states that murdered their people.*
- *Second, we had to create a system of binding international law, and act within it.*

The problem was that the current laws were not being enforced. And to enforce them we would have to break other laws (e.g. taking military action without UN approval, as we did in Kosovo).

I knew that my first belief (upholding human rights, if necessary through military force) was incompatible with the current realpolitik of international affairs. You couldn't just start bombing countries with poor human rights records. But the logic of this argument was to sit back and let genocide happen.

However, there was one issue that distinguished Saddam Hussein's Iraq from all others: his was the only regime to use weapons of mass destruction (chemical and biological weapons) against his own people. I also felt strongly that inaction in Iraq was confirming a deadly precedent: that UN resolutions were meaningless. They weren't worth the paper they were written on. In my November speech to the Commons, when seconding the Queen's Speech, I lamented the weakness of the UN, and argued that if we wanted an effective UN we had to do two things: root out the appalling double standards crippling international relations, and prove that the UN meant business. Enforce UN resolutions.

By this point the UN had passed seventeen resolutions on Iraq. In Parliament we had voted on UN Security Resolution 1441 that gave Iraq 'a final opportunity to comply' with the UN weapons inspectors. When does 'final' not mean final? When it's in a UN resolution.

Five years earlier I had argued against military action in Iraq. I had asked for Saddam Hussein to be given more time. As the vote in 2003 approached, I felt I could no longer say, 'Give him more time'. In the intervening five years, the death toll in Iraq had been 100,000, according to some estimates.

People on both sides of the argument made guesses about the outcome of military action. I summarised the worst case scenario, put to me by constituents and others, as follows: 'We attack Iraq, Saddam uses chemical or biological weapons in response, possibly aimed at Israel. Saudi Arabia and Egypt are drawn into the conflict. The war stirs further anti-Western hatred, undermining Muslim moderates and strengthening extremists, leading to new terrorist attacks on the US, Israel and possibly the UK. Israel uses a nuclear weapon in response. That is the worst case scenario of military action. The best case is very simple: Iraq gives unconditional access to inspectors and is subsequently disarmed, and war is averted. There is every indication that Saddam will have no regard for the fate of his people and will instead make illogical and disastrous decisions that result in his country's and his own destruction. It is this illogical and self-destructive streak that is precisely *why we cannot risk him continuing his nuclear weapons programme.'*

At the time, there was no doubt that Saddam had had a nuclear weapons programme, the doubt was whether it was actually still operational. Saddam had originally set up a nuclear weapons programme in the 1970s, helped at different times by Germany, France, Italy, Austria and Brazil. America also gave Iraq loans for the acquisition of 'dual use' products that could be used to develop nuclear weapons. And Britain helped Iraq with its chemical weapons programme by supplying the machinery to manufacture mustard gas. The notorious September 2002 dossier put together by Britain's Intelligence services was essentially a rehash of information previously in the public domain. Worse, however, were two claims that proved unfounded – first, that Saddam could have WMDs ready to use within forty-five minutes, and second, that he had bought uranium from Africa (and therefore was closer than expected to having a nuclear weapon). Although I have no doubt that Saddam Hussein wished to further develop his nuclear weapons programme, it remained just that – a wish.

So, if I knew then what I know now, would I have voted differently? In terms of the intelligence information, no. Even if Saddam was forty-five years, rather than minutes, from having WMDs ready to use, I believed the UN should use military force to uphold its own resolutions prohibiting genocide. After changing my mind on the issue, I finally decided that if the opportunity arose to get rid of a genocidal maniac, then we had to grasp it. This meant throwing in our lot with the so-called 'Coalition of the Willing'. It meant relying on George Bush. Had I known then that the American Government would make the monumental decision to go to war without having in place one scrap of post-conflict planning, thereby condemning Iraq to civil war, then no. I would never have voted to invade Iraq.

It was not the military action itself I objected to, but this lack of a tactical military and political action plan for the aftermath. During the early days of hostilities a senior Cabinet Minister said, 'Remember Oona, it's only the next three weeks.' I knew at the time that this was fantasy, although I could never have imagined the extent to which it proved to be so. And three weeks after the war began, it even seemed as though this Cabinet Minister might be proved right. But that was before the full extent of the Bush Administration's incompetence, corruption, ignorance and sheer stupidity became clear.

I still find it almost impossible to believe that three months before George Bush ordered the invasion, he did not know that Sunnis or Shias existed. He did not know that Islam comprised of two main sects. It's a bit like thinking you're going to resolve the situation in

Northern Ireland without knowing the distinction between Catholics and Protestants, or even that they exist. It defies belief that anyone could be so stupid. And on that basis, I strongly regret having sanctioned an invasion that was reliant on the Bush Administration for success.

16 March 2003

Dad has sent me an impassioned plea not to vote for war in Iraq. He mounted various arguments – illegality/ UN authority/ sanctions can work/ Bush is a tyrant/ oil is the real reason. And then he followed it up by saying I would make things difficult for my African–American family, who are all Democrats, and I shouldn't underestimate the fact that this could provoke some sort of catastrophic family rupture. As for Quincy, well, for the first time in almost twenty-five years we're hardly speaking. It breaks my heart, but we can barely be civil. Quincy is the self-appointed anti-war spokesperson for all our friends. I have about two hours free time per week, and there's no point spending it with her – either in a sullen silence or a blazing row. I hope one day I will get my best friend back.

18 April 2003 – The Sahara

The Sahara.

Sand dunes roll as far as the eye can see, towards sub-Saharan Africa. In the other direction dozens of camels – possibly hundreds – are scattered across the horizon. Beyond the horizon is the dusty end-of-the-line town, Mohammed, which leads us back towards Zagora, Marrakech, Spain and Europe. Out here in the desert, every second word is *Inshallah*. See you tonight – *Inshallah*. Conditions can be so harsh, it's only if God wills it – *Insha'Allah* – that what you hope will happen will happen. I hear that word a lot in Tower Hamlets. It is an Arabic word used by all Muslims. I like the way this one-word prayer rolls off the tongue.

Earlier today our four-wheel drive got stuck in the sand. Tiberio decided to hand the driving over to our expert Moroccan guide.

'I'm sorry, I don't know how to drive,' said the guide.

'But you said you could drive in an emergency!'

'Yes, I will learn to drive in an emergency.'

'Well how are we going to get out? We're surrounded by sand dunes as far as the eye can see, we haven't got much water, and the sun is scorching. What's the plan?'

'Someone will find us, *Inshallah*.'

A few hours later God willed it, and we were picked up by a small caravan of Land Rovers trundling through the sand. They brought us to the little oasis where we are now.

A formation of clouds floats overhead, making up a man's well-proportioned features: eyes, nose, two plump lips. One day Tiberio and I will float away. I love travelling. Have I said that before? We've had a second honeymoon. We travelled on horseback through a valley of palm trees under a starlit sky. Can't ask for more than that. It's so good to be back together, happier and stronger than when we first married.

11 June 2003 – Visit to the West Bank, the Occupied Palestinian Territories

I have travelled to the Gaza Strip and West Bank, accompanied by Lib Dem MP Jenny Tonge* and a team from Christian Aid. Today we visited Kalkilya, a village just north of Jerusalem. It is completely sealed off with 41,000 people trapped inside, because the Israelis have built a wall around it. On our way there we were stopped by Israeli soldiers at a checkpoint. One young soldier waved a grenade at us and told us to get back in the car, or he'd throw it. I didn't think he would, but I felt like challenging him. Young men and weapons, they're always the same. The barrier built by the Israelis is an apartheid-style construction, and it's incredibly insidious. It's not just the amount of space the wall takes up, or the fact that it cuts off Palestinians from employment or education – in the case of this village, these Palestinians are hermetically sealed off from the outside

---

* Following our trip to Gaza, Jenny Tonge was forced to resign from the Lib Dem frontbench, after saying that if she lived under the Israeli occupation she would consider becoming a suicide bomber.

world. But it's also that the Israelis have set up exclusion zones around the wall. They haven't built it on their own land, they've built it on Palestinian land, so Palestinians living anywhere near it are made homeless. It amounts to a massive land grab. I can't understand how the Israelis think that building a wall around the Palestinians will sort things out . . . I was just watching Ed, my cousin, in *The Pianist*, Roman Polanski's film. Ed plays Adrian Brody's brother. They're Jews in the Warsaw ghetto who've had a wall built around them. They had their homes taken away. They had their land expropriated. They had to get permits to do every single thing. They had their entire economy wiped out, virtually overnight. They had to suffer daily humiliation at the hands of German soldiers. And that is precisely what the Israelis are doing now to the Palestinians. It's just so depressing. Why would the Jews of all people repeat that hideous history? Possibly because we were so brutalised by the Holocaust, that today we'll do anything to defend ourselves. Anything at all. And Israelis live under the most terrible pressure from extreme terrorist violence and threats. Some Israelis I meet have clearly dehumanised Palestinians so they can ignore their plight. Otherwise it would be too terrible to deal with. They don't even know how a lot of Palestinians suffer.

For example, I met a Palestinian aged fifteen who had been blown up four years earlier with his younger brother when they stepped on a trip-wire left by the Israeli Army. OK, the Israeli Army didn't do it on purpose, but their Dad hears the explosion, comes running out of his house, and finds his two children in pieces on the ground. Literally legs over here, arms over there, they're bleeding to death in front of him. There are no ambulances, because the nearest hospital is in Israel, not in the Occupied Territories. So he calls a taxi. He puts his children, and their body parts, in the back of the taxi, and rushes to the nearest security checkpoint. The Israeli soldier won't let him through. The father's screaming and crying, 'My children are dying, please, look they're on the back seat and they're bleeding to death, I have to get them to a hospital.' The Israeli soldier says, 'Sorry, I can't let you through without a permit.' The father is desperate, but the soldier tells him, 'Fill in this form, and your permit should come through within three weeks.' So the younger son bleeds to death in the taxi, and the other one survives. He has limbs missing, but he survives. Most Israelis don't know that this sort of thing happens in their name. Can you imagine looking into the back of a car where there are children bleeding to death, and saying, 'Fill in this form and come back in three weeks?' A minority of Palestinians respond by committing atrocities, and it's hardly surprising.

But the interesting thing another Palestinian I met told me – and he's absolutely right – is that building this wall has nothing to do with religion; it's got everything to do with expansionism. Colonisation. Like I said, it's just a land grab, pure and simple. The way they're trying to wring every last drop of blood out of the Palestinians is so distasteful.

It's so short-sighted to build that wall. Look what happened with the Berlin Wall. It can't be there indefinitely in this day and age. One good thing: the Palestinians told us that lots of Israeli Jews have been demonstrating against the wall and demonstrating to protect Palestinian rights. You don't often hear that reported outside Israel – that Israeli Jews demonstrate to uphold the rights of Palestinians. They have written to their Knesset members, they have marched through the town. A Palestinian shopkeeper I met told us that his Jewish friends and business colleagues have been fantastic. But none the less, Kalkilya is literally being throttled. The Israeli Army are bulldozing houses, and not giving Palestinians compensation. It's such a familiar tale from Jewish history.

12 June 2003

Today I experienced possibly the strangest hour of my life. I slipped out of my MP's attire, into a *salwar kameez*, put on a headscarf, and went out into the middle of a Palestinian demonstration in the Gaza Strip. I was the only Westerner there. If I was white I could never have done it. But the advantage of being mixed race is that you can be anything you want to be. In Bangladesh I can look Asian, in Latin America I can look Brazilian, and today in the Gaza Strip I looked Palestinian. I attracted stares, but this was because I was the only woman walking alone, not because anyone suspected I was a British or American tourist, still less an MP.

I have written an article for the *Guardian* (12 June 2003) outlining my experiences here, which I'm setting out below:

The no man's land separating Israel from the Gaza Strip gives way to what can only be described as desecrated land. Razor wire and crushed buildings line the route. Torn slabs of concrete look like tattered cardboard on a rubbish heap. In front of us, two Israeli tanks block our path. Behind us, the border will shortly be sealed to prevent Palestinian reprisals for the helicopter attack launched hours earlier against the extremist Hamas leader, Abdel-Aziz al-Rantissi – who survived. A Palestinian woman and her young child, on their way to hospital, are dead, and thirty-five are injured.

Later that afternoon we hurriedly leave the building we are in when a missile lands nearby. As two British MPs travelling with Christian Aid, myself and Jenny Tonge are alarmed. For Gaza residents this is business as usual. More than one million Palestinians live on this tiny piece of land (smaller than the Isle of Wight), more than three-quarters of them on less than £1.30 a day. Life below the poverty line for these Palestinians contrasts with the 5,000 Israeli settlers who occupy one-third of the land and enjoy watered gardens, First World housing and protection by the Israeli army. This protection means Palestinians wait for hours – sometimes days – at Israeli checkpoints, trying to find work or get access to essential services such as medical care.

The sun is setting on Gaza. From my hotel balcony I hear demonstrations in the street below. It occurs to me that I can put on a headscarf and slip into the crowd as a Palestinian. No one will guess I'm Jewish, still less that I'm a British MP. The sounds lead me to the hospital where Rantissi is being treated. Cars rush into the compound, horns blaring, people hanging out of windows. A man carries an injured girl into the hospital. But most of the Palestinians just stand waiting. They wait for Israelis to stamp their permits, and they wait for a Palestinian state. They are no different from us: deny them human rights and they will respond with unacceptable terrorist violence.

That's what Jews did when they set up the Stern Gang and blew up the King David Hotel in the 1940s. Ninety-four people died. The leader of that terrorist group, on Britain's 'most wanted' list, went on to be the Israeli Prime Minister. Many Jews revere him, even while they abhor the terrorism that ruins their lives today. Israelis must be freed from terrorism – such as yesterday's horrific attack in Jerusalem. All terrorism, not least Palestinian terrorism, is abhorrent. But it is also predictable. When the Israeli Government chose Tuesday to launch an attack in Gaza (as it did again after yesterday's bombing), it cannot have been ignorant of its effect on the peace process and the certainty of Palestinian reprisals.

The original founders of the Jewish State could surely not imagine the irony facing Israel today: in escaping the ashes of the Holocaust, they have incarcerated another people in a hell similar in its nature – though not its extent – to the Warsaw ghetto.

Any visitor to the Palestinian ghetto can see the signs: residents are sealed off and live under curfew; the authorities view torture as acceptable and use collective punishment as a means of control; soldiers drive families from their homes, confiscate property and demolish neighbourhoods; unemployment runs in places at 80 per cent, and utilities such as water are withheld; the economy has 'client' status, and is subservient to the occupiers in every way.

As the more powerful side in the dispute, Israel must break the cycle of violence, comply with UN Resolution 242 and withdraw from territories occupied in 1967. As the occupying power, Israel must uphold the Fourth Geneva Convention and end all collective punishments. Illegal settlements must be dismantled. Repair of water, sewage, and other essential infrastructure should take place immediately.

Just under 80 per cent of all water resources in the West Bank and Gaza Strip are redirected from Palestinians to Israelis. The international community has to recognise the scale of the humanitarian disaster facing Palestinians and George Bush must put greater pressure on Sharon to give meaning to the road map. Yes, there are two sides to every story. But no story should hold within it the horrors I have witnessed here, so similar in detail to humiliations suffered by the Jews.

I have sadly come to the conclusion that, given the scale of the atrocities and collective punishment waged by the Israelis against the Palestinians, I have no choice but to boycott Israeli products. On reflection, whether Jewish or not, you might decide to do the same.

After publication I received about 8,000 emails from around the world, mainly from irate Jews, saying that I was an apologist for Palestinian terrorists. My argument that the Israeli Government's policies were 'similar in nature – though not extent – to the Warsaw ghetto' caused immense offence, particularly to Holocaust survivors. On reflection I recognise that it is important to distinguish between genocide and ethnic cleansing. The Nazis used the policies I outlined as a means to commit genocide, whereas the Israelis use similar tactics to engage in ethnic cleansing. The two must never be conflated, and I was wrong to do so. But well-meaning Israelis (even those suffering the daily threat of terrorist attack) are also wrong when they unwittingly become apologists for the ethnic cleansing that I saw in the Occupied Territories.

13 June 2003

It's the Cabinet reshuffle today. Probably won't get a promotion, never do, though secretly hope I might. Following my *Guardian* article yesterday, I did an interview on Jeremy Vine's BBC Radio 2 show. Thank God we got cut off, because he said, 'Oh, we've just lost the line to Jerusalem, but I was going to ask Oona King why she has called for a boycott of Israeli goods, particularly in light of the fact that Jack Straw has called for a boycott of Palestinian goods.'

I don't believe Jack has done that, I'm certain he wouldn't. But that would be a typical thing for me to do – to be in the national media contradicting a Cabinet Minister during a reshuffle. I never keep my mouth shut at the right time. It's 3.20 p.m. British time. My phone is uncharacteristically silent. Why can't they finish the reshuffle in the morning? Why do they have to torture us all day? Waited all day yesterday. Every time the phone rings you think, oh, maybe, maybe . . . and then at eight p.m. the news says, 'There will be no announcement of junior ministerial posts today.' Why can't they say that in the morning? Just bring the axe down and then I can relax.

Anyway, being here could make me suicidal, so I'm going to focus on something positive. I'm going to think about the best party I've ever been to in my life. It happened to be in my own home, which was a plus, and it was to celebrate Tiberio's fortieth. We put sofas and cushions in the garden – I say garden, but it's just cement slabs where the pub toilets used to be. Still, we turned it into a Moroccan courtyard covered with carpets and lanterns, brought the food from Italy (a present from Tiberio's parents), made spectacular cocktails – Moscow mules and mojitos – and the place was slamming. Incredibly, it didn't rain.

We brought over the best DJ, Gianni Gallicola from Naples, who played at our wedding. We also brought the cousins, you should never be without your cousins. We had Tiberio's cousins Emilio and Vincenzo, and my cousin Venie-B from Atlanta for the weekend, as well as Ed and Will. I only invited one MP – David Lammy – because most of the others wouldn't know what to do in a nightclub. Gianni did a heroic ten hour set. The party ran from 8 p.m. to 9.30 a.m. the next morning. As usual, I was the last person on the dance floor. Everyone was walking around saying, this is the best party ever, which was pretty cool, particularly as we didn't let anyone wear shoes.

How unlikely is that, to have the coolest party ever, and not allow people to wear shoes? It's pretty unlikely but it worked. Had to, our white rubber floors would have been ruined otherwise. It was a bit of a mosque sensation when you walked in – you had to take your shoes off, go upstairs, and put them on a rack. Then you had to dance for five hours. Anyway, now I think I have to go and listen to some music, because what with watching this apartheid wall being built, on the one hand, and knowing I'm not going to get promoted on the other, well, music, music is the only answer. Thank you for the music and the joy you're bringing.

So it's about six hours later, and I've just heard that again there's no promotion. Devastated. There are some complete nonentities getting promoted. At least I know my lack of promotion isn't because I'm crap. Lots of crap people get promoted. That makes me feel better. The other really good thing is that Fiona McTaggert, who I love, got a promotion. People say, 'Oh, Oona you're controversial, that's why you'll never get a promotion, because you don't keep your mouth shut.' But Fiona's the same, we're probably on a par, in fact she sometimes sounds off at Ministers more than I do – although not necessarily in public. I've been in meetings where she's shouted at Cabinet Ministers. I remember coming out of one meeting and saying, 'Um, Fiona, maybe it's not a great idea to scream at Cabinet Ministers, maybe we should try another approach.'

Anyway, Fiona got a promotion, despite being 'controversial'. So that means I wasn't overlooked because I'm controversial. Basically, I was overlooked because they don't like me. At least it's good to know where you stand. Following the 'direct request from the PM' conversation, Alastair put me on probation for five years. That was the end of 1999. I really wouldn't be surprised if at the end of 2004, or the beginning of 2005, he'll say, 'All right, you've done your time.' But then I think, 'No, maybe you've never done your time.' Because with these guys, you cross them once, and that's it. If you're not with them, you're against them. That's their mindset. And it's such a silly mindset.

Still, I am grateful to be a non-promoted MP in a Labour Government, rather than a Palestinian on the wrong side of the apartheid wall.

A journalist said to me earlier today, 'You didn't get promoted because you were really outspoken and controversial in the article you wrote in the *Guardian* yesterday. You called for a boycott of Israeli goods. Why did you do it on the day of the reshuffle?'

If that was why I didn't get promoted (although it wasn't) I would be proud. And I would say and write the same thing every time.

In fact, the main reason I didn't get promoted was because I was never in anyone's 'gang'. Reshuffles involve a series of negotiations between the most senior Government figures. A reshuffle is literally a power sharing agreement. Any aspiring MP who wants to be a Government Minister needs to find a power broker. If you haven't got a senior politician, ideally a senior Cabinet Minister, going to bat for you, then you're nowhere. Luck is always a key ingredient, and you might coincidentally fit what they're looking for. But beyond that, if someone isn't banging the table saying you have *to give my boy/girl a break (usually in return for something), well, it just won't happen.*

20 July 2003

Met Patricia Hewitt last week who said she had put in a word for me about a promotion.

'Sorry it didn't happen,' she said, 'but I wondered if you'd like to work for me as my PPS?'

We were in the Lady Members' room. Patricia is a Cabinet Minister, so being her PPS is quite a big deal.

'Wow,' I said. 'I'm grateful that someone in Government wants to work with me. That's fantastic.'

Everyone I speak to says I'll learn a lot with Patricia: she's razor sharp and on the way up.

I was Patricia's PPS for two years (2003–05). Her public persona and her private one are very different. In the press she's often slated as being prim and proper, someone who lectures or looks down on others. Patricia suffers from falling into one of two stereotypes the press have for women politicians: if they're serious, they're nannies, if they're 'human', they're lightweight. I owe Patricia a debt of gratitude. She was the only person in Government, other than Harriet Harman, who tried to help me reach my potential, and did so not just with warm words but strong actions. I don't think it's a coincidence that the two MPs who helped me most at Westminster were women.

29 July 2003

We've being doing the IVF palaver for about a month now – I'm sniffing hormones five times a day, injections in the thigh each night, scans all the time – but the thing is, it hasn't actually been too bad. In fact, Tiberio and I are saying to each other that we don't understand why everyone describes IVF as a terrible rollercoaster. It hasn't been that bad at all. Women on IVF are meant to go stark raving mad (I thought). But with the exception of a mild background headache, I've felt strangely normal.

The worst problem I've had so far was an uncontrollable giggling fit while interviewing a candidate to be my constituency caseworker. My two assistants, Frances and Lesley, and I sat on one side of a small desk in a small airless room at the top of my Bethnal Green office. It was during the heatwave. Four p.m. I'd started taking the drugs that morning, and expected to go mad any minute.

'So tell me,' I said. 'What would make you the best candidate for this job?'

Silence.

'OK then . . . um . . . tell us why you want this job?'

Silence.

Followed by the sound of me trying to strangle laughter.

'Sorry . . . sorry . . .' I gasped. 'I just . . .'

I couldn't think of anything to say. I tried to cover my face with my hand but burst out laughing instead. How can you go to a job interview and not come up with a single reason for being there?

But apart from this, as I said, no signs of madness. That's not to say people aren't conspiring to *drive* me mad. During the last two weeks of Parliament, it was my political friends doing this, not my enemies (of whom there are many, but with about three exceptions, I never remember who they are). So my political friends, the lead member for regeneration at Tower Hamlets Council, Councillor Michael Keith, and the Chief Executive, Christine Gilbert, told me in no uncertain terms I was mad to invite 150 Tower Hamlets residents to Parliament for a meeting about tackling gang violence in the constituency. Worse still I was naïve, they told me, to invite the Home Secretary David Blunkett along to hear their views, and tell them what the Government was doing.

'You'll attract terrible publicity,' said Christine. 'Our potential teaching recruits won't come to Tower Hamlets. And the meeting itself will be a witch-hunt.'

Michael was even more scathing. 'Frankly, you don't know anything about gang violence, and worse still you might spark a race riot.'

Between the two of them, they told me I'd be responsible for having no teachers in Tower Hamlets schools, and an explosion of race violence. Christine told me she was so worried about it she couldn't sleep. Her husband, Tony McNulty, who's one of my class of '97 mates and one of the nicest political thugs you'll ever meet, told me my idea was disastrous. The lot of them kept me awake at night and stressed me out to the point that I thought, at least I know this IVF cycle is never going to work.

My friend Ali would say, 'Breathe in light, breathe out darkness.' Calm.

The meeting in Parliament turned out to be a brilliant success. It was packed out. Louise Casey, head of the Antisocial Behaviour Unit in the Home Office, spoke. She was utterly outstanding. It was the last day of the Parliamentary session. David Blunkett did a star turn. And most impressive of all were the Tower Hamlets residents themselves, who came up with constructive suggestions and listened to each other patiently. My office also did a great job and we all walked out of Parliament on a high. No race riots just yet . . .

30 July 2003

Today's the day. We're leaving home at 7.45 a.m. to get to the hospital for eight for the egg collection. I'm apprehensive and excited. Another mini-trip. I've packed my little hospital bag which adds to the adventure.

The operation – which is less an operation than a procedure – involves my being half conscious and the doctors removing the eggs that have been stimulated by the drugs. With a needle. They poke around and dig them out.

With IVF it's not just pressure for the woman. The man has to produce a sperm sample on demand. This morning, neither of us have ever been so turned off and stressed in our whole ten year relationship. We suddenly slide into a panic that makes anything connected to sex unthinkable. No sperm sample. Tiberio is completely ambushed by the situation. I tell him not to worry, I'll call the hospital and explain we're late. I'll ask if we can postpone it until the afternoon.

The doctor is sympathetic but firm. It's now 8.45 a.m. If the sperm sample isn't at the hospital within forty-five minutes – by 9.30 a.m. – they'll have to cancel the operation. Cancel the IVF cycle. Cancel the kids. My heart is in my mouth. Tiberio is ashen.

'Tell me we've got more time,' he says.

'Yes, we've got time. Don't worry, it'll be fine.'

'How long? How long exactly?'

'Oh . . . probably a couple of hours.'

'A couple of hours, no way. What are we going to do?'

'Porn?' I venture.

'Porn.'

'Yeah, porn. Have you got any porn?'

'No.' Typical. I thought you could rely on even the nicest man to have a porn mag. This meant I'd have to go and buy him one from the newsagent opposite. From the lovely couple who think we're nice normal people, not the sort that buy porn at nine a.m. on a Wednesday morning. It's my turn to look ashen. Tiberio goes to buy some porn, but there isn't any in that nice decent shop. I go upstairs to see if I can find some proper porn on the internet. It can't be that difficult. Surely. I get at least fifty spam emails per week offering a thicker, bigger penis and God knows what else. Parents around the world are up in arms because their kids can access porn at the click of a mouse. But we dismantled our computer for Tiberio's fortieth birthday party, so the only access I have to the internet is via the parliamentary intranet.

I simply cannot use my parliamentary internet account to view porn. But I also can't throw away this chance to have children (not to mention the £3,500 already spent on the IVF treatment) because I'm worried the Sergeant-at-Arms office will start whispering about me ('You'll never believe what that Oona King gets up to in the morning'), or because I'll be caught in one of those police dragnets and read about it in the *News of the World*.

I do a Google search and type in porn. Feeling like a borderline criminal, I am drawn towards the 'No credit cards required' websites.

Click here to download now. My finger hovers over the mouse. What will my colleagues think? Never mind that, what will my constituents think? I can't bring myself to click.

Nine a.m. I should be in the operating room by now. I stare at the screen, which offers Asian babes and S & M and anal this and hardcore that.

I think about all the eggs inside me. We'll have to throw them away. The anguish makes me want to vomit.

I leave Tiberio looking at the parliamentary intranet, go downstairs and play the piano. There are only three pieces I ever play: Bach, Schubert and Schumann – all from my Grade Seven exam nearly twenty years ago. It's no wonder my fertility is clapped-out if I took my Grade Seven exam *twenty years ago*. In three months I'll be thirty-six.

At 9.30 a.m., Tiberio says the Parliamentary intranet is so slow it's worse than useless. I tell Tiberio to forget it. We'll go for a walk. Assume the cycle is cancelled. Maybe that'll help. We're putting our trainers on. Time is up. I change my mind – we can't play for time any longer, because there isn't any. Let's just go straight to the hospital. Maybe they can think of something . . .?

It's a fifteen minute drive. A miracle happens. Not a creation miracle, a parking miracle. It's 9.45 a.m. and the parking gods have smiled on us. We find a parking place – the only parking place in a road packed tightly with cars – and walk down the side street to the hospital. The sky is strikingly grey. We feel like dead men walking. In the fertility unit the consultant, Richard Howells, ushers us into a tiny room. He explains why the procedure can't be postponed.

'We gave you drugs exactly thirty-six hours ago, to stimulate the release of your eggs at,' he looks at his watch, 'well, *now*. Once your eggs are released it's extremely tricky to try and get them back. Any cramps?'

I shake my head. I'm grateful to my ovaries. No matter what the medication, I can always rely on them to be late.

'OK, well, basically you have thirty minutes at the outside . . . if the eggs aren't released before.'

No pressure then.

Various questions. 'What will happen to the eggs?'

'They'll be discarded.'

'Can't they be donated to a woman who wants donor eggs?'

'No, it'll be too late.'

'Can't you go ahead with the operation anyway, remove the eggs and freeze them?'

'No, it's illegal under current legislation to remove eggs without the sperm.'

'Is there any alternative to abandoning the cycle?'

'No.'

Richard's a nice guy. But there's nothing he can do.

Tiberio looks at his watch. 'Well, if we've got so little time left, we might as well give it a go. Come on.' They put us in a room so small you couldn't swing a cat. All around us are the noises of a busy hospital unit: other patients being led up the stairs to a consultation room above; doors opening and closing; instructions to nursing staff being shouted up and down the corridor. A clothes hook on the back of the door holds up an enormous pair of trousers for someone with a fifty inch waist. Medical weighing scales on greyish carpet. I would be less surprised to meet Saddam Hussein than I would to meet someone who conjured up a sperm sample in here.

Fifteen minutes gone. A phone rings.

Twenty minutes gone. Let's get outta here.

Twenty-five minutes gone. This is hell.

Thirty minutes gone. £3,500 gone.

We PAID for this misery. Unbelievable. And then a David Beckham moment. Only ten seconds of extra time remaining, the final free kick, all hope is lost, but he's pulled it out the bag, it's in the back of the net, GOOOOAALLLL!

I start to cry with relief at the sight of a sperm sample, but then remember there isn't time, and stop abruptly. The doctor appears with a smile, although I expect to see Saddam Hussein instead.

Within moments, we're inside the operating room, I have a drip put in my arm for the pethidine woozy painkiller. The drugs haven't been administered yet and I already feel I'm having an out-of-body experience. After all, I knew for a fact that this wasn't going to happen. A few minutes ago I was preparing myself for the psychological trauma of an abandoned IVF cycle. The fallout for Tiberio would have kept a psychoanalyst busy for years. As for me I'm so stressed I can hardly breathe. The hospital's literature says, 'Patients undergoing egg collection and embryo implantation should be as relaxed as possible.'

The doctor administers the pethidine and the effect is immediate. After a while the doctor says, 'That's great, we've got an egg.' A few moments later, 'That's two eggs, three eggs. Fantastic, five eggs, seven eggs, we're doing really well here.' There is some pain when the needle has to puncture an internal wall. But the pethidine takes care of it, and Tiberio takes care of me. He's whispering to me in Italian all the time: '*Siamo sulla spiaggia. Sopra di noi c'e un grande cielo blu con qualche nuvoletta bianca, andiamo a farci il bagno*.'

'Ten eggs. That's great.'

'*Allora possiamo restare distesi sulla sabia a guardare le nuvole.*'

'Eleven eggs, Twelve eggs . . . Thirteen eggs . . . That's an unlucky number,' says the doctor. 'Let's look for a fourteenth egg. We can't stick on thirteen.'

I don't really mind any more. I'm floating above Tiberio's white sandy beach in a very blue sky.

'Wow, we got fourteen,' says the doctor. 'Oh, sixteen.' He seems less pleased. 'Hmm, seventeen . . . eighteen . . .'

Now everyone else in the operating room has gone quiet.

'Nineteen eggs . . .'

'That's twenty eggs.'

It turns out that whereas fourteen was excellent, twenty is bad. Very bad. They're worried that I have Ovarian Hyper-Stimulation Syndrome (OHSS) which can, in rare cases, be fatal. The doctor says it looks as though they'll have to cancel the cycle. Twenty eggs is their cut-off point. If I'd had twenty-one eggs the procedure would have been automatically cancelled. My hormone levels are too high.

'You'll know if you've got OHSS in about twenty-four to thirty-six hours. Nausea, vomiting, etc. You'll be in hospital for two weeks. It's extremely serious. You'll be very ill.'

Tiberio and I leave the hospital a few hours later. We're shell-shocked. What were we saying about IVF not being a rollercoaster? This is the big dipper from hell. The next day we ring up to get the results of the sperm and egg party in a Petri dish. Did any of them hit it off? Were the sperm and eggs good enough quality? In the end, Tiberio came up with nine million sperm. The best were chosen and added to eighteen of the twenty eggs (two hadn't matured sufficiently). Of these eighteen, fourteen fertilised. We have fourteen embryos. In the IVF world this is a great result – as long as I don't drop dead from OHSS.

1 August 2003

Our embryologist Maxine – who, bizarrely, turns out to be David Lammy's cousin – is very pleased. She says they're really good quality embryos and the next day we go in to look at them and choose which two get implanted. I've had no signs of OHSS so on Friday morning the consultant says the cycle is back on again. When we go in to see the embryos, I realise this might be the closest we ever get to attending a parents' evening. In fact, given that this might be the closest we ever get to being parents, I suggest we have a family portrait. Ha ha.

Maxine says all fourteen embryos are good enough quality to freeze. So nine have been frozen and there are five for us to see. 'This one's perfect,' Maxine says, proudly showing off a very symmetrical embryo. 'In fact, it's textbook perfect.' And she goes on to explain why. The second one is less perfect and more lopsided. The four cells aren't even. And the remaining three are all over the place. They look mashed.

Maxine feigns outrage at my disdain and says that the mangled ones are better than many of the embryos some couples get to choose from. 'So which do you want to go back? I mean, obviously it's up to you both, but I'd suggest these two.'

'OK, we'll take perfect embryo and lopsided embryo, and you can hold the mangled embryos.'

The three mangled embryos go back in the freezer. I'm really not too keen on using frozen embryos, which is why we're glad we've been able to go ahead with the 'fresh' embryo transfer. All the research shows no difference at all between babies born from fresh embryos, compared to their frozen counterparts. I'm not arguing with the research, but you just never know. None of these children are over twenty yet. I wouldn't be completely shocked if children born from frozen embryos reached thirty or forty and something strange happened, like their arms fell off. Because you know how it is when you defrost things. Microwaved food never tastes quite as good. So that's why I'm pleased that somehow or other we've got this far. Having the eggs implanted is no worse than a smear test. Everyone is optimistic but I guess that's their job. Until a couple of years ago, the national average success rate for IVF was 13 per cent. Today it's 23 per cent. In the most successful clinics, including the Homerton, it's as high as 40 per cent. Because I'm comparatively young, because we have 'good quality' embryos and because I've conceived naturally in the past, they tell us our odds are a whopping

50 per cent. Amazing. Jenny, one of the nurses who takes my blood regularly, tells me to go home and relax. 'These next two weeks will feel like months.'

We leave the hospital at noon and drive to Greenwich Filmworks to watch a beautiful film, *Whale Rider*. I thought it was a better idea to go home and be very still, but everyone – consultant, nurse, embryologist – said it would be better to go and watch a film.

14 August 2003

Over the next two weeks I go in to the constituency office a couple of times (Parliament is in recess for the summer), but I mainly do admin from home. I clear my emails for the first time since last year. The first week goes by OK, but during the second week time gets slower and slower. Eventually it seems to stop. We will find out if it has worked on Friday.

On Wednesday I'm trying to finish a joint article I'm writing with Tristram Hunt on the Congo. He texts me to ask how the writing is going. Badly, I reply. I feel bad in general. I feel un-pregnant. But you never know. It's never over till it's over. Last week I thought I was definitely pregnant. This week I feel I'm definitely not. On Thursday, in a toilet in a restaurant in Clerkenwell where I'm meeting Slate for lunch, it's definitely over. I see red, I see blood. It's three years to the day that I had the miscarriage, and now, like then, I can stop hoping.

19 October 2003

Joy of joys, the happiest I can ever be: tucked up in bed with Tiberio at 8.30 p.m. on a Sunday night. Wake up at six a.m., but use all my will power to shut down my brain and go back to sleep. Wake up just after eight a.m. and lie in bed, determined to be 'asleep' until 8.30 a.m. About once every six months I sleep for twelve hours and it makes me serene.

Radio tells me Tony Blair's been taken into hospital with an irregular heartbeat. Look at my diary, which says, '6.45 p.m.,

Reception with PM for PPSs.' Well at least that's cancelled, I think. Bummer, it's still on, John Prescott will be there instead . . .

Tullio and Esia (Tiberio's parents) are leaving today, having measured and mended and cooked and cleaned and sewn and basically sorted everything in the house. Apart from the roof, which is leaking and about to collapse.

Go to Parliament, vote on the Courts Bill, then have dinner with Fiona MacTaggert and Yvette Cooper. We have a discussion about equality versus choice. I've had a bee in my bonnet about this since the last LP conference, when the *Guardian* organised a dinner for female MPs – Patricia, Harriet, Margaret Hodge, Yvette, Estelle, Tessa Jowell and some journalists – among them Polly Toynbee, Jackie Ashley, Madeleine Bunting, etc.

At dinner with Fiona and Yvette, the conversation polarised around equality versus choice, with Blairites mainly advocating choice and Brownites equality. The two don't have to be mutually exclusive.

But my concern is when choice – as a means of encouraging competition – is used to drive up standards. Often competition is the most effective way to drive up standards. But sometimes, particularly in relation to public services that preclude a functioning free market, it doesn't work. Worse, it can have the opposite effect.

Take schools, or hospitals. At the end of the day parents and patients want the same thing: good teachers and good doctors and good local schools and hospitals. The market is only of limited use, because there isn't enough capacity in the system – and never could be – to permit customers to take their children to any school they want. So it's a false paradigm. I'm hoping to find a third way on this one, but if I have to choose, I'll take equality over choice every time.

21 October 2003

Wake up at 5.30 a.m. Tiberio is already awake. Both of us are completely wound up. He's going out of his mind trying to pass an entry test to be admitted to an MBA course. The test, GMAT (General Maths and English) is suited to people who have recently finished a maths degree. Tiberio says he was *never* good at maths and he finished his course fifteen years ago, so no surprise it's killing him. I looked at some of the English tests; tricky even for me! As for the maths . . . well, anyone who isn't a maths student doesn't have a prayer. Questions like: 'John is in a lift on the twentieth floor, travelling down at six floors per minute. Susan is on the second floor travelling up at eight floors per minute. Which floor do they pass each other on?'

The really hilarious thing is that you might possibly be able to work it out in twenty minutes, but the maximum time allowed per GMAT question is one minute.

So Tiberio can't sleep because of that, and I can't sleep because I'm suddenly enraged at *yet again* not having been promoted, but having to listen to Blairites give speeches about 'meritocracy'.

Drive to Westminster for meeting with Jack Straw on the Middle East, but as I'm driving along the Embankment I hear on the radio that he's in Iran, so I decide to go to the Crossrail debate in Westminster Hall.

Lib Dems get up and make a typically vacuous statement – they have no costings or other data to back up their assertions. But then John Redwood gets up and he's just so nasty about the Lib Dems that I remind myself that no matter how irritating the Lib Dems are, they're always better than the Tories.

15 October 2003

Went to the Editorial Board meeting of *The House Magazine* for the first time this morning. *The House Magazine* is the House of Commons' prestigious magazine, written by MPs for MPs. It's run by a committee of MPs – the editorial board – which is chaired by Sir Patrick Cormack, FSA MP. Don't know what FSA stands for. Probably code for Knight of the Realm, or top banana man. Anyway, he's a charming Tory and has been around the House for decades – was probably a Cabinet Minister.

Actually, no, if he'd been in the Cabinet, his title would be RT HON Sir Patrick Cormack FSA MP TOP BANANA. Why is it that those at the top and the bottom like to garnish their names with anything to hand? It's the Mr Joe Bloggs Esq. BA (Hons) syndrome.

Anyway, Sir Patrick wrote me a letter complimenting me on my speech to second the Queen's Speech, and asked if I'd like to join *The House Magazine* editorial board. This is a generous offer, given that it's usually older MPs who have made their mark in the Commons that get asked to be on the board.

Sir Patrick started the meeting with a discussion on replacements for the departing cartoonist. Did any of the twelve MPs and peers sitting round the table know a talented cartoonist we could employ?

Austin Mitchell and Sylvia Herman made suggestions. The rest of us didn't know any talented cartoonists.

'I don't meant to be impertinent,' I ventured, 'but is there any possibility that we might have an open selection process?'

I could tell by the polite but rigid stare that fixed itself to Sir Patrick's face that the suggestion of open competition was tantamount to subterfuge. 'I just mean,' I continued, 'it's conceivable that we might be unaware of some talented cartoonists.'

Sir Patrick evidently assumes that 'equal opportunities' means asking Labour MPs to suggest their friends for jobs as well as Tory MPs.

Sir Patrick replied, 'Oona, you're a *new* MP, so you may not be aware of how we like to do things around here.'

New MP? In what other job could you be considered new after you'd been there for over six years? Patrick's a nice man. Actually he's a very nice man, so many of the bloody Tories are. But they just can't grasp how inappropriate the old boy network is. The matter was closed and we moved on to the next agenda item.

Lord Geoffrey Howe then piped up with something informed and interesting about forthcoming American and Russian elections. Was he the one that savaged Margaret Thatcher like a dead sheep? Can't remember. It's weird how all those Tories who used to run the country have just faded from memory.

20 October 2003

First week back at Westminster after the operation. Coming down with flu. Woke up at three a.m. and settled down with a Lemsip in front of a documentary on Easter Island. They were a fab civilisation, but cut down all the palm trees to build statues, virtually wiped themselves out, and were finished off by the Europeans, who brought guns and syphilis and smallpox. Captain James Cook sailed by, and I'm interested to note that he started his journey only a few hundred yards from where I'm sitting, in the Mile End Road.

Wake up to Radio 4: 'The PM will this morning address Labour MPs over their fears on Iraq.' Better get on the Lemsip and in the car. Sitting in the meeting now. Completely packed out with about 400 people. The PM looks grave and tired. Last week Jack Straw said the odds of war were sixty–forty against. The Chair of the PLP appeals for colleagues not to speak to the press afterwards, as it's supposed to be a private meeting. TB says he doesn't know how likely it is that what he says will remain private, as he hasn't asked Jack for odds yet. Jack shouts out, 'Ten to one against.' That's generous.

On Iraq, TB says that if George Bush wasn't leading on this issue, then he would be, and that he raised the link between terrorism and weapons of mass destruction in April 2001, before September 11th and before George Bush took an interest. He certainly made us vote on it back then, that's for sure.

Someone said to me the other day, 'Stop the War in Iraq.' I said, 'I haven't *started* the war in Iraq.' That wasn't us, remember, it was Saddam. He's the one that let his Army loose on the Iraqi people. And the Kuwaiti people. And the Iranian people. It's only a detail, but quite an important one.

19 November 2003

I keep winning parliamentary bingo. My numbers come up in PMQs all the time. This week I'm number eight. I'm almost running out of subjects. Not questions – obviously I always have thousands of questions, but in terms of subjects I've done most of my important ones: housing, human rights, the Middle East, youth services, Iraq, policing, poverty.

Today I asked a PMQ about the lack of women in Parliament, and in particular the lack of women on the opposition benches. Labour needs to do more – a quarter of our MPs are women. But the Tories and Lib Dems need to start from scratch. A whopping 92 per cent of Tory MPs are still men. Even worse, they all wear the same ties. And the Lib Dems only have three women MPs – in percentage terms they're worse than the Tories.

The Speaker said the PM couldn't answer for the opposition frontbench. Tony's answer was basically, 'Phew'. Can you imagine being responsible for equalities in the Tory Party?

One of the MPs I sit next to, Betty Williams, has helped me develop a new trick. She holds my piece of paper with bullet points on it, rests it nonchalantly on her knee, and I stand up, looking confident because I'm not holding an Order Paper. An Order Paper is the House of Commons daily agenda, and MPs use the back of it as a notepad. An MP with an Order Paper is like a baby with a dummy. It soothes you and stops you getting hysterical. Basically, in the House of Commons if you can't ask a question without referring to notes, usually scribbled on the Order Paper, you're considered rubbish. It's a bit of a harsh rule considering what a bear pit PMQs can be. Quite suddenly, without warning, you can lose the ability to think or speak. Your name has just been called in a packed House of Commons, your face is being broadcast live around the country, every political journalist is watching, and you can't remember what you wanted to say. You can't think why you stood up in the first place. You can't imagine why you ever wanted to be an MP. All you can hear is your heart beating louder than a cannonball, and all you can taste is humiliation mixed with adrenaline. It only happened to me once, and it wasn't in PMQs, it was in the Stephen Lawrence debate. But it was enough, and I'll never tread happily without an Order Paper again. It just *looks* as though I do, because Betty has it resting on her knee.

The PM answers my question about glass ceilings and pay gaps and work–life balance, and when I sit down in this boys' assembly, I elbow Betty in the ribs to signal appreciation.

22 November 2003

I can't believe it. I just can't believe it. England won something. It might be the first time in my life. OK, it was rugby not football and they're the ugliest sods I've ever seen, but it was beautiful to watch. A dream. Champions of the world. Beat the Ozzies. The Empire strikes back. With determination and pot bellies.

2004

The Worldwide Conspiracy
and the Sunny Uplands

14 February 2004

Valentine's Day. I'm sitting on a runway in Saudi Arabia. I'm not supposed to be here. Bangladesh Airlines – Biman – took a wrong turn. I should be extremely grateful that they upgraded me to business (BA never would) but there are mozzies in the cabin, I already have four new surgery cases from Tower Hamlets passengers, the man on my left only stops talking if he's snoring loudly, the man on my right is holding a screaming baby, the flight is eight hours late and, instead of being in London on Valentine's Day, I'm unexpectedly in Saudi. Two million people are supposed to be here for Haj, but not me.

I've had a really good trip to India and Bangladesh. I visited India as part of the APPG Friends of India, and then added a visit to Bangladesh as a follow-up to the trip I made earlier with the International Development Select Committee. Bangladesh is a beautiful and colourful country, if only the politicians could stop ruining it. It has one of the most destructive and useless political cultures I've ever come across. On the other hand, Bangladesh has a far more developed voluntary sector than Britain (admittedly of necessity – they'd have gone to hell in their oft-quoted basket long ago otherwise). Anyway, for good or bad I love the country, but like most Bangladeshis, I prefer to fly British Airways.

First we couldn't leave because the brakes weren't working, and they had to find a new plane from somewhere in the Middle East; then, once we'd boarded, the captain said he couldn't find a 'starting card'. I think he was trying to say he'd lost the keys. Hours later, as we started racing down the runway, everyone appeared to be praying. The plane was swerving and rattling like a tin can. It was the worst take-off I've ever experienced. The plane kept *not* taking off. Never mind the brakes, it was obvious the *wings* weren't working. While waiting for us to crash I did a bit of calming nonsense, intoning to myself, 'I am a calm person. My mind and my body are relaxed (and ready to die).' At least I'd just rung Tiberio and Mum and said my goodbyes. I was worried about Dad. And then, once we were finally airborne, we were told we were going to Saudi Arabia instead of Heathrow. Biman. You pays your fare, you takes your chances.

Yesterday I visited a great project in Sylhet, north-east Bangladesh – Friends in Village Development Bangladesh. They help very poor villagers, usually women, find sustainable employment by investing small amounts of capital (I don't think of a £10 note as capital, but here it is). In my speech I described the image that stays with me from the trip I made through India with Quin and Sash (one of my other best friends from school) when we were eighteen. I was in a remote village, watching a young woman in her twenties standing barefoot in cow dung under a hot sun, shovelling shit. Next to her was her ten-year-old daughter, shovelling shit. And before this woman, her mother and her grandmother had also shovelled shit. As I stood there in that earth-cracking heat I realised that the sun would more likely fall from the sky, than that ten-year-old girl escape her fore-mothers' fate. Her future was trapped in the Middle Ages.

It was the same when I visited Bangladesh with the International Development Select Committee and we visited a brothel where young girls are 'born' into prostitution. No careers advice for them, just an 80 per cent chance of contracting AIDS and a 100 per cent certainty of daily rape. Sexual slavery is alive and well in the twenty-first century. So, what was it I was complaining about? Oh yeah, this flight is a real drag.

In the end, as we sat there on the runway in Saudi Arabia, I decided to do a 'meet and greet' with the rest of the plane. I didn't feel great, but once when I was on a Virgin flight from Washington, Richard Branson came down from the mists of First Class to visit the rest of us in Economy. He shook hands with every single person on the jumbo jet. Even though he can be a bit silly, I respected his political instincts. Making yourself accessible is what it's about, not hiding beyond the reach of the people who put you where you are.

When I walked down the aisle to the back of the plane, shaking hands, saying hello, people were really pleased to see me, if surprised. Half of them were from Tower Hamlets – 'We voted for you, Ooo-nah-king! Do you remember visiting my uncle's house in Wapping, Ooo-nah-king? Thanks for sorting out my cousin's immigration problem, Ooo-nah-king! You gave out achievement certificates to my class, Ooo-nah-king! Will you come and have a curry in Daneford House, Ooo-nah-king? Can you write to Biman to complain about this service, Ooo-nah-king? We would like to offer you this sari as a gift, Ooo-nah-king. How often do you meet Tony Blair, Ooo-nah-king?'

The half that weren't from Tower Hamlets were even happier to see me, because familiarity can only breed contempt. But in general, whether you're liked or loathed, most people enjoy meeting someone they see on the telly, if only so they can say, 'I met that tosser off the TV.' Apart from the Congo, Bangladesh is the only place where my visit makes the evening news most evenings. They all know I've been in Dhaka and Sylhet over the last few days, and they're happy to have something that takes their minds off the next few hours. I am a strange smiling thing, an 'Ooonahking-thing', a single word without a first name.

In the departure lounge before take-off, I'd spoken to two young guys and promised to say hello during the flight. I found Moorshed, a slight, bespectacled twenty-five-year-old, sitting on his own near the back, looking extremely ill. He was having an asthma attack and couldn't breathe. I've never realised how frightening an asthma attack can be. For the next four hours I looked after him. Someone sitting behind him who turned out to be a first-aider, Abdul, helped me. Abdul said Moorshed needed oxygen. I asked the crew for their oxygen canisters but they refused. They said they didn't want to be held liable if anything went wrong. It took me an hour to get the canisters, but when they arrived, neither of them worked.

Later I got Moorshed a sick bag and put my hand in to open it. When I found my hand covered in someone else's vomit I got distracted and let Moorshed walk off on his own. A few minutes later I found him unconscious on the floor. Even though he was prostrate, the crew refused to put him in Business Class where he could lie down, so I did a theatrical, Bangladeshi-style, 'Do you know who I am?' routine, and finally got him and Abdul upgraded. The only thing more irritating than spending Valentine's Day with mozzies in Business Class in Saudi, is spending it with mozzies in Economy. That's where I am for the rest of the flight, because my 'Do you know who I am?' skills aren't adequately honed. On a bright note, I got a text message from Patricia Hewitt before we took off, telling me that Kitty (Ussher) has won the parliamentary selection for Burnley. Fantastic news. She'll be an MP after the next election.*

27 February 2004

I was about to start some paperwork and was rummaging about in my bag for a pen when I saw my iPAQs cute little portable keyboard and realised I'd much rather play with gadgets than work. And anyway, it's eight p.m. on a Friday night (it's quite repetitive the way I justify myself), so why shouldn't I?

This week started at four a.m. on Monday. Tiberio has been having a nightmare with his MBA. He's working as hard as he can in his day job. He wakes up to study in the middle of the night (three or four a.m. mostly) and then can't go back to sleep. The doctor gave him something to help him sleep, but Tiberio thinks it's making things worse, because when he takes the medicine his heart-rate shoots up. This Monday morning was bad. He was tossing and turning, and got up at about 5.45 a.m. to shave. I could hear him in the bathroom, really struggling with his breathing. I thought, 'I'll get up and comfort him,' and then, being momentarily evil, I thought, 'No, I'm too knackered to move, I'll go back to sleep.'

Thank God, I got up and went into the bathroom. He was leaning on the sink, both arms outstretched. We went through the deep breathing routine. I put the toilet seat down and made him sit on it. He was breathing too quickly and too hard, shallow breaths snatched in panic. 'It's the medicine,' he said, 'I'm having a bad reaction to it, it's not normal.'

---

* Kitty was elected in May 2005 and got a well-deserved promotion to become a Government minister under Gordon Brown in June 2007.

'You just have to breathe more slowly and relax,' I said, knowing it's easier said than done. I remember being in A & E, having the miscarriage, panicking, losing control of my breathing and going into spasm. But I carried on with the saccharine advice.

'Just relax.' Tiberio leaned back, eyes closed, his head tilted back.

'Perhaps you shouldn't lean so far back,' I said, 'that might make it harder for you to breathe.'

Tiberio was very composed, but he didn't seem to be listening any more.

'Babe,' I said more than firmly. 'Don't lean your head back.' Irritated, I shook him: '*Babe*, sit up properly.' The realisation that he was unconscious was so sudden it was like an electric shock.

'TIBERIO!!! TIBERIO!!! WAKE UP!!!' I shook him hard.

I pulled him towards me and everything rolled. His head rolled, his eyes rolled into the back of his sockets, and wild thoughts of unarticulated terror rolled around my mind. My husband was dying, my husband was dead.

'Tiberio!!! DON'T do this, just DON'T do this. Jesus Christ.' Lots of thoughts, less than a fraction of a second each. Recovery position. Get him on the floor. He's had a reaction to the medicine. He said it wasn't normal. Make sure his windpipe is clear. Open his mouth. Don't put your fingers in his mouth. Amazing coincidence that Quin told me that this weekend. (If someone falls unconscious, and you want to make sure they don't choke on their tongue, you mustn't put your fingers in their mouth. If they spasm they'll bite them off. Our friend had passed out just a fortnight ago at our place during a 'girls lunch'. Quin put her in the recovery position. That's the only reason I knew how).

The wild thoughts continued as I pushed and shoved Tiberio into the right position. 'Maybe he's having a heart attack. Maybe I should pump his heart. Haven't called an ambulance yet. Must leave him on the floor, don't dare leave. CALL AN AMBULANCE! LEAVE! Switch the mobile on. Why does it take so long? Why don't we have a functioning landline?'

And all the time I'm shouting at Tiberio: 'Don't leave me, don't leave me, DON'T LEAVE ME!!!'

'What, babe?'

Later he told me he could hear me screaming, 'Don't leave me,' but he didn't know why. It turns out he was having a severe allergic reaction to the medication.

So that was Monday morning. It's been a long week. The Friday before I decided to finally clean up my filthy hovel of a constituency office. I've been nagging my staff to clear it up properly for about a year. The point is, they do the most important thing, which is respond to more than 300 constituency enquiries/ emergencies/ lunacies each week, so I feel it's a bit churlish of me to go on about the state of the office. But it does my head in. There are piles of things everywhere, desks overflowing and I'm convinced most of it could either be filed or binned.

It's made worse by the fact that we don't have a cleaner. Why is it that junior HR managers have cleaners, but if you're an MP you have to clean the toilet yourself if you want it done? The last time I cleaned the toilet was about three years ago. Thank God our local LP Chair, Graham Taylor, is a diamond geezer, extraordinarily generous with his weekends, which he regularly donates to Labour Party cleanliness. A losing battle, you'd have thought.

A cleaner isn't the only basic thing the office lacks. Both here and at Westminster, we don't have adequate computers, printer cartridges, or stationery. I often exhort my staff to go out and steal Post-it notes and biros. I'm surprised Portcullis House, the new Parliament building, didn't fall off the back of a lorry. Quite the opposite. A committee of MPs (can you imagine anything worse than a committee of MPs overseeing the construction?) managed to buy cladding that cost the same as it would to cover the whole building from top to bottom in Lamborghini sports cars. Still, it's a beautiful building to work in (except when we had an outbreak of rats), so I lead a schizophrenic existence, flitting between its palatial corridors and the seedy, filthy, shit hole that is my constituency office in Bethnal Green.

At one point I decided to paint the front, so at least it looked OK from the outside. I thought green would be good, but to my horror it came out blue, which isn't good for a Labour Party office. Anyway, last Friday I decided the time had come to tackle the inside properly for the first time since I was elected in 1997. I did paperwork in the morning, went to Nando's at lunchtime with the team, sent them out to leaflet an estate for our 'Big (little) Conversation' on 'Childcare and Barriers to Employment' that we're having on Monday, and once they were gone, began to sort out the office.

I was determined to bring order to chaos, down to the very last paper clip. I estimated it would take six hours, so I'd finish at nine p.m. I know from experience things always take 50 per cent longer than anticipated, so I thought (but didn't quite believe) that I might not get out till midnight. Tiberio was at Cranfield and I'd planned a quiet night with a video. In the event I staggered out of the office at four a.m. and went next door to get a cab. I was shattered, but the office was pristine, down to that very last paper clip. I was triumphant, but then deflated when I found there were no cabs and I would have to walk the half-hour journey home from Bethnal Green to Mile End. Gutted. And, for the first time, apprehensive, as I walked along a deserted Roman Road. There has been so much violence in the area recently it's getting out of hand. Why has it suddenly got worse? Don't know. I wanted the office clean and tidy, but not at the expense of being mugged. (A few days later, Ally in my office tells me a woman was dragged off the Roman Road by three men and gang-raped.)

There's a sign just fifty yards from my front door that says, 'Warning: muggings take place in this area.' And then a week later, this Friday morning, I found the door to my office had been kicked in. They didn't nick anything, so they either wanted to get something out (a file?) or get something in (a bug? Anthrax? Paranoia?). But the most important thing was that they didn't trash the office after I'd just cleaned it up. That would have pushed me over the edge.

1 March 2004

Fantastic to visit Mum in Toulouse this weekend. Mum's bum is in better shape than mine because she walks about fifteen miles a week with her dogs. Her German shepherd, Berlioz (his predecessors were called Amadeus, Schumann and Bartok), is amazingly regal and handsome and bounds around like a lion in the Serengeti. Her stray mongrel that she got from pet rescue, Grieg, is smaller than Berlioz and looks a bit like a jet-black fox. The most distinguishing aspect of his personality is that he is hysterical in every sense. Mum has a new car, a sort of utilitarian minivan with a box built in the back for the dogs. Gone are the days of the Dogmobile which was like driving around in a kennel . . . And also gone is the fantasy I've had since childhood that I would buy her the first new car she ever owned. Can't believe I'm an MP and still can't do the basics for my parents.

Back to Westminster. David Lammy did really well as Minister today, responding to the new God-awful Asylum and Immigration Bill. He's mastered the politician's essential rule of thumb: when in doubt, attack.

Leaving the Chamber after the vote on the Bill, I bumped into Geoff Hoon, recently beleaguered Defence Secretary, bounding down the stairs with his red briefcase.

'Got any gossip, Geoff?'

'*Moi*?'

'*Toi*.'

'I know nothing.'

I was about to say, 'Well that's certainly what you told the Hutton Inquiry about why we went to war in Iraq.' But I thought better of it. He's for the chop, and there's no point dancing on graves. Having said that, he treated me like *dirt* when I was an assistant at the European Parliament. He wouldn't remember that, but it reminds me that it's never a good idea to act like an arrogant sod to people you think are irrelevant . . . they'll turn up at some point or other in another life, or worse still, you'll turn up in their book.

The vote finished at about ten p.m. It's now after midnight, I'm outta here.

Asked Gordon if he would meet with the Bengali Finance Minister. Gordon's always really helpful. But still, don't know if he'll manage it. Two weeks ago in Bangladesh that same Finance Minister gave me a box of exquisitely flavoursome home-grown tomatoes. Hope that doesn't represent 'tomatoes-for-access' New Labour sleaze.

I also asked Gordon to throw his weight behind getting some

Muslim candidates selected in safe seats, especially Shahid Malik.*
You never know how anyone's going to turn out, but Shahid, at this
stage, is at *least* as good as 90 per cent of MPs and shouldn't be
carved up like he has been. It's a scandal that the Labour Party hasn't
selected more ethnic minority candidates for safe seats. Gordon says
he'll try and do something about it. The only bit of good news in a
sea of doom is that Yasmin Qureshi has been selected in Brent East.
Hope to God she wins, if she does she'll be our first elected Asian
woman MP, in the same way that I'm the first elected mixed-race
woman MP.† It'll probably take five years for another Asian woman
(or black or mixed-race) to come along, but I hope not.

2 March 2004

Did paperwork at Westminster until 1.30 a.m. Last time I looked
at my watch it was three a.m. Why does it take so long to get into
bed? One of the things I love most is the way Tiberio hugs me tight
in his sleep when I get in to bed. We always go to sleep like that,
and after eleven years, that's not bad. Can't believe we once lived
in different countries – him in Milan, me in Brussels. But we were
young then, ha ha. Now we're old we realise how much we need
each other.

Should it be 'him in Milan' or 'he in Milan'? I think it's the latter,
but that sounds too poncey. Got Mum the book *Eats, Shoots and
Leaves: The Zero Tolerance Approach to Punctuation.* I'd have a
zero tolerance approach if my punctuation was good enough. As it
is, in my office I have a semi-zero tolerance approach, a half-
pregnant tendency to go berserk at commas in the wrong place
and semi-colons strewn about for no particular reason.

Anyway, I've decided I must write in this diary to remind me what
I did with my life. And God knows it's slipping away. I'm thirty-six
going on ninety. Actually, that's wrong, what I mean is I'm thirty-six
going on to another dimension, under a bus for all I know next week,

---

* Shahid Malik was elected as MP for Dewsbury in 2005.
† Yasmin lost to Lib Dem Sarah Teather in Brent East, but Dawn Butler won in Brent South – the
third black woman elected to Parliament. There are still no Asian women MPs in Parliament.

and nothing is down in black and white. I want it in writing. It's like I say to my constituents every week: 'But why didn't you put it in writing? Nothing's worth anything if it's not in writing.' That's one way I measure the worth of my life – whether it's down in writing. On that score, at the moment I'm worth very little. If I'm going to spend my evenings catching up on paperwork (my new obsession), then some of it better be my own paperwork, my life's paperwork.

So what did I do today? Slept in until 8.30 a.m. and missed Foreign Affairs Questions. Damn – didn't know it was Foreign Affairs, took a calculated guess it was more likely to be one of my non-PQ issues, like Rural Affairs, or Welsh Questions. Unlucky. Must manage my office better. I've told them a thousand times to put the title of the PQs in my diary. OK, let's not exaggerate, I've told them about thirty times. But the point of a manager isn't the list of things they give their staff to do, but what action they take to help their staff put systems in place. And I haven't done that, so I've only myself to blame.

So, as I was saying, missed PQs, had a couple of meetings with Ministers – Mike O'Brien at FCO about a constituent whose cousin was murdered in East Timor in the 1970s, followed by another meeting with Mike O'Brien about the recent India trip – we covered Kashmir, trade, off-shoring (outsourcing parts of business overseas to save money); followed by a meeting with David Blunkett, Hazel Blears and Beverley Hughes on Antisocial Behaviour. I was planning to tell David how well I understood my constituents' problems, because in the last two months I've received three letters from the police which begin, 'Dear Ms King, we are sorry to hear that you have been a victim of crime,' in relation to three different incidents. Instead I passed on my constituents' recommendations for tackling gang violence.

Then met (Lord) Waheed Ali in his trainers and jeans (in the middle of filming an Agatha Christie movie) to go and lobby (Lord) David Sainsbury (as in 'making life taste better'), as in, 'Please help us raise money for our fabulous Rich Mix Cultural Centre in Tower Hamlets.*

---

* The Rich Mix Cultural Centre opened its doors in 2006.

Next I was supposed to meet with the Bangladeshi High Commissioner, but he'd left the meeting by the time I got there, then I had a meeting on London's Olympic Bid for 2012, then off to Weight Watchers for a weigh-in: I'm so fat (for a slim person) that instead of looking my usual two months pregnant, I now look about five months pregnant. Met Yvette Cooper at the vote, who really is a slim person, and who really did look pregnant. Didn't dare ask in case she'd metamorphosed into a fat person, or a post-two-pregnancies with the hell-ledge-out-of-control person. Glad she's having some small victories in the area of housing as its my obsession.

Tiberio is at a concert with Tanika, so I must finish my PPS work for Patricia (Hewitt) before he's home. I'm writing a brief for MPs on the World Trade Organisation. When I was on the International Development Select Committee I would have done it properly, but now as a PPS I just cut and paste stuff from various DTI documents and SoSs' speeches. At least I know what I'm talking about when it comes to the WTO, because I wrote a report on it with the Select Committee. Being a PPS to an SoS is the only PPS job worth having, but it still doesn't hold a candle to the proper policy work done by a good Select Committee.

2 March 2004

Spoke to Jamie (Jamilla). She sometimes rings me every day. I met her after a meeting about funding the new extension of the East London Mosque on Commercial Road. One of the mosque committee members asked if I would speak to a 'sister in need'. I agreed, and was introduced to Jamilla, a young quietly spoken woman who wore a long tunic and headscarf above strong imploring eyes. Jamilla's children, Kamran and Jasim, had been taken into care and she wanted my help to get them back. Jamilla herself had been raped, suffered years of domestic abuse, and been ostracised. I wrote dozens of letters to lawyers and social workers, and eventually Kamran and Jasim were returned. Kamran, now aged ten, wrote an amazingly cogent letter to Tony Blair telling him what it was like to be a British Muslim child, and why he hoped people would vote for 'aunty Oona' at the election. 'PS,' he added, 'please sort out youth services.' To TB's credit he sent me a signed letter to give to Kamran, and I know Jamie must have been a proud mother when I gave it to her to hand to Kamran. But the most surreal thing about Jamie, the person I initially thought was browbeaten and disconsolate, is that she's thrown off her headscarf and revealed a talent as a pop star. No joke, she's got a record deal and recorded an R & B album under the pseudonym J. Da Costa. She never ceases to amaze me.

4 March 2004

I'm getting the hang of this more regular diary thing. I just start tapping on my iPAQ during those ten minute gaps that pepper my week. This particular ten minutes is in between Treasury Questions (Gordon talking about educational funding in Wolverhampton) and Patricia (International Women's Day debate in the Chamber). Hardly anyone's put in to speak in the Women's Day debate, and it is a PPS's job to run around finding MPs to fill the gaps. Failing that (which I have – all the MPs have gone to ground), Plan B is for me to write a small section that Patricia can add to her speech to fill it out. It's a six hour debate. Anything will do. I've hit on an extract from Alan Clark's diaries. I admit his diaries inspire me to keep up my own. Not because mine will be as good as his, but because it's the little things that I don't usually write about which he does so well.

So arrived at Patricia's office at midday. She's put the (Special Advisers) briefing meeting back, so she has until 12.20 p.m. to work on her speech. Go and chat with the Spads (Special Advisers) for twenty minutes. I'm sitting at Kitty's desk, she had to leave the department because she's been selected as a Labour Candidate. One of the other Spads, Jim Godfrey, shows me an article in the *New Statesman* that predicts a Labour Cabinet in 2015. David Miliband is PM, his brother Ed is Transport, David Lammy is Culture, Patricia is Health, Ruth (Kelly) is DTI, Yvette (Cooper) is Deputy PM (don't they know that's what I want?), Douglas (Alexander) is Lord Chancellor and

I'm Party Chair. Well, I should be grateful that someone – anyone – wants me in their Cabinet; the only problem is, it's certainly not the PM.

I was picked up at 6.45 a.m. this morning to go to do a radio show on the *Vagina Monologues* (I'm performing the *Monologues* with a group of women later this month). My part is: 'Let's start with the word vagina. Best case scenario, it sounds like an infection. Or maybe a medical instrument. As in, "Emergency, nurse, pass me a Vagina!" It is just the most absolutely unsexy word you could ever come across and if you try to use it during lovemaking . . . you could kill the act stone dead.' I still find it hard to even write the word, let alone say if out loud.

Now I'm sitting in the Chamber, behind PH who's just finished her speech on women. It was one of her best, and extremely powerful, especially the bit about her constituent from Sierra Leone who was raped and then had her vagina cut out. (I've been practising saying the word vagina all day today, to the point where it doesn't bother me any more.) PH nearly started crying as she described how her constituent was tortured. And as for me, well I'll cry at anything, so it's a miracle the Labour benches weren't flooded.

Earlier, about thirty minutes before PH had to be in the Chamber, she decided she had to virtually re-write the entire speech. I had been looking for the 'domestic' bit (i.e. the British section in the International Women's Day debate, so I could fit in the Alan Clark quote. I couldn't find the section, and assumed it was just missing from the copy I had. But when we went into her office, Patricia was going nuts, in a very measured way, teeth gritted, 'For God's sake, there's no domestic stuff – where's the pay gap? Where's childcare?' PH's Spad for equalities, Deborah Lincoln, was saying, 'It's been done, but it's in Jacqui Smith's "wind-up" speech.'

'Well, it's no good there, is it?' fumed Patricia. 'I'm the Secretary of State and Caroline Spelman (Tory frontbencher) is leading on domestic issues, so I can hardly avoid the subject.'

Jacqui's speech was summarily filleted. PH took a couple of headache pills and then she was gone, her takeaway Pret A Manger pesto salad pot still on her desk.

'She's forgotten her lunch!' went up the cry. I offered to track her down, reflecting that I was less of a PPS bag carrier, and more a sandwich trolley. I never mind doing things like that, and in this case it was a godsend. By the time I found her in the Members' tea room – after a four minute pit stop on the green in front of Big Ben for a *Vagina Monologues* photo shoot with Joan Ruddock and Tamara Beckwith (reality TV c-list celeb type, dunno what she does, but recognise her face) – Patricia had already got a sandwich, so I got to eat her lunch.

But still, handing out PQ forms, and having to hang round the Members' tea room while all my contemporaries – the ones I came in with, and was grouped with – get given Ministerial briefs and Whitehall experience . . . well, I can't deny it, it's gutting. I'm definitely envious of the opportunities they're being given. Problem is that I'm not in anyone's 'gang'. I don't have a patron and I toe the Government line only 95 per cent of the time instead of 100. And I said no to Alistair and Sally and was given five years' hard Labour for it.

Spoke to Yvette today. Her due date is July. She's had five years' Ministerial experience *and* (fingers and toes crossed) three babies. From where I stand, it is an abundance of riches scarcely imaginable.

Later, in Committee Room 8, I was with PH in a meeting I was foolish enough to suggest and arrange. It was on the subject of EU expansion: the new Accession States, Migration and Employment. It's amazing how MPs become like their constituents, sharing their concerns, but also their prejudices. Gwyn Prosser, MP for Dover, is basically saying shut the (flood) gates, or Britain will drown under Eastern European immigration. Phyllis Starkey, who isn't so parochial, surprises me by taking on the prejudices of her Milton Keynes constituents.

Now I'm home and the other thing scarcely imaginable in my life is a central heating system that works. House is freezing. It's been minus two degrees recently and having no heating is no joke. On Tuesday morning there was no hot water and the cold water 'splash' to get clean nearly knocked me unconscious. I'm no good with the cold. I'd be the first one to be eaten in an Andes plane crash, because I'd be dead from hypothermia within seconds. It's Mum's fault. It's the only thing I can blame her for. After she grew up in a house without heating she made sure ours was always tropically hot.

5 March 2004

My feet were killing me today. I'd been wearing the beautiful but lethal (three-inch heeled) Italian brown leather boots Tiberio bought me. It was very generous of him, although he said he had to buy them because I looked like a tramp in my geriatric (actually quite smart) Marks and Sparks easy-walking shoes which I've had for two years. Swapped into my geriatric shoes and got on the District line at Westminster. The tube trundled along to Tower Hill, where it stopped for five minutes.

About three stops later I looked up from the *Guardian* (an article by Jackie Ashley on how New Labour hasn't changed the male culture of politics even though our policies are good for women, and how we must save the world and get rid of George Bush by any means possible; I agreed with all of it). Decided I *hated* the tube driver because the train had, with no announcement, started going back in the other direction. Forty-five minutes after I'd left Westminster I arrived back there again. Jumped up and off the train, almost forgetting my beautiful Italian brown leather boots. Must stop throwing away my money and my shoes. Just six weeks ago I went to Nike Town in Oxford Circus, bought a great pair of trainers and left them on the tube on the way home, never having got them out of the box. Painful. Must NOT leave these boots on the tube.

On the next tube, going back in the direction of Mile End, I sat down opposite a Bengali Muslim wearing a tunic, a hat (i.e. I keep my head covered, I am a holy man) and sporting a trademark mosque-style beard. Even though I've criticised, in Parliament, the War on Terror for becoming a War on Men with Beards, I find that I am now more wary of men with beards. I treat people how I find them, but I find that many of the obviously religious men (with beards, hats, tunics) seem to be hostile towards me.

There could be many reasons for this, ranging from the war in Iraq (and a lot of white men without beards dislike me and everyone associated with the Government for that reason) to my Jewish background, to the fact that I've campaigned for gay rights, to mere paranoia on my part. This particular man, in his mid-twenties, fixed me with a hard and unyielding glare. Our eyes locked, without warmth or recognition, and I immediately went into every Londoner's standard 'Do not look or talk to me while I am on the tube' mode. He did the same.

I read a bit more of the paper, this time about the bomb in Baghdad seventy-two hours earlier that killed over 200 people. My mind wandered. I've been told (though I don't believe it) that Al-Qaeda are operating at the East London Mosque on Commercial Road and that I'm one of their local targets. The reason I don't believe it is because religious rivals at another mosque are saying it. Still, I wouldn't be remotely surprised if some fundamentalist group does something pretty nasty at some stage around here. And I wouldn't be surprised if I'm the target. Like my Dad always says – just because you're paranoid doesn't mean they're not out to get you.

The tube arrives at Mile End, and it floats through my mind that I hope the man with the beard doesn't get off with me.

'Excuse me?' He's looking straight at me.

'Yes?' My natural reaction is always to smile. But not to him. I'm waiting to see what he wants.

'You've left your bag,' he says, pointing at my beautiful Italian brown leather boots.

'Oh, my God, thank you so much. I've been thinking I was going to lose them and then I almost did. Thank you. Really. Thank you so much.' I stumble off the train, tripping over my gratitude and prejudices in equal measure.

6 March 2004

Lying on Nora's bed. She's given me the best chicken recipe. I'm cooking dinner for David Lammy tomorrow night. It's not really dinner, more a snack, but Nora inspires me in every department, including cooking. So, rub olive oil, salt, pepper, half a lemon and half a nutmeg on the outside of the chicken and in the cavity. Then put a pack of Parma ham inside. Twenty minutes before it's cooked, throw two glasses of white wine into the roasting dish and *le voilà*, the perfect chicken.

Nora's just had her graduation film from National Film School shown at the NFT. It was about the Friends of Israel's Defence Force, and fairly terrifying in a relaxed kind of way.

On the way home, the cabbie, Vince, tells me that the man responsible for a notorious local murder is a 'Paki'. Paki is the general term of abuse for Asians, regardless of whether they're from Pakistan. He means Bengali. Vince is a typical East Ender, in many ways decent, in many ways subconsciously – sometimes overtly – racist, the same as many of his Bengali neighbours who would rather die than see their daughters marry white men. Using Paki is the same as using nigger. You just don't do it. This doesn't occur to Vince. I'm sitting in the cab, watching the Hackney Road pass by, thinking, 'You can't let that slide.' For him to slag off Asians is the same as him slagging off black people. In fact, I think, when he says Paki, he's slagging *you* off too, Oona. I use this tactic to try and galvanise myself into action, but in fact it makes me hesitate. That's because when people slag me off, I usually let it go. There's no point taking offence, because half the time (like my wonderful and ignorant racist gran) they don't mean it. But on the other hand, letting things go leads to a culture of casualised racism that is unacceptable. I should think of a way to pull him up on it. We carry on talking about all the mad people out there. They're everywhere. Vince had a woman come into the cab office next to my constituency office, and threaten to shoot him.

'It's crazy,' I say, 'like those paedophiles in the news this week, three separate ones who tortured children, and built cages to do it in. Did you see the one who put the children under the floorboards to sexually abuse them?'

'Yeah, unbelievable.'

'Yeah, just goes to show there are sick people everywhere. All those paedophiles this week were white, but I suppose they could have been Asian, or black, or whatever. Shouldn't judge people by the colour of their skin.'

'Yeah . . .' said Vince, hesitantly, and I thought maybe he'd at least half got the message.

7 March 2004

Fourth day without hot water or a shower. Went into Westminster to have one there yesterday, but inevitably got caught up in paperwork, and would have left David (Lammy) standing on the doorstep waiting for his dinner if I wanted to be clean. Nora's chicken recipe was great, except I couldn't taste the nutmeg. Made my very own potato and pumpkin mash.

8 March 2004

No hot water again. Drives me MENTAL. House is freezing. Will have to get washed using Deo-wipes. Don't mind doing that in Bujumbura, but hacked off about doing it in London.

9 March 2004

Got in to bed at two a.m., after dinner with my friend Sara Newby for her fortieth. Earlier, performed the *Vagina Monologues* at the Criterion, a beautiful miniature wedding cake of a theatre, with Jerry Hall, Rhona Cameron, Tamara Beckwith and several MPs. Given that we hadn't run right through it even once, we MPs were pretty good. Jerry, Rhona and Tamara were outstanding. At the entrance of the after party there was a bank of photographers.

I was completely submerged under all the bags and clothes I was carrying – the suit I'd been wearing earlier, a load of constituency mail, and to finish it off, two rolls of wrapping paper that I'd bought to wrap Sara's present. I never succeeded in wrapping the present, eventually leaving it in the back of her car in a bin liner, but I *did* succeed in looking a state. A complete state. Not much better than that first time I stood in front of a bank of photographers with Bootsy.

30 March 2004

I'm sitting in a meeting at the House of Commons that's all very interesting about the experience of British MPs shadowing Kenyan and Ugandan MPs, but I was thinking I'd rather write a letter to my parents. It's a novel idea. I haven't got any news for them in particular, other than in general I'm happy, which is a reason to be cheerful. Also Tiberio is doing really well on his MBA course. He is currently working far more hours than me, which is a turnaround. The other turnaround is my cooking, which continues to be a miracle (given my standing start last January). I even cooked dinner for ten – the President of the Congolese Parliament and his entourage when Tiberio was away – and it only took me about two hours' preparation time. My white chocolate and cardamom mousse, a Nigel Slater recipe, continues to delight.

9 June 2004

It was the hottest day of the year yesterday, 31°C, and Tiberio's birthday. 'Super Thursday' elections tomorrow – locals, London, mayoral and assembly and European. I'm sitting, well, lying, on the sofa in the living room, with the kitchen door open, hot and sticky, can't imagine being cold. I have taken up gardening which means I'm now officially middle-aged (thirty-six). When I say I've taken up gardening, I should be more specific. I've bought three slim gardening books, two clematis and one plant I've forgotten the name of, and I've watered them every day (for almost four weeks now). They all had pretty flowers but are now completely barren.

I'm drinking a glass of milk, which means it must be that time of year again: IVF season. When you do IVF you're supposed to drink one litre of milk and two litres of water a day. This is the second 'fresh' IVF cycle we've done. We did two IVF cycles using our frozen embryos (born of the David Beckham last minute goal) but success rates for frozen embryo transfers are only 10 per cent, so we weren't surprised to fail. We're a bit too British about this. We're never surprised by failure, even positively expect it, but we're none the less heartbroken by it.

The good news this time round was that the run-up to the egg collection went very smoothly. The drugs really don't affect me at all (probably why I don't get pregnant!).

Even the injections aren't too bad, although remembering to sniff the drugs every four hours during a hectic Westminster day can be tricky.

The morning of the egg conection arrived, and I left Tiberio to get stressed over the sperm sample pot. I went out for a walk in beautiful Victoria Park, the park that always makes me happy to live in London. Its lustrous trees line gently curving paths. The swans and geese and ducks and deer, the canals and tennis courts: I'm drawn towards them, but most of all I love the trees as tall as centuries. They exude a calm superiority whether draped in green or completely naked.

I did some exercises in the park and felt calm and strong. The phone rang after only fifteen minutes. The sperm sample was ready to go. I had planned to spend another forty-five minutes in the park. I toyed with the idea of staying there, but decided that this was God's way of encouraging me to complete our re-mortgage application, which had been sitting on the living room table for over a month. During that time the Chancellor, peace be upon him, had announced two interest rate rises. Well, actually, it was the Bank of England MPC (Monetary Policy Committee), but the point is that although our mammoth mortgage was squeezing the life out of us, I never quite got round to filling out all those bloody forms. Went home, seized the moment, did the re-mortgage and then Tiberio and I went off to the Homerton.

Slight palaver with my veins – they couldn't find them, and dug around for a while in both arms. 'You may feel a metallic taste in the back of your mouth,' said the doctor, and five seconds later there was a metallic taste and the feeling of my head and body yielding to the table, actually being pinned down to it, in the nicest possible way. And then some quite sharp pain.

'That hurts,' I complain, 'can you make that go away?' They give me another dose, and although I stay awake, I'm not really awake.

Back to ovary hell. I wake up, without having been asleep, and know that something is different this time. I feel like I've had a backstreet abortion with a coat-hanger. I can hardly walk. It transpires that of the eighteen follicles the doctor showed me on the scan two days ago, only eight are mature enough, but the other ten had to be dug out with a needle. Tiberio tells me that after they'd finished there was blood on the floor. That's why they don't have carpets in operating theatres. I carry on bleeding quite a bit. Tiberio takes me home and I spend the rest of the day lying down. That

evening when I go to the toilet, along with the urine, something the
size of my liver comes out. I am aghast. Maybe it is my liver. Or
maybe it's an alien mutant IVF premature baby. I feel very ill.

I ring the out-of-hours IVF doctor at the hospital, the one who
showed me my eighteen follicles. He's busy in the maternity unit with
women who have got pregnant and carried babies to term. Those
women, women like my mum and your mum, they're two a penny,
yet I can't emulate them for love nor money. So much money. After
four hours, I realise the emergency C-sections are going to keep him
busy all night, so I switch my phone off and go to sleep.

On Thursday, I have some contractions, and lie still all day.
Friday, Slate takes me to the hospital to have two embryos put
back. Of the eight, five have fertilised, three have gone in the freezer
and two are waiting for the on-screen family portrait moment. Cute
little four-cell embryos. After the transfer, you're usually allowed to
lie there for fifteen minutes. Jenny, one of the nurses, says they don't
need the room and I can stay longer. This makes me very happy
because I hate having to move too soon. I know gravity isn't all it's
cracked up to be (Uma Thurman with her legs in the air in *Pulp
Fiction* springs to mind) but it makes me feel better. And anyway,
this time I really don't feel well. No sooner has Jenny left the room
than Raj arrives, starts lowering the bed and telling me to get up.
Apparently there is another transfer about to happen and they need
the room. 'Jenny said I could stay a bit . . .'

Raj gives me five minutes. He's back in about three. 'Look,' he
explains, 'at my last clinic women came in during their lunch hour
and went straight out again.'

I struggle to sit up. It feels like someone has cut my lower
abdominal muscles with a pair of pliers. Two minutes later, Raj
is back for the final time. 'OK, I'm going, I'm going.'

Saturday I spent all day in bed. I had a full day of meetings on
Monday, but I had to cancel them. I couldn't walk and it seemed to
be getting worse. My stomach was bloated to the point where,
ironically, I looked at least four, possibly five, months pregnant.
Jolita, who *is* four months pregnant, has a belly half the size of mine.
I feel as though something is wrong. This isn't how it was last time. I
don't feel strong any more, like I did in the park that day, before the
egg removal operation.

I cancel meetings on Tuesday and Wednesday, but am determined to get to the Chamber for DTI questions on Thursday. I don't want Patricia to think I'm flakey. Frances, Lesley and Kester in the constituency office and Ro and Rob in the Westminster office keep things entirely under control, and that takes a huge weight off my mind.

Still, at one point I lie down and cry for about an hour. I know this isn't going to work. How could it, when my body is reacting so badly? I was having contractions before they'd even put the embryos back. Can't be a good sign. Adrian, my acupuncturist, says it's as though I'm trying to reject them before they have a chance to reject me. Still, he also says after taking my pulse that there's no reason it shouldn't work. That cheers me up. Adrian managed to reduce my period pain by about 90 per cent after one consultation. That was after conventional doctors had tried and failed to sort them out over nearly twenty-five years. I always listen to Adrian. I saw him the week before I started this cycle. I told him I felt very calm and that I'd started a bit of meditation.

'Well, you're definitely doing something right. The only concern I have is that it's as though your body is holding its breath. You're very calm about this, but it's because you're suppressing things.'

'No,' I protested, 'I feel genuinely calm. I'm not suppressing anything.'

He shot me a gentle 'you can't pull the wool over my eyes' look. 'Maybe you don't know you're trying to.'

'The thing is,' he said, 'you have a very strong mind, and you are using that strength to keep control, but that's different to being properly calm.'

OK, it was a criticism, but to my mind, it was a compliment. 'You have a very strong mind.' That's right, I thought, and tried to keep thoughts of either my imminent period or daydreams of my child's birth from my mind. For the first time in a week I did some paperwork.

When Tiberio arrived back from Italy he told me how touched he'd been by a lovely African baby girl. 'We need to get on with adoption. We should adopt a baby from Africa, which is what you've always wanted to do. Maybe IVF is too much.'

It was that cheeky little IVF left hook again. Just when you think it's all going swimmingly, just when you're thinking, 'This isn't too bad at all,' out comes the left hook and knocks you flat.

13 June 2004

When I rang Jenny at the hospital on Monday to ask if it was normal that I still couldn't walk, she told me I either had internal bleeding (as opposed to the mutant liver thing which represents external bleeding) or a mild case of Ovarian Hyper-Stimulation Syndrome. I decided it had to be the former, because I felt like I'd been butchered. And because I didn't understand how I could get OHSS having produced eight eggs, when last time around I produced twenty eggs yet didn't get OHSS.

I made it to DTI Questions on Thursday and then went back to the constituency office and spent two hours telephone canvassing to get the Labour vote out. (We have to focus on getting Labour people to vote, rather than converting confirmed Tory voters.) At six p.m. I had a persistent sharp pain in my right ovary (it was previously intermittent) and I decided to go home to bed.

I'm finding it really hard to keep writing this because England have just lost 2–1 to France in our opening match of Euro 2004. After ninety minutes we'd won 1–0, but then in injury time we did a classic England thing and snatched defeat from the jaws of victory. It almost upsets me more than Labour getting a complete whipping in the local elections on Thursday, because at least Labour's won a major tournament more recently than 1966.

On Friday morning I got the tube from Mile End to East Putney – a ridiculous journey, given the state I'm in, but Adrian with his acupuncture needles is the only person who can make me feel better. I'm back in Whitechapel by midday to visit tenants in a block of flats. Terrible antisocial behaviour problems. The usual – heroin, and the detritus it leaves behind: foil, plastic bottles, condoms, urine, shit, vandalised property, break-ins, fear. The tenants, understandably, want me to walk up the stairs to look at the mess. I do, but by now I think my right ovary is about to pop. Frances is with me, taking notes and drawing up the list of action points we'll follow up.

I need to go to hospital. Just as we're leaving, a young woman arrives to tell me about her recent burglary. Then somebody else wants to show me the broken exit-door lock. Finally leave, ring the hospital, and they tell me to come in for a scan. I keep saying, 'I just know there's something wrong.'

The doctor slaps jelly on my tummy and waves his magic wand across, which conjures up pictures on the screen.

'Well, the lining of your womb is nice and thick, so hopefully something's going on. But your ovaries are extremely swollen. In fact they've been pushed up beyond your waist. You've got OHSS, I'm afraid. It can be a very nasty disease.'

I'm happy that he said my womb lining was thick. Thick brains: bad. Thick womb lining: good. Wow. That means I could still be pregnant.

'But how could I get OHSS this time round with only eight eggs?'

'Sometimes it's triggered by pregnancy.' Triple wow.

'With some women, you almost hope they don't get pregnant, because pregnancy makes them so ill. And you're one of them. If you get pregnant it will get much worse.'

Fantastic. Whatever it takes. I feel more optimistic than I have since the beginning of the treatment. That was Friday. Today is Sunday, the day we lost to France. I've spent the weekend in bed, and now I feel better. My stomach is like a tyre with a slow puncture, imperceptibly starting to deflate. Goddamnit, why can't I stay ill? If I'm getting better, then I guess I can't be pregnant. Five days until the pregnancy test. I'm going to start calling those tests the 'tell me something I don't know' tests.

Midnight. I'm going to bed. Don't want to hear the European election results until the morning. Just hearing about UKIP is enough to pop an ovary.

14 June 2004

I'm getting wise in my old age. I know there's no point listening to the news before bedtime. Instead of calming your mind, it does the opposite, like necking a double espresso. And news is always bad, or it wouldn't be news. Last night, my political self-restraint in resisting the news saved me a sleepless night. The UKIP bad news would have transpired to be merely the prelude to the Respect/George Galloway Party bad news, which in Tower Hamlets is a political earthquake. This is the Respect Party, as in the 'we respect everyone' party, but in the case of George Galloway, 'I respect Saddam Hussein enough to go and have tea with him.'

So thank God I didn't turn on *Sky News* to hear him declaring that in Tower Hamlets his party won the Euro elections. Both ovaries would have exploded within seconds and that would have been before I heard him declare that, given his wonderful victory in Tower Hamlets, he was now considering standing in the general election in Bethnal Green and Bow against *me*. I wasn't well enough to contemplate that news. It's exactly twenty-four hours later, and I still don't feel great, but I'm well enough to deal with the news now. It only took me an hour this evening to turn political catastrophe into sunny uplands.

It goes like this: George Galloway stands in Bethnal Green and Bow, or puts all his resources into whipping up the Muslim vote on behalf of a Muslim Respect candidate. I lose the election – a safe Labour seat turned into a losing marginal almost overnight. My political career is in ruins and I'm forced out of politics without ever having been a Minister, or – who knows – perhaps having been one for a very short time. I don't achieve my ambition of changing Britain (a bit) and am depressed for the rest of my life, although I try to console myself with plans for some nonsense media projects or writing my novel.

So that was what I was looking at, at seven p.m. tonight once I got the full election results. By eight p.m. I had another scenario in mind: worst case scenario, still get defeated. I cannot bring myself to consider other Labour seats. I am an East London person. More than that, I am a Tower Hamlets person, and I cannot contemplate going anywhere else, even if this borough goes up in flames, which increasingly I think it might. OK, never say never. Maybe I'd consider somewhere else, but at the moment I can't see it happening. And more than that, I can't ever envisage being able to invest as much of my time, my life, my consciousness and especially my heart (politician's melodrama) somewhere else, in the same way that I have in Tower Hamlets.

So there I am, an unemployed MP after the next election, with nowhere to go . . . except the House of Lords. Baroness King of Tower Hamlets. Minister in a Labour Government, under Gordon Brown, without any constituents. Did I just die and go to heaven? The more I think about it, the more I think I must *implore* George Galloway to come and stand in Bethnal Green and Bow. I'll have to deliver his leaflets. This is a once-in-a-lifetime opportunity to escape the biggest constituency caseload of any politician in Britain. My workload is at least fivefold that of the average MP. And do I get any thanks for it? Are bricks through my window thank you cards?

Anyway, I reached these conclusions at eight p.m. this evening, but at six p.m., I trotted off with all the other PLP Members to hear the PM. Well, didn't trot, more shuffled. Knew something was up when, for the first time ever, there were police officers guarding all the entrances of Committee Room 14 and saying it was full. An officer who turned me away from the middle entrance of Committee Room 14 told me to try the front entrance. The only remaining standing room was directly behind TB. He gave an amazing speech. Given the circumstances, given our recent dismemberment at the polls, his whole demeanour, delivery, conviction and confidence, all of it was completely misplaced. And yet, the thing about Tony is that if anyone on the planet can get us out of the predicament we're in (and maybe nobody can), it's him.

Or he can make sceptics *believe* he can, however misguided. That's because in TB's universe, you can't fault him. It all makes sense, it all adds up. His genius is this: it's not that he makes you think it would be *disloyal* to disagree; he makes you think it would be *madness* to disagree; a perversion of logic; a defeat for empiricism; a betrayal of socialism or at least social democracy. That is how it is in Tony's world, and so for the sake of logic and socialism, for the sake even of socialist logic, such and such 'is the right thing to do'.

A wave of nausea came over me. The hospital told me this afternoon that my blood tests showed an iron deficiency, presumably due to the blood I'd lost. This could account for the extreme lightheadedness I'd felt earlier in the day. Jenny also told me that just because the OHSS appeared to be getting better, it didn't mean it had gone. It could come back at any time, and a common symptom was vomiting and nausea. On the way over to the PLP meeting, I stopped at Boots to get iron tablets, but they'd run out, so I bought a banana and coconut smoothie instead. Drank it in the meeting to try and get a shot of sugar into my bloodstream and line my stomach. Mustn't keel over in front of 400 MPs. Mustn't vomit over the Prime Minister.

24 June 2004

As usual, everyone is getting carried away with the notion that England could win a football tournament, like we always do, and that will be followed by us being devastated that we've gone out, like we always do.

I'm aghast when I get a letter saying, 'Dear Friend, you are invited to the Labour Party barbecue that will take place on Thursday 24 June, the same date that England play Portugal in the quarter-final. A television will be provided for people wanting to watch the match . . .'

'What *bastard* thinks I'm going to go to a Labour Party event during an England quarter-final football match?'

I'm shouting in my office, waving the letter around with indignation. That's before I see it's signed by . . . Oona King. Computerised signatures are a scandal.

On top of that, I have to come up with prizes for the raffle. I'm broke this week, no cash at all, so I go round the house looking for things I can give away. A Nicole Kidman DVD. A Norah Jones CD. A silk *salwar kameez*. A necklace and matching ring. I collect these bits and bobs and head off to watch the match.

We start off far too well. Owen scores within three minutes. From that point forth we are doomed. A few minutes later Rooney got injured and was substituted by Darius Vassell. And then comes wave after wave of Portuguese attack. They equalise, then in the second half of extra time Portugal score to go two–one up. Almost miraculously, certainly heroically, England equalise, and then, even more amazingly, Sol Campbell scores a minute or so before the end to win us a place in the semi-final. To be fair, we won the match.

Then the referee disallowed the goal and so it went to penalties. (Adored) David Beckham missed his third penalty in a row – though how he even managed to walk up to take the penalty, I don't know. How do their legs function under all that stress? So England's on the plane home. I may wait my entire life to see England win a European or World Cup. That, and a socialist revolution and a baby of my own. Give me one of those – actually, be sweet, give me all of those, preferably in reverse order – and I'll die a very, very happy woman.

25 June 2004

Forgot to mention the only small piece of good news last week: managed to save money and *not* buy a pregnancy test. If I added up the money we've wasted on pregnancy tests and ovulation predictor kits over the last five years, we'd be able to buy twins over the internet by now. Get my period at Westminster. Have to go to a meeting with the Congolese Foreign Minister to discuss war in the eastern Congo, *and* miss the second half of England versus Switzerland, *and* miss having children of my own. Infertility. The pain could be overwhelming. But I can deal with it. In fact I can feel myself getting stronger, rather than weaker. Although I did burst into tears when I saw the consultant at the hospital, because I feel I'm not getting the treatment I need. Key point: I'm not walking around the House of Commons sobbing . . .

1 July 2004

. . . Unlike Cheryl thingy-bob the Tory member for Chesham and whatsit. Poor woman had a dose of the mobile phone terrors during PMQs last week. Her phone went off while the PM was speaking, she couldn't turn it off, so she tried to rush out of the Chamber into the voting lobby. She lost her step and fell flat on her face *inside* the Chamber instead. A few minutes later I walked around the back of the Chamber and found her weeping and being comforted by a small group of Tory MPs. What had happened to her was bad, but not *that* bad, not sobbing, 'childless' bad, or any of the other bad things that happen to people.

Today I met my constituent Tarek Dergoul, one of the British citizens detained without trial in Guantanamo Bay, and tortured and abused for two years. That's bad. I got a debate on his case. Was surprised when one of the clerks told me I was the first MP to get a debate on Guantanamo Bay detention centre and its human rights abuses. As I said in the debate, it's ironic that today Saddam Hussein was brought to trial in Iraq and got his day in court. This was a man who murdered 300,000 Iraqis (not to mention the half million who died after he started the Iran–Iraq war), and who today was receiving 'due process' as his trial began. And yet this most basic right to a trial, offered to even the worst dictator (as it should be) was refused to my constituent and other detainees at Guantanamo Bay by the Americans. The American Government's disregard for due process and human rights is abominable. Even more shocking is their willingness to use torture. They are morally bankrupt.

After the debate I went to a meeting at one of my LP ward branches, then took them on a tour of the Commons. Finally got home to watch the Euro 2004 semi-final, Czech Republic versus Greece. The Czechs deserved to win, but as we know, football can be cruel. And anyway so many of my friends are Greek. Realised I'd rather watch football than *Big Brother*. Must wean myself off both. But moving from fake TV to real sport signifies some small progress.

4 October 2004 – Kinshasa

Arrived in the Democratic Republic of the Congo last night. Since coming back from summer holiday five weeks ago, I've had one day off in one month – twenty-hour hours in Naples for Mattia's baptism, my Japanese–Italian godson. Now I'm sitting in the Congolese Parliament, built for Mobutu by the Chinese. It's as you would expect: huge, arrogant, a stage on which to display power, not a chamber for debate. About 500 Congolese

MPs sit in the auditorium and listen to the President of the Parliament, Olivier Kamitatu, who towers over them from the stage and exhorts them to play their part in bringing peace to the Congo. We're sitting on stage next to him, a British parliamentary delegation next to representatives from Gabon and the Cameroon.

Olivier Kamitatu referred to me in his speech. I stood up, nodded, smiled, sat down, and prepared a short speech to give to the TV crews later in French (finally Madame Borelle would have been proud). This turned out to be helpful the next day when an obstructive border guard suddenly dropped his pen and said, '*Aaah, Madame, du Parliament britannique, de la télévision.*' Then it was easy and Cath from the Rainforest Foundation was able to stop pleading with him over '*les formalités*'.

6 October 2004

Today we flew three hours north of Kinshasa, to Linsala, over untouched rainforest. Now our small delegation – me, another British Labour MP Bob Blizzard, a Belgian MP Maya, a Reuters correspondent David, a Greenpeace worker Filip, Cath from the Rainforest Foundation and three of her local partners – are all sitting in a dark room with the town priest, drinking water and eating peanuts.

We pile into a small van and drive hell-for-leather along sandy roads to visit villages affected by logging. Huge multinational companies come in, cut down the forest, give lots of promises but no employment, destroy the local resource, blow a hole in the ozone layer and leave. Local people are desperate. The forest has always been their lifeline, but now it's being cut down. This destroys their livelihood and environment. And it destroys our environment too. The villagers want to know if we can build them a school or help them get drinking water. And if not, why not? Why else have we come?

This is a good question, but we only have a weak answer – we're here to raise awareness of their problems so that we can pressure our Government to pressure their Government to make things better.

This is about the furthest thing imaginable from immediate help. Notwithstanding this, the British Government is in a position to pressure the Congolese to conserve their rainforest. And we are in a position to pressure our Government. So perhaps we can have a modest impact.*

Britain is now one of the biggest donors to the Congo. During the pre-trip briefing by the Foreign Office and various NGOs, we were told that the UK Government's position on the Congo had changed 360 degrees. One of the MPs asked why. 'Because Hilary Benn (SoS for International Development) visited the Congo, and saw for himself how critical the situation was. He understood our Government's focus in the region had been distorted, centred almost exclusively on Rwanda. He's introduced a more even-handed approach. And because of this we now have vastly increased influence with the Congolese Government. He also understands that, given the size and wealth of the Congo, if it can be stabilised, it will help stabilise the whole of Africa.'

I was reminded of a conversation I had with Jack Straw after a previous visit I made with my All-Party Parliamentary Group on Genocide Prevention to the Congo. I asked Jack if he would visit the country. He told me he couldn't in the foreseeable future, but asked if it would be helpful for Hilary Benn to go instead. Naturally I said yes. Later that afternoon I took a call in my Westminister office from Hilary Benn. 'Jack thinks it would be helpful for me to go to the Congo, and said it might be useful to have a chat with you.' And now Hilary's done the business. Hilary is an exception. Let's face it, most MPs are disaster tourists. We come, we see death and destruction, we take notes, we leave. The bravest thing we do is go without mod cons for thirty-six hours every now and then. The place we're staying in is clean, except for the communal toilets which are up a flight of stairs and must be avoided at all costs. The showers are at the other end of the corridor, and smell iffy enough for me to stick to my Wet Ones. The others have been bitten to death; Cath looks like she has smallpox on her arms, but she say's the bites don't itch. I'm feeling quite superior and bite-free, until I develop some huge growth on my

---

* At a Q & A session I hosted with Gordon Brown in May 2007, in response to a question about our most pressing challenges, I was amazed and heartened when (entirely unprompted by me), Gordon raised the issue of deforestation in the Congo Basin.

coccyx and the common consensus is that it's some sort of parasitic worm that'll either hatch or explode.

I go upstairs to my room at ten p.m., followed by a man who walks too close to me and tries to come through the door. I shut it in his face and contemplate one of those traumatic nights far from home: potential rapist standing outside my door (very likely); potential exploding worm situation in my bum (possible but unlikely); potential mosquito net choking and/or mosquito swarm hell (possible and likely); endless hot, sticky semi-conscious tossing and turning (inevitable).

After drifting off, wake up in darkness to warbling music, possibly the Islamic prayer. Gingerly check my watch. Victory! It's 4.30 a.m. and the night is nearly over. Not a single nightmare has crowded either my subconscious or my reality, and the lump the size of a hard-boiled egg in my bum is now only the size of a grape. Gratitude flows through me and I snuggle up to my travel air pillow in a state approaching ecstasy. Go back to sleep until 8.30 a.m., happy as Larry, and wake up raring to jump into a dug-out canoe and travel up the Congo river. Can't remember the last time I enjoyed a night's sleep so much.

7 October 2004

Today we set off on our mission: the Rainforest Foundation Triathlon. The plan is this: three hours upstream in *pirogues*, narrow canoes each carved from a single majestic tree; arrive in Linsala; unload bicycles and motorbikes; cycle twenty kilometres along jungle path; walk four kilometres; meet pygmy tribe; discuss impact of logging and environmental destruction on their community; sleep on floor of pygmy hut; next day do everything in reverse; be back in Linsala at midday; get plane to Kinshasa by five p.m.; sip G & T at Ambassador's Residence by eight p.m.; leave for UK the next morning.

The plan started to fall apart the moment we set off. The three hour canoe ride became a six hour canoe ride, beneath a blazing sun. We bought three catfish from a woman who tied them together using a thin piece of rope which she pushed in through their gills and out through their mouths. Clumps of water hyacinth, a weed that floats along the river, were plucked and left on the fish to stop them rotting in the heat.

8 October 2004

We arrived in Yatika, a remote logging outpost, yesterday evening, happy with our experience but fairly toasted and in no shape to cycle and walk twenty-four kilometres. In any case the decision to stay or go was stolen by the sun as it started to set. Bizarrely, a Westerner appeared to welcome us along with fifty local villagers. Dieter was a twenty-five-year-old Belgian, a modern-day Kurtz, stationed here alone by his logging company. He was clearing land to build a road and houses, and planned to negotiate with the pygmy people further inland, so he had already made the journey we proposed to do.

'I can't see you making it,' he said, 'it's hard in daylight, the path is very difficult and at places it's impossible. At night . . . well, you could try.' I thought he said, 'You could die,' which wouldn't have been far off the mark.

If we'd had mountain bikes with headlights, it might have been possible. Instead we had Chinese-style 1940s bicycles with no lights at all and, as I found to my cost later, no brakes. They weighed a ton.

So we decided to stay the night with Dieter, cook the catfish for dinner, leave camp at 4.30 a.m.; cycle twenty kilometres, walk four kilometres; speak to the pygmies; walk four kilometres back, then cycle twenty kilometres and get back to camp by midday; then get on canoe; then get on airplane; then sip G & T. Our plan involved fifty kilometres of cycling and walking through the jungle before midday.

This was where my diary entry ended. But what followed was a truly insane flight into the jungle.

We slept for a few hours in a metal freight container on the rim of the rainforest, and then set off into the interior just before dawn. It was immediately apparent that the bikes were no match for the forest. *Each bicycle tormented its rider differently. Mine had a saddle that either tipped all the way forward or all the way back, so you risked slipping off and falling on to the moving back wheel, which I did at speed a dozen times. It wasn't possible to sit down. It was like trying to balance on a vertical rolling pin. It was that, or crouch in a permanent quad-squat until cramp set in. One of the men agreed to swap bikes with me for a while, but was soon in agony (he'd chosen the rolling pin option on bumpy terrain). I was indifferent about giving his bike back, as my inner thigh was already bleeding from a protruding metal screw that couldn't be dislodged from the frame.*

After an hour I was on my last legs. By the time we'd done fifteen kilometres I wasn't sure I was going to make it. It seemed we'd been going uphill for an age. When we arrived at the end of the cycle ride, I threw the bike down and lay on my back, gasping.

'We're late,' said Cath, 'we're never going to make it in time to get the boat back to catch the plane before dark. We've got to keep going, or we won't have time to talk to the pygmies.'

Sweat stamped my clothes to my skin. It was baking, though the heat was humid. There wasn't enough water. While I'd been cycling I'd suppressed the thought of the four kilometre trek on foot, part of it through swamp. We squelched along, holding on to bits of broken logs and trees for balance, hardly daring to look up. It was only the shriek of a monkey every now and then that reminded us where we were.

When we finally arrived we were led to an open-air wooden pagoda with a thatched roof, where we more or less collapsed. I can only begin to imagine what our hosts made of this bedraggled parliamentary delegation. It transpired that the pygmies had built this structure especially for our meeting. We should have slept there the night before. We shook hands. We explained why we were in the Congo, how we hoped to achieve greater awareness of the environmental and human costs of exploitative logging and deforestation, and what we'd learned in Kinshasa. The pygmy chief said he was extremely grateful that we had come, very interested to hear what we had to say, and they would now have a brief fifteen minute meeting among themselves to consider what we'd said before offering a collective response. That was their custom.

But we were Westerners, and we all looked at our watches. That was our custom.

'Er, fifteen minutes . . . that might be a bit too long, because we have to leave in fifteen minutes . . .'

They were incredulous. So was I. We had driven, flown, canoed, cycled and walked across half a continent to meet them, and now we told then we only had fifteen minutes. But that's how those parliamentary delegations are, felled by the unexpected, they mutate into a meeting in a minute. We asked the pygmies to forgive us for our rudeness, and to tell us about their experiences with the logging company, before we had to get up and go.

The pygmies stood in torn clothing, all around five feet tall. They explained to us solemnly that they derived no benefit from the logging. They hadn't even been told that their forest had been selected for 'development'. The trucks just arrived. Here in the West we've only recently realised that deforestation is the single biggest cause of climate change. Every year logging produces eight times more CO_2 emissions than all the planes in the sky.

International corporations are being given the green light to strip the forest. The World Bank proposes a programme of logging in the Congo, or rather attempts to regulate the current situation. The Congo is the second largest rainforest in the world. Along with the Amazon, it is the planet's lungs. The pygmies are watching their land torched, their way of life tugged towards extinction. What few people grasp is that when indigenous populations in the rainforest are wiped out, the rest of us won't be far behind. Irrefutable evidence proves that environmental Armageddon is only a few decades away.*

The fifteen minutes were up, so we reluctantly got to our feet to begin our deranged journey in reverse. This time it was the canoe that proved no match for the river. After hours in the pirogue, the outskirts of Kinshasa were in sight when an unexpected storm turned the passive yet mighty Congo into a swirling rage. Within minutes our canoe was a foot deep in water, we were being whipped by wind

---

* See *Six Degrees: Our Future on a Hotter Planet* by Mark Lynas.

and rain that soaked us to the skin along with all our belongings, and we couldn't see more than a few metres ahead. We frantically grabbed everything to hand, including our shoes, to bail the water out. In the end it was too dangerous to go on, and we had to ditch the pirogue *and scramble on to the bank.*

All things considered, our trip to see the pygmies was utter madness. But it was also one of the most eye-opening trips I've ever made, and I yearn to repeat it – although next time with proper regard for the wise and ancient customs of the pygmies.

25 October 2004

2.20 a.m. The predicted date for the general election is 05.05.05. That sounds pretty likely, unless they're burning cattle in the street or something, as they were in 2001. This time around, it's Iraq that has changed everything totally, completely, utterly, and makes our chances of success seem pretty slim. But I suppose impossibly bad situations get better all the time. This one may not but on the other hand it might. More fantastic and incisive political insight. Labour's political fortunes might get better, or they might not. Iraq might be a disaster for ever, or it might not.

Things are definitely getting worse in Tower Hamlets. George Galloway is all over me like a rash. He's bought a house in the constituency; he is often at the mosque bad-mouthing me. And then the Respect lot go out and imply to my Muslim community that I shoot Muslim babies between the eyes. They've even super-imposed my head onto a photograph of a man driving a tank on a mission to kill. It's gone through everyone's letter box. And they point out that I'm Jewish, and there's a Jewish world conspiracy, and I must be part of it. They shout 'Murderer! Murderer!' all the time.

Time and again during the general election campaign my Jewish background was used as a stick to beat me with. In my experience, when someone's identity is under attack, they wrap it around them more closely. The more you attack Muslims, the more Muslim they become. The more I was attacked for being

Jewish, the more Jewish I felt. Today I feel more Jewish than ever. That doesn't mean that I go to synagogue, or fast for Yom Kippur, or give thanks during Passover for my ancestors escaping the slavery of the Pharaohs. (In fact I spend far more time in mosques than synagogues.) It means simply that I was born to a Jewish mother, I have Jewish heritage, and I feel *Jewish. The hostility of others has helped me maintain a bond with Judaism which I might otherwise have neglected. A lot of Jewish people will know what I mean. The late Peter Frye summed it up in his joint autobiography with Thelma Ruby,* Double or Nothing: *'Whether you like it or not, when you're born Jewish, there is a worldwide conspiracy to keep you Jewish no matter how hard you try to get away from it.'*

This was the only worldwide conspiracy that I encountered in Bethnal Green and Bow.

Iraq isn't ever going to go away – or at least it will at some point but that could be two years or twenty. No, not twenty years surely? Mind you the Middle East conflict has been going for more than twenty years. I'm banking on ten more years. So I'm hoping that by 2014 Iraq is more stable. Or will it just have become an ongoing conflict, like Darfur?

Some good things have happened as well, actually lots of really good things. It's just that the bad things loom larger.

We won the housing gap funding debate, which means there will be more money for housing regeneration in Tower Hamlets. Obviously it's never enough, but it's a vast improvement on the money previously available.

Another good thing is that I've just come in from a fantastic night out, the first night out in such a long time. It's always amazing when you do something with other people and you have a good time. I suppose it's called socialising. I don't do it that often now, except with MPs and that doesn't really count. I spent today with my favourite MP in Parliament, Karen Buck. Where is Tess, my former most favourite MP in Parliament? I don't know. She got out. She's so clever. I might have to get out too in May, and good things could come from that. Anyway, bloody Parliament is driving me mad.

I had a huge argument with Tony McNulty last week. I asked him, as Transport Minister, to talk to my constituents about Crossrail. As usual, I was being asked really detailed questions, questions about the depth of the tunnelling, the size of the machinery, the width of the holes being drilled. I knew all the answers, because dare I say it, I'm good, and my office is good, and we have it covered. But Tony got asked these questions and got really irate. 'I'm not here to have a conversation!' he shouted. I was truly taken aback. We were elected. Maybe we *are* here to have a conversation. Maybe that's our job. And maybe you're the Minister, and I'm only a backbench MP – you're the one that's supposed to know the answers. To be fair to Tony, these were detailed questions about the proposals in my constituency, and he can't be expected to know the depth of tunnelling along the whole route, which runs through dozens of constituencies.

If he didn't know the answers, fine, but he didn't have to take it out on me. He could legitimately say he has a quasi-judicial role as the Cabinet Minister in charge of Crossrail, and therefore he can't go into detail in an open forum. And I know he's married to the Chief Executive of Tower Hamlets, which puts him in a really difficult position. But when he agreed to come and speak to my constituents about Crossrail, what did he expect? Did he think they were going to ask him about the weather?

The next day I bumped into him in the voting lobby. I told myself to be calm and remain civil. So I said, 'Oh Tony, that was a bit of an interesting meeting . . .' and he went ballistic. There were at least 100 MPs nearby, and he started shouting at me really loudly, '*How could you be so fucking stupid,*' stabbing his finger at me, '*you're so fucking thick, you don't understand a fucking thing . . .*' He carried on hurling insults.

The thing is, he's a mate. At Westminster that's what you get from your *mates*.* It's amazing how much it stressed me out, because that night I felt sick as a dog. It's probably nothing to do with Tony, and he was probably really stressed too. I have to show some pity, because there aren't many worse jobs in Government than being a Transport Minister.†

---

* The following week Tony McNulty gave me a full apology for his behaviour.
† Although Tony got one of them when he later became Immigration Minister.

28 October 2004

I've started doing bloody IVF again. It's the best thing in the world, obviously, the chance to have a baby, but this much stress . . . In fact IVF doesn't have to be stressful, I shouldn't put people off, it's just tricky trying to do it when you're an MP, with George Galloway on your back.

Last night I was scheduled to be on the mosque radio station between ten and eleven p.m. I arrived at ten p.m. and was told they'd scheduled it to go on until midnight. They also told me I'd be on with the new Tory candidate. He's a sweet guy and a total muppet. I have a slight soft spot for him because he's just so silly, and if you ask him a question he has to write down the answer, and then read it off the paper. That might be OK in some jobs, but not as an MP. Anyway, just as I was going in they said, 'Oh, and the other guest is George Galloway.' They totally ambushed me. Obviously they'd told George Galloway that he was on with me, but they didn't tell me that I was on with him and that he'd be joining us by phone.

Spending time with George Galloway is like dipping your toe in a bloodbath. He says 'Oona King' as many times as possible in the same breath as 'George Bush'. George Bush and Oona King, Oona King and George Bush. Both of them are at war with Islam. Again and again and again and again.

'The US and Britain, two of the most powerful countries in the world,' said George Galloway, 'with *Oona King's* approval, have massacred far more civilians than Osama Bin Laden killed in New York and Washington on 9/11. The difference is that nobody cares about them because their blood is *Muslim* blood. That's very *cheap* blood in the world today, run by the rulers, George Bush and Tony Blair that Miss King supports . . . Now we have a chance to *punish* those MPs who have slaughtered Muslims in Afghanistan and in Iraq, whose blood has been shed *cheaply*. We have a chance of *increasing* the *price* of that *blood*, by *punishing* those MPs who ignored their constituents.'

I suppose I should take a leaf out of Galloway's book, and sue him for saying that I 'approve massacres'. Instead I point out that he sipped tea with Saddam Hussein, exchanged niceties with a butcher. Three times in a row Galloway responds, 'You be careful you don't libel me now.' He's great at suing people, but he can't sue me for quoting him. Can he?

The interviewer interrupted me to say that the USA had also supported Saddam Hussein back in the 1980s, it wasn't just George Galloway.

'I couldn't agree more,' I replied, 'George Galloway and George Bush were both friendly with Saddam Hussein.'

'Let's move on,' said the interviewer, 'On line one is Abdul Rahman from Canning Town.'

'It was actually George Galloway who *opposed* Saddam Hussein,' Abdul piped up, 'when he was gassing 5,000 Kurds in Halabja. It was George Galloway who was opposing that, and the Labour Party and Conservative Party in cahoots approving a CIA mission supporting Saddam Hussein against the Revolutionary Iranian regime. Oona King is simply misrepresenting the reasons for going to war . . . And isn't the real issue behind all of this – it doesn't matter how much Oona King denigrates Sharon, denigrates George Bush, the point is this – we've always got pro-Zionist policies that are being pursued one way or another. And it's people like Oona King who support them–'

The interviewer interrupted. 'Would you round it up *Inshallah*?'

'Well she's just misrepresented everything–' said Abdul, his voice heavy with outrage.

'Thank you very much,' said the interviewer, giving me a two second reprieve, 'I'm sorry, we've got to move on to the next caller.'

'First of all,' said the next caller, 'it's completely untrue what Oona King is saying.' He gave all his reasons and then finished by asking if I'd call for war on Israel. George Galloway came back to this later.

'Oona King very deftly – she hoped – dodged a question of whether she'd support a war on Israel.' George warmed to his theme, 'Well I challenge her right now, on your radio station, to table a motion to the House of Commons supporting a war on Israel to ensure the implementation of United Nations resolutions. I defy her *right now* to table a motion calling for *war* on Israel.'

'This is a cliffhanger,' said the interviewer. 'We're going to come back after the ads. Oona King, if I can ask you to just hold your response until then.'

'Of course,' I said, as I looked around the room of angry young men. It was eleven p.m. I sat back to sip cold coffee and listen to adverts about Islamic banking accounts and Haj travel deals. I wondered, in another life, how I might spend my Thursday nights. The ads ended and I reiterated my views that the Israeli Government should face sanctions for breaking the fourth Geneva Convention in the Occupied Territories.

'Those are my views which I hold very strongly. I have been contacted by the Palestinian Authority in London to thank me for the very strong and proactive stand that I take, which is pro-Palestinian, and against the right-wing Israeli Government. I do not need George Galloway to tell me what he thinks I should do.'

'So you won't table a motion for the military enforcement of UN resolutions?' asked the interviewer.

'No. That would be the most pathetic and ineffective way to actually get credible change on the ground. And that's the difference between myself and George, I want to deliver real change, credible change, whereas George lives in a fantasy land.'

'Well there we have it,' said George triumphantly. 'She was for war against Iraq to enforce United Nations resolutions, but she's *against* war on General Sharon's Israel to enforce UN resolutions. Therein lies the double standard which is the flaw at the heart of Anglo–American Bush and Blair policy towards the Middle East, towards the Muslim world. I'm glad we've cleared that matter up. The listeners are now very clear about that double standard, and I thank the mosque radio station for the opportunity to clear that issue up.'

Call after call came in along similar lines, all berating my double standards. Then the interviewer came back.

'Dear brothers and sisters, just a couple of text messages that've come through: "I want to tell Oona King that the war was wrong and ask her who gave her the right to say yes to the war on behalf of us?" Another text. "*Salaam.* Since Mrs King has been wrong and betrayed her constituents, shouldn't she give a public apology, and wouldn't now be a good time to do it, on the radio when about 70,000 people are listening?" We've got a caller on line one, we'll take that call and then come back to Oona King on the last point. Line one, Shiffil?'

'Good evening to all the guests. We're constantly being told by Mr Blair and Ms King that the war on terror is not a war on Islam. Now I want to ask Ms King – suppose this *was* a war against Islam, suppose this *was* a war against Muslims. What would be the difference?'

'Well if this was a war on Muslims,' I said, trying to speak evenly, 'I don't think the British Government would have sent troops in to Kosovo to *protect* Muslims. You have to look at the Labour Government's record, and not the Conservative Government before us – yes, they armed Saddam Hussein. Labour didn't. But the first military action Tony Blair took was to intervene on behalf of Muslims, so I think you're disregarding the facts to make an accusation like that.'

George comes in for a repetitive salvo. 'Oona King voted for the slaughter of *thousands* of Muslims, thousands, *tens of thousands* of Muslims. The blood is on the hands of all those that voted for those attacks.'

He runs through all the other reasons not to vote for me, including 'the destruction of Brick Lane by Crossrail'. In his finishing flourish he says, 'Above all, I want to remember this *Ramadan* all the Muslims that have been *slain* by Bush and Blair in their so-called war on terror, and I look forward to the day when we can democratically, peacefully *punish* those responsible for it.' He then has time for one last challenge:

'I challenge Oona King to a public debate in Bethnal Green and Bow . . . just her and me in front of the public, in front of the voters. Will she accept my challenge?'

'Oh, I'd be delighted,' I say.

It's true. I want him as my opponent a) because I have a death-wish and b) because he shouldn't get away with his outrageous behaviour. And if I *do* lose to him, well, bloody hell, I'll go down fighting. But I don't think I'll lose. And if I do, well that's pretty shocking. Maybe that's why I've got a soft spot for the Tory candidate: if Galloway splits the vote and lets him win, he'll be such a bad local MP that people will be on their hands and knees begging to have me back.

29 October 2004

OK, so I don't spend every night at the mosque. In fact I had another great night out tonight with Elaine and her girls at Crystal Events.

They had the best singers and musicians. So if George Galloway won, it would be unbearable, but I would get a life. I would have nights out like the one I just had, and that wouldn't be a bad thing at all.

16 November 2004

Money. IVF is the best way to ensure you don't have any. Added to the house falling down, and the constituency office debt – half the time I can't even buy a cup of coffee. It's really shallow, but if I could just buy things in general, even things for other people, I'd feel happier. It was Remembrance Sunday last weekend, and I didn't have £16 for the bloody wreath. I mean, come on. My grandfather would be turning in his grave. I had to borrow the money from my GLA member, John Biggs. That's bad. And not being able to buy food can also get on your nerves. I went into Pret A Manger the other day. I counted the last bit of change in my wallet. I was starving, blood sugar-levels dipping, and I thought, okay, I'll have a liquid lunch, a £1.85 banana and vanilla yoghurt smoothie. That'll be fine. I counted out the money in my wallet. £1.82. I was 3p short. So I'm standing in Pret A Manger in Victoria Street when it occurs to me that I could beg. Well not exactly *beg*, but – I mean I'm always giving money away. I think of all the £1.50s and £5 notes I give away, and I think, 'What's 3p?' It's really not much. I was about to ask a total stranger for 3p when I decided that as an MP earning £58,000 a year, it wouldn't look great. How can I earn all that money, and not have 3p? My friend John Nic says we're the new millionaire paupers – middle-class gits who got on the housing ladder, have great houses but can't afford them, have no liquid assets, and can't even buy a cup of coffee. We deserve everything we've got coming to us, which doesn't include a cup of coffee.

18 November 2004

Two little embryos were put into my womb today. I have to enjoy it because, as I've said before, this is probably the closest I'll come to parenthood: looking at those little screwed-up images on screen. For the first time, one of the embryos was at the blastocyst stage. No, it had gone past the blastocyst stage, it had started hatching. And the other one had just turned into a blastocyst. And there was a third little one that didn't quite make the grade, so that's been popped in the freezer.

Anyway I don't think I could be more stressed if I tried. Work is hell on wheels. Tiberio is at Cranfield, so he wasn't with me today. His MBA workload remains insane. I was almost tempted to do a Nicole Kidman act, you know, in the film *To Die For*. She's murdered her husband (that's not the bit I want to emulate), and then she puts on the tape and sings along to, '*All by myself, /Don't wanna be, /All by myself.*' And yeah, totally gutted to be on my own: couldn't stop crying, which is both tedious and draining. Also, not a very good mothering act towards my two little embryos. I have therefore stopped doing that, and gone back to reading the *Alan Clark Diaries*. They are always so entertaining. I put them down about a year ago, and never picked them up again. I played one of my three piano pieces. Then watched a truly dire film, *Love Actually*.

So, back to the stress. Have I mentioned that it's getting to me? Mind you, I think that injecting myself full of drugs doesn't help. On the other hand I've done four IVF cycles so far, and catastrophic failure hasn't left me too depressed, just with that general sense of desperation that any infertile person has – you know, that run-of-the-mill-exquisite-torture, wanting-to-kill-your-self-because-you-can't-have-children kind of thing. Apart from that, I'm fine.

There's a good quote in Alan Clark's book. It's him saying how pleased he is when he gets on the train, because he has some peace and quiet. 'For an hour and a half I'm isolated, trundling along, and no one can get at me with a, "Will you, can we, did you, have you, are you, if you, but you, three-bags-full query".' And then one sentence later he says, 'I must be very near a nervous breakdown.' Alan mate, I'm with you.

I recently went to great lengths to engineer a Friday night at The Pool club in Curtain Road. I was speaking to a nice guy, but of course he just wanted to talk about my job. He wanted to talk about the DTI, because he writes for a trade magazine. I smiled, and tried to talk about it, and he said, 'This must be boring for you, maybe we should change the subject.' And he stopped for about one minute, and then went back to it again. Finally my polite façade crumbled and I said, 'I can't talk about this any longer. I have to stop.'

I suppose I'm going to be talking about Iraq for as long as I remain an MP, which might not be very long. I don't know if I'm going to win or lose, but competition is good in every sphere of life, and I've definitely got some political competition.

I sent out 10,000 Eid cards, and inevitably sent one to a Hindu. The Association of Hindu Students has issued a press release condemning me for being culturally insensitive. I wish they'd get a life. I'm Jewish, but I celebrate Christmas, and if someone sends me an Eid card, I'm not going to have a mental breakdown. Life is too short. But that's the thing about politics. There's always a group waiting to be enraged, there's always someone waiting to have a mental breakdown, just need to make sure it's not me.

A social worker came to see Tiberio and me recently, because we really want to adopt, especially since the last IVF cycle failed. We've done the introductory course, and the next step is an home assessment. The social worker – twinset and pearls, very proper – walks into the house and asks if she can use the toilet. And I say, yes, follow me, I'll take you upstairs. We ran out of money fixing dry rot, so our renovations still aren't finished. We've never built the bathroom downstairs, and never put glass panels in the staircase. And its a big, high staircase because it's an old pub.

I get halfway up the staircase, and I say, 'Oh, we do realise, obviously, that we'd have to put the panels in the staircase, because you couldn't have a baby in this house as it is.'

The social worker looks really shocked, and after she's gone up the first ten steps, her eyes are bulging.

'Don't worry,' I say again, 'we're going to have all the work done, it's just that we ran out of money.'

The social worker says no, it's not that, I just can't walk up these stairs. When I asked if she had vertigo, she got very defensive and said she didn't. So I wasn't sure why I had to hold her hands and walk backwards with her up the stairs. When she came out of the bathroom, she was obviously in a bad way, and she said she was going to have to go down all the stairs on her bum, one stair at a time. So we didn't get off to the best start, but we carried on, and then she said she was going to give us some homework. She came back the next week, and said we needed to look at the logistics of parenthood. What were we going to do about childcare? I said we were hoping to get a young baby and I'd take maternity leave, because this fantastic Government of mine does make some mistakes, but at least it has brought in six months' maternity leave for newly adoptive parents.

She asks what we'd do after that. And as the conversation goes on it becomes clear that she's implying I'd have to give up my job if I wanted to adopt a baby. I say, 'I can change my hours, but it would be unrealistic for me to say I'm going to give up my job entirely. Are you saying that if I'm an MP I'm not allowed to adopt?'

'Well, no,' she replies, 'but we need one full-time carer for the child.'

'But I know others who have gone through this process, even MPs, and it's been agreed they can adopt.'

'Ah,' she said, 'but in those cases the MP was not the full-time carer, the full-time carer was his wife.'

'So because I'm a woman MP without a wife I can't adopt?'

'You have to think of the competition,' she said. 'There'll be other parents with one full-time carer.'

At this point Tiberio did his house-husband bit, and said he'd be happy to stay at home and look after the child, and I asked if we could share childcare: that's what couples do these days. In a nutshell, her answer was no. Or at least, if we did that we'd be overlooked, because it's better for the child to have one carer. I think of all the other working couples in Britain – they have kids, but they're not adopted kids. If you are adoptive parents, you can't be like normal parents, you have to jump through a thousand hoops. And that's fair enough, because they're not giving you a TV or a stereo, they're giving you a baby. But those hoops should at least be reasonable.

So the social worker says, 'I've decided it's better if we put this process on hold for a while, I don't think we'll take it any further at the moment. Wait until after the election, see what the outcome is, and then come back to us.'

She was saying that if I lose my seat they will look on our application more favourably. Tiberio was really upset because he wants a child more than anything in the world. In the back of my mind I'm thinking, 'Well maybe it's not a bad thing if the social worker disappears, because it's all too much at the moment.' So the social worker leaves and I say, 'Oh, babe, I'm really sorry, do you really feel that bad about it?' And he says, 'No, the whole thing is driving me nuts. She is dismissed.' I laughed so much. I thought *that's* my husband, *that's* my boy.

In retrospect the social worker was probably right to suggest coming back to the adoption process after the election.

I was meant to be in America for three days this week, but I had to cancel it. So yesterday I had no appointments in my diary, bar one, just thirty minutes with Patricia Hewitt. I've arranged a briefing for MPs on the launch of the DTI five-year strategy. It's just 12.30–one p.m. Only thirty minutes booked up in the whole day.

Karen Buck and I are lobbying John Prescott about affordable housing. We're basically trying to ensure that Ken Livingstone's London Plan, which provides for 50 per cent of affordable housing in private developments, is implemented. But the Conservative councils in Richmond and Westminster want to scupper it. So we need to explain this to John Prescott. The Minister who has taken the decision is Phil Hope. He says he can't talk to us because it's quasi-judicial, so John Prescott says he will see us for thirty minutes, and of course the only thirty minutes he has free are between 12.30 and one p.m.

It's always like that. There are two SoSs I need to see today, and they are both only available in that same thirty-minute slot. Why is that? Is it an astral thing? I decide I have to let down Patricia, because I can get another PPS to go to that meeting, and do what PPSs do, which is sit at the back and say nothing. I can't get another PPS to go to the meeting with John Prescott and argue about the need for affordable housing. Even when I have no meetings in my diary, I can be stressed out by meetings in my diary.

I met with Ken Livingstone last week. At the end of the meeting I mentioned Crossrail to him, because at the moment everyone's going utterly mad over Crossrail, more mad than they were over Iraq. How is that possible? Maybe because Crossrail is about transport close to home, and Iraq is about bombing somewhere a long way away. Some people confuse the two. They think Crossrail is going to bomb them back to the Stone Age, and flatten their entire community. The fact that this is ludicrous scare mongering is neither here not there. They're right that Crossrail has been diabolical in their consultation. And it's also true, as they argue, that it's all about money (when is anything *not* about money? That's all politics is, arguing about money). So of course it's about money, and if Crossrail were prepared to spend more money, they wouldn't need a worksite in Spitalfields, which is a very poor, densely populated area. Mind you, it's also densely populated with middle class, newly made millionaires in their beautiful Georgian houses. Including my very, very lovely and good mate, John, who put us up there when we had nowhere to live, so mustn't complain. Point is it's not going to be as bad as they think, but if there was a bit more money, in the region of a billion pounds, and if we were happy to add two years on to the scheme, you wouldn't need to have a worksite in Spitalfields.

I feel somewhat bounced by my staff into saying Crossrail is the devil's spawn. My staff are being very, very good at trying to get me re-elected, but I don't like doing things just because people think it plays well before an election . . . So I've been slightly bounced into saying that Crossrail is diabolically negative in terms of its impact on the community. Yes, there is some negative impact, but you have to look at the long-term benefits for East Londoners, and there are so many, and Crossrail will also help local people in some ways. But anyway, it's true, the protesters are correct – there has not been an adequate environmental assessment, or a health impact assessment, and you can't expect people to make up their mind without that information. So that's why I've made a vocal protest.

I explain to Ken that the public reaction to Crossrail is really a serious problem, and that he shouldn't underestimate either how serious it is, or how determined the people in my constituency will be to protest against it. And then I listed all the mistakes Crossrail had made, which needed to rectified. Ken's response was that Crossrail is a fantastic, important transport project, and it's going to happen.

I replied, 'Well, you know, I've got my constituents to think about, and that's not what they think. And I don't agree with you on certain issues. So I'm going to have to denounce you.' I said it laughingly, '*Yup*, I'm gonna have to denounce you.'

'That's fine,' said Ken. 'I understand.'

'OK, good, just as long as we understand each other.'

'Now what can I do to help you get re-elected?'

It was nice of him to ask.

'I don't know, just say nice things about me if you can when you're visiting the constituency. That would be really helpful.'

That's on Thursday. Trot to Sunday, five days ago. He arrives at Brick Lane to switch on the Eid lights, and I arrive just before he's going on to the podium. I whisper to him, 'Ken, remember what you said, if there's anything nice you can say about me, I'd be grateful, because I've got my back against the wall.' And he says, 'Oh, come up on the podium with me.' I say, 'No, just mention me, that's enough.' But he is insistent. So I go up and stand next to him, and he says, 'I'm very pleased to be here in Brick Lane, and I wanted to let you know that I work very closely with your local MP Oona King, and I will be working with her on various issues, and I just want you all to know that myself and Oona are going to be working *very* hard together to ensure we deliver Crossrail to this area.'

He might as well have got me up on the podium and said 'We're going to work *very* hard together to ensure we deliver *the Plague* in this area.' Thanks Ken. He didn't do it on purpose, he just forgot. I suppose.

22 November 2004

Sitting behind John Prescott, who's on the right of the PM with Gordon Brown on the left. Queen's Speech day. George Howarth is the 'old codger' MP seconding the Queen's Speech. Meg Munn is the 'whippersnapper' MP. George begins with the preamble that the MP proposing the Queen's Speech has to use, something along the lines of, 'I humbly beg and grovel to the monarch as much as humanly possible. I am a mere commoner. Lick, lick, grovel, grovel.' John

Prescott starts laughing. Not even TB can keep a straight face, and that's saying something.

Dandruff check: none of them – Gordon, Tony, John – have dandruff. That's my boys. Can't bear the usual snowfall covering men's jackets. Proximity to power. It means nothing. I'm often about twelve inches from the PM on occasions like this, and the only special insight I can provide is that it's a dandruff-free zone.

26 November 2004

John Reid, SoS for Health. I could KILL him – or his civil servants at least. A few days ago his PPS rings to say John's doing an event at Newham Hospital, and asks if I want him to do something in Tower Hamlets. 'Of *course*.'

So Lesley in my office valiantly spends forty-eight hours trying to work something out. It miraculously transpires that one of the smaller local hospitals, Mile End, is launching a big event around healthy living – minimising STDs and preventing teenage pregnancies – there will be loads of people there (nothing worse than getting an SoS along to visit a man and his dog) and it is taking place during the exact one-hour slot that John Reid has free. *Alli Akbar**, sorted. Then with sixteen hours to go, the SoS's civil servants get involved. No, no, they say, the slot John is giving Oona is a 'political' slot (which is why I was contacted by John's PPS), so it can only be used for more blatant political campaigning. But Lesley's come up with something that is 100 per cent constructive, though not bi-partisan. The local health trust is thrilled to bits, and therefore civil servants must kill it.

'The Secretary of State cannot set foot on a health premises unless it's done formally, following the correct protocol. We understand how disappointing this will be, and therefore the Secretary of State *will* come to Mile End Hospital, just not tomorrow when there's a big event going on.'

These people are deranged. But that's not why I could kill John Reid. It's because Mile End's 'consolation' prize, as arranged by

---

* *Allahu Akbar*: 'God is greatest'.

Lesley, is that I go along and do the opening instead. In two hours. Which, under normal circumstances, would be great. But under these particular circumstances I need valium, painkillers, alcohol, a wheelchair, no, a *stretcher*, and a psychiatrist. And a surgeon to operate on my tear ducts and stitch them up. We're on the fifth IVF cycle – the third 'fresh' one, as well as the two 'frozen' ones. This time we went to the Lister, which was a revelation. Not in terms of VIP treatment (i.e. privacy) – the Homerton, ironically, was better at that. But in terms of what they do.

At the Homerton we had a procedure called ICSI. ICSI costs at least £1,000 more than the standard IVF and can result in birth defects because the sperm are physically injected into the eggs. With IVF the sperm is just left alone with the eggs.

When I woke up from the egg collection thirteen days ago we were asked then and there to choose between IVF and ICSI. IVF is best, if it works, but there's a risk none of the nine eggs harvested will fertilise. ICSI is more likely to guarantee fertilisation, but there's a 3 per cent chance that the eggs/embryos could be damaged, and in the long run they don't know what the consequences of this might be.

We opt for IVF. Two days later, they ring us with the results: all nine of the eggs have fertilised. Great result. But of our nine, six (I paraphrase) are fucked. Bad result. And then slowly I start to realise it's *good*. It's starting to explain something. If two-thirds of our embryos are bad and won't implant, then it's no wonder it took me four years to get pregnant naturally, and we probably lost it because it was genetically abnormal; and the previous IVF treatment, without genetic screening, has just been blundering about in the dark. A waste of time and money, not to mention emotional strength. So I feel happier, more optimistic.

The downside of this cycle is that I can't walk. Our consultant, Marie Wren, confirms that my ovaries are 'terribly bruised and swollen, and you'll be in pain for a couple of weeks. But it won't affect whether the treatment works or not.'

The day before yesterday, I wake up at dawn feeling sick. I've never felt it before in my life, it's like a light goes on in my head. 'Wow. I think I'm really pregnant.'

At the end of my first day with morning sickness I whisper to

Tiberio, 'I'm really excited about waking up tomorrow feeling sick.'

I wake up at seven a.m., but don't feel sick. I don't feel anything. The day before, something was going on. The furnace was definitely lit.

And now, although I haven't done the test, and there's no blood, it's plain as day what's coming. The light is definitely out.

Tiberio took me for lunch yesterday at Ubon in Canary Wharf. I ate raw fish because I knew it was all over. I said, 'How will you feel if it doesn't work?'

'Like an atom bomb going off inside,' he said. 'If it doesn't work this time around, it's never going to work. That's it. I give up hope.'

So this morning I subside into tears. Grief. So much grief. How many women know what it's like to fail the fifth IVF cycle? Not many. But those that do, know you want to die. You will scream, throw yourself on the floor, collapse under the pain. You will do all these things. But you will not, in the natural order of things, put make-up on and represent the Secretary of State for Health at a family planning clinic. And that, in a nutshell, is why I could kill John Reid, or his civil servants at least. I have no valium or a stretcher so I must just get myself in the car and go right now.

I've already missed the office meeting at ten; I feel I should be allowed to take the day off work and lie in a dark room wearing a black arm band. A fortnight ago at the last office meeting, for the first time in a management setting, I started crying. It was excruciating. One of my caseworkers, Lesley, had been irate. Lesley works in my office two days a week almost as a gift of charity. She's fantastic. Her husband Mark is my intermittent 'life-coach', an amazing manager – notwithstanding a PhD in philosophy – who works in the City, and I'm indebted to both of them.

That particular morning Lesley was irate because my diary is insanely busy – often ten or twelve meetings a day, usually overlapping. Too many commitments. I say 'no' a lot, but not enough. Ironically if I were a Secretary of State, my diary would be less full. Patricia's diary isn't as full as mine. It is more important but less cluttered. So Lesley went on about my atrocious diary, Frances chipped in, and the others followed suit. It was my forty-eighth working day without a day off, and maybe that's why the tears slipped out. Or maybe it was the IVF treatment and daily injections; the adoption process; social workers and George Galloway on my case; never fewer than 300 letters/ emails/ faxes/ texts/ messages a day; not enough money from Parliament to pay my staff; worrying about their pensions; working without functioning technology; getting a court summons from the council about emergency building work on the house; a letter from a bailiff; a few hours' sleep each night. Whatever.

Before that last office meeting I'd gone across London at 7.30 a.m. to get blood taken at the Lister. They couldn't find my veins. I hate it when they dig around with the needle in the middle of both arms. I stared at the ceiling and tried to imagine I wasn't there. It can't help that on top of my demented diary I start or end most days with someone digging blood out of my veins. Each test costs between £80 and £120. I had five that week. Soon my credit card won't work. More frightening, soon Tiberio's credit card won't work, and then we're really screwed. And childless. So I sat in the staff meeting, enraged by my own tears. How pathetic. I pressed the circular plasters the nurse placed on the inside of each arm, and massaged them firmly. In my head I tried to be firm. 'Look, babe, you've had a bad morning, they've been dicking you about with needles, you haven't slept, debt collectors are at the door, but there's no need – no need at all – to be a complete tit and cry in front of your staff. For God's sake pull yourself together.'

I opened my eyes and interrupted the conversation which had become more hesitant as they realised I was crying. 'Now listen,' I said, loudly and abruptly, 'just ignore the tears, I can't do anything about them, but they're not relevant to the conversation.' After the meeting I took one of Mohammed's fags. It was that bad. Filthy habit, can't bear smokers. Mohammed himself wasn't even smoking because it was Ramadan. I wish I hadn't cried in front of Mohammed – he's only been in the office for a couple of months.

So that's why, this morning, I'm damned if I'm going to walk into another office meeting and start crying. I park the car near Bethnal Green Road, and decide to take a Royal Family approach to the situation: never complain, never explain.

'Did you forget the office meeting?' asks Frances archly.

'No, I didn't.' I casually flick through some post. 'Just thought I'd let you decide things for yourselves.'

The strategy works pretty well.

Get into the car with Lesley and drive to the hospital. 'So are you okay?' she asks.

'Oh yeah, I'm fine. Fine. So what's the name of the hospital chief Exec again?' Lesley gives me a run-down and the one page speech she's done for me. The first line is 'I'm so pleased to be opening the Sylvia Pankhurst Centre on this new site, especially as I opened the first one in 1998.'

'Did I?'

'Apparently so.'

Arrive at the centre and remember the woman running it. Gheeta. The good news is there aren't hundreds of people there – more like sixty. The bad news is, as Gheeta shows me round the new premises, almost every room is plastered with pictures – big poster pictures – of women holding newborn babies. Tears well up. I smash them back down.

We go into the largest room at the end of the corridor, one without pictures of babies on the wall. Instead, it has rails which partition off a dozen reclining armchairs. 'This is where we meet the women who choose not to keep their babies,' explains Gheeta. 'The miscarriage is induced here. We also offer counselling because losing a baby, no matter what stage, can be devastating.'

'I'm sure it is . . .' I imagine I'm on one of those reality-TV shows that try to make you crack. Gheeta explains that the women who come here need a lot of support.

As she talks, I feel my own mini-miscarriage is underway. Fab. Great surroundings, nice company. The writing's on the wall. I alter the phrase for a new generation of sub-fertile women who are devastated to get their period each month: the blood's in the bowl. You stare long and hard at a bowl of blood, and it's really not adequate compensation for a lost family.

A group of staff from a youth organisation (of which I'm patron) have arrived. They're called Step Forward, and they help young people by providing a whole range of services from contraception advice to careers advice. One of their managers is surprised to see me holding a speech. 'You must give so many, I always get the impression you do them off the top of your head.'

'I do – unless Lesley writes me one.'

So the speeches are done and dusted, the sandwiches and samosas are eaten and it's time to go back to the office. Sign some more letters. Thousands and thousands of letters have gone out to constituents in the last months. Then visit an elderly persons' day centre with Frances and Mohammed, who as usual looks like he's going clubbing. Thank God someone in my office does. Then meet Marc and Humayan and Kuddus and set off to go knocking on doors. Marc is now the Parliamentary Officer for Shelter. When he was my assistant for four years, in many ways he shaped the sort of MP I am. It was Marc's energy and commitment that kept me going out week after week back then.* Now that Iraq has turned Bethnal Green and Bow into a marginal and my arse is grass, I always say a prayer for Marc. If I win, it will partly be down to Marc. After two hours on the doorstep, go back to office, sign some more letters, amend a letter for the local press, speak to the regional organiser the LP has drafted in to help, have a chat with Frances, then drive to Brick Lane for a function and then eventually, fourteen hours after I woke up to know the fifth IVF attempt was a failure, sink into a cinema seat in Canary Wharf to watch a comedy called *I ♥ Huckabees*. Halfway through Jude Law says to his love interest, 'Why is it that the final arbiter of success with professional couples is having children? Why is that?' Elicits a 'Doh' response from me and Tiberio.

27 November 2004

Meet with LP team on Sunday morning to do more knocking on doors. Finish at 1.30 p.m. Go home. Write a handwritten letter to everyone I've met, and make notes on the issues raised. Blocked drains, overcrowding, repairs needed, lifts that don't work, security gates broken. At 8.30 p.m. I stop writing letters and start writing this. At 11.30 p.m. Tiberio says, 'You've been writing for hours. Stop writing.'

---

* In June 2006 Marc virtually single-handedly won over an entire local council ward to be elected as one of the first Labour Councillors in Bow for thirty years.

28 November 2004

Go to a Bengali wedding and a Diwali celebration. During the Diwali gathering, five minutes is set aside for meditation. I like this. Maybe I should become a Hindu. As is the fashion these days, at any religious celebration, they have representatives from all the other religions there. A nun made a fantastic speech about connections. 'Martin Luther King was influenced by Gandhi, who was influenced by Tolstoy, who was influenced by Russian monasticism, which has links back to pre-Christianity. There are chains everywhere, linking everything.'

29 November 2004

Back at Westminster. Listen to Jack Straw at the PLP meeting. Chat with David Miliband. Later, I catch Jack on the way out of the meeting. I ask him to give me a quote for the introduction of my APPG Report on Arms Control in the Great Lakes Region. The UN panel of experts have described it as a 'model' submission. Jack tells me not to worry about Galloway. 'In 1983 (or did he say 1987?) everyone told me I would lose. But I didn't. You've just got to work your balls off.'

'I am.'

I leave Jack and catch up with David (Miliband) who's at David Lammy's engagement party, hosted by Charlie Falconer in the Lord Chancellor's Private Residence. In his speech, David says that he and his fiancée Nicola met through 'my good friend Oona and her good friend Quincy'! David and Quin first met at Tiberio's fortieth. There are chains everywhere, linking everything.

2 December 2004

Jim Fitzpatrick rings me. 'Have you heard the news?'

'David Blunkett's been forced out?'

'No, George Galloway's won his libel case against the *Telegraph* and £150,000 damages.'

Fuck, fuck, fuck. That's one of the text messages that comes through from Josh, my campaign manager.

Watched Gordon deliver his pre-budget report. He was at his best. Outstanding. He wiped the floor. There is no opposition. The Tories hardly bother to attack. Gordon obliterates them both on their own terms (1.2 million additional homeowners since 1997, low inflation, high business start-up rates) and on our terms (providing extra money for the poorest pensioners, poorest children, poorest parents – and extra maternity leave for women *and* men). No disrespect to my husband when I say that listening to Gordon at his best is better than sex.

At 1.30 p.m., I run to NatWest and pay in a cheque from Tiberio. My bank manager rang today to say I was over my £9,000 overdraft and no more transactions could be charged. A cold snap has started. Cold hands. Can't buy gloves.

At 2.30 p.m., I meet with the Chief Whip. Miraculously, she's summoned me to ask what she and the Party can do to help.

At three p.m., I meet with the former Prime Minister of Bangladesh and current opposition leader. Bangladesh is sliding from a dysfunctional democracy towards a fundamentalist state, which is harbouring terror networks. I am worried for Sheikh Hasina's safety.

At four p.m., we hear that George Galloway will declare today that he's running in Bethnal Green and Bow.

At seven p.m., go to see Akram Khan, the choreographer and dancer at the Queen Elizabeth Hall. Tiberio bought the tickets. Mesmerising. I've fallen in love – not so much with Akram as an individual, but with his existence as a concept. Heart-racing dance sweeps across the stage. He displays what is fast becoming one of Britain's unique twenty-first-century hallmarks: cultural fusion, where eclecticism replaces dogmatism, and where the power and confidence of the West is used by second and third generations to turn the West on its head. Never mind New Labour, it's New Britons that are most exciting: British in a way that Britain has never seen or imagined before.

Halfway through, Akram stopped his magical dancing and pulled up the microphone. 'I want to tell you a story,' he said.

By now I was happy to be transported anywhere he wanted to take me as long as it was a place without George Galloway and infertility.

'I want to tell you a story,' he continued, 'it's about a woman who can't have children. This woman wanted children so much and so she prayed to God that she would have children but the years passed and she didn't. She had some seeds and planted them and watered them.' [I paraphrase:] 'And eventually she said to God, "Why haven't you given me children?" And he said, "Remember how much you loved those trees? Well those are your children." '

I already have trees. I bought them from Trees for London and they sent me a certificate saying I'm the proud owner of trees in Whitechapel. But if anyone thinks trees in Whitechapel are acceptable compensation for a lost family, they're barking. In this sense, trees in Whitechapel are only a notch above a bowl of blood. If you're parents, you can try this yourself: imagine your children, who you love more than you understood it was possible to love until by a miracle they arrived in your life. And then imagine your children were taken away from you and instead God gave you a tree. It's a guess, only a guess, but I think you would join with me in a loud chorus and tell God to stick his trees where the sun don't shine, and give your children back. Unless you've got really irritating kids.

3 December 2004

Attended a women's group meeting in Wapping this morning, focusing on domestic violence, followed by a meeting at the Council with Jim Fitzpatrick, and Council Leader Abbas. Knocking on doors in afternoon, followed by a visit to the Wapping Bengali Association, then a meeting at the mosque, then two meetings in Brick Lane. The mosque meeting was really good. Abbas came out strongly in favour of me, which makes a change. He wants my seat. But he's been told that unless he helps me win, the Party won't let him be an MP anywhere else. So for the first time in seven years he's explaining to the Mosque Committee that I am 'like a sister to him and should be supported'. I appreciate it, no matter how transparent it is.

George Galloway is on a victory parade in Brick Lane. The *Guardian*'s headline: 'Victor plots revenge on old party.' The article reads: 'George Galloway is to spend a slice of his £150,000 windfall seeking electoral revenge on the Labour hierarchy which kicked him out of the party, by running on an anti-war ticket against a prominent Blairite in racially mixed Bethnal Green and Bow . . . [He] announced his intention to stand against Oona King in an East London seat where ethnic minorities constitute just over half the voters . . . he denounced [me] as a New Labour stooge . . . and said he expected Labour to be thrashed at the ballot box. He made a direct appeal to Muslim voters . . .'

Rang David Lammy when I got home at eleven p.m. to thank him for the lovely message – 'Tell me what I can do to help. I'll do anything. Most people don't understand the pressure you're under. I know it's enormous.' At least I'm getting a lot of support, and at least the daily injections and hormone-baiting is over for a while.

7 December 2004

Today I took part in a five-way video conference between London, Washington, Dhaka, Columbo and Jakarta, on the relationship between politicians and the press. Norman Fowler was the other UK politician. As a former Tory Cabinet Minister, he ran the country when I was at school, but now I can't really remember who he is or what he did. Politics is so unforgiving.

Last night I took two fantastic Tower Hamlets community workers, Brian Tugwell and Shaheda Chowdhury, to No. 10 for a reception hosted by Tony and Cherie to say thank you to people who work hard in their local communities. TB started his speech by indicating at the picture of a former Prime Minister hanging above the fireplace in the large Downing Street reception room upstairs. 'It's amazing how soon people forget former Prime Ministers,' he said. 'I had a group of young people under thirty in here, and here's someone from 1960, and they ask, "Who's that bloke above the fireplace?"' Everyone laughs.

But who *is* that bloke above the fireplace? It's not Churchill, Attlee, Macmillan, Wilson . . . there's always one I forget, I must have a look above the fireplace next time. The point is that everything's utterly transitory, so there's no point getting worked up.

8 December 2004

I'm woken up by the subterranean growling of my vibrating pager. The *Evening Standard* are ringing to say they're putting me on the front page. Obviously the story must involve sex. An MEP offering me £10,000 out of his office costs for me to sleep with him. A journalist from the *Mirror* was pushing me for examples of sexism in Parliament.

'On a personal level I haven't experienced crude sexism at Westminster.'

'None at all?' asked one journalist, incredulously.

'None at all.'

'But you must have experienced blatant sexism in politics.'

'Yes, of course.' And that's when I mentioned the MEP. The *Daily Mirror* has turned my comments into an article in my name, being printed today, which the *Evening Standard* has picked up. There are serious points I make about modernisation of Parliament and the quest for a representative democracy. But of course these are submerged beneath the sex, sex, sex, angle. Will I name the MEP? Of course not. Is it one of the following three? Not saying.

The last time I was on the front page of the *Evening Standard* (also the first) was the opening day of Parliament 1997. It was a picture of me with Paul Boateng, taken a few minutes after the infamous Blair's Babes photo. Nearly eight years have intervened. I've done prominent campaigns on genocide, housing, immigration and asylum, health, arms control, crime and policing, electoral reform, Europe and education, but inevitably it's only sex that puts me back on the front page of the *Evening Standard*.

I get a text from Jim Fitzpatrick. 'The Chief Whip wants to see you.' I reply nervously: 'What about? The article or something else?' 'The article and the reaction here.' Hmmm. He's at Westminster. One of my comments might have been that Parliament was stuffed full of mediocre white men. They'll be on the warpath. I'll apologise, tell them I gave a mediocre interview.

Driving into Westminster, I'm wondering whether proper news (Iraq/ climate change/ housing crisis) has displaced me from the front page of the *Evening Standard*. I see the banner headline: 'MP offered £10,000 for sex.' Evidently not.

Later on that afternoon, on my way in to see the Chief Whip, a journalist stops me in the lobby.

'The hunt's on for the MEP. Can you give me any more information?'

'No.' I feel partially consoled by the fact that I've forgotten the MEP's surname. If *I* can't even remember his name, then surely they won't track him down? But this morning the *Evening Standard* journalist said, 'You've said that he was an MEP for more than ten years. That means he came in in 1979. We can narrow it down.'

And then I think, was it ten years? Maybe it was only seven or eight. I really can't remember. But as long as I don't say anything, it should be OK. I really don't want to ruin this man's life. The only other two people who know his identity are the two MEPs I complained to at the time – Glyn Ford and Glenys Kinnock. But even if they were asked, I don't think they'd remember. Glyn's office rings me. The *Daily Mail* have been on to him. I ask them not to say anything.

At about five p.m. I'm in the Chief Whip's office. Hilary sits down with me and says she's been having to fire-fight all day, that it's not very helpful, it gives the impression that Labour's undisciplined.

'If we're going to help you properly (to win the election), from now on everything you do and say has to go through the regional press office.' As it happens, I'm clutching some 'lines to take' that Joe Derrett, the LP London Region press officer, has drawn up for me on Galloway. I'd be delighted to go through Region. I'd be delighted to get some proper help with the press. Unless you have someone working on it for you it's madness. You make a few remarks and whoosh . . . everything goes up in flames. These 'lines to take' that I'm holding are the first help I've received from an LP press officer since I was elected in 1997. When you go on *Question Time*, the LP gives a briefing on some of the main stories in the news that week, but that's different to a press officer providing direct assistance.

Hilary continues, in a very relaxed fashion, to ask what she needs to know. 'Is it anyone who's still a serving politician – in Brussels or in the Lords?'

'No.'

'Who is it?'

'I'd rather not say. I'm the only one at Westminster who knows. If I don't tell anyone else, it can't get out.'

Failing, as ever, to live up to the stereotype of a Chief Whip (in the whipping sense) Hilary says, 'Fine'.

Just when I think I'm getting out of the office unscathed, I say something flippant and Hilary becomes sharp. 'It's your political judgement that's being called into question.'

Well, yes and no. Actually it's a question of an older man in a position of authority making an indecent proposal to a younger woman. You'd think it would be his judgement that was called into question, not mine. This story about the MEP first appeared in an interview I gave about six years ago. It didn't cause a ripple. Several of the journalists I've spoken to said they'd read it last time round. Why should it make such a splash now?

'Because it wasn't just before a general election,' says Hilary, 'because they *liked* us then.'

She's right. You just can't risk it. Even though I said no to an indecent proposal, I've put me and sex in the same headline. Won't go down well at the mosque. Won't inspire nice white male MPs to come out and campaign for me. Maybe I should have said I wasn't aware of any sexism.

Leaving Hilary's office I bump into the same lobby journalist.

'Was she hard on you?'

'Not really.'

'What did she say?'

'Not to speak to journalists. Bye for now.'

Get a few icy stares in the voting lobby, but also get a lovely message from Patricia Hewitt. 'Good on you for talking out.'

Get about fifty messages in total. Reply to twenty.

I'm home at ten p.m. I get a text message from the journalist at the *Evening Standard*. He's named the MEP. I can't work out how he figured it out. His message says, 'The MEP says he was only joking about the £10,000. We need your reaction urgently.' My reaction is, you must learn there is *nothing* the press won't find out. I'm gutted about the MEP. Why did he say he'd done it, even if it was only as a joke (which it wasn't)? They probably tricked him by saying, 'Oona's named you, what's your reaction?' Feel very guilty. If I wanted him to be punished for what he did, I should have taken him to a tribunal at the time – not let the press ambush him thirteen years later. It never crossed my mind that they could identify him. He was

one male MEP out of forty. Although being an MP for seven years
has made me incredibly guarded in almost everything I say, I resolve
to be even *more* guarded with journalists in future.

9 December 2004

Got a text message from (BBC journalist) Tim Franks this morning.
He's going to present the *Today Programme* for three days between
Boxing Day and the new year. Surely he's got the most amazing voice
in radio. He says he's got a face for radio. I say he's got the brain of
Britain. I haven't spoken to him very much since he was in Iraq. I
can't forgive myself for choking during a conversation we had while
he was in Basra. I was terrified that my friend could die in a war I had
voted for. The thought of anyone dying in Iraq makes me feel sick,
but it would be a lie to pretend that the death of a stranger hits you as
hard as the death of a friend. Tim sounded so near, as though he was
in Bethnal Green. He said it was really dusty, he was hallucinating at
the thought of fresh vegetables, the gas masks weighed a ton. And
when he was reporting for the *Today Programme*, you could hear
bombs falling. I kept thinking of his wife Sarah. What right did I
have, in London, as someone who voted for the war, to be worried
for his safety? I didn't ring him for months after that. Almost a year
later in Morocco, when a guide in Fez took us to the old Jewish
quarter, I bought him a beautiful silver Jewish symbol, similar to the
'Hand of Fatimah', inscribed in Hebrew. But when I got home I
realised that if I gave it to him he'd think I was buying it out of guilt.
So I kept it. It's the only Jewish symbol I've ever bought, but I love it,
it's next to my pillow, and it reminds me that one day I will re-learn
my own Jewish heritage.

I managed not to look at a newspaper until five p.m. today. I'm
quite good at ignoring the press. The *Guardian* has a huge photo of
me (but at least it's only page thirteen) with a headline quote: 'MEP
offered me £10,000 for a night of sex.' No he didn't. He offered me
£10,000 annually out of his office costs allowance to sleep with him
on an ongoing basis. I'm hardly going to quibble, but their facts are
wrong. I've never said those words ('£10,000 for a night of sex') and
yet they've put them in a headline with quotation marks round them.

Bloody cheek. My beloved *Guardian*. Making things up as they go along. Or to be more precise, manufacturing Chinese whispers as they go along. At least they haven't printed the MEP's name. I hope no other papers have, but I haven't looked.

Mum arrived from France. So good to see her. Thank God she didn't buy the *Guardian* when she got off the plane.

12 December 2004

Today is my family Christmas day. Decided to have it early, when everyone can make it. The deal is that Miri pays for it, I put it on, and the rest of the family turn up: Ed and Amie, Will and Linzi, Emilio and Mito and adored godson Mattia, Esme toddling around, the spitting image of Ed, Miri and Chris, Cat and Zac, Mum, Slate and Kate, Tom, Daphne my piano teacher for sixteen years, my bridesmaids Quin and Nora, John Nicolson, because in my book if you give people somewhere to live you become family, and me and Tiberio. Twenty adults and three kids – a good ratio.

Tom was on good form. He said that for the first time in his life he's giving himself a break and not imposing a deadline for writing the next play. His trilogy, *The Coast of Utopia*, got rave reviews. We talk politics for a bit. I do my really good trick which is to more or less cook a roast dinner involving seven dishes for twenty people and then wander off and leave my friends to get all the last bits sorted, and everything on the table, chop the parsley and serve the baby carrots.

Go back into the kitchen, where Daphne and Quin have got everything under control. Quin has been lecturing me on speaking to the press.

'Why would you do it?' she says. 'What's in it for you? Nothing. They get a story, you get screwed. From your point of view they're the enemy. Stop talking to them.'

This morning, while Mum and I were wrapping presents, Tiberio read out a profile of me in the *Independent on Sunday*. It's somewhere between Chinese whispers and fiction. Dad, I read, has gone off to start a new life in Australia. Actually, he lives in Atlanta. According to the paper, he refused a medical exam for Vietnam. In fact, the Vietnam war didn't figure in anything Dad did. I read that I 'narrowly' escaped de-selection last year. I admit it wasn't a bed of roses. But I won my re-selection by something like thirteen votes to five. How can you describe a politician who got two-thirds of the vote as someone who 'narrowly escaped defeat'? I'm interested to hear that my former boss Glyn Ford MEP has 'already chewed me out in an angry phone call'. I haven't spoken to Glyn.

The main thrust of the article is that my political judgement is flawed and I'm always whining about not getting a promotion. I've never publicly said anything about promotion. I write about it in this diary. I've never said it out loud. Ever.

Glenys is quoted: 'Many of us expected her to soar but it just hasn't happened yet for whatever reason.' People always ask me what the reason is. I just smile and say, 'It's politics.' I was never in anyone's gang. I've never had a senior Cabinet Minister banging the table for me. And I rejected the 'promotion' I was offered first time round as a PPS, because I wanted to stay on the International Development Select Committee. I remember the conversation I had with the Chief Whip, Hilary Armstrong:

'I'm offering you a PPS to the leader of the Lords.'

'I don't want to be a PPS. I want to do policy.'

'But you need to be a PPS.'

'Why?'

'You won't be promoted otherwise.'

'Why? Other MPs are.'

'Like who?'

'Yvette Cooper, Douglas Alexander, David Miliband . . .'

'But Oona, those MPs are all linked to the Prime Minister or the Chancellor. You're not.' She was right. I didn't have their connections and in politics, as in life, it *always* comes down to who you know.

On Friday night, a journalist rang and asked: 'What do you say to allegations that you exaggerated or lied about this incident, and to rumours that this is a media stunt to help you in your battle against George Galloway?'

It's as though they work in a fiction factory. On Thursday, the *Daily Mail* ran a story: 'Why is Labour MP Oona King telling us now that an unnamed MEP offered her £10,000 for sex thirteen years ago . . .? Some suspect this headline-grabbing claim might help Miss King, thirty-seven, defend her constituency at the election.' Oh really? Since when has a sex scandal gone down well with the Muslim community? And as for the answer to their question, 'Why is Oona telling us this *now?*' Well, it's simple. There's no conspiracy. I was just waiting to go into that video conference with Norman Fowler. There wasn't anyone to take me up to the studio, and while I was waiting for someone to come down from the twelfth floor, the *Daily Mirror* rang. If they'd called two minutes later when I was in the lift, they'd have got my answer machine. I wouldn't have repeated the anecdote that was printed six years ago, the *Standard* wouldn't have picked it up the next day and put it on the front page, and none of this would've happened. According to the profile today in the *Independent*, I provide 'a case study of how years of serious but worthy work can evaporate with one misguided interview'. According to the *Daily Mail*, it's part of a cunning plan. The best bit comes at the end of the *Mail* piece, when the journalist (using the name Ephraim Hardcastle) writes: 'Miss King is a coquettish lassie. She gave a mutual friend her pager number and told him, "Vibrate me sometime".' It's the oldest trick in the book. It's the 'the woman is a slut' number. At least the boys are predictable.

The family Christmas day is fab, a really nice atmosphere, everyone having a good time. As John and Quin are leaving, they say, 'You've got a great family, lots of interesting people, there's never anyone you don't want to speak to.'

It makes me realise something for the first time: I've got a great family. A *fantastic* family. The only person missing is Dad. I spoke to him yesterday. Better warn him he's started a new life in Australia. This reminds me, returning briefly to the fiction factory, that a journalist rang me to say they've got hold of the old rumour in circulation that I had an affair with Jack Straw. The first time I heard it, I'd never even had a cup of tea with Jack Straw in private. I'm not sure who made it up. In 2002 a friend of mine, Michael Keith, told me he'd read it on an American website. I've never mentioned it to Jack because it seemed so absurd.

On Friday afternoon, went to the Guantanamo Bay service to mark International Human Rights Day. I was invited by Corin and Vanessa Redgrave. I'm going to try and get a parliamentary debate on the men in Belmarsh Prison. I've got to stick to the important stuff and remember that today's newspapers are tomorrow's chip paper.

14 December 2004

Lots of MPs are doing gags about being paid £10,000 for sex. I tell them that that was then, this is now, a tenner will do. Jack comes up to me with a couple of other MPs, cracking jokes.

'Actually, we'd better not joke about this,' I tell him, 'because there are rumours that we're having an affair.'

'Really?' He's mildly entertained.

'I've been told it's on an American gossip website and a journalist rang me this weekend and said they were going to print it. They haven't, but they might.'

We move through the lobbies. We're voting on the Mental Incapacity Bill – aka euthanasia. See the Chief Whip and tell her today's crisis – George Galloway is suing me.

Eighty young Labour Party Members are waiting for me to speak to them over in Portcullis House. But first I have to do a five-way conference call with LP lawyers and others.

15 December 2004

The pressure. It's starting to fizz. Music, the antidote. Haven't done any exercise – even stretching – for a month. First thing in the morning, put on 'Sounds of Blackness', gospel house music.

'The pressure . . . my back is against the wall . . . playing on the tensions that lure your mind astray . . . you can fight it, you can win.'

The lawyers are telling me I have to apologise to George Galloway. They say I can't spend the next five months, when I should be fighting an election, locked in a legal battle with Galloway. And anyway, they add ominously, 'Can you afford it?'

Can I afford it? I can't afford a pair of gloves at the moment. Money. Debt. That reminds me, builders are arriving any minute with someone from the council – the council has slapped a Dangerous Structure Notice on our house and says we'll be taken to court unless it's sorted out. What a coincidence, there was a photographer from the local paper outside my front door when they arrived.

16 December 2004

A headline in the *Evening Standard* today says, 'Galloway calls in lawyers in battle with Oona King.' As a story, it's starting to bore me already. What can I say about why he's suing me? Not much.

The good news is that the meeting that Karen (Buck) and I had with John Prescott has paid off. He's changing the decision on the percentage of affordable housing that must be included in all new property developments in Westminster. That will effectively act as a precedent for the rest of London. It's another VH Day (Victory in Housing Day) to go along with the £180 million for Tower Hamlets VH Day. It's still not enough, as any of the 20,000 families on the Tower Hamlets housing waiting list will tell you, but it's *incomparably* better than what went before.

At ten p.m. last night I got a message from Quin. She's ecstatic, and I can't quite figure why, until I realise she's saying David Blunkett's resigned. Shocked. Sorry for him on a personal level, but don't have any sympathy if he really fast-tracked his lover's nanny's visa, or for his totalitarian views. Any Home Secretary who presides over the detention without trial of suspects in Britain should have a big cross next to his name.

Charles Clarke will take over as Home Secretary. I found out this morning that Ruth (Kelly) is in the Cabinet. Breathtaking. It doesn't seem that long ago that we had a 'reshuffle day' conversation. 'Surely he's got to promote *one* of us,' we said to each other at four p.m., when neither of us had heard anything. And then she called me when I was shopping in Safeway at seven p.m. and told me she'd been offered the Treasury. Safeway is now called Morrisons. Ruth's no longer a junior Minister, she's in the Cabinet. And I'm no longer on my Select Committee. Instead I hand out PQs to MPs I meet in the tea room.

I momentarily imagine the parallel universe I inhabit somewhere: I played my cards right at Westminster. I didn't say no to the Prime Minister early on, I didn't say no to the Chief Whip when she offered me a PPS job on the first two occasions, and I didn't concentrate on the policy areas I was drawn to, instead I concentrated on gaining the patronage of a senior Cabinet Minister, who ensured I got promoted. David Miliband said to Quincy, in 1997 when he was still at the No. 10 policy unit, 'All she has to do is keep quiet for two years, and she'll definitely be promoted.' Wise words I wasn't able to – or didn't wish to – follow.

In some sense it happened incrementally, going from being Channel 4's 'Rising Star' to the *Parliamentary Companion*'s 'over-tipped, under-promoted MP languishing on the backbenches'. But in other senses it happened dramatically, there was a clear choice I made early on and I can't regret it. I can regret (deeply) working in an environment where healthy dissent is mistaken for treason, but I can't regret my decisions themselves. So it's my bed and I'll lie in it.

Something tells me, despite her meteoric rise, that Ruth won't be Prime Minister. But I hope she is, not least because she's a genuinely decent person and might let me play a part in front-line British politics . . . Derek, her husband, also cooks fabulous barbecued vegetables, and that's got to count for something. They're a genuinely friendly, down-to-earth, decent couple.

Finally, TB made a really clever move promoting Ruth over David Miliband – it will mean David's a more powerful Cabinet figure when he gets there, and will have a slightly tighter grip on TB's crown.

20 December 2004

The last day of Parliament before Christmas. I was in my office, forced to go over and over the George Galloway stuff. I understand why the Labour Party want me to roll over. They can't risk losing a court case in an election year, they have no insurance to cover it, and therefore they want the legal side closed down. They will only pay for one more set of transactions between my lawyer and his. And that transaction in their opinion should be me saying (I paraphrase): George, you are the truth and the light. I am a bad person. In fact, please take my seat at your earliest convenience.

My lawyer reads out the letter GG's lawyers have drafted, which will settle the whole thing.

'Will you sign it?' All the advice I've received from everyone (except my staff) is that I should sign it.

'Will I sign it? . . . Umm, highly unlikely.'

'Well then, Oona, you have to come up with some evidence. And you've got one hour to do it. It cuts no ice even if these allegations were published in virtually every national newspaper. The libel law regarding repetition is very strict. You can't just prove that he was *accused* of these allegations. You would have to prove the allegations were *true* or that you had some other defence. You need to bring me evidence, otherwise on the instruction of the LP I'll have to withdraw my services. I'm sorry. I'm in a difficult position.'

'How long did you say I've got?'

'An hour.'

'Fine. I'll get back to you in an hour.'

I put the phone down and look out the window at Big Ben. Bloody ridiculous. How can I come up with anything in an hour? There's nothing else on the internet and I don't know where else to look. I ring Kester in the constituency office.

'We *have* to find some hard evidence. We need to find someone who was at that bloody press conference in 1987, or the War on Want Committee members from that time. Someone must know something.'

'John Denham MP was around at the time. Speak to him.' I ring John's office, grateful for a lead. I ask for his pager number.

'He doesn't have one.'

'OK, then his mobile.'

'It'll be switched off but you could text him. He should be in the House listening to a statement on Belmarsh.'

Belmarsh . . . detention without trial. I wanted to hear that statement too. At least there was a chance I might actually find him. I look at my watch and then outside again at Big Ben. Twelve minutes have passed. What with finding John's constituency office number, keying in a text message to him, entreating Kester to find something on the internet, telling Ro to put back a meeting, ringing the regional officer to pass on the lawyer's ultimatum . . . twelve minutes have passed, forty-eight remaining. I suddenly feel like I'm in one of those drama/thriller movies, a combination of Julia Roberts in *Erin Brockovich* and Kevin Costner in *No Way Out*. Move!

I grab my jacket and run out of the office. Down from the fifth floor of Portcullis House, past the expensive fig trees in the open plan foyer space, and down the escalators, taking them two at a time, through the underground passage beneath Westminster Bridge Road and under Big Ben. I glance up at the CCTV cameras just before Palace Yard. How many times have they recorded me running hell-for-leather towards the Chamber or a meeting room, or the voting lobby? But never as fast as this. Run past the Royal Mail's collection point and up the back stairs, past the Government Whip's Assistant's office, and out into the Members' lobby.

'You look like you're in a hurry Oona,' says one of the men-in-tights '. . . for a change!'

'I am.' I'm gasping to catch my breath. I pull up short outside the inner door to the Chamber, and comb the Labour benches looking for John Denham. I think I've found him, but then have a doubt. Damn, all those middle-aged white men in suits look the same. I have an unfortunate habit of confusing John Denham and John Hutton. John Denham resigned over Iraq. John Hutton didn't, and he has rosier red cheeks and curlier hair. Still, best be on the safe side. I get the nice man-in-tights, who's in his pagoda-style throne next to Churchill's bronze foot, to double-check.

He confirms it's John D. At that moment the Speaker stands up.

'Statement, the Prime Minister.'

Double damn.

Bloody Prime Ministers pop up at the most inconvenient times. Now John won't leave the Chamber. Forty-three minutes left. I walk in to the Chamber, don't even attempt to register what Tony is saying, and start formulating what I wanted to ask John:

'I know you'll want to hear the Prime Minister's statement, but I just wondered if you could step outside a minute, because I've got forty-three minutes left to get some material for my defence against Galloway, without which he'll sue me and take my home, make that forty-two minutes . . .'

When I'm still twenty yards away from John I'm surprised to see him stand up and start to make his way out. I run out of the nearest exit, and into the voting lobbies. I catch John just as he's about to slip down one of the numerous back door exits. He sympathises with my plight, tells me not to get entangled with Galloway (it's a bit late), and suggests I ring some of the War on Want committee who were there when Galloway was General Secretary. He mentions names – Martin Plout, Ken Ritchie. Ken! I *know* Ken. We've worked together, campaigning in favour of proportional representation. He's the Chief Executive at the Electoral Reform Society. By now John and I are walking through the Members' cloakroom. I thank John and go running on towards Portcullis House, under Big Ben – still thirty minutes left – and up the escalators towards the atrium with the posh fig trees. Jump in the lift and up to the fifth floor. Dive on to the phone, directory enquiries, Electoral Reform Society, Chief Executive's office, it's Oona King, I must speak to him urgently. Ken! Thank God you're in your office!

Ken is somewhat bemused by my urgency. Within seconds he is giving me more names and numbers.

'Evidence? Would you like an auditor's report? They found that Galloway had, "in good faith", spent some of the charity's money on expenditure "that was not wholly and exclusively in connection with his employment". Is that the sort of thing you're looking for?' It was as though an angel had alighted on my shoulder.

'Yes, that's the sort of thing I'm looking for.'

In fact, the auditor's report was not sufficient and I was advised that there was no defence to his libel action. I therefore settled the case and apologised. For legal reasons I have had to leave out many interesting sections of this diary relating to George Galloway that followed on from the above entry. When either I or he is six foot under, they can be exhumed. Until then, suffice to say, there is already enough in the public domain that gives pause for thought about the way George Galloway chooses to operate. Once the press reported that Mr Galloway was suing me in December 2004, more and more people contacted my office with information about past events, many of them still incandescent with rage at Mr Galloway's behaviour – even years later. I had been unaware that his career trajectory often followed a pattern: initially received with open arms by a group or organisation placing great faith in him, they then felt betrayed, and denounced him in the strongest terms.

In 1988, after he had been elected an MP, his local Labour Party passed a vote of no confidence in him. The local Party Chair, Mrs Johann Lamont, said, 'The constituency has expressed its condemnation of the behaviour of the MP.' The no-confidence vote was reported in several newspapers, including The Scotsman *under the editorial headline 'Time for George to go' (24 February 1988). 'There is little point in examining the murky trail which has brought Hillhead's MP, George Galloway, to his present plight,' said the editorial, 'what matters now is that he has lost the confidence of his constituency Labour Party, the very people who chose him as their candidate, worked for him, organised his election campaign and helped ensure it ended in victory.' This reflects almost exactly the sentiments expressed to me today by disillusioned Respect members.*

2005

The Remedial Stream
and the Emergency Parachute

New Year's Day 2005 – Paris

It's a strange time, the planet's cracking up. Last night, New Year's Eve, Tiberio and I celebrated our thirteenth anniversary. But you can't celebrate with a global catastrophe unfolding in the background. Tsunami. A natural calamity on this scale should happen once a century, but with the world falling to pieces, or falling on its axis, there's the suspicion that calamities – man-made, natural, or both – will visit us with increasing frequency.

The first reports on Boxing Day said that 10,000 people had died. The next day it was 25,000, then 30,000, then 40,000, 100,000, and as of yesterday 150,000.* With such a high number it's almost impossible to register the individual human loss. It was caused by a huge underground earthquake, with its epicentre in Indonesia. It was so powerful that it tilted the world on its side, coasts in some areas moved twenty metres in a second and giant waves swept everything before them – humans, hospitals, coastlines, hotels, villages. At least 80,000 Indonesians have been killed. Eighty thousand. Apparently Britain was hit by a tsunami in 5,000 BC. Suddenly Noah's Arc jumps from myth to reality. And yet the numbers are still too big to digest.

3 January 2005

We got the Eurostar back from Paris last night. Our friend Daniel hosted a fab New Year's Eve party at his studio. Tiberio and Vanessa

---

* The eventual death toll was estimated by the UN as in the region of 220,000.

had to march me home against my will at five a.m., no sort of time to
give up the ghost on New Year's Eve. But my period pains sucked the
fight out of me. For all I know I won't have another night out until
after the general election in May. The French crew gave us a great
time though, and I'm really thankful for our French friends, like our
Greek friends and our Italian friends. They're people we're growing
up with, living our lives with, and it makes a difference to see the
world from different angles.

8 January 2005

Tiberio's friends – Aldo, his wife Keiko and their two children,
beautiful Japanese–Italian mixed-race kids, Luca and Lea – were in
Thailand when the Tsunami hit. They visited us last year. But now
they're gone, a whole family swept away. I wish I hadn't written that
'it's almost impossible to register the individual human loss'. Because
when it's people you know, it becomes instantaneously possible. I
suppose it's the scale of each individual loss that we can't digest. Feel
sick. On the way back from Paris we read their names in an Italian
paper. A few hours later, going through the post at home, I handed a
Christmas card to Tiberio to open. But he grimaced, drew one hand
to his chest, and leaned the other on the table for support.

'I think it's from them.' He pushed the card back towards me. The
envelope was made from transparent frosted paper, our address on one
side, and on the other, when I looked more closely, was a multicoloured
Christmas tree with pictures of each of them, smiling and happy,
hanging as decorations on the tree. Aldo, Keiko, Luca and Lea. Those
smiling faces. What horror clouded them when they saw that wave?

Tiberio still stood leaning against the table. 'Put it somewhere,
hide it, I just can't see it.' I didn't tell him that it had their pictures on
the front. Posted from Japan, ten days before they died. Their friends
and family all over the world, knowing they were listed as 'missing,
presumed dead', were receiving pictures of the happy family through
the letterbox. Their card arrived with our friend Tiziana in Torino
the next day. It disturbed her so much she cried all day and couldn't
go to work. I hid the card away. It transpired that Aldo and his son
survived. His wife and daughter tragically died.

9 January 2005

Decided to have a lie-in on Sunday morning, but was shocked to find it was afternoon when I woke up. I had forty-five minutes to get to the AGM (of the Greater Sylheti Welfare and Development Council). They always hold their meetings in the Bangladeshi community on a Sunday. Tiberio jumped out of bed and made scrambled eggs on brown toast and went to the shop to get the papers. Would've been Christmas all over again if I could've stayed on the sofa eating a Sunday brunch and reading the *Observer*. Started to make mental notes for the speech instead, beginning with a few sentences in Sylheti. I arrived at the meeting near Brick Lane. There were two other women in a room of about sixty men. It's almost impossible to know whether organisations you visit as an MP are good or bad. It's easy enough to put on a good show for an hour. But aside from the gender chasm I get the impression this one's pretty good.

Leave at three p.m. and drive to Party rooms in Bethnal Green. My plan is to do five hours' straight work on the George Galloway 'dossier', no interruptions. I'm gobsmacked to find the place humming with activity. Claire and Rachel are co-ordinating a mail out, our GLA member, John Biggs, is sitting stuffing envelopes with five other volunteers. Josh, my campaign manager, is upstairs with Tim, our new LP organiser seconded from the PLP, plotting my campaign grid.

Graham, my agent, is breaking down the wall of a small ground floor office to increase space and capacity. He's already laid a new carpet in the main meeting room and painted it, and recently washed all the floors. Later on I ring Frances, my senior caseworker, because I can't access her computer, and thirty minutes later she walks through the door. 'I was coming in to stuff some envelopes anyway.'

I'm amazed. It's a Sunday afternoon and my office is like Piccadilly Circus. Good news: we're all seriously gearing up for a major political battle. Bad news: this heralds the beginning of seven day working weeks, every week. And I'll never get my own work done. Graham is the last to leave at ten p.m. I finish the document just before one a.m. and lock up. Make a mental note to get new fire extinguishers.

11 January 2005

Visit Central Foundation Comprehensive School with Lord Putnam, and watch students perform a non-ballet version of *Swan Lake*. Next I go to Whitechapel Art Gallery. There's been an announcement of a grant from the Heritage Lottery Fund that will enable the Gallery to almost double its current space by expanding into the next-door library. The library is being moved to the council's new 'idea stores'. The tour of the library and its semi-abandoned vaults gives the glimpse of the archives that'll be opened up to the public for the first time, old documents from the borough, naming luminaries such as Attlee, or pictures of visiting speakers such as Picasso. In fact, everyone seems to have tossed up in the East End, from the Romans, to the Normans, to Sylvia Pankhurst to Gandhi to Stalin.

Meet a *Today Programme* journalist who's doing a profile on the constituency. I take her on a little tour, looking for somewhere to record the interview. 'And here's a mosque that was previously a synagogue, that was previously a church.'

Next I drive to Westminster for my 2.30 p.m. meeting with a Metropolitan Police Officer. He's a white Christian guy, very nice, who's come to complain on behalf of his Bengali, Muslim friend and former colleague, who was suspended from the police force and then sacked after being sent to jail for punching a black guy who had been beating up some Asian guys.

The conversation turns to surveillance, and he tells me there's a new thing his Special Services colleagues do, which is to tune into the 'channel' of your mobile phone, even when it's switched *off*, to get thirty second bursts of your conversations. Then they have to tune in again to get another thirty-second burst.

Later on, we vote in the Commons. I remember why MPs won't ever do away with voting in person entirely (i.e. rather than electronic voting). I transact five mini-meetings in fifteen minutes:

- Tell Jim Fitzpatrick about the (unproven) allegations of Al-Qaeda connections to the local mosque.
- Ask the Chief Whip, Hilary Armstrong, to let me know when the new PPS will be appointed to the DTI team. It's a strain being a person down, and I need to be spending less time at Westminster, not more.

- Speak to Peter Hain, who asks me if it would be helpful for him to come and visit the Muslim community in the constituency, both in his capacity as Leader of the House, and as someone formerly involved with the ANC liberation movement.
- See Karen Buck. Why don't the very best people get to the top in politics?
- Speak to Neil Gerrard who comes up and offers to go to visit constituency as an 'anti-war troublemaker'.

And then Jack Straw finds me and we sit down in the Members' lobby. He tells me a journalist has contacted him – someone from the *Daily Mail* – saying that they're going to publish this ridiculous story about the affair.

'They can't really publish it,' he explains, 'because they have not one scrap or shred of evidence, as there is none, so we could take them to the cleaners. But the main thing I wanted to warn you about is this: if they contact you again, don't either confirm or deny it.'

'What?' I look at him incredulously. 'You mean if they ask me "Are you having an affair with Jack Straw?" I answer, "No comment"?'

'No, I mean you say something like, "I won't even dignify what you've said with an answer." Otherwise they'll turn it into a story.'

And then he told me about a time when he'd been Home Secretary, and an entirely fictitious rumour that he had a terminal illness had been doing the rounds. 'If I'd been quoted saying it wasn't true, the headline would have been "Jack Straw denies terminal illness". That would've immediately created a bigger story and probably made people think I *was* actually dying.'

So much nonsense in this business, it's insane. The bells, the bells. They're ringing, but happily it's for the adjournment.

I drive to Quin's. Tiberio's in Cranfield all week and I'm doing my MBA widow bit. I take Quin the case I've prepared against GG, and we spend a couple of hours discussing it.

I hide my mobile phone under her mattress and duvet for the duration of our talk, just in case those gadgets really exist.

Get home at midnight, do whatever it is at night that takes up time when I get home, like tonight, exceptionally, feed the cats (Tiberio usually keeps them alive), put the rubbish in the garage outside, fold the washing. Write this. Look at my watch: 1.30 a.m. Staff arriving for a campaign meeting at my house on Saturday morning. Seven hours' time. Goodnight.

Sunday 23 January

My first day off since New Year's Eve. It's such a luxury not getting suited and booted to go to an MP gig, I can hardly get over it. Tiberio's got adult chicken pox (shingles), a medieval disease. He's no longer in outright agony, but it's not pretty. I hadn't scheduled chicken pox into my general election campaign. Drove to Canary Wharf and then went for a forty minute walk–run along the Thames river path. Slowly, slowly starting to get fit after the carpet-bombing of IVF.

I've lost half a stone over the last two months, which is due to a combination of not being on all those drugs, and starting to do exercise, plus the fairly reliable general election diet. The general election diet is bad for your health, but great for shifting weight. It basically involves the following: breakfast: a longing glance towards the kitchen as you stumble out the door; elevenses: lots of biscuits and caffeine to jump-start your system; lunch: sandwiches, which remain in your bag; tea: more biscuits and caffeine; dinner: the sandwiches you brought for lunch. Nightcap: a few spoons of ice cream followed by a few spoons of Night Nurse medication. This diet works perfectly in conjunction with sixteen hour days and lots of caffeine and running around like a nutter.

We went to David Lammy and Nicola's wedding yesterday. It was a fabulous service, with a black gospel choir at St Margaret's where Winston Churchill got married, next to Westminster Abbey.

David and Louise Miliband were there with their baby, Isaac. David is the most besotted new father I've ever seen. He must have kissed Isaac at least two dozen times over the duration of the service and reception. Quite right too. Thank God he's a fully paid up human being.

The image I have in my mind right now is from the bank of the Thames this morning. It was a perfect blue sky. At one point when I looked across the river, the sunlight on the water nearly made my eyes water. Life under grey cloud isn't life. Let's face it, I'm a sun queen, trapped in Bethnal Green.

25 January 2005

It's 4.30 a.m. and I can't sleep. I have an evil sore throat and nights are always a punishment when you're ill. Plus, I desperately need to sleep so I can survive an ordeal with George Galloway tonight at a public meeting aimed at saving one of the fire engines in Bethnal Green. George will inevitably turn the conversation from fire engines in Bethnal Green to bombs in Baghdad. How can we spend so much money murdering Iraqi children under the direction of George Bush, TB and Oona King, who, incidentally, eats them for breakfast, when we haven't got enough money for an extra fire engine in Bethnal Green? The audience of about 400 people will construct a scaffold to hang me from. Naturally, the real reason for the deployment of a fire engine from Bethnal Green to an outer London suburb will remain as obscure as Osama Bin Laden's hiding place.

In a nutshell, the Fire Authority is doing two things: spreading safety from fire risk more equitably across London, and moving the onus from saving buildings to saving people. Tower Hamlets has more fire stations than any other borough in London. We also have more fires, but they are predominantly secondary (kids setting fire to rubbish bins) than primary (a block of flats or a warehouse on fire). Fire-fighting response times and resources were set in an era when the City of London was prioritised over residential areas. One of the fire engines in Bethnal Green was used in the event of fires in the city. So, empty office blocks around the Bank of England enjoy more fire protection than people living in outer London, where the population has grown. The Fire Authority's proposal to move the fire engine from Bethnal Green to outer London is completely rational.

But I, as local MP in the run-up to an election in a marginal seat with George Galloway on my case, am duty bound to say, 'Screw pensioners in Surbiton. They can burn in hell. Actually, they can burn in Surbiton. My only concern is for pensioners in Bethnal Green. I don't care how rational or equitable it is to move our fire engine. I will form a human fire ball if necessary to prevent this happening. Oh, and please vote for me and not George.'

26 January 2005

To be fair to George, he didn't get onto bombs in Falluja for at least forty minutes. In fact, because his first salvo included no sustained personal attack on me, I was caught off guard. The SWP lot started screeching about the dismantling of Public Services under Labour, and how we were hell-bent on stealing from the poor to give to the rich (hello?).

George congratulated everyone on the pressure they had placed me under, and said that it was only their pressure that had brought me before them this Thursday evening and that, as my constituents, they ought to place me under more pressure.

'Well, yes,' I conceded, 'it's true. I came because I was asked. But talking of pressure George, no amount of pressure would induce *you* to meet *your* constituents. Your constituents are in Glasgow, while you're down here in Bethnal Green.'

The crowd of about 200 people started booing me.

'It doesn't matter,' Josh reminded me later. They're either SWP and were never going to vote for you anyway, or they're not local and can't vote.' And then he sent me an email today saying '1. You rocked and 2. Don't be late for campaigning sessions.' My reply said, 'Cut the crap, I was shit.' And I was.

Silver lining came in the shape of my friends Lauren and Soren. Soren was filming the event for Channel 4 news, Lauren came along for the ride. Lauren's riding high on her Clarice Bean children's books, which are nearly selling as well as Harry Potter. Soren's just come back from Andaman Islands. He was also at Beslam, the Russian school blown up by Chechen rebels, filming charred children's bodies, and, before that, Iraq. They came home for a drink and after two glasses of prosecco I'd washed the trot-fest from my mind. After they left I listened to Jamiroquai, always a top option.

Today MPs voted to partially revoke the modernisation changes to working hours. Stupid wankers. Those of us that attempt even the smallest concession to being normal are thwarted at every turn. Not to mention the concept of a modern (1950s) democracy as opposed to something nineteenth century. Most of them just want to sit in the bars at night without feeling lonely. Which is fine. But why do they have to hold the rest of us hostage?

I went to the Tower Hamlets Holocaust Memorial event in Stepney, where I listened to a survivor, John Wemer, give an extraordinarily moving account of his time in Auschwitz and other concentration camps. Got up to speak after him and started crying to the point that I couldn't speak for a while. People said they were amazed to see such humanity in a politician. They don't seem to understand that being a *bit* human in politics can be good. But being *that* human is just downright weak.

I speak to Quin about it later. She says I have no reserves left. 'You can't scrape the barrel to pull out your last reserve of strength – the strength to keep yourself composed – because it's already gone.'

Why did this particular speech upset me so much? It's boring the way I harp on about always giving speeches on genocide. But I do. Some people close their eyes and ears because they don't want to see or hear about genocide. I've sought it out, year after year, because I wouldn't forgive myself if I hadn't. After all, people like us, we only have to *observe*. We don't have to *endure*. So it's the least we can do, observe, campaign, and financially support charities like Amnesty or Human Rights Watch. And as part of my campaigning I give speeches on genocide all the time. I talk about human depravity without skipping a beat.

So why couldn't I stop crying this time? Answer is simple. The pressure is getting to me. Just need a good night's sleep. Something now far less likely, thanks to my Westminster colleagues who voted to return us to working at night.

30 January 2005

I'm ill again. Still, at least it's Sunday, so I don't have to get up early. I'm starting to obsess about needing sleep. I'm working approximately ninety hours per week, so it doesn't take a brain surgeon to work out why I'm under the weather.

Last week I was talking to Harriet (Harman) briefly on my way to the Westminster Hall debate on fire safety. A good opportunity to talk about fire engines and high-rise blocks. I told Harriet how I was (stressed, knackered, ill) and asked her how she was.

'This morning I was in the Cabinet meeting. A Cabinet Minister was speaking, and Tony wasn't even pretending to listen to him. It was embarrassing.' Harriet doesn't like it when people behave in this way. Politics at its best is about innovation – art and possibility. At its worst it's about tyranny, power and brutality. At its most humdrum, it's about putting people in their place, quite simply by ignoring them.

Tiberio has announced he's going to train for a ten kilometre run. Quite funny, since both of us are bedridden. Still, he finds the energy to make the best miso soup. Later he puts on *The Outsiders*, a film by Jean-Luc Godard. It's diabolical that I find it easier to watch a bad film from the 1990s than a good film in black and white from the 1960s.

The Times on Saturday described me as 'a passionate advocate for the war in Iraq'. You know me, I love war, just can't get enough. What I am is a passionate advocate for getting rid of dictators in Iraq and enforcing UN resolutions. And so now, in every article written about me, I'm described as the 'pro-war MP Oona King'. I want to say to people, so if I'm pro-war what are you? Pro-genocide? Pro-murderous dictators? Pro-doing nothing? Because when you're an MP and you have to vote on something like Iraq, you don't have a range of options open to you. Unless you're going to abdicate responsibility, you only have two options: vote yes or vote no. Vote for change or vote for the *status quo*. And nothing would induce me to vote to keep a man like Saddam in power. Especially not after I was involved in the International Development Select Committee inquiry into the situation facing Iraqi civilians with Ann Clwyd and other MPs.

We began the inquiry in 1999 and concluded in 2000, before George Bush stole the White House the first time round. While we took evidence from Iraqis in exile and heard descriptions of Halabja and Saddam's torture chambers, George Bush was still playing with his oil wells in Texas. The UN stated that Saddam's abuse of the oil-for-food programme led to the deaths of half a million Iraqi children. That was the *status quo* for Iraqis under Saddam: death. So it's very reasonable to be anti-war, but just remember that a lot of Iraqis construed that stance as being pro-death. Their death. But their deaths continue now at a rate possibly faster than before (although given the previous combination of malnutrition and death squads, that statement is questionable).

Today is the day of the first Iraqi election. They are dying to vote. Literally. We can agree on the past, that America and Britain among others funded not only Saddam Hussein in the mid 1980s but also the *jihadis* who eventually spawned Al-Qaeda. But what of the future? Are we going to fund democracy or will we just create mayhem and leave?

I rang my little brother Akasi in New Zealand tonight – for once it was the right time to ring the other side of the world. His reading has improved dramatically, although he was fairly monosyllabic, but that's the prerogative of a ten-year-old talking to an older relative. It's funny to think I was twenty-seven when he was born. Demographic change is almost up there with climate change. Went to a seminar on climate change this week and it's clear that global warming won't be pretty. It's not so much genocide (meaning destruction of a particular race, *genus*) but more *homicide* in its wider sense: the destruction of mankind, the entire human race. Unlucky. Particularly unlucky that of all the human beings on the whole planet, the one with the most power has a brain the size of a peanut: George W. Bush.

As for TB, apparently he's cracking up. I take this on good authority, from an article in *The Times* quoting a handwriting expert. Someone got hold of his doodling, and the expert concluded that he was 'unstable' and 'stressed'. They compared it to his handwriting on the letter he wrote Peter Mandelson in 1998 accepting Peter's (first) resignation. The handwriting expert looked at the way Tony wrote, 'Yours ever,' and concluded, 'The *y* is almost maternal, cradling, as if to say, "Don't go".'

Last week I received a letter from Tony signed, 'Yours ever,' so I compared it with the one in the paper from 1998. Identical. Presumably that's because he doesn't want me to go, and when my existence bobs into his head I make him emotional, and he has something to drink before he signs a letter to me. Journalists. Handwriting experts. Ridiculous.

Still, it reminds me. I must bother the poor, emotional, stressed-out man again. In his letter to me (I'd written to him about a youth event), he added at the bottom, 'You've been immensely brave over Iraq, I know it's tough but we will give you every help. Yours ever, Tony.'

I don't want to be churlish but 'every help' is not how I would define one LP organiser (the blessed Tim). I desperately need more case-workers in my office. At present we can only open an advice line on Tuesday and Thursday afternoons, which is a disgrace. Otherwise it's impossible to deal with the 200 weekly enquiries that come in via phone, fax, post and email, mainly from the poorest and most desperate people in England, who are being evicted, deported and convicted. They want their MP to look at their case. But I can't do that and fight a general election against the Member for Baghdad. TB is probably the only person (even if he doesn't realise it now) who would be as irked as me to have the Member for Baghdad back in Parliament. Time for bed, but when I wake up I'll pen the PM a line to suggest that 'every help' he mentioned could at least extend to an extra caseworker.

31 January 2005

Went to visit a group of Bengali women on the Ocean Estate, organised by Shaheda Chowdhury.

Shaheda is one of my favourite people. I first met her when I was chairing the Ocean New Deal for Communities Board. She was one of the only Bengali women to get involved. She's young, in her thirties, came to the UK when she was eight, grew up in Stepney on the Ocean. At first she found the NDC meetings terribly intimidating, and hardly said a word. I was very enthusiastic about her being there, so I did everything I could to encourage Shaheda, though after a while she didn't need much encouragement.

It wasn't long before she set up the Ocean Women's Association, and had hundreds of women relying on her to deal with their problems. Shaheda kindly says I'm her inspiration for being involved in community politics – it's funny, because these days she's one of the people who inspire me.

As its name suggests, the Ocean estate is seemingly endless. Row after row of enormous rectangular blocks, often ten storeys high, thrown up after the Blitz.

I pulled up on Harford Street opposite Queen Mary Westfield University at the intersection with Shandy street. I was looking for Moray House and once I found it, I did a U-turn towards the densely packed grey brick block. A young Bengali guy was walking on the other side of the street. He nodded towards me, recognition on his face. He looked familiar, but that's probably because, one way or another, I've met a third of all young Bengali people in this part of Tower Hamlets. I rolled down the window.

'Hi.'

'Are you Oona King?'

'Yeah, have we met?'

'I don't think so.' He looked at my car, evidently surprised it wasn't a Jaguar.

'Oh.' I'd done it again, needlessly starting up a conversation with a random stranger.

'What are you doing round here?' he asked.

'I'm often round here,' I nodded towards Mile End tube station. 'I live five minutes away and I do a lot of work on the Ocean.'

'What are you doing today?'

'I'm visiting some women in Moray House.'

'What for?'

'To ask them about their problems. To tell them what I do.'

'What d'you think of the current situation?'

'The current situation where? Here in Bethnal Green or in Iraq?'

'Iraq.' He was direct, but pleasant, dressed in youth worker chic, casual but stylish. He looked about twenty-five.

'Well, whatever anyone thinks about going to war in Iraq, and I'll assume you passionately disagreed with it, most people agree that it's a good thing for Iraqis to be able to vote and decide their own government. So I think the elections and the high turnout are good.'

I returned the question. 'What do *you* think?'

'I'm a member of Hizb Ut Tahrir, and we're against the elections. We think they're bad.'

Hizb Ut Tahrir. Weren't they the extremist group that wanted me stoned to death? I couldn't remember.

'Don't you think it's good that Iraqis get to elect their own government?'

He squatted down on his haunches, one arm holding on to the car window, level with me in the driver's seat.

'No, because we don't really think Iraqis can decide anything for themselves when there's an American occupation. That's why we don't think people should vote.'

'What's your name?'

'Abdul. Abdul Azziz.'

'But Abdul, if people don't vote, things won't change.'

'We think change needs to go beyond anything electoral systems can offer. Don't get me wrong though, I think it's good that you do your job. It's good that you come down here and talk to people on this estate.'

'Well, look at this estate Abdul.' I pointed behind him to the dilapidated brick blocks. 'What's going to change this? While you're waiting for a revolution, another generation of Bengali children will grow up in slums.'

'Yeah, but you have to change the whole system, everything. And until it changes I don't want to work inside the system.'

On the surface, radical Islam is just like the SWP.

'I respect people who take the view they don't want to work inside the system, if they then do something constructive. But do you respect people who *do* work inside the system? Or do you think we're all bad?'

'Oh, no,' he looked slightly affronted, 'I think you're good. I just think . . .' I looked at my watch. I was late for the women.

'Would you ever have time to meet up for a chat?' he asked. 'It would be good to discuss a lot of things.'

'Yeah, it would be good, Abdul. Only I have a bitch of a diary. But I'll give you my number.' I wrote down my mobile number and handed it through the window. I wouldn't mind getting to know a reasonable person from Hizb Ut Tahrir, the same way it's important to understand why reasonable people join the BNP.

I made my way to Moray House and met with eight women crammed into a tiny living room.

1 February 2005

Today I had lunch with a group of white pensioners at Toynbee Hall, and then another meeting with Bengali women. I've written to thousands of white women about the new Child Trust Fund, and met with them at a public meeting that Gordon Brown addressed. Notwithstanding gross cultural generalisations, white women read the letters, and come along to public meetings. First generation Bengali women have significant problems with language, and unless they've received an invitation by word of mouth, they're less likely to attend, so I have to rely on meetings with community organisations to reach them.

Anyway, at the meeting 150 people clapped and applauded Gordon Brown, just for walking through the door. It reminded me of 1997. Applause before you did anything. These days you get booed before you do anything. Alan Milburn was talking about it the other day. He said, 'D'you remember our honeymoon? It just went on and on and on. And on. Tony could do no wrong. It created huge expectations that we could never fulfil. Today we're living with the consequences.'

Most of the Bengali women I meet today are on very low incomes, living with families of up to twelve people in two- or three-bedroom flats with serious damp problems, leading to health problems and family breakdown. I outline what the Government is doing to help the poorest. New money for housing, new money to help parents through the Sure Start programme, a new health centre on the Ocean, new money to tackle drug addiction, a new childcare centre, new money for babies, new money for this, new money for that. 'But what about our heating bills? The Government doesn't pay them.' I had mentioned the extra money given to pensioners this year for their winter fuel payments.

'No, you're right, the Government can't pay everyone's heating bills.' I was starting to get exasperated. We're under attack from middle England for being too preoccupied with the poorest, and yet when I speak to low-income families, they're just angry we haven't given more.

'We're trying our best. In Bangladesh the Government doesn't pay for *anything*. Here we pay for a lot.'

Speaking in Sylheti, the woman replied, 'But in Bangladesh, it's the husband's responsibility to pay the bills.'

This woman, sitting in her sari and slippers in one of the poorest parts of Tower Hamlets, was deeply unimpressed by my argument. She was right to be, but it was a second generation Bengali women's health worker that articulated it best.

'I don't agree with your argument Oona, because the point is, we're not in Bangladesh.'

She was right. Britain is not Bangladesh. It's the fourth biggest economy in the world. Mothers shouldn't be bringing up children in overcrowded, damp, cold, unfit housing. So the Government has a responsibility to give housing even greater political priority. But it's a two-way street. The community also has a responsibility to meet the Government halfway. We are fighting a losing battle if we try to house families with as many as ten children. The health worker is right. We're not in Bangladesh. Parents must take responsibility for how many children they bring into the world. And in fact, if we were in Bangladesh we might be doing a bit better – the birth rate in Dhaka is lower than in Tower Hamlets!

2 February 2005

Today I attended a big meeting in Spitalfields on Antisocial Behaviour. I regularly organise meetings on this subject, so that residents can get up and say, 'Politicians don't listen to local residents.' The residents want three things: policing priorities set by residents instead of police; Brick Lane police station open at night; and extra, visible community police officers. We are delivering each of these things: neighbourhood police teams where residents set priorities; evening opening hours for Brick Lane; dedicated police officers for all areas. Are the residents happy? Is Saddam Hussein a social worker? From the back of the hall, Tracy, for the third time this evening, starts to shout: 'When are you going to do something, Oona?! When are you going to *listen*?!'

Tracy is waving a brick that was thrown through her window in the studio where she works. I've already said that I understand how upsetting it can be to have a brick thrown through your window, as the same thing happened to me.

'Oona's only had a brick thrown through her window *once*,' says Tracy. 'I get it all the time'

Mia at the front has a stammer, which doesn't deter her from interrupting the meeting (good for her) more than a dozen times, but it does prevent her from finishing her sentences once she's got the floor. Vera gets up to say that in the 1950s there was a very nice bobby in Spitalfields called Roddy. Dave, who will be the police officer in charge of the new Safer Neighbourhood team for Spitalfields, says that he doesn't work twenty-four hours a day, but if they want him there at two a.m., he'll be there at two a.m.

Tracy starts up from the back again, unable to help herself. 'When are you going to *do* something?! When are you going to *listen*?!'

'Tracy, we *are* listening. That's why we're here. That's why we've taken on board a lot of what you've said, and we'd like to . . .'

'Why won't you *listen*!!'

By now I've lost my voice, and can't shout her down even if I wanted to. The Borough Commander says that he's certain that in Spitalfields – as in the other areas where Safer Neighbourhoods teams have been introduced – residents will see a noticeable difference and he'll come back to meet with them again, and listen to their experiences.

After the meeting, Tracy comes up and thrusts her brick into my hand. 'Feel the weight of this.' I consider telling her the truth – that it weighs about the third of the brick thrown at my living room window – but decide against it.

'I know you've had a terrible time, Tracy, but what I'm trying to say is . . .'

'I don't believe a word you say.'

'Well, Tracy, if I said the same to you, that I don't believe a word you say, and if I wouldn't let you get the words out of your . . .'

'I've heard it all before.'

'Yes, but you haven't had six new police officers just to deal with crime in Spitalfields before, have you?'

Tracy was winding me up. The Tracy in question was world-famous artist, Tracy Emin. I wanted to say to her. 'Listen, Trace, why don't you take that brick, pop it in your gob, pour some formaldehyde over it, and exhibit the latest Tracy Emin Brit Art installation IN SILENCE outside Brick Lane police station, say, perhaps, hanging from a noose?' It had been a long day, and a Tracy Emin lecture wasn't the best way to end it. Earlier in the meeting Tracy pointed out that Antisocial Behaviour should be taken much more seriously, because it affected her creativity and her income. Rich, coming from the wealthiest person in the room.

Later that night I drive Frances home and she reinforces Tim's message that despite working seven days a week, if I take off Wednesday afternoon until Monday as planned in March (for a family holiday with my Mum and aunt and cousins and Tiberio, that's been in my diary for a year), it will damage my credibility and goodwill in the Labour Party regionally and 'with No. 10'. She adds, 'I'm only taking three days off in February.' I don't point out that she's just returned from one week's holiday, because a) she's not the candidate, and b) she doesn't want to discuss it because I 'won't listen'. I spend my life listening to people who say I won't listen. At least if I lose the election I can stop listening to them all.

6 February 2005

Spent yesterday, Saturday, canvassing – knocking on doors in Wapping in the morning, Spitalfields in the afternoon.

Wapping is a surprising place. Exciting in parts, desolate in others, it's most often a cross between Essex and Bruges. Man-sized brick houses run along municipal canals, bordered with glass-balconied flats. A young new LP member was there, Tom from Bethnal Green via Nigeria and Norway. Nice, engaging, normal – what a treat. Josh and Rachel arrived, making it a dream ticket for the dreariest task imaginable. Well, not dreary exactly. Canvassing on a cold miserable Saturday morning (knocking on doors uninvited) is not dreary, but for a normal person, it requires supreme mental effort. That's why the vast majority of normal people don't do it. Once you begin, it's not so bad. You'd be surprised how nice a lot of people are when they open the door. And here was a group of nice normal people coming with me to knock on doors to support a Labour Government and a Labour MP.

'We're calling from the local Labour Party to find out if people will vote. Would you normally vote in an election?'

'Yes.'

'And d'you know which party you most closely identify with? Is it Conservative? Lib Dem, Labour, Green, Respect, Monster Raving Loony Party or none of the above?' Amazing how many people will look you in the eye, smile and say Labour. It'll be funny if I read this again after losing the election. But I don't think so.

Ruth (Kelly) lives just round the corner, so I give her a ring on the off-chance, and drop by for a cup of tea. Derek has taken three of their four children to a play-theatre and Ruth is at home with the youngest, plus three older relatives. The table is set for lunch. Nieve has grown so much. She's already eighteen months, but it's the first time I've been round to see her. Ruth looks great, she's lost lots of weight and she's really enjoying her new job in the Cabinet.

'Nothing's gone wrong yet,' she says. Both of us are aware that every week in politics without a 'beyond-your-control' event is a week to be grateful for.

Ruth is suspending her work–life-balance rules for the next three months, which means less time with the kids and more time at work. It's fair enough – after all, you only get promoted to the Cabinet once in your life. Unless you're Peter Mandelson. The opus Dei stuff is the only trouble so far. That's classic beyond-your-control stuff. And *The Da Vinci Code* has fanned the media fire to give the story prominence it wouldn't otherwise have.

Ruth mentions wanting to visit a Tower Hamlets college. I'd written to her about Ibrahim College, which I'm very impressed with, although some rival Bengalis dismiss it as a 'Madrassa'. The preferred day for the Bengali community, as ever, is Sunday. 'Out of the question,' says Ruth. 'I still don't work the utterly insane hours you do.' Ruth is the only person in British history to be a Cabinet Minister and have such young children. She's calm and serene because she won't engage in nonsense. Ruth initially went for my seat, before the selection was suspended (first due to allegations of dodgy dealings, then due to the court ruling banning woman only shortlists). When we both arrived in Parliament, we thought I was the lucky one. I had the safe seat, a plum inner-London constituency twenty minutes from Westminster, a guaranteed job for life. Now things look very different.

Today twelve LP members arrived to help stuff envelopes, a really decent number for a Sunday afternoon. Slate came round and picked up a batch for him and Kate to stuff at home. The picture he took of me recently in his bathroom – because it was raining and we couldn't go out into Victoria Park – is now being pushed through thousands of doors.

Earlier this week I argued with Tim, who's seconded from the L.P., about taking off three working days in the middle of a four month campaign. My argument is that it's one third of a year and I need one long weekend break during that time. His argument is that I should work six days a week, not seven, and I then wouldn't need the break. He's partly right, but anyone who thinks a candidate doesn't need to work seven days a week is dreaming. He says he's not sure we're going to win. Sitting with him in my car near the Party rooms after another freezing canvassing session, I still have a sore throat and headache, and I'm trying not to let my voice crack with emotion (politician's melodrama) because I want to scream: 'Don't you get it? I'm ill. If I don't get a rest, you won't have a frigging candidate. How old are you anyway? Twenty-eight? How long have you been working at this pace? Since January. I've been doing it since August last year and for twelve years before that. I CAN'T DO IT ANY MORE!'

Instead I say we should compromise.

Later in the week, after listening to Tim and Frances, I ring the travel agent and pay a penalty to change my flight. Instead of leaving for the break on Wednesday lunchtime, I'll leave on Thursday night. All this grief to get one sodding Friday off. In general though, it's always good to listen to Tim.

7 February 2005

My APPG report made the front page of the *Observer* business section yesterday. The report is on resource exploitation in the Democratic Republic of Congo and recommends that the DTI should be more proactive in enforcing the OECD guidelines on best business practice. Which would be great if it didn't slag off the DTI, when I'm the PPS to the Secretary of State at the DTI. This is the first APPG report that I have delegated entirely, allowing a Lib Dem to lead on it. Should've known better. To be fair, he didn't really slag off the DTI. On the *Today Programme* – which I declined to go on –

when they said, 'So, you're attacking the DTI?' He replied, 'No, we're not concentrating on the DTI. We're drawing attention to the problem more generally.' But the journalists wanted to spin it a certain way. Patricia is not impressed.

9 February 2005

It's strange how days slide into weeks. Yesterday I was absorbed in the APPG-DTI story. The bells started ringing and I jumped up from my office in Portcullis House, all pale blue carpets and wooden panelling, and ran with only three minutes left towards the Chamber. I caught a glimpse of one of the monitors on the way over. 'The Belmarsh Judgment.' Voting on the Belmarsh Judgment?? I hadn't seen that in the Whip. What aspect of the Judgment? I met Joan Ruddock on the way down the escalators.

'We're cutting it pretty fine.'

'I know.' She was holding the Order Paper with Amendments. 'But I'm trying to work out what we're actually voting on.'

Trying to read the Order Paper's dense type while running is a challenge. 'I need my glasses.' She rummaged in her bag, and I took the paper from her. 'I'll read, you interpret.' It was a Lib Dem Amendment, basically saying that Britain shouldn't detain people without trial, especially not by derogating from European Convention on Human Rights.

'Well I agree with that,' I said.

'So do I,' said Joan. The night before, for the first time ever, I had accidentally voted against something I really agreed with – the admissibility in court of phone taps – because I was in such a rush. I can't do that again.

We were at the bottom of the stairs leading up to the Table Office, behind the Speaker's Chair. 'Let's not go up the stairs,' I said. 'Once the Whips have us in their clutches, it's curtains. Let's go round the corner to consider our options and the Order Paper.'

After some reflection (i.e. one minute) we decided we *would* vote on the Government Amendment, which was essentially motherhood and apple pie, but we *wouldn't* vote *against* the Lib Dem Amendment, because we agreed with it. We agreed that it is wrong, under any circumstances, to detain people without trial and derogate from the European Convention on Human Rights. It's ironic that many of the Lib Dems locally would welcome detention without trial for any of the 'foreigners' walking the streets in Tower Hamlets.

Avoiding/evading the Whips is best done in company, which helps strengthen the spirit. Too often it's either politically, tactically or logistically (too many clauses on too many subjects) impossible for MPs to make up their own minds even if they wanted to.

Joan gives me encouragement in the BG & B street fight. 'I know what it's like when other people are playing nasty. When I was Chair of CND at the height of the Cold War, M15 had a phone tap on me. It was the most chilling thing when I pressed the phone receiver down in the middle of making another call, and heard my own voice. It was a recording of the conversation I'd just had. I pressed it again and I heard myself speaking again. It was on a loop.'

At the office meeting that doesn't finish until eleven p.m. we discuss the fact that we have to get the office swept for bugs. The bloody Home Office won't do it. They say if they have to do it for one MP then they have to do it for everyone. Ridiculous. I'm not aware that most other MPs are fighting the sort of fight that's going on here.

22 February 2005

Went to the 'Make Poverty History' campaign launch at the Museum of Immigration in Spitalfields, followed by a meeting with the Minister for Postal Services, Gerry Sutcliffe, and a chance for local residents to vent their fury. Then there's a meeting with Alastair Campbell for MPs and their staff, entitled 'How to Get Your Message Across'. Due to the angle of the projector displaying the meeting's title, 'How to Get Your Message Across' is stamped across Alastair's forehead while he speaks. Alastair tells anecdotes about the 2001 election campaign, how Tony is the only person he knows who can give someone (Alastair) 'a bollocking while smiling', and how John Prescott rang him up to say he'd 'punched some bloke'. 'Does the press know?' asked Alastair. 'Well, it was filmed live on Sky,' says JP.

Leave the meeting none the wiser (apart from how to get your message across your forehead), and slip into meeting room in Portcullis House, where the Home Secretary, Charles Clarke, is attempting to sell his new policy on Detention without Trial to Labour MPs. This is basically 'Detention without Trial *Lite*'. Terrorist suspects will only be detained without trial for seven days before a judge rules whether they think the Home Secretary was justified in locking them up. The rules apply to only a handful (or 'handfuls' as Charles puts it, less than 100, more likely about thirty) of suspects who the security services believe are intent on blowing up British citizens, but for whom they don't have evidence to stand up in court.

Following the Law Lords' ruling that detaining prisoners in Belmarsh without trial was 'disproportionate' and therefore unlawful, Charles has brought forward these new measures. Instead of getting the judge involved *after* the Home Secretary's taken the decision, why can't it be before? I have a fundamental problem with people being locked up on the word of a politician. Charles argues that it should be an accountable politician (the Home Secretary) that takes a decision as grave as that, and it's unfair to argue that politicians are inherently corrupt, or can't be trusted. I lob in my two pennith, penn'orth, however you want to spell it: 'It's not that politicians are psychologically maladjusted. It's just that we need a separation of powers. Checks and balances. And detention without trial is a line most of us here can't cross.' On the screen, Caroline Flint is arguing about drug policy. I wonder which aspect of drug policy we'll be voting on in a few minutes. In an ideal world I'd go and check, but for the moment I have to concentrate on Detention without Trial. I am simultaneously missing meetings with Alan Johnson, Minister for Works and Pensions; Margaret Hodge, Minister for Children; someone at the House of Commons Public Bill Office, who needs the title of my Youth Services Bill which I'm presenting to Parliament; Tony McNulty, who's giving a parliamentary briefing on Crossrail which is critical to my constituency; and Brian Sedgemore, MP for Hackney, who I need to ask for advice about parliamentary privilege in relation to the ongoing GG saga.

It's no wonder MPs never concentrate on anything for longer than ten minutes. The meeting with Charles is adjourned while we go and vote on some aspect of drugs policy. I speak to Charles in the lobby. 'You're going to ask Labour MPs to vote on this, and then the Lords are going to block it and send it back to us. You'll have to make the concession we're asking for (and the Lords are asking for) so that you safeguard the legislation, i.e. let judges review the decision *before* instead of after it is made. So then you'll ask Labour MPs to troop back through the lobbies in favour of what we're calling for today, but you're saying we have to vote *against* tomorrow. Is that about right?'

Charles is patient, considerate, but seems unlikely to be correct when he says, 'That won't happen.' Something along those lines is about to happen. I chat to Vera (Baird) about it after the meeting, and although she was previously pressing Charles on various other aspects, she tells me my objections don't stack up. 'Your point is judicial oversight. The new proposals grant that. Seven days is neither here nor there. We already lock up people for fourteen days without giving them a trial. You have to accept that whether the judge sanctions detention or rejects detention, on day one or day seven, it makes no substantive difference.'

'If that's true, then why won't they let the judge do it first?'

'You can just as easily turn your argument on its head.'

Fifteen minutes earlier, in the meeting, Charles makes his way through the thicket of MPs' questions. 'On Oona's point of checks and balances, the new proposals, in my view, provide those balances.'

Although he's very good and he goes on to outline the judicial role, he slips into the ministerial habit of tautology. I've also asked why his briefing says, 'The legislation will be fully compliant with the European Convention on Human Rights. If necessary, to ensure this is so, the Government will derogate from the ECHR.' In other words it says, 'We'll be fully compliant with the ECHR. And to make sure that's the case, if necessary we'll ditch the ECHR.'

I catch up with Brian Sedgemore in Central Lobby and we go to the Smoking Room. I'm irritated it's so smoky, usually it isn't. I order two drinks. I'm asking Brian's advice about using parliamentary privilege – in relation to Galloway – because Brian is something of an expert on it. Brian advises me not to fight Galloway. I accept his advice. (*It later transpires that Brian comes out in support of*

Galloway against me. In April he defected from Labour to the Lib Dems.) Go back to issue of Detention without Trial. Jim Fitzpatrick, my Whip, wants to know if I'll be voting with the Government tomorrow. He texts me just before ten p.m.

'And the decision of the Bethnal Green jury is . . .?'

My reply: 'Sadly, it's a no . . .'

Within a flash he texts back, 'You're kidding!'

I ring him. 'Look, I don't agree with it. It's where I draw the line.' He's still quite friendly. He's a mate. 'I know you're being nice,' I say, 'when really you want to break my kneecaps.'

'That's not my style, Oony.'

I like it that he always calls me Oony with a pleasant Scottish accent. 'I just think it's crazy', he says, 'to have been through everything you've been through on Iraq and then throw it all away on this.'

He's talking, obviously, about my political career.

'Jim, my political career's been on the line for a long time now. But like I said, I just don't agree with it.'

The fact is, if I was a Minister, collective responsibility would push me through the lobby. It's a clear quid pro quo: your beliefs in one area, traded for your influence in another. That's what politics is. That's how the system functions, and it's the price you pay for greater influence. But I'm not a Minister and I'm not voting with the Government.

24 February 2005

I've been sitting writing this in Lancaster Gate, where the PM's hosting a reception for the Africa Commission. I don't do receptions but I thought it was a round table, so here I am . . . in the toilets which are like a living room, while 150 people are milling around in the reception room next door. The hum of conversation has just lowered by an octave, which means the PM has arrived and is now circulating. People carry on chatting, some being nonchalant in a forced way; others craning desperately to catch a glimpse. Love him or loathe him, most of all they want to see him. The trick is to wait until it goes completely silent, and then make a quick escape when everyone's straining their necks in the other direction. I hate spending time drinking orange juice and eating canapés. When Tony gives his speech he's flanked by the other Commissioners, notably Bob Geldof who proves that pop stars without Botox are the only people to age faster than Prime Ministers. Bob's sipping red wine, something a Cabinet Minister probably wouldn't do so prominently any more, and certainly not a Prime Minister.

I chat to Hilary Benn and arrange for him to visit the constituency. Harriet is there with a consultative document she has drawn up with all her African diaspora communities, aimed at feeding in their views to the Commission. She's a brilliant MP at a visionary level, but, more importantly, at a nuts-and-bolts level. Thank God my safe seat has turned into a marginal one. It's made me a much better MP, I'm better at everything – management, multi-tasking, delegation, consultation, communicating, delivery: the works.

25 February 2005

Sunshine followed by snow blizzards. It never snows like it used to, but the snow is still spirited. As I walk along the canal to work, through Victoria Park, listening to 'California Soul' and watching the snowflakes fall, I'm momentarily overjoyed. Music is even better than coffee in the morning, especially in contrast to the addiction of the *Today Programme*. A gaggle of geese eye me in a guarded way, so close I could offer my hand to peck. Or hack. They're like Government Whips. Every now and then they can be vicious, but it's not their fault. It's in their nature.

I walk past a newsagent on Old Ford Road. A billboard for the local paper says, 'Crackdown on Yobs Urges MP Oona.' I'm listening to Brazilian jazz. I would really like to see a billboard that says 'Everyone Should Have a Little Dance Urges MP Oona.'

26 February 2005

Sunday afternoon, knock on doors in Bow. Sunday evening, work on my pledges to constituents. Pledge to my husband that we'll see each other. Pledge to each other that this is the last time in our lives we work this hard. Round off Sunday evening with a trawl through all my bank statements. We've just re-mortgaged the house for the millionth time, and this time it's the last time. We've reached the limit. In a good cause of course. We asked for £20,000 but they'll only give us £15,000. It's to pay for repairs to the front of the house and for babies. Or to be more accurate, it's to pay for emotional trauma and invasive surgery and wishful thinking. My overdraft's crept up to £10,000 again. Tiberio says he'll put £10,000 from the re-mortgage into my bank account to pay the debt, on the condition that I don't spend any money on anything.

'You're not going to the supermarket on your own. You spend too much. You come back with that stuff for your hair [Frizz-Ease] and things that we don't need. From now on you're not buying anything, not even shampoo or Nurofen or whatever else. I'll buy everything. And you're not spending any more money on meals or drinks. That's it.'

It's true; my generation needs a mighty slap. Voting on the Consumer Credit Bill next week. It's about people like me. Tiberio's final word: 'I'll give you some cash tomorrow and you give me your credit card. It's over. Anyway, I can't believe we've just got a cheque for £15,000 and it's disappeared like water in the desert.'

The light was off, we were lying in bed.

'That's great, I like that. Water in the desert. I'm going to write it down.' I switch the light back on. He continued, exasperated, as I started to write, 'And why would anyone want to know what I said about money disappearing like water in the desert anyway?'

I'm about to say, 'I write a *diary*. That's what diaries are. Descriptions of what people say and think.' But I don't.

2 March 2005

Today I'm meeting the Borough Commander, followed by PMQs, followed by a meeting with the PM, followed by a public meeting in the constituency with Hazel Blears, the Home Office Minister whose brief ranges from graffiti to terrorists. Fifty local residents have arrived to tell Hazel about serious problems with Antisocial Behaviour, and to ask what the Government is doing about it.

My speech is becoming well worn: 'It can be frightening to face intimidation from a group of fifty youths, or have a brick thrown through your living room window, or have your car broken into. I know, because all those things have happened to me as a local resident. But I also know there are solutions, and that things can get better. Things are improving.' Cynical politician's blather? No, the extra police officers in my Safer Neighbourhoods team have genuinely made me feel safer. OK, I'll probably be mugged tomorrow, and maybe I had a brick through my window because of my stance on Iraq, but I doubt it. Too many friends and neighbours had similar experiences, and they didn't vote on Iraq.

The meeting goes well. Residents are introduced to their new police officers. Later, I return to Westminster, pondering that ancient MP debate: who has it easier? London MPs living near Westminster, or everyone else? The swings and roundabouts in this argument are well travelled. As a London MP I have the absolute privilege of returning to my own bed each night. I only have one home. I don't have to pack twice a week. I don't spend Thursday night travelling. On the other hand, because my constituency is so close – thirty minutes on the District Line – I spend virtually every day in a continual whirl between Bethnal Green and Westminster. I rarely sit chatting in the Members' tea room. Every day I'm hurtling back and forth.

'But she's only down the road!' cry constituents. Legislative scrutiny doesn't cut much ice in Stepney. Earlier today I met with the PM to discuss youth services in Tower Hamlets. Whenever he's in his office after PMQs he's always surrounded by an ocean of sundry articles for him to sign: House of Commons bottles, books on Parliament, coffee mugs, in the past even footballs and T-shirts. At no point do his eyes glaze over. In fact, apart from carrying on signing, he seems to have no greater interest in anything in the world than youth services in Tower Hamlets. Now there's a politician.

3 March 2005

I'm at my office in Bethnal Green at nine a.m. for a 'media briefing'. This is a new meeting in my diary every Thursday morning, on the day the local papers are out, so we're up to speed with the local press. At 10.30 a.m. I drive to Westminster, and arrive at eleven a.m. for DTI Questions. Flick through the Government brief that Ministers respond from. The theory is that a PPS sits behind the Minister with this brief. From here, we might suddenly spot in the brief something the Minister hasn't, or find part of the brief the Minister's lost, and casually fling it towards the Despatch Box in time to save the day. Suffice to say, I have only had one moment of glory, when officials gave the Secretary of State a brief for one PQ that, at ninety pages, wasn't brief. It allowed me to prove that I can read. Fabulous job satisfaction.

DTI and Women's Questions pass without incident, and I leave with Patricia to attend the Labour Friends of India event in Regent Street, where we're both hosting a table. The chief guest is the PM. We have a fabulous curry, which of course the PM can only glance at. It's a great bash, but it's time to slip away for the Decent Homes Standard debate in Parliament. Another speech on housing. Until every British person has a decent home, equality of opportunity will remain elusive. The Decent Homes Standard (a ten-year target has been set, with the aim of bringing all social housing up to a decent standard by 2010) is one of the Government's most radical initiatives. Again, it costs money, but in my view decent houses are as vital as decent education or decent healthcare. Keith Hill MP is, as ever, one of the more entertaining ministers at the Despatch Box.

4 March 2005

During an 'outreach' surgery I meet residents on a local estate and discuss their housing problems. There are 20,000 Tower Hamlets residents on the council waiting list. They want to know why housing isn't the most important item on the parliamentary agenda. 'I'd love house arrest,' says one homeless person staying with relatives, 'at least it would mean I had a house.' Later on I meet a group of mothers to talk about the Child Trust Fund, followed by a meeting back at the constituency office on Crossrail with Councillor Michael Keith. Crossrail is fantastic in theory, but many Tower Hamlets residents are utterly opposed. Many, including me, have argued that to create a construction site slam in the middle of the most tightly packed residential area in the borough – Spitalfields – is not the best plan.

Friday night begins with a speech at eight p.m. to mark the impending International Women's Day, and ends with a speech at eleven p.m. from the visiting Bangladeshi Finance Minister, at one of those posh Park Lane Hotels. It's exactly the sort of place I can't bear to spend my Friday nights. Chandeliers dripping from the ceiling, rich people gliding along marble floors. I'm having dinner with the Finance Minister and fifty others. The Minister gets up to give his little speech which meanders on for forty-five minutes. Stephen Timms and Jim Fitzpatrick are sitting next to him, staring stoically into the distance and nodding. Claude Moraes and his wife Barti sit on the other side of the table. On the other side of London, Tiberio is lying on our sofa watching TV alone. At eleven p.m. there's a mass exodus and I drive John Biggs, Claude and Barti home.

'It's astonishing how anything could ever be so boring,' says Claude as we sit in a traffic jam on the Embankment. We all agree. Purgatory.

So that was Friday night, and tonight, Saturday night, I'm at the mosque. My second biggest fear is of losing my seat at the general election. My biggest fear is winning it. And spending Friday and Saturday nights like this for another five years.

5 March 2005

A morning canvassing session. Oh, the joys of fighting a 'battle-ground' seat in the run up to an election. We have one session in the morning, one in the afternoon, and in the evening I visit members of the Council of Mosques in Whitechapel.

7 March 2005

Alan Johnson, SoS for Works and Pensions, is visiting a group of pensioners in my constituency. These are original East Enders, the ones who were here during the Blitz. Both Alan and I are keen for them to claim their entitlement, and many of them do. Over 6,000 pensioners in my constituency are claiming the Pension Credit with an average award of £68 per week. Not bad, but needs to be higher still.

Later that day I go and speak to Queen Mary University students. The conversation naturally turns to Iraq. I explain to them that I'm less pro-war, and more anti-genocide. But if they've already made up their minds that Iraq is the one issue to determine their vote at the general election, they must recognise that other consequences will follow: the amount of money we have for housing on the estate opposite; for education; for our public services. I quote Robin Cook, who, said, when he recently visited, 'It would be perverse if people who, like me, opposed Iraq were to inadvertently reward the Tories.' Or, I add, other parties like Respect. Conservatives will be heartened to know that the most likely outcome of a large Respect vote for George Galloway will be a Tory MP. That's what happened in Tower Hamlets in September in a local by-election – people voted Respect, and they got a Tory. (*And how wrong I was!!*)

8 March 2005

I'm at Westminister in the morning, then back to Tower Hamlets at lunchtime to celebrate International Women's Day, then back to Westminster in the afternoon. Meet the new Deputy British High Commissioner in Dhaka. The last time I saw him was somewhere near a temple in Cambodia, on a visit with the International Development Select Committee. Later that evening I return to Tower Hamlets for a meeting with trade unionists.

9 March 2005

The long-running saga around the proposals in the Anti-Terrorism, Crime and Security Bill is reaching a climax. I first spoke against this legislation in 2001, and haven't changed my view since. As I write this, the final shape of the Government's Bill is uncertain, so I'll withhold judgement. But in Tower Hamlets, no matter what's going on nationally, it's always the local housing situation that takes priority. I'm on an estate looking at where the £30 million 'gap

funding' is needed from Government to enable refurbishment. After
lengthy negotiations with the Treasury and ODPM, Jim Fitzpatrick
and I have got the agreement we want. Our constituents in Tower
Hamlets will see the change. Not instantaneously, but they will see it.
They will see new houses built.

15 March 2005

Today I attended a meeting I'd arranged for Helen Mirren and two
Oxfam representatives to see Jack Straw. Helen has recently tra-
velled with Oxfam to northern Uganda, where 90 per cent of the
population have been displaced by the savage conflict between the
Ugandan Government and the Lord's Resistance Army, the LRA. As
Jack says during the meeting, a good way to get items into the
Foreign Secretary's agenda is to get meetings into his diary. Then he
has to deal with it, to some degree at least.

We're a bit early and so someone from Jack's office offers a tour
of the Foreign Office, which is stuffed full of Renaissance paint-
ings, gold-rimmed ceilings and marble pillars. It oozes empire.
Unusually for me these days, I'm wearing high heels, and we
clatter along the wide corridors. Helen has on a beautiful black
and grey skirt with a classic black top. Our conversation moves
from the need for easy walking shoes to facial mutilation. In the
last month the LRA has cut off people's ears and lips – the
message is that they're listening to the wrong things and saying
the wrong things.

Helen and the Oxfam people are delighted that today Jack has
announced a major breakthrough on an International Arms Treaty.
So am I.

Overall, this is a dream of a meeting from Jack's point of view. No
proper briefing required, no pressure. But I ask him to deliver us 'just
one thing'. A public statement pushing for work on stabilising the
region and highlighting the involvement of the ICC. Jack agrees, and
sips tea with a film star.

We get up to leave, and Helen gasps – her beautiful designer skirt
has virtually fallen off. Jack possibly can't believe his luck. Reminds
me of the time I went with the Select Committee to meet Kofi Annan

at the UN and my sari fell off. After the meeting I have a quick word with Jack about a couple of journalists' jibes regarding the 'affair' story. The *Sun* has quoted an anonymous source (e.g. the journalist) saying, 'Oona was very cosy with the Foreign Office during the war in Iraq, now she's terrified George is going to accuse her of being in bed with Jack Straw.' Journalists and their games.

16 March 2005

Budget day. I've been looking forward to this for ages, because Gordon Brown's budgets are like magic shows. The rabbits he pulls out are legendary. And given that Alan Milburn's getting it in the neck for buggering up the Labour election campaign (a bit unfair but that's politics), the stage is set for a Gordon Brown spectacular. It's days like this I love being an MP. What a privilege to sit in the Chamber and soak up the atmosphere, and be on the inside. So now that I look at my diary more closely I'm gutted to see I'm going to be nowhere near the inside of the Chamber, instead I'm going to be on a Tower Hamlets estate, wandering around the political wilderness. Tim, thanks for blatantly butchering my diary and putting me in my place.

18 March 2005

Finished work at ten p.m. and went to a 'Black Women Mean Business' event. The girls at Crystal Events put on a wicked night. Angie Brown and Mary Pierce were amazing. I love dancing with them, it's like diving into the surf. Hernandez, the sexy boy, wasn't bad either. David Lammy's sister, Lavon, my party girl, came with me and I want to set her up with Hernandez. Then I could listen to him sing whenever I want. Another great Friday night courtesy of Elaine. In an instant I forget the ongoing Galloway libel saga.

Now it's 2.20 a.m., and the alarm is set for nine. I ponder the fact that this evening I've been with Afro-Caribbean people who all love me. Tomorrow have to go back out on Tower Hamlets estates where a significant number of white and Bengali people loathe me.

20 March 2005

I shouldn't be so negative. Out on Tower Hamlets estates this morning a significant number of white and Bengali people loved me. I was at a Bengali wedding at two p.m., Ali came with me and acted the perfect political spouse in a room of 800 men. The women were in a hall next door with a screen, on to which the live camcorded proceedings from ten feet away were projected. I gave a three minute speech, then drove to party rooms where there were about ten people stuffing envelopes. A group of young Fabians had come in to help, as well as Alf Dubs from the Lords. God bless him, he's been amazing, more energetic than most people half his age. He's the only person on my campaign who always says, 'Oona, your diary is insane, why don't these people ever give you any time off?'

The day began with George Galloway in an ITV studio in Gray's Inn Road. He can really put you off your eggs on a Sunday morning. He's always threatening to sue me. He loves hiding behind the skirts of a judge.

I sit down in the ITV studio with the Tory candidate, Faruk, in between us, and Nick Ferrari, the right-wing presenter to my right. Galloway's telling viewers, 'Oona King is in the papers nearly every day with stories of affairs . . . *is* she, *isn't* she?' (Reference to concocted rumours about Jack. Allegations about being offered £10,000 for sex) '. . . she's a poster girl.'

It was pure Galloway: a brilliant diversion and a cheap sexist tactic. it was also a bit rich coming from a self-confessed Romeo with the nickname 'Gorgeous George'. He got the sobriquet at a press conference in the 1980s after he stunned journalists by talking about his 'carnal knowledge' of certain women, thereby diverting interest from the original subject of the press conference – a furore surrounding his personal expenses. Needless to say, the headline-writers and political cartoonists had a field day, and the fact that he later 'voluntarily' repaid money to the Charity Commission got little coverage.

Nick Ferrari: 'Are you a poster girl?'

Me (something like): 'Well, you can get into sexist language if you want, but the issue is . . .'

'Are you a poster girl?'

'Are you a poster boy?'

'Obviously not, look at me. Now I don't mean this to sound rude, but *are you a poster girl?*'

Later I speak to Kester from my office. He reminds me I should've said, 'The answer's No. I'm an MP,' But it's live TV and I don't think of anything as obvious as that. Instead I'm feeling a knot in my stomach. I resent having to deal with juvenile sexism. It's so last century. The punch can knock you off-centre if you're not 100 per cent prepared for it. And I'm not. Somewhere inside I'm still genuinely surprised that in 2005 a woman politician has to put up with this.

And there's the other fact, that I've already been knocked off-centre by one of the TV mic guys. I must have had at least 200 TV mic guys (and they're always guys) attach a mic to my shirt before a TV interview. But this guy just shoves his hand up my shirt and starts groping me. Full on. I'm enraged. 'GET YOUR HAND out of my shirt.' I don't want to make a scene, especially not next to Galloway, or in front of Nick Ferrari, but this mic guy is bang out of order. Maybe he didn't mean it, in which case he does his job as carelessly as a heart surgeon accidently removing your lung. Or maybe he did mean it, in which case he needs a hard bloody slap.

'Thirty seconds till we're live,' says the floor manager.

I can only make light of it in sarcastic tones.

'Well, I know where to come if I need any excitement.'

'Fifteen seconds till we're live.'

'Hey love,' the mic guy comes back towards me, 'don't accuse *me* of trying to touch you up. Is that what you're trying to do?'

'Ten seconds till we're live.'

One part of my mind is preparing to do battle with Galloway. The other part is shouting at the mic man. 'You cheeky little wanker.'

'We're live.'

'Good morning, welcome to *The Week*,' Nick Ferrari smiles. 'We'll be looking at one of this election's biggest battlegrounds, where Oona King, the Labour MP, is locked in battle with her former colleague George Galloway.'

Later on Galloway says, 'Oona King is paying me thousands of pounds . . . she's voted for all of Tony Blair's wars, she's backed terror legislation and detention without trial.' Should I sue him for lying? He keeps saying I voted for things I didn't.

The outcome is a draw. Which isn't good enough. And Galloway, Ferrari and the mic man combine to almost capsize me in a sea of slimy men. I need to surround myself with my lovely men, the men who give men a good name – Josh, Tim, Marc, Kester, Mohammed, Ullah, Alan, Graham and, more than anyone, Tiberio.

That afternoon, after canvassing the estates around Bethnal Green, I go to a young people's focus group, where we're asking them their views on Antisocial Behaviour, youth services, affordable housing, ID cards and immigration. The conversation turns to politicians.

'They're boring. They ain't cool, you can't talk to them,' says Fokrul, nineteen.

'Is that what you think of Oona?' asks Alan. Fokrul's eyebrows shoot up.

'Oh no! Oona's different. She's a cut above the rest.'

That'll do me.

22 March 2005

Nine a.m. this morning seems like aeons ago. It began far, far away in the ministerial meeting rooms on the seventh floor of the DTI building in Victoria Street. Walked into the meeting, behind Douglas (Alexander) and Mike O'Brien at two minutes past.

'You look dour boys, what are you talking about?'

'The elections.'

Douglas is still reeling from being effectively sacked from the party's general election campaign, in the fallout from the Brown/Milburn sumo wrestling. Earlier, Douglas told me how amazed he was, that when push came to shove, talent didn't mean a thing. I pointed out that becoming the Minister of State for Trade, serving jointly in the FCO and DTI, a position Alan Clark described as 'the most important job outside the Cabinet' (which it was until immigration became the most important job outside the Cabinet) wasn't a bad consolation prize.

'Most Ministers and MPs would kill to have your job.'

'S'pose so.' Douglas is also Minister for Bangladesh, a role it's now my job to pursue him in.

When we arrived, the meeting had started. Patricia sat in her usual place, on the far side of the room with her back to the window, with maybe twenty officials, DTI Ministers, PPSs and civil servants. Outside, Victoria Street was rainy.

Two minutes past nine, and we'd already missed this week's DTI business, which in theory it was my responsibility to ensure had a proper PPS rota. Last week I arrived ten minutes early – possibly for the first time ever – to find that Pat had cancelled the meeting thirty minutes before.

After ministers gave their updates, the civil servants were asked to leave so we could have a political session with Geoffrey Norris from No. 10 on the business manifesto. It was interesting, but what struck me most during the discussion that followed was how intelligent Douglas is, and how much I've had the policy beaten out of me since the Government decided to place me in the remedial stream of being a long-term PPS. My job, from a parliamentary perspective, could not be more dull, repetitive or low-skilled. In fact, the more correct term is *un*skilled. How much skill does it take to sit behind a Minister? How much skill does it take to write out a rota? After all the years of ambition and determination which combined (as it does for all MPs) with astonishing good luck to propel me into Parliament, only the second black woman ever elected, what job did they give me? Writing out the rota. And while intelligent friends like Douglas gained years of experience, which has magnified their ability, I felt my own innate ability begin to shrink. Like a muscle that isn't exercised.

When I leave the DTI, it's still raining. Decide to go for a walk in St James's Park and hum 'Singin' in the Rain'. The yellow daffodils are mesmerising. Very happy, just for a moment, and really love every second outside.

Later in the evening I host a screening of *Hotel Rwanda* at the Genesis cinema, Mile End. About 200 people turn up, it's a really good crowd. I explain why I founded the All Party Group on Genocide Prevention, and then we go in to see the film. In some ways I'm angered because it doesn't show enough of the agony. It gets the terror right, but not the agony. Quin says it's good though, because showing too much means 'more is less'. But the scene of someone driving along the road by a river completely covered in bodies as far as the eye can see has a huge impact. Reminds me how much I was affected by my visit to Rwanda.

Cath Burd, our friend and architect, comes back home with Quin. Cath has a six-month-old and a two-year-old. She finally got her longed-for family. Sitting in my living room with a glass of wine, she tells me and Quin how things are going.

'It's hell. My two-year-old is driving me crazy. She wakes the baby. Bud and I sleep in separate rooms to keep the kids apart, sometimes for a fortnight. What sort of life is this . . .?'

Everything will be fine in a couple of years or less, but it's a reminder that dreams are paved with nightmares.

'Anyway,' says Cath, 'Wasn't it a problem, you eating that hot dog in front of Muslim constituents?'

'What hot dog?' I'd been famished when I arrived at the cinema, and eagerly considered my general election diet menu, which offered a choice of hot dogs or popcorn for dinner.

'The hot dog made of pork,' said Cath.

'Pork? I've never really thought about what's in a hot dog before.'

'How can you not know that a hot dog is made of pork?' Cath is incredulous, but this allows Quin to warm to a theme.

'You're talking about the fourteen-year-old who was a vegetarian, tucking into a huge slab of pâté on toast, and then freaking out when I told her it was meat,' said Quin. 'And she also had no idea that canals were man-made.'

'Why should I know they're man-made?'

'Because they're straight lines. If you looked at the map, you'd know.'

'I never looked at a map. And anyway, it's not the sort of information I'm interested in absorbing.'

'I know,' said Quin. 'It's also because your brain works in a different way.'

I give some thought to whether there might be a clinical term for not connecting hot dogs with pork. Mild concept dyslexia? Quin continues:

'It's like when Oons rang me up and asked if I wanted to go to the El Greco exhibition, because she was taking Tiberio's parents. I thought, "Wow, that's good, I didn't associate Oona with high art." As we're standing in the queue, Oona turns to me and says, "Now, Quin, tell me. *El Greco*. Person, place or concept?" '

Canals don't interest me. Inanimate objects other than tasteful interior decorations don't interest me. But although I make no connection between a hot dog and pork, men and canals, I make *loads* of connections between people all the time. People interest me. And I'm better at making connections between people and *with* people than virtually anyone else I know.

Go to sleep at about three a.m., and momentarily wonder if today, sitting behind Patricia and listening to the budget statement, was the last time I will ever sit on those green benches?

23 March 2005

Driving home tonight, I'm staring at the bright lights and plasma screens of Piccadilly Circus. For the first time ever, due to a fluke combination of pastel glowing colours and original graphics, it looks tasteful. In fact, it looks like a modern art installation. I'm snatched out of my night-dreaming by a shriek:

'OOONNNAAAA!'

There's a cabby beside me gesticulating wildly. I roll the window down.

'Hello, mate?'

'How's it going in Bethnal Green?'

'Yeah, it's OK.'

'Have you got time for a drink?'

'Nah, can't. My husband's cooking dinner.'

It's eleven p.m., so this sounds suspect. Lights change. We move off, still talking between our windows which – thanks to my left-hand drive car – are adjacent.

'. . . to your right!' he's shouting, perhaps about politics, but in fact about a car.

'It's really good to meet you Oona, if you can't do a drink, how about a quick Chinese?'

'Mate, really, I can't. My husband . . .'

'To your right!' We continue down Haymarket towards Trafalgar Square.

'You better beat that fucker Galloway.'

'I won't if I kill us both in a car crash first. I've got to go.'

'Did you see *Seven Up*? The TV programme?' He's shouting at the top of his voice above the roar of London traffic. 'That's me, Tony, the one from *Seven Up*. They've filmed me every year since I was a kid.'

'Yeah, I remember that programme. I'll look out for you Tony.'

'TA-RAA,' and he careers off towards Chinatown, Tony from *Seven Up*.

Sometimes I feel like I'm in *The Truman Show*. Just sitting at the traffic lights, or buying the newspaper, or queuing in the bank or walking along the road, all day long, people come up and say, 'Hello, Oona,' or, 'Help me, Oona,' or, 'Way to go Oona,' or, 'Fuck you, Oona.' And I watch them go by. In a nice kind of way.

4 April 2005

Today was the day the PM didn't fire the starting gun for the election, because the night before last, the Pope died. All parties suspended political campaigning as a mark of respect. Except for Respect who were out in force, with George Galloway marching up and down Columbia Road Flower Market. Frankly, I think they got it just about right, as the last time I checked, Britain wasn't a Catholic country. We decided to go to a Bengali/Muslim estate, but called it off when a white person complained. It's nuts.

I've decided to ask Nora if she wants to make a documentary about the campaign. I don't trust the other offers we've had so we've turned them all down. But then I thought, 'I want a record of this; at least I should get a friend to do a bit of filming. Who could do a decent job? Nora. She's a documentary filmmaker.' And from there it seemed obvious that a documentary could be on the cards. So I ran it by Nora. She thought it was a great idea and immediately started to talk about how she would make it from a personal angle, and how it could be more interesting and personal than all the other documentaries about political campaigns. She stressed that she didn't agree with my position on Iraq, asked if it was a problem, and I said it wasn't.

So then I emailed the eight core members of my campaign team and office to say, 'I'm thinking about doing a documentary with my oldest friend.' All of them unanimously said it was an extremely bad idea that could only have a negative outcome in terms of the election, either because it would prove a distraction, or because Nora would inevitably have to show me in unguarded moments that portrayed me or the Party in a bad light.

One of them said it might contribute to Labour losing the council elections in 2006 (I can think of many other things that will do that) and another said, 'It's out of the question. You can't do it. You have no choice.' Always a bad tactical line to take with an MP. So I'm doing it. Not for the hell of it, but because I think it could be helpful in the long run and a really unusual piece of political TV that might connect with people. Let's hope I'm not proved wrong by eight to one. After I'd made the decision, one of the team suggested a more immediate benefit.

'If she's really your oldest friend then send her in to film George Galloway's campaign team meetings and we can see what he's getting up to every night. How funny would that be?' I agreed it would be hilarious. But I don't want to go in for dirty tricks.

On the subject of dirty tricks, Prince Charles must think someone's orchestrating a campaign against him. He announced today that instead of being at his own wedding this Friday, he now plans to be at the Pope's funeral. I can't imagine anyone who'd want to be in Prince Charles's position. He can't even get married without appealing to European Human Rights Legislation, and then he has to cancel his wedding day so he can stand in for the Queen in Rome. Frances says Tony Blair should become the new Pope.

Closer to home, God will be landing in Bethnal Green and Bow in a few hours. *Fantastic* news that Gordon Brown has decided to launch my election campaign. *Alli Akbar*. I couldn't ask for more. After all, if the PM arrived here it would be a nail in my coffin. And anyway, he's a bit tied up tomorrow. He drives to Buckingham Palace at 11.30 a.m., and as soon as he leaves the Queen to drive back to Downing Street, the starting gun is fired. About bloody time.

Here in the East End we've been fighting this campaign virtually full on since the run up to the European and mayoral elections in May last year. A year is too long to inflict a general election campaign on anyone. It seems fitting that this is the last entry in this particular journal. The first (and only) entry before this year was May 1997, and an account of the hustings meeting that made me the candidate for Bethnal Green and Bow in April, exactly eight years ago. Eight years is a long time in politics. It's long enough for an American president, and it's long enough at Westminster. And I'm going to have to fight like a dog to stay there. So tomorrow TB will fire the starting gun. I'm calm, but also excited. Let the battle commence.

18 April 2005

At this point in a general election campaign weeks don't start or end. The hours just pass along with the doors and the constituents and the eggs.

But still, it was a good start to the week. I am amazed that my fight with Galloway has become national (and according to some of the foreign journalists, international) news. *The Times* editorial today is entitled 'Pearly King' and says, 'Bethnal Green and Bow should re-elect its MP.' Amen. *Inshallah*.

Still, I asked Miri for Valium. She said it's not listed any more (it was a 1950s housewife's drug) and prescribes Librium instead. But Tiberio's doctor told him Librium is a 1980s drug, so I decide against a trip to the chemist. I just like carrying the prescription around in my bag. Respect slashed my tyres and trashed the car. It's OK but then again it's not. They're howling, 'Murderer, murderer', and it's fine at the time, but twelve hours later in the middle of the night my heart's beating really fast and I'm choking on panic. Is that an anxiety attack? I've always wondered what they're like. Or perhaps I've got post-traumatic stress syndrome. Why wasn't I afraid at the time? Or maybe it's nothing to do with the thirty kids, the pack on your trail.

20 April 2005

Super Wednesday. The campaign changed for me today. Everything kicked off. Van loads of police. Van loads of media. Ken Livingstone came to the mosque to support me. Later, we're in a meeting on the fourth floor with twenty members of the Muslim community, and the police tell us we can't leave the building because there's an abandoned car outside and it might be a bomb. Ken's been fantastic.

This appears to be the high point of his visit so far. He is definitely the politician most helpful to my re-election campaign. Five minutes later the police say we can leave, there's no bomb.

We walk along Commercial Road and then turn up Brick Lane. This is the first time in the campaign that we've had a proper presence on Brick Lane. Twenty-five of us walking up the street with media and camera crews in tow. Ken and I hand out 'Oona' posters. Ken says he's wearing his cheapest clothes, so it doesn't matter if we get pelted with eggs. I've got a spare change of clothes in the car. I wonder where all the Respect lot are. They're nowhere to be seen. Then we turn left on to Hanbury Street and I see they're being held behind police barriers. We arrive at Salique's restaurant. Respect advertised the event by saying that Tony Blair would be here, as a way to get their protesting numbers up. But in the event there are only about forty of them. I'm half expecting a brick or at least an egg. Nothing materialises.

Inside, Salique tells people to vote for me. I like his straightforward approach: 'My friend, if there were a better Bengali candidate then I would support them instead of you. But there isn't. And you work hard, you are honest, so I support you.'

The food is good.

After the meeting I do interviews with BBC and Channel 4 news, then go home to prepare for the hustings with Galloway this evening. He's pushed me off the front page of the *Standard*, which was going to lead with me getting my tyres slashed, but is instead leading with the story that GG was attacked by a mob from Al Muhajiroun. All very suspect. During the course of the day I realise things could spin out of control. People could get hurt because the mood is turning really ugly. I remove all my attacks on GG from my speech. Gotta take some of the heat out of this campaign, or we'll all live to regret it.

Hustings goes well. Later in bed, I can't sleep. After two hours I start to panic about the fact that I can't sleep. Must sleep. Take a sleeping pill at four a.m., knowing I'll be drugged through the morning. Wake up four hours later at eight a.m., feeling like someone's hit me over the head with a hammer. Ten times. Tiberio, who had come back from Cranfield to sit in the front row during the hustings, had already left to go back to his MBA hell. Tim led me across Victoria Park towards the daily campaign meeting at 9.30 a.m. and two or three times I thought I would just have to lie down on the grass. Too tired to appreciate the yellow tulips. At the meeting, I told the campaign team we'd have to stop any personal attacks on GG. Discuss possibility of cancelling an interview with the *Evening Standard*'s main political correspondent, Andrew Gilligan. I'm not in a good way. The interview goes ahead, but the campaign team are awash with clemency and let me go home to sleep for two hours. In the event I can't sleep, but I put on a meditation CD for the first time in eight months, still my mind, then return to the office for the meeting I've called with GG and Borough Commander.

Diane Hayter answers a 'withheld number' on my mobile. I'm swaying. She scribbles down, 'No. 10'.

'Who wants to speak to me from No. 10?' Although I ask the question, I assume the answer will be Tony. Whenever an MP's diagnosed with a terminal illness or something bad's happened, the PM steps into his pastoral role.

'It's Tony,' says Diane, before handing me over to the No. 10 switchboard operator.

'Hello?' Yes, it's definitely Tony.

'Hi Tony, it's Oona here.'

'How are you? It sounds pretty bad.'

'I'm fine. It sounds worse than it is.' I should be excited – or at least interested – that I've made the front page picture and story for the *Guardian*. I buy the *Guardian* most days (although I often don't get round to reading it). Today I've failed to buy it all day. It's midnight now, and I still haven't seen it.

Tony asks some more about the campaign, and what it's actually like out on the estates. I ask him for a people carrier, which sounds fairly random, but is the most significant thing we're lacking. It's not the hardest thing he's ever been asked. For all I know it's illegal, but then most things these days seem to be illegal when it involves politicians and their campaigns.

'I'll sort it out,' says Tony. 'Take care of yourself darling and lots of love to you.'

He's also offered me the President of Iraq if that would be helpful.

Friday 22 April 2005

Yesterday, after the phone call with Tony, I went across the road to Bethnal Green Police Station for the meeting I'd called with GG and the Borough Commander. It's the first time I've been in a non-confrontational encounter with GG. My team – Kester, Graham, Tim – and I make a series of proposals aimed at calming the situation and keeping our two camps apart. I'm not surprised that GG agrees to almost anything we say as he's suffering from the Pandora's box whiplash moment. The forces he thought he could harness are way beyond his control. One of my requests is that Respect don't sabotage our events. They stay away from us, we stay away from them.

27 April 2005

Peter Hain came to the constituency today. Our paths only crossed for about twenty minutes walking down Roman Road in the rain. Still, it's great to see a pro in action. But the rain is draining. Tim says I have no discipline about going to bed. It's after midnight and I'm writing this next to my sleeping darling Tiberio. Miss him so much, we never see each other at the moment. The one thing inducing me to sleep sooner rather than later is the need to see Victoria Park before Oliver and Anna arrive at 8.15 a.m. to take me away.

The morning school gate visit today was cancelled when one of the school girls got run over, and Anna, a nurse at the Royal London, and my assistant during the campaign, had to take charge of the situation. It's the first time I've felt paralysed since the election was called. It would have been in bad taste to canvass while a child was being treated by the ambulance crew. And it would have been in bad taste to stand with all the other gawpers. So I stood in between the school gates and the ambulance, looking from one side to the other, until we returned to the office.

Victoria Park was full of spring this morning. Budding leaves, cherry blossom, hatching chicks, wild geese. Love it. Maybe I should move to the country. Was also inordinately pleased by a couple of rainbows. Reminded me of leaving Westminster for the very last time after Parliament was dissolved – possibly never to return – and driving in the car towards Westminster Bridge with Big Ben on my right, before turning left on to the Embankment. I was mesmerised to see the brightest, largest rainbow I've ever seen, standing tall over the London Eye. My jaw actually dropped when I looked higher still and saw *another* rainbow, the big mama rainbow, presiding over the first rainbow. Where do double rainbows come from? Why hadn't I seen one before? I stared at them all the way along the Embankment, and by the time I saw a third and fourth rainbow over Canary Wharf, or somewhere to the east, I had decided I was the Messiah and would whip Galloway into oblivion. Or at least force him out of Tower Hamlets. The mood of reconciliation during the meeting with the Borough Commander has passed. Things have been quieter over the last week, but trouble is looming again. A young Bengali man told me he had all his tyres slashed because he had my poster in his car.

Last night David (Lammy) and Nicola came down. On one estate in Shadwell, I became separated from the main group. Marc rang to say there was a group of boys I should avoid. A car with five young people pulled up, and they were shouting, 'Jewish bitch, get out of here.' It only affects me on an anthropological level. 'How interesting these people hate me so much because my mother is Jewish. I am Jewish.' The day before, Ro spoke to a Bengali man who said he wouldn't vote for me.

'Why's that?' asked Ro.

'Because I don't agree with Oona King spending her parliamentary salary to pay the Israeli Army to bomb the Palestinians.'

Where d'you start?

On the same day, one white man said to me, 'I'm not voting for you because you receive £500 per week from the *Hackney Gazette*.' Hello??

And another white man said, 'I cannot vote for you because you have chosen to pay for your son to go to a private school.' I told him that a) I didn't have any children, b) I was a passionate advocate for, and product of, comprehensive education, and c) he was confusing me with the one other black woman MP, Diane Abbott. He didn't believe me. 'No it's you, it's Oona King who pays for her child to go private.'

No mate, I should've said, I'm the one that spends all my money on IVF treatment. Later on got doorstepped by Reuters about the Attorney General's advice on the legality of war in Iraq. Don't know who tipped off the journalist and a photographer that I'd be at a residents' meeting talking about Antisocial Behaviour in Bow.

2 May 2005

Yesterday I did an 'extreme sports' version of canvassing. It involved running and jumping up innumerable stairs in tower blocks for about nine hours. The tactic is called 'blitzing' and I go with about ten others who spread out along the balconies knocking on doors. While the ten canvassers ask people if they're voting, I run from one to the next, saying hello to as many people as possible. I've done it many times before, but never running instead of walking and never in so many fifteen storey buildings where lifts were broken, and never for nine hours straight.

We run to the top of the blocks each time and then start working our way down. Often, as we all reach the ground floor, someone calls over the balcony that they're sorry they missed me and can they meet me? So I run up six flights of stairs again, say hello, then run back down. It's the first hot day of the year. I feel OK at the time, maybe even buzzing. I'm wearing trainers and I like jumping up the stairs, two at a time. Josh has transformed himself from campaign leader into personal trainer. 'Come on, faster, keep running, keep moving, less talking, more voters.' He's a gorgeous twenty-eight-year-old boy with rippling muscles who goes to the gym every morning. I'm feeling quite pleased that I keep up with him.

At the morning meeting the day before, I told the team what Tiberio told me. When you run the marathon you have to pace yourself. A marathon has two halves. The first half is the first twenty-three miles. The second half is the last three miles. Some of us in the Bethnal Green and Bow Labour Party have been working at a crazy level for a year. In the office this morning the sign on the wall says 'Three Days Till Victory'. We're running down Pall Mall, win or lose, we're going to cross the finishing line. And then my extreme canvassing takes a heavy toll. Wake up at four a.m. with a sore throat and a temperature. FUCK. How could I fuck it up so close to the end?

Go to the 9.30 a.m. campaign meeting this morning, then cancel all 'blitzing' and go home. Sleep for four hours. Could've slept for four days, but Andrew Gilligan won't do interviews over the phone. He quizzes me on corruption allegations relating to the electoral register. I'm exhausted and don't know what he's talking about. No idea. Haven't even heard about it.

Just another three days. Someone told me that a minute during an election campaign is like a day. These three days seem like an eternity. Maybe I'll spend them in bed and they'll have to carry me over the finishing line. Anna says, 'Come on, Oona, you're not doing a Paula Radcliffe (when she collapsed in the Athens marathon). We were thinking more a Kelly Holmes.' I think of that book, *Touching the Void*, when the guy is left for dead inside a glacier and then has to drag himself miles over boulders with a crushed leg. He arrives barely conscious at base camp, unable to crawl another inch and says, 'This show goes no further.' That's what I'm thinking. 'This show goes no further.'

Months of sleep deprivation combined with excessive exercise means I've lost one and a half stone. Funny to think I went to WeightWatchers last year and couldn't shift a pound. Now I'm slim but exhausted and unhealthy. Often too tired to sleep, until I get ill. But the bottom line is that I wouldn't have missed it for the world. So this show will go just a little bit further, up Pall Mall and then into an ambulance.

4 May 2005

At midnight tonight '05.05.05' will turn from a catchphrase into today. The date seems like a long lost relative I've been waiting for ever to meet. I've written a victory speech, but no losing speech. So many people have come out to help me, some from other parties and some with no affiliation but mainly, of course, from the Labour Party. Given some of the bad press I get and how often I'm described as a murderer, I'm overwhelmed that so many people have come to show me so much support, and invest so much faith in me, whether they agree with my views or not. Their kindness could kill me, or at least turn me into an emotional wreck. Cannot, cannot, *cannot* afford to start crying. But I cry at EastEnders. What hope have I got? Actually, I remember what'll keep me strong. Respect/SWP will behave like a bunch of tossers. They're always reliable in that respect, and that'll keep me strong. Must think ice maiden.

Tiberio turned the news on and I asked him to turn it off immediately. There's no point listening to the news now. It's all too late. Got a text message from Louise Casey: 'I hear you're doing well on postal votes. Fab news.' I ring Josh: 'Why hasn't anyone told me about postal votes? What are the results?'

'Of what we've had in so far, you've got 50 per cent.' I'm wowed. I expect he's going to say, 'The other 50 per cent is split between the other parties.' Instead he says, 'And the Tories have got 50 per cent.'

What the hell does that mean?

'It's what we expected,' says Josh. 'A high percentage of affluent Tories will vote by post. If that's all they get, that's fine. Respect are nowhere.'

I know the theory of what he's saying and if I were to bet on the result I'd say I'd get a majority of 5,000, give or take . . . But that's the theory. I'm not going to sleep all night. Maybe I'll write my 'losers' speech instead.

5 May 2005 – Election Day

The most difficult part of today was reading the 'losers' speech in my office:

> It seems clear that Britain is set for another four years of a Labour Government, and I am very happy for the country as a whole, because I know that only Labour is committed to delivering on health, education, jobs, housing and the police. The voters of Bethnal Green and Bow have made a different choice, and will no longer be represented by a Labour MP. That is their right in a democratic society. And while, of course, I am very disappointed not to have won

this election, I am not afraid to accept the verdict of the electorate because I have always believed that democracy is worth fighting for . . .

Tough.

Tiberio and my cousin Ed are downstairs with Mum, watching the election night drama begin on TV. The exit polls say it'll be a Labour victory but with a reduced majority of sixty-six. My biggest fear tonight isn't about the result. My biggest fear is that whatever the result I'm going to start crying uncontrollably. If that happens I'll never forgive myself.

Ever since Galloway started suing me, and the pressure started to fizz, I promised myself I'd pop a couple of Valium on the big night. But I never got further than the prescription for Librium from Miri which is still at the bottom of my bag. I've been carrying it around like an emergency parachute. Too late to get it now. Instead I run a bath and try deep breathing to calm my racing heart. And then I remember the solution. Why didn't I think of it before? Music. It will get me through anything. I lie in the bath listening to 'California Soul' by Marlena Shaw. As if by magic, all the anxiety I've stored in my body over the last year just melts away. My heart slows. I feel entirely calm. By the time I've listened to the song three times I'm raring to go. Victory, defeat, whatever, it's performance time and I'm up for it.

Nora knocks at the door while I'm doing my hair. She comes in with the camera and we have a chat. It's 11.30 p.m. 'Aren't you a bit late?' she asks. It reminds me of the last time we were together and I was getting ready for a big appearance – my wedding, eleven years ago. We shared a room the night before in Naples. We got up at nine a.m., and the wedding wasn't until five p.m., but we still managed to be late. It's nice to have my oldest friend, my bridesmaid, here tonight. I take another swig of the Day Nurse. Nora calls it legal speed. It's keeping my temperature down, and my throat isn't too bad. It would be nice to be on top form physically, but that's not the most important thing. Mentally I now know I'll hold it together, and that's all that matters. Why hadn't I thought of music before? I pack my iPod for the count.

We arrive at St Margaret's Church next to York Hall in Bethnal Green. The police have cordoned off the road. Inside about 100 Labour activists are milling about, pouring drinks into plastic cups. One room has music, the other has a widescreen TV. Outside police officers, residents and Labour Party members are wandering around in front of the barriers. The Borough Commander, Mark Simmons, is waiting for me on the pavement, and calls me over to see him before I go in.

'Good evening, Oona. Sorry to have to tell you this, but we have reports that an unspecified attack by an extreme Islamic group is a possibility this evening.'

'OK,' I say evenly, 'do I need to know anything else? Can I go inside now?'

The Commander seems concerned, almost agitated. But I want to go inside because I know people are waiting for me. I ask the Commander to discuss any security concerns with Louise Casey. Louise works for the Home Office, and security concerns are right up her street. I leave Louise and Mark on the pavement and walk inside. I get rapturous applause. I go on to the stage and give a speech. Everyone cheers everything, except when I say: 'I'm going to ask you to do one thing. Just for ten seconds, visualise us losing tonight. You have to imagine it, just for a moment.' I am about to say, 'So that we're prepared,' but people have already started booing. So instead I say, 'Before we consign it to the dustbin of history.' Sometimes you have to give people what they want to hear.

The people in this room have sweated blood and tears for me. They deserve all the optimism I can muster.

I tell them how great they are. It's true. It breaks my heart to think how hard they've worked for me. I speak to one young guy in his mid-twenties, who I've seen a few times before. He lives outside London, but he says, 'I had to come to the East End to fight for you. This is my equivalent of the Spanish civil war.' I start laughing. 'No, really,' he's completely serious. 'I had to come. I believe in you.' I start to get a bit choked, and am relieved when Louise interrupts the conversation.

'There is a problem,' says Louise, 'and I need to discuss it with you outside.' We walk back up the steps.

'The Borough Commander says there is a specific threat against you, Oona, from an Islamic group.'

'Well he didn't say that to me,' I say, thinking, 'What else can they pop into the mix to raise my stress levels tonight?'

'He probably didn't want to worry you,' says Louise, 'but that's what he's told me. Also he's concerned about security, because people are walking in here without ID. He would be very relieved if you cancelled this event and went straight to the count at Canary Wharf, because it's secure there.'

I consider my options:

1. Go to Canary Wharf and leave my supporters to get blown up.
2. Go back into my own bash and get blown up with my supporters.
3. Cancel the event, even though there is only a miniscule risk of anything happening. After all, that's what gives terrorists the advantage – they only have to plant the seed of terror, and you do the rest.

The police are crawling all over the place. They even have plain-clothes police officers inside. I've had enough death threats to know they don't want to kill you, they just want to scare you. So I go over to the Borough Commander, thank him for his concern, and go back into the party. My friend Elaine has arranged some great live music, so Tiberio and I dance. There aren't that many people dancing with us, because they're all in the other room glued to the TV. We stay for an hour. Eventually they drag me away from the music and we drive to the count at 1.30 a.m.

There are loads of photographers and press at the entrance. It's a spanking new large glass atrium called the Winter Gardens, worlds apart from the municipal sports hall where the previous two counts were held in 1997 and 2001. There are floor passes and balcony passes. I'm handed a candidate pass. I can hardly believe the scene up on the balcony, where it seems half the world's media are jostling for position.

I ask Graham, my agent, how it's going. 'Fifty-fifty,' he says.

'You're kidding?' He shakes his head. I've been utterly convinced for the past two weeks that I'm going to win, and win well. Although I tried to imagine losing, like a sort of practice run, I didn't think it would happen. Graham's answer pulls me up short. I wander around the room, and have a chat with the Bengali Lib Dem and Tory candidates. Both the candidates and their families tell me they hope I'll beat Galloway. I can't help smiling when one of them asks if I can put in a complaint about Galloway's behaviour on *their* behalf.

The room is a hum of activity. There are rows of tables with different ballot boxes, each marked with different wards. In front of them are rows of cardboard boxes, each marked with a candidate's surname. As new ballot boxes are opened, each party representative tries to get a good position to see how their candidate is doing. I stand behind one teller as they open a box. I hold my breath as I count eleven consecutive 'KING's. I'm not doing *that* badly I think, until someone tells me it's a Bow ballot box. Apparently Bow is giving Galloway a big thumbs down. Which is what some of the other wards in the south of the constituency are doing to me.

Interminable waiting and counting. As I walk around the counting agents, all the Labour counters who are monitoring the tellers say it's too close to call.

Rageh Omaar is up on the balcony, reporting for the BBC. I'd love to speak to him. I haven't seen him since one of Quincy's parties – they were at university together. I start to walk towards the balcony staircase to have a quick chat with him, but get beaten back by a dozen journalists. They all want a quote. 'How are you feeling, Oona?' 'What's your prediction, Oona?' 'Do you expect to retain your seat, Oona?' I smile at the journalists but remain silent. Mum is also up on the balcony with Anna. I wave to them and go back into the main room. Tiberio, Ro, Rush, Tim, Josh, Graham, Claire, Rachel, Lesley Pavitt – they're all on the floor with 150 others.

At three a.m. there is a flurry of activity. I get excited, but it turns out it's the result for my neighbour, Jim Fitzpatrick. We know Jim will be all right. The candidates are called on to the stage. Jim has won with a majority of 7,000. Cheers and jubilation. Jim has saved my life more times than I can remember, and I'm thrilled he'll be going back to Parliament. Then back to waiting for the Bethnal Green and Bow result.

After another hour I'm told we're still nowhere near getting the result. I go with Tiberio to watch a bit of TV in an adjacent room that has been set aside as the 'candidates' area.' *Sky News* shows TV footage of me, taken a few minutes earlier in the main room. Breaking news. It feels like an out-of-body sensation. The headline running beneath the picture says: 'Oona King has lost to George Galloway by 2,000 votes.'

There is no way this can be correct, because everyone who knows anything – i.e. the tellers on the floor – say it's too close to call. But then I start to doubt myself. Maybe I missed the result. Maybe they called all the candidates on stage in the last three minutes while I was in here. After all, it's on the news – it must be true! Have reports of my political death been exaggerated, or am I a loser? Go back out on to the floor and sit on a table, chat to Tiberio, Tim and Josh and listen to my iPod. I play 'California Soul' again. Maybe I'll go and live in California.

The waiting is just interminable. Interminable. Interminable. Change the song on my iPod to 'Elevate Your Mind', a great dance music version of the Sly and the Family Stone track. I listen to the music, tell myself I will elevate my mind, and then do just that. I feel fine. My mind is up above, but fully under control. My very greatest fear, my fear of losing it in the slang sense as opposed to the ballot sense, has gone. It's not about being an ice maiden. It's about being cool and relaxed. I feel as though I have an invisible shield around me. Nothing will pierce too deep, whatever it is. I'm thinking, 'Come on, let's *do* it.' Over and over. And still, when the announcement finally comes, 'Would candidates and agents for Bethnal Green and Bow make their way to the Returning Officer,' it feels somehow unexpected.

I am furthest away from the Returning Officer, maybe 200 yards, and it takes me longer than the other candidates to walk around the counting benches towards her. The room and the balcony hush, like a theatre when the actors appear on stage. The noise of my shoes clacking on the ground suddenly sounds conspicuously loud, and I feel every eye trailing me. The 200 yards seem miles. When I reach the Returning Officer, Christine Gilbert, the only place I can squeeze in is by her shoulder. Christine is the Chief Executive of Tower Hamlets, wife of my favourite political bovver boy, Labour MP

Tony McNulty. Pressed against Christine's shoulder, the sheet with the results is abruptly in full view. I immediately look for the letters G and K. Political enemies, alphabetical neighbours. I scan the figures. I've lost. I've already turned away as Christine starts running through the housekeeping before moving on to the results in a hushed voice.

What do I feel? I feel deep, deep shock. But then again I don't. Somewhere I feel devastation. But most of all I feel it's not the end of the world. Most of all, actually, I feel fine. This surprises me so much that a smile nearly slips onto my lips. I think of the first time I waited for the result of a make-or-break count, when I was selected in 1997. My agent Dino scanned the figures and shook his head almost imperceptibly. I had my heart in my mouth.

Today, eight years later, I know the suspense for my team on the other side of the room is unbearable. I want to let them know we haven't made it. I turn towards Josh, Tim, Rachel, Clare, Lesley, Rushanara, and the others standing with Tiberio. My wonderful team. And so many more back at the Labour Party event. Rohema, Frances, Kester, Mohammed, Brian, Fred and Ruby, and hundreds of others. I genuinely love them. I shake my head from side to side almost imperceptibly. For them this signal ends a year's campaign, and five decades of Labour parliamentary representation in the heart of the East End.

Then I turn back to Christine and the other candidates. The Labour Party says we must challenge any result where the margin is less than 1,000. I ask what the majority is, and Christine says 'About 800.' Graham immediately interjects. 'I request a recount.'

Christine shakes her head. 'I cannot authorise a recount.'

'The majority is less than 1,000,' says Graham, 'I request a recount.'

Christine refuses again. Graham requests again. Christine is implacable.

'There are no circumstances in which I will permit a recount.'

'I request a recount,' says Graham for about the fifth time.

'The decision is final,' says Christine in her calm but firm manner that in other circumstances is often pleasing.

We are called on stage. I stand next to Galloway. I smile at him, shake him by the hand, and then lean towards him momentarily.

'Congratulations George, you got a great result.'

His eyes flicker from me, and then out to the audience and the TV cameras. I get the impression that he doesn't reply, but maybe he is uncharacteristically inaudible, or maybe I don't absorb what he says. I stand behind him while he gives a very loud, air-punching acceptance speech. He reminds me of an American evangelical preacher. He calls on the Returning Officer, Christine, to resign – the person who just refused me a recount, and fast-tracked his victory. He says the Council is corrupt. He's starts talking about Iraq. Half the council workers get up and walk out. It's as if he's giving his 'losing' speech, because he didn't expect to win.

He leaves the stage, and the Respect lot are going wild. In fact everyone leaves the stage, except for one stray candidate who I think lost his deposit. No one is handing me the microphone, and in fact they expect me to leave the stage without saying anything. Exit my political career without a word? No. I take the microphone. I'm as calm as I've ever been. And I feel strong, perhaps stronger than I've ever felt. I know I fought a decent campaign, one which avoided vicious sectarian politics. I was right to do it that way, and Galloway was wrong. It won't take long for the constituency – and the rest of the country – to see through George Galloway. And in any case Galloway is a one-man band, a man that skillfully exploited a particular community for his own ends. He will vanish from the East End as quickly as he appeared. In contrast, despite our mistakes and my personal failings, I know the Labour Party will be in the East End for generations, and this makes me enormously proud and happy.

I walk down the steps of the stage and hug Tiberio. Then hug the others. I look at my watch. It's almost five a.m. Almost time to start a new life. But first I want to get back to my Labour Party members in Bethnal Green. Going out into the entrance hall of the Winter Gardens I walk past the new MP for Bethnal Green and Bow. He is surrounded by a media scrum. Less than an hour ago all those journalists were desperate to speak to me. But I am no longer the MP, I am no longer the story.

Mum takes my hand for a minute. Someone gives me a flower. People ask if I'm OK. Yes I'm fine, I'm really fine. We drive the ten minutes back to Bethnal Green. When I walk briskly into the room where the band played earlier, one of the first people I see is Nora with the camera. But then I am greeted by a sight I hadn't prepared for. At least half my Labour Party members are crying. The other half look equally devastated. Their collective despair and anguish is the only force strong enough to pierce my mental armoury. I can easily handle George Galloway's contempt, but not the grief of those I'm indebted to.

I am handed the microphone. I get angry.

'I was fine,' I shout, 'absolutely fine, I could deal with it all, until I saw *you* lot!! Now I'm a mess!!' Tears roll down my cheeks. I see Slate standing in the crowd. His hand covers his mouth, as if to mask a sharp intake of breath, or a terribly bitter pill. Carli is sobbing, Carli who mobilised so many NUS (National Union of Students) members to turn out in the East End. Mohammed, my caseworker, has cheeks streaked with tears. I hug Mohammed long and hard. He has fought my turf war week after week on the most aggressive ground, outside the mosque. Mohammed's mum is here too.

Then I see the Wing Commander arrive. That's our nickname for our election supremo, Alan Barnard. In 1997 Alan was the 'Key Seats' officer for the Labour Party, and then head of Labour's elections department. His original polling at the beginning of the year predicted I'd win, but only by 800 votes. He was nearly spot on, it's just the result was the other way round!

As the early morning light creeps into the room, I finish my speech by reminding everyone that the Labour fight back in Bethnal Green and Bow starts in the next few days. We can have the weekend off, but that's about it. People clap and cry and hug each other. It's a new day, a new dawn, so we decide to go to the café for a fry up. It's the café next to the Labour Party offices that, until eight hours ago, was the nerve centre of our Battle for Bethnal Green. It is just after six a.m. and there are twenty of us left. I order baked beans on toast but can't eat it when it arrives.

At 7.30 a.m. Tiberio leaves for work. Others start to slip away. By ten a.m. I'm left with my cold baked beans, and three of the people who worked hardest for me. Tim, Alan and Rushanara. As a generous gesture Rushanara clicks into her former parliamentary assistant mode.

'If you could do anything right now, what would it be?'

'Er . . .' I think for a while and draw a blank. 'Go to the job centre?'

'Personally,' she says, 'I think you need to relax. How about a massage?'

My eyes light up. Rushanara is a genius. I'm so glad she's here. She shared the beginning of my career as the MP for Bethnal Green and Bow, and it seems fitting that she's here to share the end.* And yes, if I could choose to do anything right now, it would be a massage. *Whoosh* . . . here comes the upside of defeat! Had I won, at this very moment I would be writing press releases and arranging my first constituency visits for later today – no doubt what George Galloway is doing right now.† I would be knocking on doors to thank my constituents for the next weeks and months. I would be utterly traumatised by the vast numbers of promises I'd made and would work day and night to fulfil them. Instead it dawns on me that for the first time in eight years I am *unaccountable*. I am a free individual, not a representative of a collective. I don't owe anyone my job, because I don't have a job. It's 10.30 a.m. on Friday 6 May, 2005, and for the first time in a year I can properly relax.

As this thought washes over me, this foreign sensation that I am 'allowed' to relax – in fact I can do whatever I want – I decide to write out a to-do list. It involves a spot of retail therapy, and is entitled 'Oona's new life list – things to buy':

1. Make-up remover.
2. Pair of trainers.
3. Swimming costume.
4. Blank diary.

From where I'm sitting in the café in Bethnal Green, this is all I need to get my new life off to a flying start.

---

* Two years later, Rushanara was selected to be the Labour Party Candidate for BG & B at the next general election. The East End deserves an MP like her, someone in politics for the right reasons who does not favour a particular group or community, and is entirely dedicated to the constituency where she grew up. Rushanara would also help realise my long-cherished dream of a more representative democracy. The most damaging attack Respect have levelled at her is that she was my assistant from 1997 to 1999. They also lie about her supporting the war in Iraq when Rushanara was one of the many Labour Party members who marched against it.

† In fact George Galloway was about to leave the constituency to spend a week in his holiday home in Portugal, followed by a trip to Washington, followed by a speaking tour of America.

Cherie calls from No. 10. I wonder how many phone calls she has to make this morning. She has always been extremely kind to me, and came down to help during the campaign. Gordon (Brown) rings. 'Oona, I just wanted to let you know that your speech was so dignified it made me cry.' Maybe I need a hearing aid.

I ring Stephen (Twigg) because he's lost his seat too. In different ways, we both know what it's like to symbolise a British election.

'Hey honey, I suddenly have a clear diary next week, how about lunch?'

'Great,' he says, 'my diary's just come free too!'

In the next four days I receive 700 text messages and over 2,000 emails.

I laugh out loud as I read some of the text messages coming in.

'Hey guys, people are saying I was dignified!'

Tim and Alan look at me sceptically, with my smudged eyeliner, sitting next to my soggy baked beans.

'Well that's a result in itself,' says Tim.

It's a huge result, and I'm overjoyed. As the morning wears on I start to realise I didn't mess things up. OK, I messed up the 800 extra votes. I should have got those. I should have won the election. George Galloway should not have a platform. Bethnal Green and Bow should still have a Labour MP. I should still have a political career. But maybe that's not the most important thing. The more I try to measure my gut feeling, the more I realise it is a sense of relief intertwined with pride. I didn't let myself down. I didn't let my supporters down. I got the goal in the back of the net.

How can I say that when I lost the match? Simply because it's how I will always visualise general election night 2005. Yes, I may have been 'the biggest symbolic defeat of the Blair Government' on that night, but I had some personal objectives that were separate to the political headlines beamed into Britain's homes. Those objectives were to avoid sectarian politics, and encourage others to do likewise. To treat others as I would wish to be treated. And to accept victory or defeat with grace.

With hand on heart I can say that those objectives were incredibly important to me, even more important than winning. And I achieved them. So when I close my eyes and think of that night, I visualise the perfect penalty. I see someone under great pressure walking to the penalty box. For the whole match they've been deafened by the opposition's angry roar. They feel all eyes on them, they feel great fear of failure. But they place the ball on the penalty spot and slot it calmly in the back of the net. And although their team loses the match, they know they did their best. And in fact my team won the championship. We're in Government.

'Shall we go?' says Tim.

'Yeah, let's go to the West End.' The sun is shining. My aunt Miri says we can use her living room in Mayfair as our luxury headquarters. The four of us get into Alan's banged up car and drive along White-chapel Road, then past the Tower of London, and on to the Embank-ment. The blue sky screams spring. We pull up at the traffic lights by Westminster Bridge, with the London Eye behind us, about to turn right towards Piccadilly. The House of Commons looms large, filling my entire horizon. But only for a moment. I look up at Big Ben. It is time to go. I am no longer a Member of the House. A lump in my throat. I doubt I will ever be a Member of Parliament again. It was the best of times, it was the worst of times. A message comes through from a friend. 'At least you got out with your life.' The light turns green and a tear slips down my cheek. Not only will I get out with my life, but this morning I will step *in*to my life. *Inshallah*.

Postscript

Right Said Fred

'I know an Oona,' says Fred, the man next to me on a flight into Heathrow. Fred is in his late sixties, a white Geordie. I think he's about to say '. . . an Oona who was Charlie Chaplin's wife.' That's what older people often say. Instead, a bit later he says, 'I suppose you're not interested in politics.' The way Fred looks at me, sizing up my trainers, jeans, and iPod, he's obviously thinking, 'I *knew* she wouldn't be interested in politics.'

'Oh, I'm interested in politics,' I say, 'believe me.'

I don't add anything further for fear of triggering the 'what was it like being an MP?' conversation. Or the 'please can I have your address and phone number?' conversation. I don't mind giving people my details, and I like to hear from them. It's just that their unanswered letters and emails stack up like paper mountains or electronic sediment, and I worry that they think I'm rude. So I say nothing further to Fred.

A moment later Fred strikes up the conversation again.

'You might not know,' he says, 'but in Bethnal Green and Bow there was an Oona King who had a *terrible* time at the election. She had that dreadful man, George Galloway, come down from Scotland and turn her constituents against her.'

I stare at him wide-eyed.

'You'd never imagine what a bad time that Oona King had,' continues Fred. 'Did you not hear about it in the news?'

Before I can answer, Fred shakes his head, tut-tutting in a 'you young people never watch the news' way.

'I *really* don't like that Galloway,' continues Fred vehemently. 'I'd tell him to his face if I ever met him. I felt so much for that Oona King. And I'd like to *tell* Oona King—'

'You can tell me Fred. It's me.'

'What?'

'It's me. I'm Oona — King that is.'

Fred doesn't believe me. The person he's read about in the newspapers can't be the 'young girl' as he calls me (thanks Fred!), the person in torn jeans and trainers sitting in the back of Economy. In the end I show him my passport to prove who I am. He says it is the most amazing coincidence he's ever had in his life. He says it is pre-destined.

I hear my story from others over and over. But it is only when I hear it from Fred that I grasp the significance of these other re-tellings: though symbolically alone on stage that night when Galloway left in triumph, in fact I was surrounded by a sea of people and their heartfelt support. I couldn't see them at the time, but I meet them every day – in the street, on the bus, on the plane. They send me letters, cards and emails. They tell me *their* story of *their* outrage, and in doing so they release me from mine. I am outrage-free. And that is a priceless gift I cannot repay. It gives me a sense of peace that transforms losing my seat into winning my life.

'Right,' said Fred as the plane came to a standstill near the terminal. It had been a long trip. 'All the very best to you, Oona.'

'And to you Fred. Thank you. *Really*, thank you.'

Afterword

The Penalty Shoot-out and The Last Emperor

The days and weeks immediately after the election were cathartic. As soon as you're dead you win the sympathy vote hands down. My political obituaries were generous, though this was as much to do with Mr Galloway's drawbacks as my own appeal. In the constituency the shock was palpable, though in some areas they were probably dancing in the streets. Regardless of party affiliation people were suddenly falling over themselves to tell me how grateful they were for my work in the community, and to rail against their new MP. In the eight days after the election I received more love and affection than in the previous eight years combined.

But a lot of people didn't even notice the election. They didn't realise I was no longer their MP. Even now, constituents sometimes stop me in the street to ask if I'll help with their case. When I say I can't they often get indignant. 'But you've got to help me. You helped me for years.'

'I'm not your MP any more, I lost the election.'

'What election?'

Losing MPs were given one week to clear out their Westminster offices. Our passes were revoked and we were told we would be 'escorted from the premises' if we used them. When I tried to retrieve emails and contact addresses from the parliamentary IT system, I was told I'd missed a one-week deadline. All my emails from the previous eight years were deleted, and I wasn't allowed to retrieve any of my documents. But there were nice moments too. A fortnight after the election I walked into Strangers' Bar and was astounded when 100 people gave me a standing ovation.

I wrote in my diary that evening, *I like this walking-on-water stuff. I'm more used to wading through shit. I met the Congolese*

Ambassador today, who said that President Kabila and senior Cabinet Members wanted to contact me about the election. 'People in Kinshasa were watching you on election night in your white suit. We feel like we've lost our friend in the British Parliament.' People in Dhaka, Kigali, Seoul, Sydney and Washington told me they saw the count too. It amazes me that people around the world were watching, and actually took an interest in the result in Bethnal Green and Bow.

Back in the constituency, the result itself was under scrutiny. Local residents, led by a determined and impressive young woman Gurnam Kaur, began a campaign to get George Galloway's majority of 823 votes overturned. Apparently 1,500 Bow residents (Bow voted overwhelmingly for me) were disenfranchised because their houses were left off the electoral register. They arrived at polling stations to vote for me but were turned away. They wanted the election re-run. They had a strong case because the Council admitted liability for leaving them off the electoral register. But it transpired that only people *on* the electoral register can challenge an election result in court. Their whole complaint was that they were left *off* the electoral register. It was a Kafkaesque, *Catch 22* situation which was grossly unfair. But I was partly relieved when their lawyers said they could not challenge the election or get it re-run: can you imagine fighting the Battle for Bethnal Green and Bow twice?

As many people predicted, Mr Galloway left the constituency shortly after the election result. His superb performance in Washington in front of the Senate reminded me what a wasted talent he is. In the meantime my office was still dealing with desperate housing cases in Bethnal Green. Letters and emails flooded in from around the country, from a cross-section of people – students to pensioners. Several of the pensioners told me to take heart from Churchill's experience at Gallipoli. This was Churchill's 1915 plan to break the deadlock in World War I. The military campaign was based on information contained in a 'dodgy dossier'. The campaign was disastrous, and resulted in terrible casualties and the Allies' biggest humiliation of the war. Churchill resigned from Government, assuming his political career was over. History proved him wrong.

I was more likely to take heart from Churchill than from some sections of my local Labour party. They were understandably aggrieved that between me and the Government, we'd managed to lose a safe Labour seat. The CLP's post-mortem at the end of May 2005 had a great turnout of around 100 people. About one in five of those who spoke said, 'Oona's a liability and she's why we lost. She can't be the candidate next time round.' Many others passionately disagreed and said I was the only one who could guarantee the party would win the seat back. I refrained from saying I'd rather die than be the candidate again.

The problem was, I no longer wanted to be the MP for Bethnal Green and Bow. I immodestly believed it was one of the toughest jobs around, and that I'd done it pretty well, for the most part unsupported. The support only flooded in when my head was on the block. During those pressured times I so often imagined the relief of walking out of my constituency office for the last time . . . finally closing the door on the 20,000 cases, many of which kept me awake at night. The door finally swung shut in September 2005.

In some respects it was harder for my campaign team to come to terms with defeat than it was for me. Mohammed, our *yoot* representative, got everyone saying, 'Allow it'. Depending on intonation, it means let it go/ never mind, as in, 'Ah well, we lost the election, never mind.' *Allow it*. It took me a long time to get used to my new-found freedom. I was a bit like an institutionalised person who's chucked out of jail. I kept going back to Westminster for meetings, almost as though I was programmed to do so, meetings with my All Party Group, meetings to lobby Ministers, meetings with former colleagues.

These days there are few things I love more than being in my own living room in the evening. The biggest privilege I have as a non-MP is getting my evenings back. I may still often visit Westminster, but when the bells ring at seven p.m., I get on the District Line and go home. I marvel at being home, as though it were an illicit activity like money laundering or identity theft. I have stolen an identity with a life, and I don't want to give it back.

To quote Tony Benn, I'm leaving Parliament to spend more time on politics – but only the politics I'm passionate about: human rights, poverty, international development, housing, young people, youth services, political engagement and building strong communities. It's enough to be getting on with, and I'm grateful to leave the rest behind.

My biggest challenge during my first year out of Westminster was resisting reality TV. During that year most of the work I did was unpaid political work or TV commentary (people are surprised to hear that you're usually not paid for going on the news, or programmes like *Newsnight*). I was still working on issues close to my heart. This included a grass roots advocacy project, aimed at making local people's voices heard at Government level, and lots of canvassing as an ordinary member of the Labour Party. That year I earned £4,000. Tiberio pointed out that we had a mortgage to pay. *I'm a Celebrity, Get Me Out of Here* offered £60,000 for three weeks' work. Obviously I was never going to say yes, but I confess I came close with some of the other programmes in the dreaded reality TV genre. My favourite, the one I secretly yearned to do (avert your eyes now) was ITV's *Dancing on Ice*. I've always loved ice skating. I dreamed of triple sulcos – or at least staying upright on a pair of skates. Tiberio said he would divorce me. Quincy and Nora said I would irrevocably ruin my reputation and career.

'*What career?*'

'People will be so disappointed. They'll think terribly of you.'

The thought of learning how to ice skate, dancing to music, getting fit, *and* being able to get money out of the cash machine . . . it nearly tipped me over the edge. Thankfully my friends, and particularly Tiberio, pulled me back from the brink. If you ever see me dancing on TV, I can only apologise in advance.

Senior politicians contacted me and encouraged me to come back to the Commons. Gordon Brown invited me into the Treasury to give me careers advice. Though he and Tony are viewed as chalk and cheese (Tony a relaxed, charismatic media performer, Gordon media-shy and dour), in fact they come across as remarkably similar in private – nice and normal. Gordon wanted to know which seats I was looking at. Like everyone, he was taken aback that I didn't want to return to Westminster. It's not that I don't want to go back, (I loved being an MP, I would love to be an MP again) it's just that I don't want to go back to the *life* of an MP (I hated it, and I don't want to be the moaning, miserable person that it made me). It's a shame, but there it is.

When I went to Downing Street for a seminar on a public service reform, people looked at me like they'd seen a ghost. I bumped into John Prescott.

'What are you doing here?' He didn't hide the note of surprise.

'Going to a seminar on the "strategic state" – something you wouldn't need to know about John.' It sounded harsher than I'd intended.

'You mean more of that New Labour rubbish?'

'Yeah, summink like that.' I trotted up the stairs with the pictures of former Prime Ministers peering out from their political deathbeds, the last one being John Major. Tony didn't want his portrait up there as soon as others would like.

After the meeting I bumped into him.

'Oona!'

'Tony . . . why does everyone look at me like they've seen a ghost?'

'I'm not looking at you like I've seen a ghost. It's just I can't help thinking of that awful man . . .'

'Well anyway, I'm fine. In fact I'm really enjoying it.'

'Really?' He looked doubtful. 'So what are you up to?' I ran through the usual list.

'I've turned down *The Oona King Show*.'

'Why?'

'Because that's not what I want to do.'

'Why not? *The Oona King Show* sounds quite good to me.'

Maybe I *will* end up doing it, and it won't be half bad. But compared to trying to make the world a better place, having a TV show doesn't quite cut it.

The best political moment for me since the general election came at the local elections in June 2006. Pundits predicted that Respect could take over Tower Hamlets Council from Labour. Instead, the People's Republic of Bow, for the first time in decades (other than during the 2005 general election), voted overwhelmingly Labour. Across the country there was a swing against Labour, but my area bucked the local trend with a 30 per cent swing to Labour – it saved the Labour Council, and stopped George Galloway taking control of the town hall. And who are the new Councillors? Josh, Marc, Carli, Claire, amongst others – they are a new generation of young Labour people who battled to the death for me. I am so, so proud of them, and inspired by them.

The Last Emperor

Putting politics aside, after the election the last thing I wanted to do was start IVF again. But I was thirty-seven years old and the clock was ticking. A few months later I went along to begin a new cycle. The first scan showed something was wrong. I needed an operation just to get back to first base. Instead of starting a family or getting a life, I risked having operations and doing rounds of IVF for years. So in March 2006 Tiberio and I decided to look into adoption again. Our social worker Sara explained that adoption could take anything from nine months to four years.

Sara picked up the adoption magazine *Be My Parent*.

'You have to be realistic,' she said, 'you're unlikely to find a baby.' She flicked through pages of small faces.

'Of all the children listed, this is the only baby.' She pointed to a small caramel face.

'He's seven months old, and his birth background is a black mother and Italian father–' Sara stopped in her tracks. Adoption bingo.

'That's unbelievable! He'd be the perfect match for you!' She was almost breathless.

'It's unlikely he's still available, but do you want me to find out more?'

Tiberio and I were caught off-guard. We'd only come in for a chat. But Sara told us not to get our hopes up: even if the baby – called Elia – wasn't matched, we had a mountain of bureaucracy to climb. With the best will in the world it was unlikely we could pass the legal checks in time.

I tried not to think too much about the baby called Elia (pronounced E-*lee*-a). I only had twenty words underneath his photo to go on: 'He eats well, sleeps well, and is easy to care for. His foster mother says Elia is a little angel.'

But things soon got difficult. We were given Elia's medical background. Devastation. He had received a cocktail of drugs in the womb. No folic acid or omega-3 fish oils for him. The list of his medical problems went on and on. We wanted to know how much the drugs he'd been exposed to might stunt his development. Irreparably? Not at all? The doctors couldn't tell us. I kept his picture from the magazine and looked at it all the time. My baby. I didn't care if he had developmental problems. Then a few weeks later some more medical information. More complications. This little angel might well become seriously ill. The social workers said we had to know the worst. It was quite possible he would need a liver transplant. We might have to manage a chronic medical condition. I hadn't absorbed that blow before the next one arrived. He had difficulty breathing and eating. He couldn't swallow solid food, he had a heart condition, he might need two operations. Tiberio said we had to rethink, we couldn't just run headlong into life with a disabled or sick child without considering the consequences.

He was right of course, but I clearly remember thinking, 'I will do whatever I have to do to persuade Tiberio to give me my baby. *Our* baby. I will not lose this child. Unless he is terminally ill – I'm not strong enough for that.' From then on, every time we got medical information it was more bad news. I started wondering how a baby could have so many things wrong with him. The least worrying one was a squint, and also asthma. But a bit of good news came through: he'd started trying to walk around nine months, which signified good motor skills. He was meeting all his developmental milestones. It was too early to say whether or not he'd be developmentally delayed.

I looked at Elia's photo over and over, marvelling at his wise Mona Lisa smile. I decided that birth parents don't choose their children, so why should we? On one level becoming a parent is not a choice. You are the parent of whichever child arrives, regardless of their physical and mental health.

'That's different,' said Tiberio, 'birth parents haven't *chosen* a sick baby.'

'Nor have we,' I said 'he just arrived.'

Our pregnancy lasted four months. The social workers at Norwood Adoption Agency and Newham Social Services were outstanding, and our family only exists because of their remarkable commitment. These people were the exact opposite of *Daily Mail* stereotyping. They went the extra mile again and again to make the impossible possible.

Finally it was time for our baby to be born into our world. We met Elia's foster mother, Katrina, at a social services building, and then drove to her home to meet Elia himself. When the car pulled up outside a pleasant suburban house, I saw a thirteen-month-old baby on the doorstep in the arms of his foster-nan. I stared and stared at him from the back seat of the car. From this distance, he looked almost indistinguishable to pictures of Slater as a baby. Tiberio got out and walked the twenty yards towards Elia. But for me, after waiting a lifetime it was suddenly too soon. I sat in the back seat and let the tears tap my eyes. I looked away. I had opened the car door, but now closed it again.

I took a few deep breaths before sliding across the back seat of the car. Then I slowly got out and walked towards my baby. He was real. The biggest shock was his beauty. His head was sculpted. Two perfect almond eyes sat like dark wishing wells above lips that cupid would die for. There was no sign of a squint. The perfection of his lips and soft twirling curls around his forehead was mesmerising, and that was before I noticed his dimple. He stared at me.

'Hello baby boy, how are we today?' I smiled but didn't touch him. He looked back quite solemnly, enquiringly. Then he pursed his round lips in the shape of a plump diamond, as if to indicate he had completed his initial assessment.

Tiberio's first impression was that we had the wrong baby. 'Who is this beautiful baby, and what have they done with ours?' We were expecting a poorly baby, perhaps a darling lopsided baby. Instead we were greeted, in Tiberio's words, by a little God. Even taking account of parental bias, that's not much of an exaggeration. He was the sort of toddler a casting agent would choose for *The Last Emperor*, the sort of baby that could be garlanded and placed on a throne. Tiberio and I were transfixed.

After ten minutes we touched Elia fleetingly, in an exploratory fashion – a chubby leg here, a chubby cheek there. I couldn't get over how real he was. The thing about miscarriages, failed IVF, and infertility, is that they make babies so unreal. You spend your time obsessing about them, but your own baby can never exist, can never be touched. Yet here he was, gurgling and laughing. We could reach out and touch him. Elia's three foster siblings, George, fifteen, Louise, thirteen, and Jayne, eight, were in the living room. Elia clearly had a fantastic relationship with his whole foster family, and especially his foster father Anthony. He had been with them since birth, and they loved him as their own. He had never suffered even a minute's neglect or abuse, and it showed in his sunny, confident personality.

His foster-nan, Pam, told us how lucky we were.

'Elia is a very special character. Wherever we go people want to play with him. They stare at him. He's very social. But most of all, he's just so clever.' Clever? That wasn't in the script.

'What about all his health problems?' I asked.

'Health problems?' Pam was clearly sceptical. 'There's not a single thing wrong with this baby. Look at him. He's healthy and beautiful.'

I thought I was dreaming. In my desperation to have a real baby I must have dreamed it all up.

'But we were told he could be chronically ill. Developmentally delayed . . .'

'Elia?!' Pam laughed as though we were deluded. 'Not Elia! You just wait until you see how lucky you are. He's bright as a button. I suppose the social workers have to tell you the worst-case scenario but, believe me, Elia is the best-case scenario.'

Our amazement grew throughout our first two-hour contact session with him. It was true. He was clearly intelligent, gorgeous, social, affectionate and funny. He loved to laugh, and was brimming with health. He was clearly a miracle.

An old-fashioned honest-to-goodness miracle.

These days it feels as though Elia has been our son since before he was born. Even though I see him every day, every day I pinch myself. There is no other child in the world I could love more than Elia. Happily for me, one of Elia's greatest loves is music, and especially house music. Early on we took him to the Notting Hill Carnival. We came out of Ladbroke Grove tube station to an unbelievable din – the roar of hundreds of thousands of people, and pounding bass lines shaking the pavements. For a minute I thought Elia would cry. He was thirteen months old, we'd only been his parents for a fortnight, and perhaps we'd been foolish to bring him. After a split second Elia threw his head back, pumped his fist in the air to the beat, and laughed loudly. We put him on the ground and he stamped his feet, doing a crazy-jig dance. The only time he cried was when we dragged him away from the dancing carnival procession to avoid him being trampled.

As I watched Elia pump his little fist, his face peeled back in giggling delight, I realised an amazing thing. I love Elia to the point that I'm grateful – deeply grateful – that I'm infertile; otherwise I wouldn't have him. It sounds absurd or exaggerated, but it is true.

This is something other adoptive mothers have told me too: they love their adoptive children so much, they panic at the thought they might never have had them. I didn't know it at the time, but my 'bad luck' with infertility was the best luck I ever had.

With Elia here, I could never go back to being an MP working a ninety-hour week. Winning and losing Bethnal Green and Bow were two of the three best things that happened to me this past decade. But the best thing was becoming a parent. People ask if I've given up my political ambitions. No, it's just that my life ambitions are greater. I've let go of my political career, but not my politics. I have no idea if my political career will find me again. When Stephen Twigg and I met up for lunch after the election we thought we might like to do a job-share as London Mayor one day. Or maybe I'll be an aerobics teacher for pensioners. Or writer. Whatever. I am chairing an inquiry into youth services, and I chair the Institute of Community Cohesion. I'm passionate about political engagement. I choose the campaigns I'm involved with, which also still involve housing and genocide. And I am lucky enough to make television and radio documentaries on subjects that interest me, ranging from immigration to cooking.

But more important than any choice I make, is the choice Britain makes about its politics. Will we open up politics and let ordinary people in? By ordinary people I mean the overwhelming majority of the British public who do not spend every waking hour obsessing about politics. Will we devolve power, not just to regions, but to *individuals*? Will we make consultation meaningful? Will we consider job-sharing for MPs, Mayors, and other elected positions? (It's not as difficult as it sounds, the difficult bit is finding the political will to change.) Will we support politicians who modernise our political institutions? Will our political institutions have life breathed into them by the views of the people they serve? Will we re-negotiate the settlement between citizen and state?

Some people spend a lifetime in politics, which is possibly too long, but everyone should spend at least a decade. By that I mean everyone should engage with their local community, and take responsibility for promoting change, however small. We need more normal people in Westminster; and we need normal people to be more political. Never mind my politics, what about yours?

Acknowledgements

My heartfelt thanks to the following:

Alexandra Pringle – the queen – at Bloomsbury for constant encouragement, zest, and saving me from the title *A Woman in the House* . . . amongst much else; Mary Morris at Bloomsbury for her efficiency, warmth, indulgence and determination not to crack – *Allahu Akbar*, we did it!; Gillian Stern for being a fantastic editor and friend; Simon Trewin, my literary editor at PFD – thanks for good advice and sorry your bike was nicked during the Bloomsbury meeting that led to this book being published; my television agent Sophie Laurimore at William Morris Agency for encouragement and advice; fellow judges of the Jewish Book Awards for discussions about writing, life, and the future of Jewish atheism – Julia Pascal, Eliane Glaser, and Dave Schneider; and Margaret Stead for trying harder than *Hansard* to curb my slang-ish writing.

Quincy Whitaker, my best friend who shares my life and tries to save me from it, thanks for a lifetime of world-wide travels and armchair adventures; Nora Meyer, one of the most emotionally intelligent people to grace the planet, what a result we've been together from the start; thanks to Natasha Walter for invaluable criticism; Rachel Blake for lending me her living room and being an all-round star; Esia e Tullio, grazie, dal piu' profondo del mio cuore, per la vostra incredibile generosita'. Non avrei mai immaginato di avere un giorno dei suoceri meravigliosi come voi; Mum and Treena for stepping into the numerous childcare emergencies this book threw up, and limitless affection; and to Sue, Aneesa, Zahida, Farjana, Suria, Naz, Syeda, Jaqueline, Kochi and Carlton amongst others at the Ocean Children's Centre in Stepney for flexible childcare.

Thanks to Nick Fox and Louise Restrick for giving me the chance to be an MP. Thanks to Johann Hari for agreeing to come with me to the Congo, and using his talent to communicate its vast suffering. Thanks also to the many Labour Party members, officials and constituency assistants who worked with me in Bethnal Green & Bow: Josh Peck, Tim Nuthall, Marc Francis, Graham Taylor, Frances Simmons, Rohema Miah, Kester Dean, Lesley Rogers, Lesley Pavitt, Mohammed Choudhury, Dianne Hayter, David Triesman, Victoria Silver, Chris Weavers, Abi Hewitt, Clare Hawkins, Sybil Yates, Tim Bennett-Goodman, Rushanara Ali, Alan Barnard, Andrea Pastorelli, Carli Harper-Penman, Beatrice Stern, Anna Lynch, Brian Boag, Oliver Gell, Jo Miller, Chris Drinkwater, Caroline Gordon, Andrew Hobson, Alaha Begum, Rukia Begum, Lucy Potter, Mia and Belle Harris amongst many, many others; to all my volunteers, and to those whose names aren't mentioned, thank you for putting up with everything, including our low-quality LP office biscuits. Thanks also to Ken Clarke, Joe Derrett and Julian Ellerby at London Region Labour Party. Thanks to the outstanding co-ordinators of my All-Party Parliamentary Group on the Great Lakes Region: Stephen Carter, Mark Pallis, Ben Shepherd, Anya Bensberg and Ben Crampton, and a shout out to the staff at the House of Commons who always shared a joke and never once arrested me.

Thanks also to those who indulge my 'phone-a-friend' moments: Tristram Hunt, Waheed Ali, Karen Buck, David Lammy, Jim Fitzpatrick, Mark Hannam, Tim Franks and Ted Cantle. And for various acts of benevolence or brilliance: Kwame Kwei-Armah, Valencia King, Anneka Van Woudenberg, Richard Stone, Ben Bilboul, David Mann, Eric Joyce, Taneka Gupta, Anne Longfield, Craig Jones, Jo Meek, Kate Taylor, Stuart Young, Ian Katz, Michael Wills, Torben, Barbara Tonuit, Adrian at Empire, James at War Child, Sarosh and Susan at HW Fisher, and Paresh and Mina Patel at Coburn Corner. I must also acknowledge that I've often danced to house music late at night with Ben Bradshaw, so I guess I'm not the only MP to love house music.

I particularly want to thank the 20,000 constituents who came to see me or contacted me during my time as MP for Bethnal Green & Bow, and shared their stories with me. And to all my incredible staff who helped me link casework to policy campaigns to reduce poverty and disadvantage.

To one of the other politicians in Tower Hamlets who knows what it's like to suffer opprobrium – Michael Keith – thank you for always choosing your community above your comfort. And for your kindness.

I also thank the many people who inspired me in Tower Hamlets through their dedication to community work, including several labour Councillors, as well as the extraordinary people who build community unity every day, in particular Shahida Choudhury, Brian Tugwell, Brenda Daley, Kofai Bibi Choudhury, David Robinson, the Rev. Philippa Boardman, and Linda and Carol – amongst so many others.

Finally, thanks to my youngest brother Akasi and my godchildren Tex, Inca, Otis, Mattia, Maggie and Evie, and my American family for showing no resentment over prolonged absences. Mum, Dad, Slate, Miri, Christopher – thanks for always, always being there. And back to the future, grazie Tiberio, amore mio, di tutto.

Oona
July 2007